Journeys West

Journeys West

Jane and Julian Steward and Their Guides

VIRGINIA KERNS

University of Nebraska Press
Lincoln & London

Library of Congress Cataloging-
in-Publication Data
Kerns, Virginia, 1948–
Journeys West : Jane and Julian
Steward and their guides / Virginia
Kerns.
p. cm.
Includes bibliographical references
and index.
ISBN 978-0-8032-2508-4 (cloth : alk.
paper)
1. Steward, Julian Haynes, 1902–1972.
2. Steward, Jane Cannon.
3. Anthropologists—Great Basin—
Biography. 4. Archaeologists—Great
Basin—Biography. 5. Indians of
North America—Great Basin—
Antiquities. 6. Indians of North
America—Great Basin—Social life
and customs. 7. Anthropology—
Fieldwork—Great Basin—History.
I. Title.
GN21.S78K46 2010
301.092′279—dc22
[B] 2009030685

Set in Galliard.

For Ronald

Contents

Illustrations

Photographs

Map

Preface

During the many years I worked on this book and its predecessor, I made more than a dozen journeys west and had the privilege of seeing most of the places mentioned in the pages that follow. The mountains and deserts of the American West have an astonishing and enduring beauty that nearly two centuries of rough use have not yet destroyed. The native people who live there, and whose ancestors lived on that land for many generations, have also endured despite the odds.

This book tells a story of adaptation and survival, both before and after an ecological crisis in the desert West. It is at the same time an inquiry into ideas and methods in cultural anthropology. The narrative centers on fieldwork that Julian Steward carried out in the West in 1935 and 1936. That research resulted in a classic ethnography known to generations of readers by its shorthand name, *Basin-Plateau*. It told how native people adapted to specific localities in the arid West before American colonization and settlement. The book, which became a foundational work in ecological anthropology, also helped to introduce the concept of cultural adaptation.

Over the years many anthropologists and other scholars have disagreed with some of Steward's ideas and conclusions. The test of a classic work, however, is not whether it is "right" in every respect but whether it continues to be read and to raise questions that lead to more research. Steward's ethnography has met that test. It has provoked so much research and commentary—which continues to reach print in the twenty-first century—that simply commenting on the commentary would require a volume beyond this one.

While this book is an outcome of my research on Steward and the dozens of Indian elders who served as his cultural informants, it also draws directly, if not as obviously, on my own experiences and memories as a cultural anthropologist and teacher. Decades after Steward's fieldwork drew to a close in western America I had an experience of fieldwork with native people in the western Caribbean. Like him, I sought out elders as cultural informants. My informants, like his, had lost their ancestral land to invaders but so many years in the past that firsthand memories of those events had died a century earlier with the first generation of survivors. Exiled to a new and distant land, they adapted and survived—with great hardship. Their past is a variation on a theme that runs through the history of the American West and the Americas in general.

Years after that fieldwork ended, and in the course of a long career in teaching, my students raised questions about all aspects of research, including some perennial queries about objectivity. I thank my students not only for their questions but also for their patience with my musings about the term *objectivity*, a word with varied meanings, and about memory. I also want to thank several university administrators—who to my surprise questioned whether fieldwork qualifies as research. Their doubt is perhaps a measure of how esoteric and poorly understood ethnographic fieldwork remains, even in universities, and despite some well-known critiques by literary critics in the late twentieth century.

I wrote this book as an extended reply to questions I have heard from students and others—and to my own questions. Telling the story has taught me much about the mélange of memories, words, observations, and experiences that become ethnography. It has also deepened my admiration of the elders who took part in Steward's research, as well as my appreciation of them as distinct individuals. Every man and woman brought a unique set of life experiences and memories to the encounter with Steward.

In my efforts to learn about each of them I purposely did not seek out genealogical descendants, although I did encounter some over the years. The sheer number of elders and other cultural informants—more than fifty—dissuaded me from that plan. In the unlikely event that I managed to complete the task, I knew that the results would fill volumes, not just a single book. Current concerns, and conflicting views, about family privacy also led me to search for public records about individuals while forgoing family history and oral tradition for the most part and avoiding mention of descendants' names.

I used public records very cautiously, given their gaps, inconsistencies, and errors. I reconciled these as best I could, usually by searching through five or six censuses taken over the course of decades and then choosing the most consistently recorded name or age or other detail of identity. When that failed I tried other means, drawing on what I knew of cultural and historical context. In cases where I had no name—only a set of initials, an estimated age, and an indication of gender—I searched census records and located names by using a process of elimination. Then I looked for supporting evidence that I had found the correct name. The records, as is always the case, were partial and often raised as many questions as they answered.

To reconstruct Steward's fieldwork and his encounters with the elders and others, I pieced together details from a variety of sources. Julian Steward and his wife, Jane, kept a field journal in 1935 and 1936, and their sons, Michael and Gary Steward, kindly allowed me to read it and quote from it. The journal has since been deposited with the Julian H. Steward Papers at the University of Illinois Archives. Because the journal contained so few entries for the second round of fieldwork, in 1936, I drew almost entirely on the records and letters that I located at the Smithsonian Institution, the University of California's Bancroft Library, and other universities. Jane Steward's memories of their earlier travels, in 1935—memories that she shared with me more than fifty years later, but long before I began working on this book—helped to clarify and extend the written record. Letters that she wrote and received from her parents and other family members during the 1930s helped in turn to deepen my understanding of what she had told me. Those letters, part of a collection of family papers recently deposited at the University of Utah's Marriott Library, also added new details.

To trace their routes through the desert I studied old road maps. To provide context for places and events I turned to other primary sources, from newspaper articles to photographs taken at the time, and to a range of works by anthropologists, historians, geographers, and other scholars. Seeing nearly all field sites for myself helped to answer some questions I had not even thought to ask—one of the great advantages of naturalistic research.

Names, of peoples and of places, have changed in some cases since the time of Steward's journeys, and not uncommonly the spellings have changed as well. In some instances I have followed the usage of the 1930s, and in others, that of the present. In general I have tried to avoid confusing readers of this book or offending people named in Steward's book—a hard balancing act in some cases. I use the word *Americans* to refer to settlers in the nineteenth century, but not to Indians because most American Indians did not attain full rights as citizens until well into the twentieth century.

It was my good fortune to write the first and the last chapters of this book at The Mesa Refuge, a writers' retreat in Northern California and a place of sustaining beauty and solitude. My first thanks are to Peter Barnes and the Common Counsel Foundation—and to fellow residents at the retreat whose presence and questions affected, in ways both subtle and direct, the shape of the book.

During the two years between residencies, I lived in Utah and wrote most of this book. I am grateful to Mary Dickson for her many insights about Utah life, past and present, and for her friendship.

Forrest S. Cuch, executive director of the Utah State Division of Indian Affairs, provided important guidance about Utah history and Utah Indians. I thank F. Ross Peterson for a tour of Cache Valley during his last year as director of the Mountain West Center at Utah State University and for hospitality during a return visit I made to Deep Springs College in California soon after he began to serve as its president. Elaine Thatcher, program coordinator of the Mountain West Center, offered suggestions and assistance that led me to the Bear River and Bear Lake regions of Utah and Idaho. Patty Timbimboo-Madsen, manager of cultural and natural resources for the Northwestern Band of the Shoshone Nation, kindly permitted me to visit the Shoshoni Tribal Cemetery at Washakie, Utah.

I hope that my very deep debt to the late Jane Cannon Steward, and my respect for her and for all of the elders, is evident throughout the book. I also want to thank several people whose names appear only in passing in the text, belying their importance as my other informants: Sidney W. Mintz and the late Robert F. Murphy, Dorothy B. Nyswander, and William C. Sturtevant.

The staff of many museums and archives assisted in various ways, and without their help this would be a different book. I especially appreciate the assistance that William Maher, Chris Prom, and Linda Stahnke provided at the University of Illinois Archives over the course of many years. I am grateful as well to Robert Leopold of the National Anthropological Archives, Smithsonian Institution; Stan Larson and Lorraine Crouse of the Manuscripts Division, Marriott Library, University of Utah; Beth Sennett Porter, Eastern California Museum, Independence, California; and students at Deep Springs College, as well as current president David Neidorf, who allowed me to reproduce photographs of Jane and Julian Steward taken there in 1935. I also thank the staff at the following libraries, museums, historical sites, and public agencies: the National Archives, Washington DC; the Bancroft Library, University of California, Berkeley; the Paiute

Shoshone Cultural Center and Museum, Bishop, California; the Nevada Historical Society, Reno; the Northeastern Nevada Museum and Historical Society, Elko; the Research Center at the Utah State Historical Society, Salt Lake City; Special Collections, Salt Lake Public Library; libraries of the Church of Jesus Christ of Latter-day Saints, Salt Lake City; Swem Library, the College of William and Mary; the Shoshone Bannock Tribal Museum at the Fort Hall Reservation in Idaho; Scotty's Castle in Death Valley National Park, California; the Golden Spike National Monument, Promontory, Utah; regional offices of the U.S. Forest Service and the Bureau of Land Management in Nevada and Utah; and the Utah Division of Wildlife Resources.

I owe a special debt to Don D. Fowler and Nancy J. Parezo, who reviewed the manuscript, and to other scholars and writers who read and commented on it, in full or on specific chapters: Ronald A. Hallett, Mary Dickson, and Dawn Marano. At the College of William and Mary, which supported a portion of the project, I appreciate the assistance of Raquel Nava Cerball and Tom Trovato in preparing the bibliography and illustrations. At the University of Nebraska Press, Matthew Bokovoy, acquisitions editor for Indigenous Studies and American West, and Elisabeth Chretien, associate editor, guided the manuscript through review and into production. Ann F. Baker, senior project editor, and copyeditor Katherine Hinkebein were patient and helpful at every turn during the long process of turning the manuscript into a book.

My husband, Ronald Hallett, was my first and last reader and a true Renaissance man who gave guidance on matters ranging from the literary to the automotive. I am grateful for his unfailing support.

Journeys West

Introduction

Remembering

The story went like this:

> Long ago and in a different time, a man and a woman set out on a journey through the high desert. They had just begun a life together when science took them there, to a place of beauty so spare that they saw the bones of the earth. A fierce sun shone each day, and the sky turned from blue to flame to black. Heat ebbed into cool as day gave way to night.
>
> The land that they crossed, much of it still remote, lay between high plateaus on north and south and imposing mountains on east and west. Roads were mere tracings on the surface of a landscape so open and immense that the rare human construction—a ranch house, a fence—had the look of a work in miniature. Names shown on maps, in English or not, told what people prize in an arid land: Deep Springs Valley and the Deep Creek Range, Tonopah and Pahrump—"pah" meaning water.
>
> In seven months and two trips, they saw as much as they could of that country.

A few years passed, and then a book appeared in print about the desert and the people they had met on their journeys. It told how Indians had once survived in that land—or rather, what elders remembered of an old way of life, and what explorers in the past recorded about the land and the people. One of those explorers gave the desert—America's largest—the name it still bears, the Great Basin.[1]

The book's title sounded scientific, suitably abstract if also hard to recall exactly. Even the author sometimes got it wrong. Later readers often used just the first two words of the title, *Basin-Plateau*. Despite its start as a scientific report published by the Government Printing Office, and a slightly awkward title, the book became a classic. It remains in print today.[2]

The author of *Basin-Plateau Aboriginal Sociopolitical Groups*, a young anthropologist named Julian Steward, had spent seven years of his life in the Great Basin, mostly in eastern California and Utah. That time included seven months of fieldwork with his wife in the 1930s, when they also traveled through Nevada and Idaho. Only one name appears on the cover of the book, but any reader who listens carefully can hear many voices in its pages. Very attentive readers will see that dozens of Paiute and Shoshone elders offered their knowledge and memories. Their initials are scattered throughout the text.

"GR rated pine nuts as most important," Steward wrote, "because in years of good harvest enough were gathered to last through most of the winter." In some cases, men and women long dead spoke through descendants, who recalled their grandparents' words and memories. "TS's grandfather described a hunt in the Sierra Nevada Mountains west of Owens Lake," Steward reported, "in which several hundred men from throughout the valley participated."[3]

Black-and-white photographs of the open landscape, taken by Steward, appeared as illustrations in *Basin-Plateau*. They show sweeping views of austere mountains and desert valleys and close-up shots of stoic desert plants: Joshua trees, with branches held high as if in supplication for rain; screw-bean mesquite trees the size of bushes, stunted by their chronic thirst; lonely stands of bunchgrass and sagebrush, which simply hold their ground and wait.[4]

There is not one portrait of a person in the book: neither GR nor TS nor any of the elders whose initials attest to their presence. The photographs show a land without people. The look of the desert landscape—the open sky and strong light, the contours of mountain and valley—had endured into the twentieth century. But a way of living based on hunting and gathering, foraging for wild food on wild land, survived for the most part in memory. People had moved with the seasons in search of food for generations until a flood of settlers entered their country: farmers, ranchers, merchants, miners, and workers who came from other places, mostly in North America but also from points beyond, in Europe, Asia, and Mexico.

The absence of human portraits in *Basin-Plateau* is apt, but only metaphorically. Paiutes, Shoshones, and Utes—The People, *Nimi* or *Newe* or *Nuche*, as they call themselves—did not disappear. They adapted to wrenching changes to their world, including ecological damage done by mass settlement. They had lived far more lightly on the land, and in much smaller numbers than the newcomers. Their survival as hunters and gatherers required it.

Perhaps most destructive to their hunting and gathering grounds were the herds of grazing animals brought by settlers. Cattle and sheep—domesticated animals not indigenous to the Americas—ate native plants that Paiutes and Shoshones and Utes gathered for food and that offered food and shelter for wildlife. As Steward noted in the opening pages of *Basin-Plateau*, the animals "grazed the hills, decimating native food plants."[5]

John Muir, the naturalist and early conservationist, called sheep "hoofed locusts" because of the ruinous effects of overgrazing on western lands. But the settlers' herds also devoured a way of life along with the wild plants they ate and the wild game they displaced. More than half a century later, elders remembered that the human intruders came in small numbers at first, followed by more and more who "sat down" instead of moving on, occupying their lands. To borrow from Muir's famous phrase, they had reason to regard the settlers as locusts in boots and bonnets. For their part most Americans—and the federal government—saw the wild lands as "waste," and transformations of the land as signs of "progress."[6]

Times change, and so do ways of speaking and of seeing events of the past. Today it might be said that a sustainable way of living on the land came to a sudden end, a result of unsustainable practices that degraded and damaged the fragile ecology of the desert.

I never met Julian Steward or any of the elders. Some of them died sixty years before I began to write a book about Steward and his ideas, the precursor to this book. He had thought about the environment and how people adapt to it—the links between environment and culture—in ways that seemed unusual for his times. After seeing a desert valley where he spent three formative years as a student, I wondered if his own experience of the desert had shaped those ideas. His insights about land and labor and technology provided the foundation for what he later called *cultural ecology*, a framework for understanding links between environment, the quest for food, and the structure of human groups.[7]

The first person I approached with questions, and one of the oldest, was Julian Steward's widow. She told me that she had gone with her husband on his field trips in the 1930s and had met nearly all of the elders who contributed to his book. When she recalled how old they seemed to her then, she laughed. She was in her twenties at the time of those trips, but when we met, she was a full decade older than some of the elders. Like them she had a keen memory that took us back in time more than half a century.

I spent a week with Jane Steward in Honolulu, where she moved after her husband's death. She had left their home of twenty years, on the Illinois prairie, for a new life in Hawaii. She lived happily in a high-rise building in the middle of the city, not far from the beach at Waikiki.

The muted din of traffic, far below us, drifted in through the open windows, along with the mild Hawaiian air, as we talked about long-ago events in another part of the world. That place of memory—a pale land of limitless space and sand, little water, few people, and searing sun—stood in complete contrast to the world she saw around her. Honolulu's beaches, fringes of white sand by limpid blue water, drew thousands of people each day to take part in latter-day sun worship.

Here and there, now and then: we leaped back and forth, from one place to another and one time to the next during conversations that continued for a week. Jane's memories looped around the events of a long life, as each recollection stirred another. They arose as memories often do, in a welter, not one by one or in strict order.

She had vivid recollections of traveling with her husband in the Great Basin in 1935 but said little about the second field trip, in 1936. Few specific memories came to mind about the many Paiutes and Shoshones whom she and her husband met—except in California, where some were old acquaintances from his student years. She did not mention meeting Shoshones known as Goshutes, or any Utes.[8] As I later learned by reading their fieldwork journal, Jane spent very little time with most of the elders—a few hours or a few days—which explained why she recalled so little about them. Her husband had a highly nomadic approach to fieldwork. With limited time and a vast region to cover, they rarely lingered in any place for more than a few days, and sometimes only for hours.

Although Jane lived firmly in the present, my questions drew her back fifty and sixty years into the past, to what she saw as another time, when life was very different. "Those were more innocent times," she said, with a trace of regret in her voice. It was so long ago, she added. Later, as other memories came to mind, she smiled and said that it seemed more like yesterday than half a century ago. She told me what she recalled of the journeys through the high desert with her husband, and about the later years of their life together as well as the early years of her own. I soon realized that it would take time for me to make sense of all these memories—to sort through what she had said and to return with other questions, asking her to explain what I had not understood or had not thought to ask.

Learning so much about Steward's life only deepened the sense that I knew almost nothing about his nearly invisible collaborators and guides. Who *were* those elders whose memories became ethnography? While searching through his papers I had seen several photographs of Paiute and Shoshone men, and a few women, taken during the field trips of the 1930s. Later, using his fieldwork journal and other records, I began to match names with some of the initials; and with his photographs, I put faces with a few of the names. Those faces had the contours and lines of lives spent in the open air, under the sun in all seasons. The expressions ranged from impassive to knowing.

Years passed, but their faces continued to come to mind. Learning some of the names and finding a few portraits did not satisfy my curiosity about the elders as individuals or dispel a strong sense that they had something of value to teach me, if only I knew more about them and their lives. Clearly, Steward had learned much from them in the 1930s and had left a record of their knowledge in his book—but any such record is always partial and a product of its own times. I thought that they had something more to teach us who live in the twenty-first century.

I began to search for photographs and records that could help me to identify all of the elders. Collaborators in a landmark book, they had remained unknown to nearly all of its readers. The search slowly yielded results. Initials became full names, and the outlines of lives—each one unique—emerged. Predictably, I learned more about some than about others, and, as is always the case, my knowledge remained partial. From the start I realized that I would always know far more about Julian Steward, who kept a journal and wrote books and sent and received thousands of letters, than about any one of the elders. I had read Steward's own words. I could hear theirs for the most part only through others' words about them.

As I slowly learned more about Steward's research, I was startled by how much his approach seemed to differ from mine, which I had accepted, with limited knowledge of its history, as standard practice for what came to be termed *ethnographic fieldwork* in the twentieth century. Like many cultural anthropologists of the later twentieth century, and the twenty-first, I assumed that fieldwork involved intensive and extended contact with a community, not interviews with one or a few individuals at a series of sites. I began to think of Steward as a nomad, while many other cultural anthropologists were sojourners who settle in one place for the requisite year or more as I had done.

Later, after repeated readings of *Basin-Plateau*, I realized that Steward's fieldwork was in the tradition of early journeys to the West, especially the scientific expeditions whose reports he cited in his book. I wondered how that single difference—moving on or staying—affects the questions that cultural anthropologists ask, what they see, and what they know of the people who answer their questions. I had also learned, to my surprise, that Steward paid the elders, and sometimes interpreters, an hourly wage to work with him, and that this was customary at the time. The use of interpreters in fieldwork, as I knew, had for the most part ended long ago. Reciprocity had in nearly all cases replaced payment of a wage.

As I learned more about the elders, I also began to wonder about questions Steward had *not* asked them. He asked how they lived before outsiders occupied their lands. Given his interest in ecology, why did he remain largely silent about the environmental effects of settlement? Why did he say so little in *Basin-Plateau* about how they adapted to an ecological crisis in the mid-nineteenth century, and how they survived conquest and colonization?

The usual explanation is that anthropologists of his day engaged in what came to be termed *salvage ethnography*: documenting nearly "extinct" ways of life before all memory of them vanished. But the aims of Steward's fieldwork in the 1930s, I had discovered, were more complex. He did want to document the past, but above all he was searching for evidence in support of a theory. That aim, as well as his approach to fieldwork, affected the questions he asked—but as I came to see, so did the times. Today's questions about the environment—and perspectives on the history of the American West as a history of colonialism—are informed by events, and interpretations of events, that Steward never knew about or that he learned of late in life.[9]

As I understood more about Steward's fieldwork, asked other questions about the elders, and saw the desert and mountains and the places where they had lived, a series of stories came slowly into focus. They were comprised of the many recollections that elders in the nineteenth century passed on to their descendants; the memories that those descendants, as elders themselves, gave Julian Steward and other anthropologists in the 1930s; the personal memories that Jane Steward recounted to me more than a half century later; and firsthand accounts of places and events that I found in written sources, ranging from the journal that she and her husband kept and letters they wrote to the yellowed pages of handwritten records, typescripts, and old books.

There is the story of their fieldwork in the American West: journeys made in the hard years of the Great Depression by a young anthropologist and his wife who were in love with each other and who at first embraced the romance of the road. For Steward, the journey was a quest for science, yielding results that he later reported in *Basin-Plateau*, about how Paiutes and Shoshones and Utes lived before losing their lands to colonizers in the mid-nineteenth century. He told how they had survived as hunters and gatherers in the high desert, using intimate knowledge of plants and animals and place to make a living from the land.

There is the later story, only hinted at in *Basin-Plateau*, about how settlement of their lands by massive numbers of outsiders—food producers who lived by farming and ranching, as well as miners—caused an ecological crisis for native people. The changes to desert lands soon destroyed the foragers' food supply, the seeds of wild grasses and the other native plants and animals that had long sustained them. And there is the linked story of how the survivors survived, of their flexibility and resilience as they adapted to a radically changed world, often by using old skills and knowledge in new and creative ways.

Most of the men and women who answered Steward's questions were not only elders. They were also first-generation survivors, as I suddenly realized while reconstructing the outlines of their lives. They had witnessed and lived through the Catastrophe. The severe ecological damage done to their homelands, and the loss of land, formed a central part of their life histories.

Woven into their lives, as I came to see them, is an overarching narrative about major environmental change caused by human activities. I began to wonder if what Steward did *not* report—the hardships that the elders faced when their world suddenly changed, and how they adapted to the change—could tell us something about the possible shape of the future. They experienced an ecological crisis on a local and regional scale, but by a century and a half later the dimensions had increased. The prospect of ecological change on a global scale, in the form of global warming and climate change, finally entered wide public consciousness in the early twenty-first century.

When I left Hawaii I planned to return within the year, armed with many more questions. I had no way of knowing that Jane Steward, vibrant and life loving, was in the last months of her nearly eighty years of life.[10] Like her late husband, who questioned several elders who soon died, I had recorded memories that would have vanished just months later when a life ended. They were memories of a distant time and of little-known places and events.

Some of the places, as she told me, had changed almost beyond recognition in half a century, from open desert to city sprawl, a startling mutation based on importing water from faraway rivers. Other places, as I would later see for myself, remain thinly populated. Many of them retain the desolate and singular beauty that certain travelers in the past, including Julian Steward, admired. To this day the high desert landscape of the Great Basin attracts some people who happen to pass through its vast reaches. Others, disturbed by a lack of green and by the openness and unexpected scale, do not linger and look at a place once known as "the interior of California" and still called by many names: the Sagebrush Sea, Basin and Range, the Big Empty. Western Shoshones, who claim much of it as homeland, call it *Newe Sogobia*, the People's Land, and *Bia Sogobia*, Mother Earth.[11]

Although she did not say very much about the elders she met so briefly, Jane did have memories of fieldwork, especially of the first trip, in 1935. She recalled the foods she and her husband ate, how they got water and carried enough to reach the next source, where they stayed, and other details of daily life as they traveled through California and Nevada. In an odd and apt way, her memories ran parallel to her husband's research, the questions he asked elders about how they had once lived in that arid land.

On our last day together I asked Jane why her husband had turned away from fieldwork after the 1930s. She looked puzzled and considered the question carefully, as if for the first time. Finally she cited complications and commitments of life: children, competing work demands, and ill health. But when I asked how she and Julian had fared during their desert journeys, how she remembered the time and the place—and their time together in that place—she answered at once, with feeling.

"That was Eden," she said.

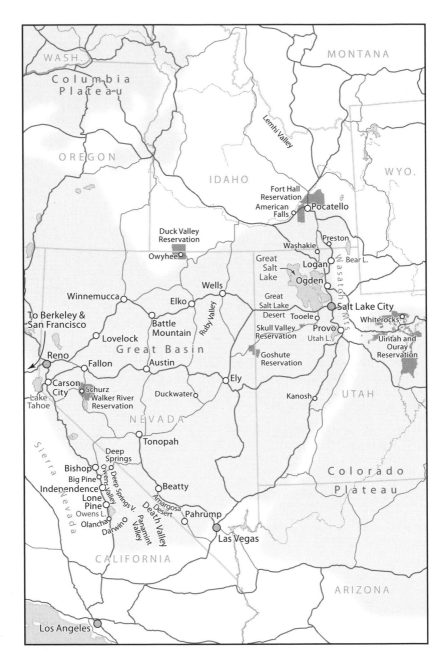

1. The Great Basin

PART I. California, 1935

1. Going There

IN SPRING 1935 Julian Steward was thirty-three years old, happily married to his second wife, and temporarily out of work.

He had given up a promising position in anthropology at the University of Michigan in 1930 in order to marry his first wife, a psychologist, and join her at the University of Utah. So unusual was that decision for the times, one friend recalled, that all of his colleagues thought him "mad." He had traded a place at a major university for one with fewer prospects. He had also married a woman who was eight years older and successful in her career, a poor choice of helpmate as they saw it. Only three years later he lost his position at the university and left under a cloud of scandal.[1]

Unhappy in his marriage he had separated from his wife in 1932. Then a love affair with a young woman who belonged to a prominent family came to light, with damaging—some suspected ruinous—results for his academic career. Julian Steward married Jane Cannon in Mexico in 1933, a few months after leaving Utah. He and Jane settled in Berkeley, California.

Their joy with each other and their life together spilled out in letters to friends and family. Even Julian's colleagues at the university noticed. "We have been so gloriously happy and alive here in Berkeley," Jane told her father just months after they arrived. To her sister she reported celebrating their fifth month of marriage. Her brother summed up her new life in just one sentence. "In spite of unsettled conditions and a decided pinching of the bank account," he assured their parents, "she is the happiest person in the world."[2]

What had drawn Jane and Julian together, besides the instant attraction, were their skepticism and an urge to resist, quietly, some conventions of the time. Both had rebelled against what they saw as the dogma and restrictions of organized religion. They recognized each other as fellow rebels from their first meeting.

Jane Cannon descended from one of the earliest Mormon settlers to enter the western territory of high mountains and high desert that became Utah. Her grandfather also served for many years as one of Brigham Young's closest advisors and as Utah Territory's representative to Congress. She could not have had more distinguished ancestry in her community unless she had descended from Young himself, who led the Mormons west in the 1840s, or from their prophet, Joseph Smith. Her father had always planned that she would marry a man in good standing with the church—not a man of uncertain beliefs who was not Mormon.

Julian Steward also had ties to one of the new churches that emerged in America in the nineteenth century. His mother converted to Christian Science, joining the Church of Christ, Scientist, when he was nine years old; but his father, the child of a minister, remained a staunch Baptist. His parents' religious differences, among others, finally led them to separate when he was fifteen, marking the end of a shared family life. He entered a boarding school the next year, in 1918.

Later, as a college student, he chose science for his life work and put aside the claims of religion. It was the era of the Scopes trial, called "the trial of a century," when a jury deliberated for just nine minutes before finding that schoolteacher John Scopes had broken the law by teaching about evolution. Like many other people of the time, Steward viewed science and religion as completely different ways of understanding the world. He later told his devout father-in-law very frankly that the "basic assumptions, the methods, and the proofs" of science shared almost no common ground with religion.[3]

Long before they met, Jane and Julian had begun to smoke cigarettes and drink coffee, practices that were not just personal habits but a way of expressing dissent. (Both Mormonism and Christian Science strongly discourage the use of nicotine, caffeine, and alcohol.) They drank alcohol socially, beginning in the 1920s, during the years of Prohibition when nearly all of the alcohol was bootleg. To keep peace with her parents, with whom she lived happily, Jane did not smoke or drink in their presence or with their knowledge. She thought of these as small rebellions, bohemian, and regarded Julian as a fellow *bohême*.[4]

Their differences also drew them together. Jane, light-eyed and fair-skinned, always remembered that she had been attracted immediately to Julian, in her eyes the prototype of the tall, dark, handsome man. Her effervescent good humor rarely failed, and she liked to laugh. Julian's friends approved of her from the start. She was "high-spirited," in the language of the day, and made friends quickly. By contrast, Julian, usually serious and at times withdrawn, often depended on Jane's buoyant spirits to lift his own.

They settled in Berkeley because Julian needed to find work, and Berkeley offered the best prospects. In those years of the Great Depression, jobs remained scarce and the unemployment rate high. New positions on university faculties had nearly vanished. Six years earlier Julian had earned a PhD in anthropology from the University of California, and he hoped that his contacts in Berkeley would help him to locate professional work.

In the meantime they moved into a small apartment near the university. Jane, a skilled stenographer who could take dictation and type, found work as a secretary. Previously she had helped her father run a small family business, the Cannon Supply Company. By the age of twenty she felt like the de facto assistant manager. "We are going to hang out a shingle, 'J. J. Cannon & Daughter,'" she joked to her younger brother. But then the Depression descended, the Cannon Supply Company went out of business, and she found a position as secretary to the president of an advertising firm. And then she met Julian.[5]

By spring 1935 her new husband had held a series of temporary jobs, including one term when he taught courses in place of his former teacher, the well-known Alfred L. Kroeber, who had a leave of absence. After Kroeber returned to Berkeley, Julian cast about for other opportunities but found nothing. Jane's parents continued to send encouraging letters, as they had from the start. Her father had earlier advised them not to worry too much about just such a lapse in Julian's employment since Jane was working. "He can spend his time perhaps more usefully to himself and you in his [research and] study than in a teaching position," he told her.[6]

Resolved to have a career in anthropology, despite a complete lack of prospects, Julian searched for grants to support fieldwork. He wanted to extend his previous research with Paiute Indians in California to Shoshone and Ute Indians in Nevada and Utah. He finally applied to the only two foundations that seemed likely sources. Then he and Jane marked time, awaiting letters about funding. "If I had a penny for every day I've waited for mail on jobs, divorce, etc.," Jane told her parents cheerfully, "I'd be able to take us on a world tour."[7]

In the late 1920s, as a graduate student, Steward had spent weeks at a time during two summers doing fieldwork with Paiute Indians. That research took him back to the region where he had attended boarding school, in eastern California. He worked at the northern end of the Owens Valley, a high desert valley that stretched for more than eighty miles along the rugged eastern face of the Sierra Nevada.[8]

Following standard procedure for the time, he sought out elders to question about their way of life in the nineteenth century, at the point just before conquest and settlement by Americans. Many changes, ecological and cultural, took place in the aftermath of struggles with American soldiers and settlers in the 1860s. As Steward later wrote, after 1870 the people of the Great Basin were "rapidly dislodged from their native habitat."[9] That habitat also quickly degraded, a result of intensive mining, ranching, and farming.

In the 1920s Steward, like most American anthropologists, saw his task as reconstructing and recording an earlier way of life, not as documenting current life. Before all memory of it vanished, he wanted to learn how Paiutes had once lived in the place American settlers called the Owens Valley. Working mainly with elders as cultural informants, he recorded old stories and songs and collected kinship terms and life histories. During the second summer he also collected more unusual material. He decided to compile detailed lists of the wild plants that women had once gathered and the game animals that men had hunted. Using techniques he had learned the previous year in a field geography course, he also mapped the location of old Paiute villages, trails, and hunting grounds. He reported to Kroeber on what he called "this more or less geographical study."[10] In the future he would instead term his approach *ecological*.

When he returned to live in Berkeley seven years later, in the mid-1930s, he developed a long-term plan for research. His interrupted employment had one benefit: freed from the crushing demands of teaching, which had taken him by surprise at the start of his career, he had time to think more deeply about his ideas. Jane Steward clearly remembered his "pronouncements," as she called them, about how he would begin by studying the smallest, simplest human societies—those based on hunting and gathering wild foods—and then move on to more complex societies. He woke up one morning in Berkeley, she recalled, and announced that he had "a twenty-year research plan."[11]

Years earlier, as a student, Steward had been intrigued to learn that Paiute languages belong to the Uto-Aztecan language family. Paiutes and Aztecs spoke distantly related languages. They shared ancestors, yet Paiutes in the Owens Valley had long lived as foragers in small groups while the Aztecs had created a large empire to the south. Aztecs farmed the land and built a city of such splendor that Spanish invaders in the sixteenth century admired it even as they set about destroying it. The Aztecs qualified as a civilization, or what came to be termed *complex society*. In contrast, Paiutes, like other hunter-gatherers and most indigenous people, were categorized in the early twentieth century as a *primitive society*. (Later generations of anthropologists would abandon that term, which sounded pejorative, and define more specific ones, such as *band* and *tribe*.)

Steward was working out some unusual ideas about the ecology of human groups, and he had an important insight—at the outset, just a hunch—that needed supporting evidence from fieldwork. He thought that the food-getting quest had predictable effects on the structure of social life. Similar ways of getting food—or forms of subsistence—would probably result in similar social structures, which he came to call *culture types*. This could help to explain a puzzle: why Paiutes and Aztecs, despite shared if distant ancestry, had developed into such different types of societies, especially in terms of size and complexity.

Starting with the smallest societies, hunter-gatherers, Steward identified two culture types, which he termed the *patrilineal band* and the *composite band*. The patrilineal band had five defining characteristics, he said: "land ownership, political autonomy, patrilocal residence, band or local exogamy, and patrilineal inheritance." It was a politically independent and land-owning group of male kin. In other words, it claimed and defended exclusive rights to a defined territory. The men of a patrilineal band were related as fathers and sons, brothers, and so on; they inherited rights to land passed down through men. Women married in from other groups, as required by rules of band exogamy and patrilocal residence.

The composite band was also a land-owning group, but in contrast to the patrilineal band, it had a highly variable form. Steward defined it largely in terms of how it differed from the patrilineal band, or what it lacked. The composite band did not have strict rules of band exogamy, patrilocal residence, or inheritance of land by patrilineal kin. He also alluded to a third type of band, which he termed the *matrilineal band*, but he said little about it.

Instead, he drew on published writings that described male-centered local groups. Some anthropologists of the time thought that these groups had originated during the earliest stages of human life and then diffused widely. Theories of diffusion had gained popularity as a way of explaining why different cultural groups—often neighbors but sometimes not—shared traits: for example, a style of basketry or a type of ceremony. These cultural traits had presumably diffused from one group to another.

Anthropologists also used traits to classify cultures. They had divided native North America into what they termed *culture areas*, placing groups that shared many traits and spoke related languages within each specific area. Kroeber was recognized as the world's authority on California Indians and the California culture area. He also had field experience with Indians of the Southwest culture area and others.

Since the boundaries between culture areas, like those between racial categories, were arbitrary, the debates between lumpers and splitters proved difficult to resolve. Which cultural traits (or physical traits, in the case of race) were diagnostic? Where should lines be drawn between categories? There was no consensus about the number of culture areas in native North America—or the number of races in the world.

Steward did not take part in most of these discussions and debates beyond questioning the importance of diffusion.[12] He wanted to find a more scientific way of classifying cultures than by content; that is, other than by using every sort of cultural trait, from designs on pottery to beliefs about spirits. Identifying culture types—based on ecology and social structure—seemed less arbitrary and more scientific to him. A culture type such as the patrilineal band might be found all over the world, not in just one geographic area. If the patrilineal band had existed on nearly every continent, something other than diffusion probably accounted for that. He thought that "something" was ecology, the relation between people and the natural environment. His reading, and some of his own experience, led him to think that the patrilineal band developed among hunters and gatherers who lived in arid places or in other environments with a limited food supply.

Where the food supply was limited, he reasoned, the population had to remain small and population density low. People lived in small groups, bands of no more than about fifty or sixty. Foraging on that land could not support more people. Because men hunted, they had greater economic importance, Steward believed, than women, who only gathered wild plants for food. Men, as hunters—and, he assumed, as the main providers of food—found advantage in remaining in their familiar home territory. Presumably that enhanced their success in hunting and promoted group survival.

Steward also said that "innate male dominance" favored male-centered groups. In that single phrase he expressed a common belief among Americans at the time, and among many members of his own profession, about the nature of male-female relations. Decades would pass before gender inequality—in fact and in theory—was called into question by anthropologists.[13]

His earlier research with Paiutes in the Owens Valley convinced him that they had lived in composite bands, not in patrilineal bands. Reports about hunter-gatherers elsewhere in the world, however, led him to think that patrilineal bands had existed in many places, including the deserts of Australia and Southern California. The groups that Australian Aborigines lived in, termed *patrilineal hordes* at that time, seemed to resemble what he called the patrilineal band. William Duncan Strong, his friend and onetime roommate in Berkeley, had written about Indians in Southern California who lived in groups he called *patrilineal clans*. These too seemed to qualify as patrilineal bands. Steward believed that he might find evidence of such bands in the deserts of the American West—if not in the Owens Valley then perhaps among Shoshones who lived in the desolate Death Valley region or in the austere desert lands to the east.[14]

One day, a month or two after he submitted grant proposals, the mail brought Julian and Jane good news. A letter from a foundation informed him that he had been awarded a small grant. Kroeber offered him the additional funds he needed for about six to eight months of fieldwork with Paiutes and Shoshones in eastern California and Nevada. The funds came with strings attached. Kroeber was directing a research project that he called the Culture Element Distribution Survey. It had the immediate goal of recording detailed lists of cultural traits from many groups of western Indians. He planned to subject the lists to statistical analysis at a later point, looking for patterns in the distribution of traits. Several of his graduate students had already set to work.[15]

Steward took no interest in the project, which struck him as ill conceived and even pointless. His training in the natural sciences—in geology and zoology, which he studied as an undergraduate—had taught him to ask questions about causality and to frame hypotheses at the outset of research. His ideas about bands reflected his earlier training in science, not his experience as Kroeber's student.

When he had raised questions about causality, Kroeber made it clear that he doubted that anything noncultural "caused" anything cultural. "I am interested in phenomena, not causes," Kroeber told his young student more than once. He seemed to regard the quest for causality as an exercise in futility. Steward, in contrast, would come to think that natural, or ecological, features such as scarcity of water or the migratory habits of wild game might have causal effects on human social groups, helping to shape their structure.[16]

The culture element survey had no bearing on Steward's questions about ecology, but for practical reasons he agreed to cooperate. Kroeber, then approaching the age of sixty, had achieved eminence in his profession during a long career and had the respect of colleagues in the United States and abroad. Steward needed Kroeber's advice and goodwill as he continued the search for employment. He also needed the money that Kroeber offered for fieldwork.

On a Saturday in mid-April Julian and Jane left Berkeley. Jane had just given up her job and they had also given up the lease on their apartment, putting most of their belongings into storage. Their worldly possessions, she remembered, did not amount to much, although their financial situation during those Depression years was never desperate, in contrast to many Americans. They always had the money to buy necessities. Still, unsure about their whereabouts in the near future, she considered every purchase carefully, wondering if it would pack. "The nomadic life agrees with me," she told her parents, "and Julian is happy, so we are all right."[17]

They drove a standard passenger car, a Chevrolet coupe, which Julian had fitted out for camping in the desert. To combat the hot dry air, which felt like a blast from a forced-air heater as it blew in through the car windows, they carried desert water bags. Each canvas bag held about two gallons and could be hung over a window. The rush of hot air over damp canvas caused evaporation, cooling the air as it entered the car.

At night in the desert the blistering daytime heat gave way to cold as temperatures fell by thirty or even forty degrees. The bedroll that Julian had made—a large, thick quilt filled with ten pounds of wool batting and covered with flannel—would keep them warm during the nights. Since it was so bulky, and the car trunk so small, he wrapped it in a canvas tarp and fastened it to the front bumper when they traveled. The same tarp could be attached to the car, to serve as an awning on days when the car was parked for long hours. When lowered at night, the tarp looked like a cross between a lean-to and a tent.

A skillet and a pan and a coffee pot—along with matches, a can opener and knife, and a supply of canned food and coffee—sufficed for campfire cooking. They had a few sturdy dishes made of metal. The large tanks of water that they carried would allow them to do dry camping, staying in places without a stream or spring nearby. Spare parts for the car, two or three gas cans, a jack and a spare tire and tire pump, and Julian's skill in car repair: these offered the only insurance against serious trouble on a lonely road.

Their gear also included a first-aid kit and what Jane called an "umbrella chair." The umbrella, attached to a folding chair, protected mainly against sun, not the rare cloudburst. It provided shade when the awning was not set up and a protected place to read and write. Long hours in the desert sun could cause illness and severe burns to skin. Lotions to prevent sunburn did not yet exist, and Jane later recalled that she usually wore a hat to protect her fair skin and to shield her eyes from sunlight. Despite those measures, she soon began to tan. "I am even browner now than last summer," she told her father, alluding to a research trip that she and Julian had made to the Southwest.[18]

They did not wear tinted sun goggles, later known as sunglasses, for travel. Sun goggles were still strictly for Hollywood and the beach. Their conservative clothing and hats were more appropriate for the work ahead. Whenever the hard sunlight hurt their eyes, they pulled down their hat brims.

Besides the camping gear, Julian took his typewriter, paper for field notes and letters, a small notebook that served as their field journal, and maps. Keeping the journal would give them a record of where he and Jane went, the people they met on their journey, and noteworthy "incidents of travel," to borrow a favorite phrase of earlier travelers. The road maps, some sketchy, would help them choose routes through remote areas of Nevada. Sometimes they simply made their best guess when they came to a turnoff and then drove in that direction. There were so few cars on the roads during those years, and settlements stood so far apart, that they could never count on asking other motorists or anyone else for advice.

Their collection of U.S. Geological Survey maps provided more than help in choosing a route. The maps showed features of the landscape, including water sources, which held a central place in Steward's ideas about culture and ecology. As he learned from elders where people had found water and hunted and gathered in an earlier time, he located those places on the maps. If the sites were fairly accessible, he tried to visit them. The elders gave him guidance about location but did not often go with him. In some cases they lived on reservations far from the sites.

A seasoned desert traveler, Steward had already made many trips—on foot and horseback earlier in life, and later by car—across the arid lands of eastern California and western Utah. Just a year earlier he and his wife had driven thousands of miles through the desert West, visiting prehistoric sites such as Chaco Canyon and old settlements, including Zuni Pueblo and Taos Pueblo. They crossed Arizona and New Mexico and returned to California by way of Utah and Nevada.[19]

He left Berkeley well prepared for this journey because of past experience. No doubt he could have recited the staple advice given to any motorist who planned to travel on rough roads in the desert: "An adequate supply of water should be carried, for the traveler and for the radiator; also gas, oil, and food. . . . In sand, stay in the ruts and drive steadily. . . . If wheels sink in the sand and the car will not move, clear away the sand and throw a canvas tarpaulin or brush in front of the wheels to obtain traction. Be careful in crossing dry lakes." Rutted and rocky roads in the desert and mountains, as he knew from prior travel, posed still other hazards to a car. They caused blowouts and could tear off the oil pan.[20]

He and Jane took the southern route to the Owens Valley, driving on a two-lane highway through the green San Joaquin Valley to avoid the deep snow of the Sierra Nevada. The northern route, which crossed the mountains, often remained closed until June. After spending the night in Bakersfield they continued on, crossed Tehachapi Pass, and descended into the pale desert land of eastern California. They turned north toward the Owens Valley and higher terrain. With an elevation of more than four thousand feet, and fewer than ten inches of rainfall each year, the valley floor qualified as high desert.[21]

Julian knew the Owens Valley well and always felt a sense of homecoming when he returned, having lived nearby for three years. The unusual boarding school he attended was a working ranch as well as a college preparatory school, the creation of a lawyer and entrepreneur named Lucien L. Nunn. He had used his wealth to put some innovative ideas about education into practice. Nunn wanted students to learn not only in the classroom but also outside it: to work with their hands and use their minds to solve practical problems, learning by doing. He thought of education as life training, not simply as book knowledge. Its lessons included responsibility and cooperation and concern for the common good, not just for personal gain. He hoped to train generations of leaders for public service.[22]

At the school he founded in Deep Springs Valley, about twenty male students attended classes in the morning and did ranch work outdoors in the afternoon. Some of the hired ranch hands were usually Paiute men, most often from the Owens Valley. On ranches throughout the region, the cowboys were Indians: Paiute, Shoshone, and Washoe men. Julian had first met Paiutes as workers at the ranch during his student years at Deep Springs. Six years after leaving the school, in the late 1920s, he had seen some of them during summer research as a graduate student in the Owens Valley. Now he planned to draw on those contacts once again.

As he and Jane traveled north, they drove along a road called El

1. The ranch in Deep Springs Valley. (Photo by Julian H. Steward, courtesy of Deep Springs College)

Camino Sierra. The very name of the valley's only highway attracted tourists to that scenic place. The level two-lane road also offered a respite from the narrow dirt tracks that crossed much of the western desert, saving wear and tear on vehicles and travelers alike. Its graded surface of gravel, oiled to keep down the dust, gave way here and there to short and welcome stretches of smooth pavement. Dirt roads intersected with the main road, and billowing clouds of dust rose in the wake of any car that left the highway for a byway.[23]

Midway along their route through the valley, Julian and Jane passed the town of Independence, California, once the home of writer Mary Austin. She had died months earlier in Santa Fe, New Mexico. Austin's well-known book, *The Land of Little Rain*, had established her as a writer and brought the people and landscape of the Owens Valley to the attention of the American reading public in the first years of the twentieth century. She called the area that they were driving through, east of the Sierra Nevada, "the Country of Lost Borders."[24]

The region shown on their map as the Owens Valley fell within the boundaries of Inyo County and the state of California; and the towns, incorporated and bounded, bore names such as Lone Pine and Independence and Bishop. It was the ancestral home of Paiutes who called these sites by other names, often by names of landmarks. Lone Pine was known as Yellow Pine Place in the language of the Owens Valley Paiutes.[25] Just as their place names differed from those shown on the map, their stories of the past differed from those recorded in history books.

They had lost most of their territory to conquest by the United States in the early 1860s. The Paiutes struggled to keep out the rising number of American intruders, but the conflict ended after three years. Their land was opened to American settlers under public-land laws. Living near the western edge of the continent, Paiutes could not be pushed much farther west, and they resisted attempts to send them to distant reservations.

In 1935 more than a thousand still lived in the valley, only about half the number who lived there when Americans arrived in the nineteenth century. Warfare, hunger, dispossession, and disease had soon created a downward spiral of premature deaths and declining numbers. The population of Paiutes, in the Owens Valley and elsewhere, remained low after American settlement.[26]

The survivors had lost not only their land but also their livelihood and a way of life as hunter-gatherers. As Steward already knew—from reading historical works, living in the area, and talking to elders—the ecology changed suddenly in the nineteenth century when American settlers streamed into the valley and brought a different way of living on the land. Their herds of livestock grazed on wild grasses, eating the seeds that Paiute women had long gathered to feed their families. Settlers cut down pinyon trees, the source of the pine nuts that provided the Paiute staff of life during the winter. Irrigated farm fields and orchards occupied places where other native, edible plants had grown. Roads crossed the valley floor, and railroad tracks soon skirted the bordering mountains. Privately owned land, with boundary markers and fences, replaced what had once been open space. The human population doubled, and then doubled again, and again. Wild game dwindled in the face of massive habitat loss, and Paiute men found less and less to hunt.

This happened in the course of a single generation. Paiutes who were born in the mid-nineteenth century experienced an ecological crisis and witnessed the transformation of their world.

The new need to buy some of their food left men and women with no choice but to sell their labor. Like many before them, they went to work for wages because they had lost their land. The United States government transferred—sold or granted—most of the Paiutes' territory to American settlers and enterprises, including railroads and mining companies.[27] A faraway city eventually gained exclusive rights to the river's water. What the Paiutes had inherited from their ancestors—a place to live and a way of living there, drawing sustenance from wild foods—could no longer be passed on intact to their children and to their children's children.

Many of the men found work on the ranches and farms that were the very source of so many changes in the land and in their way of life. Others hired out at mines or joined crews to build roads. Women often worked as laundresses at the same ranches and farms, or for settlers who lived in the valley towns. Farmers also hired them as threshers during the wheat harvest, preferring them to threshing machines because of the women's skill and the low cost of employing them.[28] But even before the 1930s and the hard times of the Great Depression, these jobs had grown scarce as farmers and ranchers, and then many of the merchants and other town residents, left the valley.

In the early years of the twentieth century, agents of the City of Los Angeles, using disguised identities, had quietly begun offering option contracts to farmers. In exchange for a cash payment, a landowner agreed to sell the land for a specified price in the future. When many of the farmers had signed contracts, the city exercised its options and claimed the land. City officials did not want the land itself but rights to the water of the Owens River, which ran through farmland. They planned, and soon began to build, an aqueduct to carry the water more than two hundred miles to Los Angeles, a thriving and thirsting metropolis. The secret maneuvers looked like water rustling but were not illegal.[29]

This set in motion yet another transformation of the Owens Valley. Farmland that had produced bumper crops of wheat and potatoes and apples, and pastures that had supported large herds of cattle, slowly reverted to high desert. Sagebrush came to dominate a landscape where, before the entry of American settlers, tall stands of wild grasses and other native plants had also grown, providing much of the Paiutes' food.[30] And water from the streams and river that Paiutes had always used freely now belonged to a distant city that many of them had never seen.

The ecology had changed, even if the geology of the valley gave an appearance of constancy. Travelers still saw the sharp peaks of the Sierra, gleaming with snow; and the Owens River continued its southward flow, fed by springs and snowmelt. But the lives of the Paiute people had changed irrevocably as a result of losing their land and the wild plants and animals that had once sustained them.

Farming and ranching had transformed the ecology of the Owens Valley in the nineteenth century, and even the abrupt departure of so many farmers and ranchers could not reverse the change, restoring what was lost.

In 1935 the oldest Paiute men and women in the valley had memories and knowledge of the land that reached back to the middle years of the nineteenth century. Their geography of the region differed from the lines shown on maps issued by the State of California and by the

United States Geological Survey. Anthropologists of the day, including Steward, made a practice of questioning elders about their remembered territories. They wanted to record knowledge of territories and borders before it was completely lost. Their ambitious goal was to identify all of the native cultures of North America before contact and conquest by Europeans and Americans and to learn their locations—and dislocations—thus creating a map of culture areas.

Yet even the maps that anthropologists published in monographs could not fully represent the memories and perspectives on which they were based. The maps offered simple graphic renderings of a complex remembered past, expressed in words and in response to persistent, and perhaps confusing, questions. Anthropologists struggled to frame comprehensible questions about territories and boundaries and to understand answers, a slow and often difficult process. Fraught with confusion on both sides of the cultural divide between Indian informant and non-Indian anthropologist, it required the patience and goodwill of both parties.

Only a month after Steward set to work in the Owens Valley, Kroeber wrote to a young graduate student named Omer Stewart. He was doing fieldwork near the coast in Northern California and felt frustrated by the task of determining territorial lines. Kroeber advised him not to worry too much about boundaries. "If you do not think too much about them," he said, "they have a way of settling themselves." He suggested putting the questions in terms of how land was occupied and used. "This will show in a great many cases," he explained, "that one group of Indians claimed a creek but recognized the priority claims of another group to a creek on the other side of a ridge or divide. The watershed thus forms the de facto boundary, and can be so entered on the map, although no old Indian might so state explicitly."

Shifting from practical advice to larger questions of cultural difference, he commented, "Their whole point of view was the opposite of ours. We begin by delimiting a state by such and such surveyed lines; then we survey some more lines, and whatever is inside a set of four becomes a county." Instead of beginning in this manner, with an outside frame, an Indian "begins with the spot where he was born," Kroeber said. "Around this is the territory where he habitually wandered over and got his food from. Farther up the creek, or in the hills, is territory where he might occasionally hunt. His mind works outward from a spot, or a group of spots; the edges are hazy."

Returning to practical matters, Kroeber advised getting "all the information which he really has from his own angle," because that would probably make it possible to put boundaries on a map. "You will certainly find some cases where there is no boundary, whenever the land was not utilized by the Indians," he added. He cited the example of very dense stands of redwood trees, which offered little by way of food.[31]

As Jane and Julian drove north through the Owens Valley, they crossed and recrossed the aqueduct built by the City of Los Angeles to carry the river water to its distant destination. The city now owned most of the property in towns and 95 percent of what had recently been farmland. Some of the farmers and ranchers had resisted the loss of land and water to the city, just as Paiutes and Shoshones had once struggled against encroachment by settlers. The valley residents engaged in one of the first and fiercest water wars in the American West, conflict that escalated into armed violence in the 1920s. Finally, in defeat, most sold their land to the City of Los Angeles and left the valley. In an effort to erase any reminders of the recent past and to put a stop to resistance, the city cut down orchards, razed farmhouses, and plowed up pastures and fields.[32]

Jane, a new visitor to the valley, saw a dry land and a sea of sagebrush that reminded her of the Utah desert south and west of Salt Lake City. The Owens Valley in fact marked the western border of the Great Basin: a region of high desert valleys and hundreds of mountain ranges, stretching from the eastern side of the Sierra Nevada across the state of Nevada to the foot of Utah's Wasatch Mountains. Because of tall mountains and plateaus surrounding the desert on all sides, water from streams and rivers did not reach the sea. Its final destination was salt flats, where the water evaporated completely, or shallow lakes of saline water. Great Salt Lake was the largest of these, and Jane had grown up just miles from its shoreline in Salt Lake City. The Owens Valley also had a saline lake, although little trace of it remained in 1935.

Julian, unlike his wife, had memories of Owens Lake and the valley that reached back seventeen years, half of his lifetime. He recalled green orchards and pastures and the shady, tree-lined lanes that once led to well-kept farmhouses. All of that had vanished by 1935. He had witnessed the second ecological transformation of the valley in its brief recorded history. Like the first, it was extraordinarily rapid and the outcome of human activity, political and economic.

At the hamlet of Big Pine they turned east and left the Owens Valley. Crossing a high pass between the White and Inyo mountains, they descended into Deep Springs Valley. With an elevation of five thousand feet and an area of about fifty square miles, Deep Springs Valley was higher, smaller, and drier than the Owens Valley. Springs at one end of the arid valley were a source of some of its water as well as its English name. A creek, too small to attract the notice of a faraway city, also supplied water. When L. L. Nunn bought the ranch for his innovative school, he had secured the rights to Wyman Creek.[33]

Indians had lived in the valley for generations, always in small numbers, but even those numbers could not be sustained after ranching began there. Like the Owens Valley, the ecology of Deep Springs Valley had changed when grazing livestock entered the area and consumed the native food plants. This created an ecological crisis for Paiutes who could no longer hunt and gather what they needed to survive.

2. Julian and Jane Steward (*on left*) with Deep Springs students, April 1935. (Courtesy of Deep Springs College)

They left the valley after 1880, and most went to live in Big Pine and other settlements in the Owens Valley. Over the years a few returned to Deep Springs to work as ranch hands.[34]

The sole inhabitants of the valley in 1935, mostly male, lived at the school and ranch. These included the students, about twenty young men; several teachers and their wives; the ranch manager; and the ranch hands, including a few Paiute men. Julian had agreed to give some lectures in anthropology at his old school in return for room and board. He and Jane stayed for nearly two weeks, visiting with the teachers and their wives and the students and preparing for fieldwork.[35] With limited funds for research, which would barely cover living expenses, gasoline, and informant fees, they needed this subsidy of food and lodging.

The school also offered a quiet place for thinking and for writing. During his stay at Deep Springs Steward finished revising an essay on the ecology and structure of patrilineal and composite bands. It was his first statement in print about the two types of bands, the outcome of years of research and reading that also spurred his upcoming fieldwork. Later in life he called the essay his "first major theoretical work." He drew on primary data from his own field research with the Owens Valley Paiutes in writing about the composite band. But he had not yet seen evidence of the patrilineal band in his fieldwork. He found it only in print: in secondary sources, books and articles that gave fragmentary descriptions of male-centered hunting societies. As he candidly admitted, those accounts were "inadequate" and "incomplete."[36]

With the deadline looming, Steward mailed the essay to Robert Lowie in Berkeley just days before leaving for fieldwork in Death Valley and beyond. Lowie, one of Steward's former teachers and his graduate advisor, was Kroeber's longtime colleague in the Department of Anthropology. Lowie was editing a volume of essays written in honor of Kroeber, soon to be published and presented to him on his sixtieth birthday. That Lowie included Steward's essay, which diverged from Kroeber's thinking in almost every respect, testified to the nondoctrinaire atmosphere of the department.[37]

The day after he wrote to Lowie, Julian and Jane took time off for an excursion with the students. They went to Eureka Valley in one of the ranch's pickup trucks, sparing their Chevrolet coupe, if not themselves, a punishing overland trip. The remote valley, a nearly waterless place, was home to towering sand dunes but not to any people. Excursions to climb the Eureka dunes, which Julian made as one of the school's first students, had quickly become a tradition at Deep Springs.[38] Jane had no experience of hiking in the desert, and she wore a dress for the festive occasion.

3. Jane Steward in Eureka Valley, April 1935. (Courtesy of Deep Springs College)

Steward left Deep Springs with his wife in late April, in search of Shoshone elders to serve as cultural informants for the Death Valley region. Before leaving California he also intended to finish his work with the Owens Valley Paiutes, questioning elders who lived in the southern portion of the Owens Valley and finding an informant for Deep Springs Valley. Then they would head for the Nevada desert to look for Shoshone elders along the western border before moving on to more distant points in the north and the east.

The Death Valley region and the desolate reaches of the Nevada desert seemed the most likely places to find the evidence that Steward sought. He was going there in search of the patrilineal band.

2. Shoshone Territory

ON THE ROAD into Death Valley the elevation dropped by thousands of feet and the temperature climbed. Still in the first month of spring, it was already 100 degrees Fahrenheit in the sun, and the open landscape and cloudless sky offered no escape from the heat. Not even a cloud shadow gave them respite. Steward took a photograph of Death Valley that showed the blistered land, a sandy track that passed for a road, and a sweep of sky.[1]

In this first stage of fieldwork he wanted to learn about the people who had long lived in an expanse of eastern California that extended over thousands of square miles: from the slope of the Sierra Nevada to Death Valley and bordering valleys. Kroeber had published his masterwork, the *Handbook of Indians of California*, ten years earlier. Many questions remained about the identity and the boundaries, both cultural and territorial, of Indians who lived in this vast desert domain.[2]

In Grapevine Canyon at the northern end of Death Valley he and Jane found only a few people at Scotty's Camp. Others had already gone to their summer camps at higher elevations, escaping the valley's rising heat. Death Valley had recently gained federal status as a national monument because of its natural wonders, but it was also home to a man-made wonder, the famously lavish Scotty's Castle. Built between the early 1920s and the 1930s, the sprawling Moorish-style structure had cost about $2 million, an enormous sum for the time. It featured fourteen fireplaces, an indoor fountain, ornate chandeliers, and imported furnishings.[3]

Indian workers had helped to build Scotty's Castle, and several families of Shoshones lived outside the gates, at the place called Scotty's Camp. Shoshones had lived in that area for generations. They spent winters at a village located by the spring in Grapevine Canyon. Scotty's Castle now took most of the spring's water for household use and for the gardens, which included palm trees, olive trees, and shrubbery imported into the valley.[4]

Steward introduced himself and explained his purpose. He often told potential informants that he wanted to record stories and the old ways of living so that their descendants could read about them a thousand years in the future. Besides having questions about the past, he also had money from two museums in the East to pay for specimens for their collections. He could offer ready cash for objects that people had made from natural materials and could make again. This eased the problem of *entrée* in fieldwork: how to enter a community and be seen as a visitor or guest, not an intruder. As his wife said, having funds to buy specimens made "contacting the Indians a pleasure to them, for a change."[5]

Steward asked two men about their place of origin and learned that both were Panamint Shoshones. One of the men, Wilbur Patterson, was only about forty years old and had a work history as a farm and ranch hand. In more prosperous times he would have been at work during spring in the Owens Valley. The other man, John Hunter, was his uncle. Steward judged him to be sixty and just eligible by age to serve as a cultural informant if he were willing. Both men could speak English.[6]

Hunter, who lived with his wife, Sarah, and a twenty-year-old son, had been born in Saline Valley. A low, hot valley located northwest of Death Valley and due east of the Owens Valley, it had little water and in earlier times had been home to a small number of people. They harvested seeds from plants that grew on the valley floor and gathered pine nuts and hunted deer in the bordering mountains. The people of Saline Valley also traded salt for goods or shell money with the

Owens Valley Paiutes, who in turn sometimes traded it across the Sierra Nevada, traveling on foot.[7]

The valley had nothing to offer American settlers who farmed or ranched. But by the time of Hunter's birth, an American company was already mining borax from a salt marsh in Saline Valley. Borax, a white crystalline salt, was in demand in America and abroad as an antiseptic and cleansing agent. To outsiders seeking profit it seemed to be Saline Valley's single valuable resource.

In nearby Death Valley, the site of large borax works in the late nineteenth century, the famous twenty-mule team wagons hauled in supplies for the miners and hauled out tons of borax at a time. Like anything extracted from the land on an industrial scale and for profit, borax was subject to mining's boom-bust cycles. Prices rose and fell with shifts in supply and demand in the international market. At one site in Death Valley a pile of borax, judged too impure to bring any gain, still marked the place where a borax works had stood fifty years earlier, around the time of John Hunter's birth in the 1880s. Some of the abandoned equipment had been taken away to other places. As Steward and his wife would see in the coming days, Shoshones in Death Valley country sometimes found new and creative uses for castoffs from old mining sites.

Most of the borax works closed long before Steward visited the area in 1935. They left behind not only rusting tanks and boilers but also land shorn of mesquite trees and creosote bushes. Workers had cut them down to use as fuel for heating the boiling pans. The National Park Service, having taken charge of Death Valley National Monument, established a nursery of mesquite and other native plants to use in restoring fragile land stripped of its cover. Other scars on the land—left by mining for gold, silver, lead, copper, talc, and zinc—still remained and proved hard to erase.[8]

John Hunter, born about 1885 according to census takers, was probably younger than Steward judged, perhaps only fifty. He had very little to say about earlier times. Steward wanted to learn about the period before 1870, before American settlers poured into Shoshone country. Since he preferred firsthand knowledge and memories, he needed to find cultural informants who were older than sixty-five. Hunter provided only a few facts about Saline Valley.

Disappointed that he had learned so little, Steward at first mistook as unwillingness what may have been puzzlement about the questions and uncertainty about the answers. "Reluctant informants," he noted tersely in his journal, describing the women as "speechless."[9] The women may not have spoken English fluently. But the men, who did speak English, clearly had trouble with the questions, and not only because they were younger than Steward thought.

As he later told Kroeber, they were not actually unwilling. They simply found it difficult to make definite statements about their culture.[10] What he termed *culture*—the central concept of anthropology and the preoccupation of most anthropologists—was completely alien to them, and to most other people at the time who were not anthropologists. Steward no doubt avoided using the term, but he may have asked some rather abstract questions relating to his interest in band structure and the patrilineal band.

Like any cultural anthropologist in the field, he faced the challenge of trying to frame questions that could be understood, and then trying to understand the answers, whether given in English or another language. He would be working with people who spoke different languages and dialects within the Numic branch of the Uto-Aztecan language family: Northern Paiute, Southern Paiute, Panamint Shoshone, Western Shoshone, and Bannock, among others. Major field studies of some of the languages, still poorly known to linguists in the 1930s, would not be carried out for decades.[11]

To help sort out linguistic and cultural boundaries, Steward planned to collect lists of core vocabulary from some of his informants. The list included words for numbers, colors, parts of the body, natural objects, and animals such as *coyote* and *wolf* and *antelope*. Since he had to cover an immense area in a matter of months, learning one or more languages—or even knowing what to learn—was impossible. As a practical matter, and like many cultural anthropologists of the time, Steward asked questions in English, using an interpreter if necessary.[12]

He preferred to work with cultural informants who were bilingual and spoke English. This spared him the trouble and expense of hiring an interpreter, and direct communication was almost always preferable. But because most Paiute and Shoshone elders had not learned English early in life, unlike their children, even those who spoke English did not necessarily speak fluently or pronounce words as he did. Sometimes both he and his wife struggled to understand elders' names.[13]

Julian and Jane spent the night at a nearby auto camp, a public campground for motorists in Death Valley. Tourism had grown in the valley, in part because of proximity to Los Angeles and improved roads. Auto camps with tent sites served some visitors; small hotels and an expensive new resort welcomed others. The resort offered tennis courts, an outdoor swimming pool fed by warm springs, and other luxuries, at a daily rate that exceeded a week's wages for most of the people at Scotty's Camp. It also exceeded what Julian's fieldwork budget allowed for a week's lodging.[14]

He and Jane returned to Scotty's Camp the next day, but again they met with little success. Julian decided just to buy some specimens, but he apparently bought nothing from Sarah Hunter, who made baskets, perhaps because she had none on hand. He paid for the artifacts, gave up on the questions, and headed south with Jane. They drove more than a hundred miles to Panamint Valley, also simmering in late April, to seek out George Hanson, a Panamint Shoshone and "famous as the oldest Indian," Julian wrote in their journal.[15]

Hanson, a widower, was about eighty years old according to census takers, and at least ninety according to other estimates. He lived with his daughter, Isabel, at a place called Indian Ranch. The closest settlement, Ballarat, with a population of ten, was sliding toward ghost status. In earlier times hundreds of people lived in Ballarat, which served as a supply center for the mines in that district. When mining declined, so did the town. By the 1930s only a few adobe houses and a saloon still stood below a deeply eroded flank of the Panamint Mountains. The remains of other houses, as well as broken bottles and assorted refuse, were strewn across the desert floor.[16]

George Hanson, who lived about five miles away, qualified as the most notable resident of the area, and not only for roving anthropologists. A guidebook informed all visitors to the Death Valley region that Indian Ranch was "the home of Panamint George, a handsome, white-haired old Indian, who knew most of the white men who came here in the early days. He guided Dr. George in 1860, and assumed his name." Dr. Samuel G. George, a physician with a bad case of silver fever, was searching for the lost Gunsight Lode—unsuccessfully, as it turned out. The legendary silver lode remained lost. Hanson later prospected on his own but never got anything for his work, he said, aside from "grub and promises"—and once, a worthless check.[17]

Although George Hanson spoke English, his command was limited. He and Steward had some misunderstandings, including the identity of Hanson's daughter. Steward thought she was Hanson's niece, and he judged Hanson to be about ninety: "He is healthy but his sight poor. Said he wanted to move because he can't see the rattlesnakes." Hanson had reason to worry. The Death Valley region was home not only to the sidewinder but also to the Mojave rattlesnake, one of the most aggressive and dangerous rattlesnakes in North America. It did not always signal before striking, and its venom contained a potent neurotoxin. There was no antivenin in the 1930s.[18]

Hanson agreed to work with him the next day, and Julian and Jane made camp in his front yard where tall cottonwood trees provided shade. An old stagecoach with torn side curtains rested nearby, a reminder of the years when people poured into Ballarat. The fence that surrounded Indian Ranch was made from rescued material: barbed wire, old iron wagon wheels, and other manufactured goods of the market economy. What others had bought and used and then discarded in the desert as valueless, Hanson had gathered to make a fence.[19]

This fence marked the perimeter of a piece of land but could not keep out unwanted visitors. Jane and Julian never spotted any rattlesnakes, but they did unknowingly share their bed that night with a poisonous companion. In the cool desert night, the warmth of a bedroll sometimes attracted scorpions and spiders. When they crawled out of their bedroll the next morning a black widow spider crawled out with them.[20]

The two men set to work, and Isabel Hanson also answered some questions. She was about fifty-five years old and wore the style of clothing that Shoshone and Paiute women adopted after American settlement: a loose-fitting cotton dress with a high neckline and a long hemline, and sleeves that reached below the elbows. Her father usually wore denim overalls and a long-sleeved cotton shirt, standard for Paiute and Shoshone men at the time.[21]

One of Steward's acquaintances in Berkeley, Jaime de Angulo, would later publish *Indians in Overalls*. The title reflected a shift in American anthropology that began in the 1930s. Studies of acculturation—written in present tense and centering on cultural changes brought about by contact and conquest—slowly began to appear in print. Steward and many other anthropologists, however, still took more interest in the precontact past, and continued to reconstruct it through archaeology and ethnography.[22]

Julian asked Hanson some questions about the clothing the "Old Ones" had worn. According to Jane, Hanson "spoke poor English but was willing and informative when he got the idea of what we wanted." Julian took out a piece of buckskin he had brought on the trip, "hoping," Jane said, "that a demonstration would be easier for us to understand." Hanson folded the buckskin, beckoned Jane, and, explaining that a skirt would be fringed, draped it around her. Then he sat back on his heels to admire the skirt. "'Pretty fine looking the old way,'" he said happily as he studied this sudden vision of the past.[23]

Language problems kept Steward from understanding some of Hanson's answers. "George is affable," he remarked at the end of the day, "& we secured some information, but his Eng. is insufficient for fine points without an interpreter." Hanson told him that there was no "ownership," as Steward put it, of the land where Panamint Shoshone women gathered seeds.[24] Steward understood Hanson to say that no family or larger group held exclusive rights to harvest seeds on a specific and clearly bounded piece of land, and to keep others from gathering food there. People had not "owned" land in the way that Steward thought a patrilineal band owned land.

He interpreted Hanson's words in terms of American legal concepts of private property, without investigating Shoshone cultural understandings. Eliciting and recording their complex knowledge of the land—not only its use but also its care, a spiritual matter—would have taken far more time than he could devote to it. Not only was it a subject rife with "fine points," it also held practically no interest for Steward.

Symbols, values, religious beliefs, and other "subjective" matters had no place in his theoretical approach, with its focus on the "objective," meaning the external: what could be observed and, ideally, measured. That approach shared common ground with behaviorism in psychology, which had influenced his thinking, as had another new field of science, ecology. He concluded simply that no one owned bounded tracts of land. Several male informants would later agree

4. George Hanson, April 1935. (Photo by Julian H. Steward, courtesy of University of Illinois Archives)

with Hanson about access to seed lands; one of the few women Steward identified as an informant would disagree.[25]

Before Julian and Jane left Indian Ranch that day, George Hanson agreed to have his photograph taken. He was used to that request from visitors. Instead of wearing overalls, he put on some posing clothes: a pair of pants with a slight drape, a clean cotton shirt, and a hat with a wide brim. Standing with hand on hip, he struck a jaunty pose in front of the old stagecoach.

His visitors, after stowing the camera and camping gear in their car, headed toward a place called Darwin in Panamint Valley. They pressed on through rising winds and swirling dust, the beginning of a dust storm. Now and then Jane glanced at a thermometer they kept at hand while driving through the desert. It registered 110 degrees Fahrenheit inside the car when it was 100 degrees outside, and even higher when they rolled up the windows to keep out the dust. They reached Darwin in the evening and camped there.[26]

With a population of fewer than one hundred and falling, the old mining town had seen better days. At the peak of Darwin's biggest boom, following the discovery of silver and lead, more than a thousand people had lived in a place nearly devoid of water. Decades before Los Angeles began taking water from the distant Owens Valley, the town of Darwin piped water from a spring miles away in the Coso Mountains. Panamint Shoshones, once known to settlers as Coso Indians, had undoubtedly made use of the spring before the waters suddenly started flowing to another place.[27] The Darwin pipeline—the Los Angeles aqueduct in miniature—gave early evidence of an American penchant for importing water to any place of profit in the desert.

The next morning Julian and Jane visited some Panamint Shoshones who lived on the outskirts of Darwin and who gave them the names of three men who might serve as cultural informants. Two of the men, George Gregory and Charlie Wrinkle, were brothers who had once lived in Darwin. Their different surnames came from two different settlers. Taking the name of an employer had become a common practice in the region during the years after American settlement. Gregory was about ten years older than his brother.[28]

Julian decided on Gregory because of his greater age and perhaps also because his daughter was married to George Hanson's son. Knowing Hanson created a personal connection in advance, one that might prove useful when he asked Gregory to serve as an informant. He and Jane left Darwin and headed toward Olancha, where Gregory lived. They drove sixty miles through the gusting winds of a desert storm.

Their route took them past Owens Lake, once a shining blue haven for thousands of migrating waterfowl and now a dry salt flat. The Los Angeles aqueduct had diverted the river water that long fed Owens Lake and supported the ducks that Shoshones hunted there in the fall. Even before construction of the aqueduct, farmers had used so much water from the valley's streams and river to irrigate fields that the water level of the lake began to drop. In just decades a lake that covered more than a hundred square miles went dry, and the ducks disappeared. Columns of billowing dust, kicked up by the wind, rose high above the lakebed giving vivid testimony of the loss.[29]

Keeler, once a busy port and supply center for the famous Cerro Gordo mines, now stood marooned on the old shoreline, its population dwindling. A company had built a soda ash plant nearby. It mined alkali, or soda, from the dry bed, removed the impurities, and sent the soda ash to market for use in the manufacture of soap, detergents, paper, and other products. Like the ravens that circled in a blank blue sky, swooping down to feed on carrion, the company had found gain in the lake's death by dehydration.[30]

Near the old Cerro Gordo mines, in the Inyo Mountains above Keeler and the lakebed, slopes once covered by pinyon trees looked almost bare. The trees had provided pine nuts that people gathered in the fall for their winter food supply. When mining began in the area, charcoal kilns were built and the pinyon trees cut down to make charcoal for the smelters. The trees did not grow back.[31]

Shoshones had long lived along the southern shore of Owens Lake at a place they called by a name meaning Water End Place. Now the name held a new and grim meaning, at least in English translation. The hamlet of Olancha, population seventy-five, occupied land south of the dry lake. Shady cottonwoods gave it the look of a small oasis in the desert, presided over by towering Olancha Peak.[32]

George Gregory, who was seventy-five years old and Panamint Shoshone, lived with his wife, Mamie, and seven other family members: their daughter and her husband, a granddaughter, and four other children. George had been born about 1860, probably in the area around the Coso Mountains. Mamie may have been the same age or as much as ten years younger than her husband. In photographs taken around the time that Steward met them, they look directly at the camera, each with an air of quiet dignity. Their age, upbringing in the desert, and ability to speak English made them ideal candidates to serve as cultural informants. They agreed to work with Steward the next day.[33]

While talking to George Gregory, Steward learned, to his annoyance, that one of Kroeber's graduate students, Harold Driver, had preceded him in Olancha. Just a month earlier Driver had recorded culture element lists for Indians living on the western side of the Sierra Nevada. He worked around Porterville and the tiny hamlet of Badger where, he reported, "mail service is only 3 times a week and I will only be here 2 or 3 more days so I don't know what good it will do anybody." At some point he evidently drove south, crossed the mountains, and recorded another list at Olancha. Unlike Steward, Driver had genuine enthusiasm for the project, certain that statistical analysis of the lists would yield important results.[34]

Since Driver had already worked with George Gregory, Steward could avoid the tedious and time-consuming task. It required learning whether specific cultural traits, numbering in the thousands, should be recorded as present or absent for the group in question, no easy task. Had they used nets in communal rabbit hunts? Had they used a hooked pole to collect pine nuts?[35] Those were simple matters. Queries about religion and ritual and political leadership were not, and the answers did not always fit neatly into one of two authorized categories, present or absent.

With the next day settled, Jane and Julian drove to nearby Cartago, population thirty, a relic of the 1870s silver boom. It had once served as the landing for steamers that plied Owens Lake, carrying cargo from the Cerro Gordo silver mines. Now standing watch over the dry lakebed, Cartago had little to offer travelers beyond lodging at a private auto camp with cabins, precursor of the motel. Years later, Jane remembered the cabins at auto camps in small desert towns as crude structures. They were built by anyone who could nail two boards together, she said, and who hoped to earn some money from weary and mildly desperate travelers.[36]

In Cartago Julian rented an auto cabin for a good price. Despite its shabbiness and the two black widow spiders that he evicted, it offered comforts, including running water, a bed, a small stove, and shelter from the wind and choking dust that they had breathed for the past two days. Dust storms had grown steadily worse in the area after Owens Lake lost its water and dried up. The alkali-laden dust burned throats and eyes, and it caused respiratory problems for people living there.

Julian and Jane carried water in two thirteen-gallon tanks and had carefully rationed it for days. Water for drinking had the highest priority because dehydration could be deadly. They each required as much as a gallon a day, two or three times the amount needed in a humid region. They also kept water in reserve for the car radiator in case it overheated on a lonely road in a waterless place. The most arid parts of the Great Basin lacked surface water for a span of hundreds of square miles.

They never had enough water to wash clothing and sheets or to bathe fully when they camped, but they kept themselves reasonably clean, Jane recalled. They used water for more than one purpose if possible. After cooking potatoes, for example, they boiled eggs in the same water. They cleaned the car's windshield with water they had already used to wash their faces and hands, or to wipe the daily coating of salt and dust from their arms and legs. Perspiration dried almost instantly in the dry heat, leaving a salty residue on the skin.

Because of their frugality with water, they saved enough for Julian to shave every day. "He was meticulous then," Jane said. He dressed with care during fieldwork, she explained, because he treated it as a professional activity. When he hiked in the Sierra with friends, she added, he stopped shaving and looked just as disheveled as the other men.

In the blessed shelter of the auto cabin they had water to shower and to hand wash their sheets and dusty clothing. (Electric-powered washing machines with hand wringers did exist, but public laundries with coin-operated machines were still on the horizon.) They wore light-colored cotton, which had two virtues: it did not absorb as much heat as dark colors in the strong sunlight and it more or less matched the desert dust. Jane usually wore a sleeveless blouse and long pants, and Julian, a tailored shirt and pants. Besides that everyday clothing, Jane added, they each carried a set of "city clothes" for the times when they stayed in towns. Hers consisted of the light cotton dress and scarf she had worn for the trip to the dunes in Eureka Valley, but thereafter saved for town.

Their housekeeping cabin—unlike a less expensive sleeping cabin— also offered a sheltered place to cook and to eat. They used the two-burner stove to cook their meals and the desert refrigerator to store a few perishable items: luxury foods for desert travelers, which she and Julian bought whenever they had the chance. Jane remembered desert refrigerators as a framework of wood with burlap tacked to its sides and with a door that gave access to the shelves inside. They resembled a large cupboard, she explained, with an interior cooled by evaporation. A small spigot on top dripped water on the burlap, and the evaporation of water in the dry air kept the food slightly cool. Butter and fresh milk and eggs—delicacies after their camping fare of mostly canned foods—could remain unspoiled for a day or so. Meat had to be cooked and eaten more quickly.

An orange or an apple was their usual dessert. Sometimes they stocked up on oranges from Southern California before leaving a town. Paiutes and Shoshones, Jane recalled, and anyone else living in a remote corner of the desert, treasured the fragrant fruit. Eating oranges—savoring the sudden burst of tart and juicy sweetness—counted as a rare luxury. She and Julian often gave the fruit as gifts to informants and others they met on their journeys.

Now and then they received a gift of pine nuts in return, but they never counted on hospitality during those lean years of the Depression. Too many people lived at the edge of hunger.[37]

The next day, rested and clean, Jane and Julian returned to Olancha. Julian spent the day questioning George Gregory and his wife, although he did not list her in print as an informant or double the fee for their work. "Spent day with Geo. and his wife Mamie at $2.00," he recorded in his journal. His frequent practice when married couples served as informants was to list just the husband's name in his records, or the man's initials in print, and to pay him. (A year later, when George and Mamie Gregory served as informants in a different project, each was named.)[38]

Like her husband, Mamie Gregory had a long work history. For many years when they lived in Darwin she had earned money by doing laundry and cleaning the house of a white family. Her employer, Elizabeth Mecham, recalled that Indian women walked five or six miles to Darwin from the places where they camped with their families. They washed the laundry by hand, hung it to dry, cleaned the house, ironed, and walked home, each with a dollar in hand. Some of their employers also provided breakfast and lunch. Later, many of the women and their families moved near a small wash, a dry channel that bordered the east side of town. They lived in tents and other shelters; still later some built small houses at another site on the edge of Darwin.

Mamie and George Gregory, Mecham recalled, "were fine people. . . . Mamie made beautiful baskets, as did others." Women used willows to weave baskets for carrying and storing food. Some were so tightly woven and sealed with heated resin from pinyon trees that they held water. These woven water jugs, which allowed people to travel far from springs while searching for food, served as important tools in the food quest.[39]

To weave a basket took many hours and great skill, especially when the basket maker created an intricate design. In the early days of settlement in the Owens Valley, women had begun to produce baskets for trade or sale besides making them for their own use. The baskets met the settlers' need for storage containers and the women's need for food or money to buy food.

In the early twentieth century general stores began to sell cheap manufactured containers, which both settlers and Indians purchased; some of the women continued to make baskets, selling or trading them to collectors. Scotty's Castle in Death Valley had a collection on display. One of the largest collections in the Owens Valley belonged to the pharmacist's wife in Lone Pine, who recognized the beauty and fine artistry of the baskets. She purchased some and traded medicine for others. Storekeepers also sold baskets to tourists and other visitors as souvenirs. And anthropologists, acting as agents, bought baskets for museum collections—as well as for their own collections. Steward bought several baskets himself, although apparently not from Mamie

Gregory. Years later, she and Isabel Hanson and Sarah Hunter, among others, would achieve renown far beyond the Owens Valley, their baskets regarded as art, not merely craft.[40]

Steward's work with the Gregorys went slowly. Most of his questions elicited only a "yes" or "no" or answers that seemed contradictory to him. Frustrated but persistent, he returned the next day to record kinship terms and to ask more questions. At the end of the day he reported that he had at last "got light on bands." He continued the next morning with more questions about bands, covering a wide range of topics that related to band structure, and especially to patrilineal bands. Kinship terms, genealogies, marriage customs, population figures, food-getting practices—all was evidence that provided clues.[41]

On that day, the third spent with George and Mamie Gregory, Steward realized that the family was in desperate straits. Nine people lived on four or five dollars a week. Two women earned that money as laundresses, and a son who lived elsewhere gave some money now and then. The men had little prospect of finding work: George Gregory was old, his son-in-law disabled, and many jobs had simply vanished in the grim years of the Great Depression. In the Owens Valley the ranching and agricultural economy had declined even before the 1930s, jobs for ranch and farm hands disappearing along with the valley's water. Some Paiute and Shoshone men left the valley to find work; a few, despite the bitter irony, moved to Los Angeles.[42]

During Steward's worst period in Berkeley, when only his wife was employed, their income for a household of two had amounted to fifteen dollars a week. They were still living on about the same amount of money and spending much of their research stipend for gasoline, which was expensive, and for informant fees and lodging. Still, the contrast between that life of "semi-poverty," as they thought of it, and the Gregory family's was stark.

Paying Gregory, if not his wife, the standard informant fee of two dollars a day provided a windfall but did not solve the family's problems. Steward knew that if George Gregory, at his advanced age, had looked for paying work he would not have found any; and he understood that bureaucratic complexities did not make it easy to collect relief payments from the government, especially for people who did not read or write English. Most of the elders Steward worked with were not literate.

The family lived forty miles from the town of Independence, the county seat, and Steward decided to take George Gregory there himself to find out about relief. After a few frustrating hours they ended up with a five-dollar grocery order and a promise to investigate Gregory for government relief or an old age pension. They bought groceries and drove forty hot and dusty miles back to Olancha.

The bureaucratic snarl had put Steward in a bad temper, and the whole ordeal had cost him half a day of work time and the equivalent of a half-day's informant fee to pay for the gasoline. Gregory made no comment about the groceries, and the family simply smiled when they saw them. Expecting a different reaction, and perhaps a word of thanks, Steward felt exasperated but said nothing. His frustration spilled out later that day: "The inability and/or unwillingness of these people to express themselves is incredible," he wrote in his journal. Previously, and in print, he had used more measured language, alluding to the "reticent attitude" of Great Basin Indians. Irked by the lost work time that day, and by the slow progress of research, he wondered irritably if they lacked powers of abstraction. The ongoing dust storm added to the burden of a tiresome day. "Wind still roars," Steward recorded, "and the Owens Lake salt bed is swept into the sky obliterating the mountains."[43]

The task of trying to learn about band structure had been wearing work, made difficult not only by language problems but also by different styles of expression. The silences, or long pauses followed by short answers, which he sometimes interpreted as resistance or inability, may well have had different cultural meanings to the Gregorys and previous informants. They may have indicated careful consideration of the questions, or reluctance to express certainty, or unwillingness to speak for other people, among other meanings.[44]

Steward's interest in abstract and unfamiliar matters such as band structure and political organization, even when he did not use those words, may also have created confusion once again. His skill in asking questions would increase as the weeks passed, and his comments about reluctant informants would decrease. As he gained more understanding about the structure of groups, he asked better questions, which his informants grasped and which yielded much more than "yes" or "no." A question such as "Did married men live near their fathers and brothers?" would probably produce only "yes" or "no"—or, confusingly, both (because in fact some did and some did not). He could learn more by asking open-ended and concrete questions such as "Who lived at that place?" and "How were they related to each other?" With experience, Steward also began to understand the answers more easily.[45]

Experience was in truth Steward's only teacher. He had not received any formal training for fieldwork, either in archaeology or cultural anthropology—but neither had his teachers, Kroeber and Lowie, and nor would most of Steward's own students. Kroeber did not believe that students could be taught how to do fieldwork. He would reply to specific questions, such as the one Omer Stewart sent from the field, asking how to determine territorial lines, but his famous advice to students who asked for general direction was to take plenty of paper for field notes. (The sink-or-swim approach persisted for many years. Training for ethnographic fieldwork did not become common until later in the twentieth century, and even then it was not offered in all graduate programs.)[46]

A few days later when Steward wrote to Lowie about his research, he remarked, "[T]he principal difficulty has been with political entities."

45

His questions to John Hunter and George Hanson had yielded very little, and only his tenacity—and George and Mamie Gregory's tolerance—had finally resulted in a breakthrough about the social and political organization of Panamint Shoshones. As he explained to Lowie, "There is no such idea and it practically requires a third degree to get any light on it."[47]

Since Jane did not take direct part in most interviews, she did not share Julian's impatience or frustration, and she had used her time to study the Gregorys' house closely. The frame, built of discarded timbers, was covered with scraps of corrugated metal on the outside. Lengths of cardboard from boxes formed interior walls that kept out the wind. Pictures torn from newspapers and magazines—including one of radio evangelist Aimee Semple McPherson—covered the walls.

McPherson was often in the news, even ten years after gaining national notoriety when she disappeared from Los Angeles. She later claimed to have been kidnapped, but witnesses swore under oath that they had seen her with a man at a secluded cottage in Carmel. A sensational court case dragged on for months. McPherson's name appeared in print once again when the man's wife filed for divorce, and other controversies followed. Reports of the glamorous evangelist, often illustrated, reached every part of the nation, including Olancha, where they found a home on the Gregorys' walls.[48]

The floor of their house was belting, "from some defunct soda works probably," Jane guessed. It might have come from an old soda ash plant near Owens Lake. They had gathered all of these "odds & ends," as she called them, and put them to good use. The natural, more flexible but less durable materials—such as grasses and willows—that they had formerly gathered to make shelters, had been superseded by these durable castoffs of industrial society. "It is small," she concluded, "but they just love it."[49] It saved them the trouble of building anew, and now that they lived for long spells in one place, their sturdy shelter proved more practical.

George and Mamie Gregory's skills as gatherers and hunters, with long experience of "living off the country," to use Julian's phrase, also helped them get by during the Depression. As Jane remembered years later, many of the Paiutes and Shoshones they met, and especially those who did not live in towns, still gathered some seeds and pine nuts and hunted small game. When they explained how they had lived in the past, they sometimes drew on recent experience, not just distant memories of the old ways.[50]

Now in the fifth day of the dust storm Julian and Jane drove south to look for another informant, a man from Panamint Valley named Tom Spratt. George Gregory had told them about Spratt, but he identified him culturally by an unfamiliar name. They left Olancha in a roaring wind, clouds of the alkali-laden dust from the dry bed of Owens Lake still filling the sky. "The mts. to the east of us here at Cartago are obscured ¾ of the time," Jane recorded. As they drove through the dust, they had the choice of keeping the windows closed and sweltering or rolling down the windows and choking. The corrosive dust, which could damage the paint on vehicles, covered their car, turning it light gray.

Passing the hamlets of Little Lake and Brown, they drove up into a more protected place, a canyon in the Sierra Nevada. They found Spratt, whom Jane described in their journal as "Pleasant person, ½ white." Born around 1880 according to census takers, Spratt was in his midfifties and lived by himself. His mother, Nancy Spratt, had died about fifteen years earlier. Census takers listed her as Shoshone. Evidently Tom Spratt had a white father because they categorized him racially as half Shoshone and half white. They did not categorize him culturally and linguistically as Shoshone.[51]

Steward later described him as "one half white" in *Basin-Plateau*, and in another publication only as "one-quarter Shoshone, one-quarter Kawaiisu," without specifying his non-Indian ancestry. He generally preferred informants who were "full blood Paiute" or "full blood Shoshone," to use the language of the census. His reasons had to do with culture, not race. His education at Berkeley—with two men trained by the famous anthropologist Franz Boas—taught him that differences in biological ancestry had nothing directly to do with differences in cultural behavior and language. That idea of Boas's ran contrary to popular thinking of the time. At any rate, Steward simply wanted to work with men who had grown up as Indians, living among Indians. Elders who spoke English had usually learned it, however, through long contact with non-Indians.[52]

Steward quickly decided that Spratt qualified as a linguistic informant, in part because he was still unsure about his cultural identity. Too young to offer firsthand help about the period around 1870 or earlier, Spratt did provide the names of the various groups who lived in the region. Steward also recorded a short vocabulary, hoping to resolve the question of Spratt's identity. According to that day's journal entry, "We procured a vocab. which seems to check with Kroeber's Kawaiisu." Steward later referred to the vocabulary in print as Panamint Kawaiisu. (Kawaiisu, like Panamint Shoshone, belongs to the Numic branch of the Uto-Aztecan language family.) This established "the fact," he said, "that these people had occupied most of Panamint Valley and mixed in the northern part of it" with Shoshones.

Elsewhere he wrote, "They were mixed with Shoshones in at least the central part of Panamint Valley." The boundaries—linguistic, cultural, and geographic—were complex and not easily drawn. In contrast, culture types, such as the patrilineal band, seemed to have the virtue of sharp boundaries. There was no ambiguity: a group either met his definition of a patrilineal band or it did not. Regrettably, and perhaps because of his age, Spratt did not have much to say about bands.[53]

Backtracking forty-five miles Jane and Julian spent their last night at the auto camp in Cartago. They planned to leave the next day. It was already early May, and they wanted to move on to another area. Julian intended to work with Shoshone and Paiute elders in Lone Pine, just twelve miles north in the Owens Valley, drawing on contacts he already had there.

Before leaving Cartago he wrote to Kroeber to report on his fieldwork. The several lists of vocabulary that he had already recorded from Death Valley and nearby seemed almost identical, he said. He had not yet completed a trait list (formally, a culture element list) because his "best informant" to date, George Gregory, had already worked with Harold Driver. As Steward explained, "there seems little use in repeating." He also expressed his skepticism, obliquely, about the value of the lists. He suggested to Kroeber that "it is necessary to define the groups first," before collecting trait lists from informants.

Kroeber had defined groups in this region of eastern California by using linguistic criteria. Steward inquired, politely but pointedly, about why his earlier publications contained inconsistencies about the identity of some groups. Instead of categorizing on the basis of language or clusters of cultural traits, Steward had come to think that environment and "ecological relations" provided a sounder basis.

He considered aridity the hallmark feature of the environment from eastern California through Nevada and Utah, but he understood that water and food were more abundant and reliable in some areas of that immense region than in others. As he knew from his own experience, in advance of fieldwork, this was true even of neighboring valleys: the Owens Valley had much more, Deep Springs Valley had less. And already, in the essay on composite and patrilineal bands that he had finished writing just before leaving Deep Springs, he had tried to establish correlations between features of the food supply and food quest and the structure of social groups. He realized that the Owens Valley Paiutes of the past had lived in a much more favorable environment—with more water and more abundant and varied foods—than the Panamint Shoshones of Death Valley country. And he had learned that they lived in very different kinds of groups—a result, he thought, of those differences in environment.

All of this bore on how he reported his first findings to Kroeber. The Shoshones from the slope of the Sierra Nevada to Death Valley, including adjacent areas of Saline and Panamint valleys, appear to have formed "something of a single band," he wrote. "But they were divided into some 6 or 8 sub-bands, each habitually utilizing definite territory & apparently hunting rabbits & dancing together [at yearly festivals], and also named." These named groups were linked through intermarriage. Because of those ties, and because of ups and downs in the food supply from one year to the next, he explained, "they had reciprocal gathering rights."

In other words, since pine nuts and other plant foods might well be abundant in a certain place one year, but scarce there the next, people could look for food in places beyond their own local area if need be. By implication, although Steward did not say this, the six or eight groups shared this great expanse of eastern California desert in common. Saying that they had "reciprocal gathering rights" was another way of stating that they occupied, held claims to, and used a large common. This probably promoted their survival. It was *adaptive*, to apply a term from evolutionary theory and ecology that Steward came to use. If each group had owned a part of it as private property, each would have had the right to exclude hungry neighbors and kin from afar, even during times of local plenty—and to be excluded by others during times of local scarcity. Holding land as private property would not have promoted survival.

Steward's general framework supported this interpretation, but his concepts of *property* and *ownership* did not because they were based on widely shared American understandings of private property. This may explain why he made no reference to a common: land inherited jointly by members of a community, who occupy and use it and pass it on to future generations. Like American courts of the time, he did not recognize a common as real property.

A decade later a Supreme Court justice, in *Shoshone Indians v. United States*, wrote, "Ownership meant no more to them than to roam the land as a great common, and to possess and enjoy it in the same way that they possessed and enjoyed sunlight and the west wind and the feeling of spring in the air."[54] That single sentence of certainty revealed how little he knew of a way of life that differed from his own. The Shoshones' land, unlike "the feeling of spring in the air," had provided the food that sustained them. In Panamint Shoshone territory, people had survived by sharing access to land and to the food they found there.

Steward showed less certainty about some of his recent findings. "This comes near to being a woman's economy," he told Kroeber, "as seeds are almost the whole story." He had learned that men's hunting did not provide nearly as much food as women's gathering. "The main foods were vegetable," he later wrote in *Basin-Plateau*, avoiding the phrase "a woman's economy" in print. He said more about wild game and hunting than about edible plants and gathering—perhaps in part because he thought that differences in game and in men's hunting practices explained why some bands were composite and some patrilineal. Like most anthropologists—and Americans—of his time, he thought of men's activities as more important, economically and socially, and as meriting more attention.[55]

In several respects what he had just learned about Shoshones of the Death Valley country seemed highly anomalous. It did not conform to the theoretical ideas that he had recently laid out in his essay on composite and patrilineal bands. It also called into question two of his ideas about bands. He thought that bands owned specific food tracts and bounded territories; but he had just discovered reciprocal rights to harvest food throughout this large region. What he had learned also challenged his assumption, then widely shared, about the primacy of men and hunting in the food quest. In the "woman's economy" of the eastern California desert, seed-gathering by women provided more food.

For the moment Steward put aside these anomalies and turned his attention toward the Owens Valley Paiutes. He had already published a report on Paiutes living in the northern part of the Owens Valley, drawing on his research around Bishop and Big Pine in the late 1920s. Now he planned to concentrate on Paiutes living in the southern part of the valley.[56]

3. Valley of the Paiutes

JANE AND JULIAN ARRIVED in Lone Pine late in the day and found a comfortable cabin in an auto camp. With a population of just 360 the town seemed cosmopolitan after Olancha, Cartago, and Darwin. Located at the foot of Mount Whitney, the tallest mountain in the forty-eight states, Lone Pine enjoyed a brisk tourist trade. Hikers and mountain climbers passed through on their way to the snow-capped peak of Mount Whitney or other points in the High Sierra.

Film crews from Los Angeles also visited, often lodging at the Lone Pine Hotel while they shot footage for Westerns in the nearby Alabama Hills. Its rugged and open landscape, with lofty peaks of the Sierra Nevada as backdrop, made the Alabama Hills a favorite location of Hollywood directors. Among other amenities, the town had a theater that showed some of the latest movies.

Most of the residents of Lone Pine were white, but Paiutes and Shoshones lived on the outskirts of town. Long before American settlers arrived in the valley, at least one Paiute village had stood along Lone Pine Creek, now also the site of the town. The Paiutes who lived in Lone Pine fell under the jurisdiction of the Bishop Agency, as did the Panamint Shoshone Indians Julian had worked with around Death Valley. The Bishop Agency was one of many administrative units of the Bureau of Indian Affairs, itself part of the U.S. Department of the Interior. A census showed that most of the Indians who lived in Lone Pine were Owens Valley Paiutes. Some Panamint Shoshones had also moved to the town years earlier from Saline Valley and other parts of the Death Valley region.[1]

Since Julian and Jane had arrived too late in the day to look for an informant, they took the rest of the day off and went to a movie that night. Time in town also gave them a chance to buy a newspaper and magazines and catch up on the news. Most cars did not have radios, and most radio stations did not report much in the way of news. The front page of the *Los Angeles Times* carried a few lines that day about Amelia Earhart, the world-famous aviator. She had put off attempting a nonstop flight from Mexico City to New York City due to a spell of bad weather. Another story told of refugees who had fled worse weather, the severe drought on the Great Plains. A hundred destitute families were streaming into California each day, many without any place to live. In the Imperial Valley, hundreds of miles south of the Owens Valley, some found shelter only under trees. One state official recommended action "'to stop this influx.'"[2]

The next morning, rested and ready to work in Lone Pine, Julian and Jane spent hours trying to locate a Paiute informant. Finally they found Andrew Glenn, whom Julian had met during summer fieldwork in 1928. Glenn had briefly served then as an informant and remembered Julian. He agreed to help the following day because he was too busy working in his garden with some relatives to answer questions that afternoon.[3]

Glenn was in his midfifties and a widower. When he was young, his two older brothers had married wives who were sisters. As Steward would learn, this was a preferred form of marriage not only among Paiutes in the Owens Valley but also among native people in other parts of the Great Basin. Likewise, a brother and sister might each marry a woman and a man respectively who were siblings. Spouses always came from unrelated families; this was prescribed, not just preferred.

After one of Glenn's brothers died, his widow observed a year of mourning as was customary. Glenn then married her. Steward later recorded that marriage as a case of the *levirate*, the term for the practice of a man marrying the widow of his deceased brother. The levirate too was prescribed, not simply preferred. The only way to avoid it was to make payment to the woman's family.

Steward also learned of another practice, known to anthropologists as the *sororate*, which required a man whose wife died to marry one of her sisters or to make payment. Glenn said that sometime after marrying his brother's widow, his other older brother died, and then Glenn's wife died. When the mourning period for his late wife ended, the parents of the older brother's widow—who were also the parents of Glenn's late wife (because his older brothers had married two sisters)—tried to force him to marry her. Although he had agreed to the levirate, he balked at the sororate, refusing to marry his late wife's sister because he considered her too old. He had not remarried since that time.[4]

Glenn lived a few miles from Lone Pine along Tuttle Creek, on land where he and his relatives raised melons and vegetables. They sold some of the produce in town. Glenn reportedly had a legal claim to an eighty-acre tract of land by the creek, in ancestral territory. (Some Owens Valley Paiutes had adapted to farm life so quickly that beginning in the mid-1870s they filed on homesteads.) A Paiute village had once stood along Tuttle Creek and west of the Alabama Hills. Its name meant Behind Granite Hills.[5]

At some point a rancher occupied land along Tuttle Creek. When the ranch later changed hands, the new owner put up a fence, forcing the Glenns to move farther up the creek to a rocky area unsuited for gardening. The experience of displacement and losing land had begun in the valley of the Paiutes during the previous century. The dislocation continued in the twentieth century. As Steward later wrote, "Loss of food lands since the coming of the white man has produced extremely variable residence and much moving." Old rules governing where people lived after they married were not observed in the new and difficult conditions.[6]

With time on their hands Julian and Jane decided to drive seventy-five miles to Deep Springs to collect any mail that had accumulated during the ten days of their absence. They also looked forward to having dinner with several of the teachers who were friends. While they were there they happened to see Tom Stone, a Paiute man in his forties who had previously, in the late 1920s, served as an interpreter and one of Julian's informants in the Owens Valley. Julian remembered him well, as a skilled interpreter and one of his best informants. He was pleased when Stone greeted him warmly.

Stone, while too young to have direct knowledge of life during the 1860s and earlier, had listened carefully to his grandfather's stories about the past. He had an exceptional memory and spoke English fluently. Steward made arrangements to work with him once again during the following week, cheered by the prospect of some very productive days, and without the usual strains. He had more questions for Stone, and he also wanted him to serve as interpreter for a woman in her eighties, Mary Harry. Steward had known her at Deep Springs during his student years. He also worked with her briefly during his summer fieldwork in 1928.

Returning to Lone Pine, he spent some time the next day with Andrew Glenn, but he soon concluded that Glenn knew very little about earlier times. At the age of fifty-five, he was slightly too young to have firsthand memory of the old ways. Although he could sing some of the old songs, he did not know the meaning of the words. The hymns he heard in church in Lone Pine had probably grown more familiar to him.

Glenn had made a highly unusual decision to be baptized sometime after an Irish miner, in an alcoholic haze, severely wounded his leg with a blast from a shotgun. It required amputation, and afterward Glenn always wore a wooden leg. He converted to Christianity, began attending church, stopped drinking and smoking, and years later learned to write. The sale of his eighty acres to the City of Los Angeles, which was still buying land in the valley to assure its claim to the water, promised to give Glenn an income. Called a "cripple" by some people, he had few ways to earn money aside from selling produce from his garden—and offering his services to a visiting anthropologist.[7]

Steward quickly realized that Glenn did not qualify as a good informant, but that he could help locate elders who were more knowledgeable and he could assist as an interpreter. During the afternoon the two men tried to find Shoshone informants but had no success. One, a man named Dee Lacy, was working and hence unavailable. The other man was drinking heavily and also unavailable. Julian finally gave up and spent the rest of the day working on his field notes and writing letters.[8]

The next morning Julian and Jane drove fifteen miles north to Independence, population four hundred. As county seat it was home to the Inyo County Courthouse, which stood a few blocks from the brown, two-story house on Market Street where Mary Austin lived when she wrote *The Land of Little Rain*. The Eastern California Museum had opened a few years earlier and occupied space in the basement of the courthouse, a stately building bordered by shady trees. Two librarians had charge of a collection of old documents, newspaper clippings, photographs, and artifacts. Julian left Jane there to look over the collection while he drove a few miles north to Fort Independence to try to locate an informant.[9]

About two hundred Paiutes had once lived in a village at the site, which they called by a name meaning Oak Place. In 1862 a military post had been built there to house the troops who put down the "uprisings" of the 1860s, a last stand as Paiutes and Shoshones tried to protect their land from invading American settlers. Years later, in 1915, some of the land that the government had taken for the fort was set aside for the use of Owens Valley Paiutes; and Fort Independence gained official status as a reservation. Almost nothing remained of the fort. It had long ago fallen into ruin, and only a dilapidated cabin still stood as a visible reminder that it had taken military force to strip the Paiutes of their land.[10]

George Robinson, who lived nearby, was seventy-one years old and silver-haired. Born in the mid-1860s, two years after the fort was built, his life spanned most of the valley's recorded history: from the early years of military occupation and settlement to the later water war with Los Angeles. His wife, Jennie, was just a year younger. Both of them could speak English.[11]

Robinson and his wife had planted about five acres of land with fruit trees, vegetables, and hay. The sale of surplus produce from the garden—including strawberries and grapes, just two of the exotic plants that settlers brought to the valley—must have given them some income. They occupied "more imposing premises" than many of their Paiute neighbors, according to Steward. While their house was not large—just one room, with extra space provided by a tent—the land around it had a tended look.[12]

George Robinson was hard at work plowing a field when Steward drove up to his yard, but he agreed to stop at once. The two men sat down and set to work together. Robinson's left hand rested immobile at his side. It appeared maimed, as if by an old injury, but he had found a way to plow and to tend his garden without having full use of two hands. Growing up in the hard years after American settlement had given him long practice in finding a way through difficulties.

Steward asked questions about what he called "the band ecological material" in the journal entry for that day. He learned that Robinson was born at a place that came to be called George's Creek, and he recorded what Robinson told him about that community as well as others in the valley. About two hundred people lived in two villages, one at George's Creek and another at Shepherd's Creek. Steward surmised that the two villages were allied into what he called the "George's Creek band." In the northern part of the valley, Steward had previously learned, villages were usually independent and each constituted a band.

Robinson told him that pine nut areas on the eastern side of the Owens Valley, in the Inyo Mountains and White Mountains, were divided into family plots. They had known boundaries defined by natural landmarks. Trespass without invitation, whether by other families or by outsiders, led to conflict but not bloodshed. At George's Creek, he said, women owned the plots; through matrilineal inheritance, the plots generally passed from mothers to daughters. They sometimes invited others—especially kin, but sometimes members of other bands—to collect pine nuts on these plots. In some areas to the north, including Big Pine, men owned the plots. Through rules of patrilineal inheritance men received rights to the land from their fathers or other male kin. Women harvested pine nuts on their husbands' plots.[13]

Steward would later say in print that Paiutes in the southern part of the valley had shown a strong preference for matrilocal residence. He suggested that this pattern, in which women stayed in their home community even after they married, was "perhaps connected with female ownership of valley seed plots." Women did not leave the place where they owned food lands or would inherit them from their mothers. "This tended to convert small villages into female lineages," he added, "which approximated but failed actually to be exogamous matrilineal bands." He had learned that the people did not always find their spouses in other communities. The practice of marrying out was termed *local exogamy* by anthropologists. Marrying within the community, termed *local endogamy*, was accepted if the marriage joined an unrelated man and woman. The villages thus did not meet his definition of a matrilineal band, a culture type in which he would never show interest, and he said no more about it.[14]

Steward talked with Robinson for several hours that morning, asking questions on topics that ranged from pine nut collecting and communal hunts to leaders and conflict. The two men finally stopped for lunch. Steward returned to Independence to meet his wife. After lunch he drove back and spent a few hours on kinship terms, which "as usual," he wrote, "were almost too much for all of us." His words suggest that Jennie Robinson also helped with kinship terminology, but he did not include her as an informant in *Basin-Plateau*. He listed only her husband's initials, as he had also done in the case of George and Mamie Gregory. He paid Robinson for a full day's work and returned to the museum in Independence, where he picked up Jane and then drove back to Lone Pine.[15]

The next day he and Andrew Glenn looked for another informant. Steward still wanted to question Dee Lacy, a man in his sixties who spoke English. Since he was working again that day, Steward settled for a Shoshone woman, Susie Shepherd, who came from Saline Valley. Although he thought that she was only fifty-five years old, her recorded age was about sixty-one. Steward spent several hours with her crosschecking what he had learned about Saline Valley from George and Mamie Gregory.[16]

She added little to what he had already heard, but she did insist that entire families inherited specific pine nut areas. George Gregory, like George Hanson, had told Steward that people did not hold exclusive rights to food areas, which he interpreted to mean no ownership. Later, in *Basin-Plateau*, Steward tried to reconcile their differences. Families did usually go to the same tracts each year, he wrote; and in good years, when a family could not possibly collect all of the pine nuts, others were "allowed freely" to gather there as well.[17]

In the afternoon he returned with Jane to record some origin stories told by Shepherd's sister, and Glenn went along as interpreter. The two women lived together. Jane and Julian had some trouble understanding the older woman's English name. They heard it first as Patsy Widson but finally decided it was Patsy Wilson. "They are very reluctant about telling their Indian names," Jane observed. Julian later, mistakenly, listed Wilson's age as fifty, and Jane described her as "an old lady." According to a census she was sixty-six at the time.[18]

One of the stories from Saline Valley that she told Julian and Jane explained the origins of the four-month winter season: why winter lasts for the length of four lunar cycles. As in so many of the stories that they heard elders tell, Coyote, the trickster-creator, took a central role. (The story might have reminded them of George Hanson's sensible caution in watching out for rattlesnakes. Coyote, often too clever by half, rarely showed such good sense.)

The Length of Winter: Coyote Is Bitten

Coyote, Owl, and Whippoorwill were making the year. Coyote was fixing the length of the winter. Coyote said, 'It should have as many months as the hairs on my back.' Owl said, 'No, it should have as many months as my feathers.' 'No, there are too many feathers and hairs,' Whippoorwill said, 'it should have 4 months.' He flew away singing, 'Watsa mu'a (4 months).'

Coyote became angry and ran after Whippoorwill, but could not catch him. While Coyote was following Whippoorwill, he came to some red berries. As he sat eating them, a rattlesnake bit him. He wanted to tell someone that he had been bitten. He found a man and told him to tell the people. He [the man] went a short distance and came back. Next time he went farther and came back. He kept doing this until he finally got tired. Coyote died while the man was going back and forth.[19]

Patsy Wilson told several stories that day that featured Coyote and his misadventures, including one about how he learned to fly. "They were told through an interpreter," Jane noted, "and so lost some fine points, but they are really amusing." She had listened very carefully, perhaps recording them in shorthand as Wilson spoke and Glenn interpreted. Her skill in taking dictation and typing from the notes would have proved useful because some of the stories were long, and time was already short.

Julian paid Wilson $1.00 for three hours, slightly more than the usual rate of $1.00 for four hours. His stipend gave him about the same hourly rate for his own labor, but he spent it on travel expenses. He also bought three baskets from Susie Shepherd for $6.00 and later sent one of the three, made for winnowing and parching seeds, to a museum. Although he paid a standard price, it offered small compensation for the many hours of labor devoted to weaving each basket, as he himself realized.[20]

The next day he and Jane went back for more stories, and they were surprised to find Patsy Wilson in an entrepreneurial mood. She demanded $2.50 for the previous day's work. Julian agreed instead to pay her $1.50 for that morning's work—about twice the usual rate—but later remarked with asperity, "At the prices they sell baskets, they have worked at 3 to 5 cents an hour." Wilson told nearly a dozen stories, making her the major contributor to the collection he published a few years later under the title *Some Western Shoshoni Myths*.[21]

That afternoon, with Glenn still assisting, Steward once again went to look for Lacy. This time they found him, and Steward crosschecked material from Robinson that he had recorded two days earlier. Learning that Lacy, who was in his midsixties, came from Fish Springs Creek in the Owens Valley, he asked some questions about genealogy and compiled some census figures. Steward had visited the area and seen surface archaeological evidence of what appeared to be a fairly large village.[22]

That ended the work at Lone Pine and with Glenn, whom he judged more willing than able. They settled accounts, and as they were parting—"bosom pals," Steward later remarked with heavy irony—Glenn asked his name.[23]

With Wilson's stories already written up, Steward spent the next morning working on field notes. The material he had just compiled centered on the bands of Owens Valley Paiutes who lived in the southern part of the valley. He had learned that the bands were not as large as those in the north, where he had worked in the late 1920s, and that some were "female lineages," comprised of women related as mothers and daughters, sisters, and so on. But they did not meet his definition of the matrilineal band. All of the Owens Valley Paiutes, he later wrote, lived in "true composite land-owning bands." In the south, "bands were essentially the same [as in the north], though many were smaller," he added.[24]

In his previous fieldwork, in 1928, he had mapped village sites in the northern part of the valley. In the southern area of the Owens Valley, he saw surface archaeological evidence that a village was located on every stream that ran down from the Sierra Nevada to the Owens River. Each village, as he observed, stood near the edge of an alluvial fan—a mound of debris washed down from the mountain, which spread out from the mouth of each canyon. Situated two to four miles from the Owens River, these sites offered a good supply of excellent water and were close to many food sources.

As Steward later said in *Basin-Plateau*, the Owens Valley's "extraordinarily varied environment afforded all essential food resources within 20 miles of the villages." In contrast to Shoshone country around Death Valley, and other areas he would soon visit in Nevada, in the Owens Valley people did not need to go far to find food. "Although people sometimes remained away from home for several days," he said, "it was usually possible to return within a day or two."[25]

The more sedentary life of the Owens Valley Paiutes would prove to be one of the key differences between them and most Shoshones. That difference, as Steward saw, had roots in the environment, and especially in the supply of food and water. With access to sources of food and water that were fairly reliable, abundant, and nearby, the Owens Valley Paiutes had been able to lead an unusually settled way of life for hunter-gatherers. He had also begun to grasp how mobility or stability—moving often or staying mostly in one place—affected the size and structure of groups.

During the afternoon he took time to drive down to the Owens River, in search of sites of former Paiute villages. He qualified as an experienced archaeologist, having spent three years in the early 1930s working mainly in archaeology while on the faculty of the University of Utah. At the time he was the sole archaeologist at the university and perhaps the only professional in the state.[26]

He and Jane drove along the road that ran between Lone Pine and Keeler until leaving it at a point where it crossed the Owens River. Steward made a quick surface survey along the eastern bank of the river and observed that despite swampy conditions, some villages had stood there as well. The river was home to two important native species of fish. Owens Valley Paiutes had told him that they caught the fish using spears, hooks, baskets, and nets.[27]

Although the car got stuck in the sand, that nuisance was offset when he found a good surface site. He saw some tools—including re-touched flakes of obsidian, a glassy volcanic rock—and scattered pieces of pottery. Pottery making, like basket making, was women's work in the Owens Valley. Steward knew that from experience. By the time of his first fieldwork in the late 1920s, only a few old women still made pots. As he also knew, the use of clay pots, which are both heavy and fragile, was rare among hunter-gatherers. It testified to the unusually settled way of life of the Owens Valley Paiutes, at least in the period just before American settlement.[28]

Before leaving the river that day, they discovered a beach, "which delighted Jane," Julian noted in their journal. That night they saw another movie in Lone Pine and made plans to leave the next morning.[29]

When they arrived at Deep Springs on the following day, hoping to stay for a week, they found the school trustees there for a meeting. They spent the night but left the valley the next morning. Guest quarters were limited, as was the school's budget, and the trustees did not necessarily approve of long-term guests. In Big Pine, about twenty miles away in the Owens Valley, Julian looked up Tom Stone and Mary Harry and arranged to work with them the next day. Then he and Jane drove a few miles north to Keogh's Hot Springs, once the site of a Paiute village. A small resort now stood there instead, offering rustic charm and a range of amenities to tourists. As agriculture and ranching declined in the valley, tourism had grown. The loss of its water to Los Angeles brought an influx of tourists—mostly from Los Angeles.[30]

Out of deference to Jane, and also in the interest of work, Julian by-passed a public campground and bargained instead for a rock-bottom weekly rate at the resort. He had recently told Lowie, "Jane has taken to the trip like a veteran and has been no end of help." In truth, while she did not complain, she had grown up in a city, had no experience of camping, and liked her comforts. "I was a pure city type," she said years later. A bedroll on the hard ground held no appeal, no matter how scenic the surroundings. Throughout their journey, she and Julian would camp when necessary and stay in an auto cabin or in other lodging when possible. Having a table and chairs and electric light gave them several more hours at night to work on field notes and trait lists and to transcribe and type Coyote stories.[31]

The next day they returned to Big Pine, a hamlet about half the size of Lone Pine. Julian knew it well from his student days at Deep Springs as the closest place to purchase food and supplies. Tall oaks and maples shaded wooden sidewalks along the main street. Most of the white residents lived in small frame houses on side streets. Big Pine also had a small community of Paiutes on the outskirts, where some still lived in shelters. Like the Paiutes at Lone Pine and Fort Independence, those at Big Pine fell under the jurisdiction of Bishop Agency. Big Pine Colony had gained reservation status in the early 1920s.[32]

Before conquest, one of the valley's largest villages stood at the site that became the town of Big Pine. During the wars against the Americans the valley's once independent bands joined together for the fight. In the north they united under the leadership of the chief at Big Pine, and in the south, under the chief at George's Creek.[33]

Tom Stone had no direct memory of those events. Born in 1891, around the time the frontier was declared closed, he grew up in the Owens Valley after American settlement and the first ecological transformation. He learned to speak English and to read and write. His paternal grandfather, born before American settlers entered eastern California, had told him many stories about the old times and the old ways. Stone recounted some of those stories to Steward during his fieldwork in the late 1920s. His grandfather's recollections, which he held in memory and passed on to Steward, appeared in print with others', in the form of ethnography in the early 1930s. The University of California Press had published Steward's *Ethnography of the Owens Valley Paiute* just two years earlier.[34]

Stone, who lived in Big Pine, had resided for many years in Bishop, fifteen miles north and home to a larger community of Owens Valley Paiutes. He had married several times and had children by each of his wives. Serial monogamy was not uncommon. Earlier in life he had earned a living as a farm or ranch hand, but he did not have steady employment during the Depression years. Tom and his third wife, Lena, separated for a time in the early 1930s; he lived with several of the children, and Lena lived with the others.

Like her husband, Lena could speak English and had learned to read and write. Their children were also literate. Indian schools had been set up in the Owens Valley by the 1890s, decades after American settlement. For many years Paiute and Shoshone children did not attend public schools with white children.[35]

In contrast to Tom Stone, Mary Harry spoke very little English, and she was far too old to have attended school in the valley. Most of the people who now lived there spoke a language that she had not heard as a child. That testified to changes in the course of one lifetime. She had been born into one world and now lived in another.

A life of hunting and gathering had given way to one in which she bought food with money that she sometimes earned as a laundress. Washing sheets and clothing in a tin tub, using a manufactured washboard made of wood and corrugated metal, had not been part of her earlier life. She had not always lived in a segregated world where racial categories and class divided people. Fences and roads had not divided the land of her childhood.

She vividly recalled first hearing of white men when she was a little girl, perhaps six years old. A report of two white men with pack animals crossing through the country reached her people, and she fled with them into the mountains to hide. This probably happened during the 1850s—following the discovery of gold in California in 1848 and of silver in Nevada soon after—when a flood of hopeful miners rushed into the gold and silver fields. The number of native people in those areas plummeted, a result of disease and bloodshed. Mining began east of Fish Lake Valley by the 1860s at a place whose English name, Gold Mountain, was both ominous and alluring: ominous for the welfare of those living there because it was alluring to miners of many nationalities who were intent on striking it rich no matter the cost.[36]

Eighty years later Mary lived in a place where non-Indians vastly outnumbered Indians and where trucks had almost replaced pack animals. Only a few old prospectors—and greater numbers of tourists hiking on trails that had once served as Paiute trade routes across the Sierra Nevada—still used pack strings of donkeys to carry their supplies. And now she was going to earn money by answering questions about her former world, put to her, for rather obscure reasons, by a white man who drove a car. She had first seen him almost twenty years earlier, when he lived with the other young men at the ranch in Deep Springs Valley.

Mary was a widow and probably in her mideighties. Her late husband, Captain Harry, had worked at the ranch, irrigating the fields, while Steward was a student. Captain Harry, of Shoshone and Paiute ancestry, died in 1921 at an estimated age of eighty or eight-five if census takers were correct. They listed his birth date as the 1830s or 1840, but it was impossible to know the exact year. Steward and the other young students at the ranch thought he was much older, probably a centenarian.[37]

Captain Harry met Mary at a festival in Fish Lake Valley, located across the White Mountains from the Owens Valley. She was fifteen or sixteen and he was about thirty, and a widower, when they met, probably in the 1860s. They were attending a fall festival near Pigeon Spring, in the mountains at the eastern end of Fish Lake Valley. The festival took place during the season when people gathered pine nuts, one of the few times during the year when there was enough food nearby to feed a large gathering for a week or so. People danced, gambled, visited, and courted at these festivals.[38]

After they married, Mary and her husband moved to another place in Fish Lake Valley. People called it by a name that may have meant Cottonwood Tree Place; the English name, Oasis, explains why a ranch soon occupied that favored site where water flowed. They did not live with Mary's parents, unlike most young married couples who stayed with the wife's family until they learned to provide for themselves. Steward would hear repeatedly of this practice, which anthropologists came to call *initial matrilocal residence*, as he traveled elsewhere in the Great Basin. It did not augur well in his search for the patrilineal band. He expected to find patrilocal residence, with women joining their husband's group. In the case of Captain Harry, he was older than usual and an experienced hunter when he married again and had no need to join Mary's family.

After he and Mary had lived at Oasis for about two years, she bore a daughter. Her mother had died earlier, and her maternal grandmother acted as midwife and then took care of her in the days following the birth. She bathed Mary and, as was probably customary, instructed her not to be "a lazy mother." The child was named Wino'hekuwa after Captain Harry's sister.[39]

American settlers entered the valley sometime during this period and established several ranches in an area of nearly a thousand square miles. The herds of livestock grazed on native grasses and other plants, soon destroying the Paiutes' supply of plant foods. Before contact, Mary remembered, her people sometimes suffered from hunger in the spring, when stored seeds ran short, but she insisted that they never starved.[40] After contact, the declining supply of native plants made hunger a pressing problem, and earning money to buy food became a matter of need, not of choice.

Captain Harry and his family left Oasis when he went to work at the McFee ranch, and during that time, when their daughter was three, Mary gave birth to a son. He was called Robert, perhaps because the family now lived on the fringe of an English-speaking world. Robert Harry learned to speak English and may have learned to read and write.[41]

Sometime after the birth of their second child, they went to Deep Springs Valley to visit Captain Harry's sister for a month. She lived there with her husband, a man known as Big Mouth Tom who served as leader. He organized festivals and rabbit drives—communal hunts in which men, women, and children took part—in Fish Lake Valley and in Deep Springs Valley. A leader, known by a Paiute word that meant "talker," was supposed to have speaking skills, which may explain Big Mouth Tom's name. Although a son or other male relative would normally have succeeded him, Captain Harry—his brother-in-law—became the next leader.[42]

After that visit, Mary and Captain Harry returned to the McFee ranch. Their third child, another son, was born during this time. Several years later they moved to Deep Springs Valley. When a ranch was established there, cattle grazed on the native plants that Mary had once gathered to feed her family. Captain Harry worked at the ranch occasionally, and Mary sometimes worked there as a laundress. During Steward's student days the family lived in a shelter, not in the stone buildings that housed the white students and teachers or in the old ranch building where some workers lived.[43]

After her husband died in 1921, Mary burned the shelter and all of his possessions, the custom after a death. She moved to Big Pine to live with one of her children. When Steward went to see her in May 1935, she was living with her son Robert Harry and his wife, Emma. Robert, widely regarded as "a good worker," was a ranch hand who also farmed. Emma worked as a laundress. They lived in a small house constructed from wood and other salvaged materials.[44]

Julian and Jane drove from Keogh's Hot Springs to Big Pine to see Tom Stone and Mary Harry on a Monday morning, and Julian continued to work with them for six days. Jane, who had brought along some skeins of turquoise wool, planned to finish a new addition to her wardrobe. It was an economy measure during those Depression years and also a way to pass time during the long hours Julian spent asking questions and taking notes. She often sat in the umbrella chair, knitting and listening while he worked nearby in a shaded spot with an informant. Since she had already knitted a skirt, she now had to consider whether to use the rest of the yarn for a sweater or a jacket. When Julian offered to carve some wooden buttons, she decided on a jacket.[45]

Julian felt an immediate sense of "pleasant relief," as he put it, at having Tom's help while he questioned Mary. He wanted to know what she remembered about the times before 1870, more than sixty-five years earlier, when she was a child and a young woman. Working with informants who spoke no English, or very little, or who did not grasp his questions, took more time and more money. He had a limited

5. Tom Stone, May 1935. (Photo by Julian H. Steward, courtesy of University of Illinois Archives)

supply of each. The dragging pace of the work, the need to rephrase and repeat, had tried his patience at Lone Pine and Olancha and Indian Ranch. Still, he had managed to maintain an aura of calm as he worked, yielding to temper only at the end of long workdays and in private—in journal entries and to Jane, who always sympathized.

He liked Tom Stone as a person and gave him high praise as an assistant: "Smart, cooperative, and more than friendly," he remarked. Stone had an easy smile and a manner that matched. His dark hair, combed back from a broad forehead, framed an expressive face. He often wore denim overalls and a shirt, but that day he was dressed in pants and a long-sleeved shirt sewn from rough cotton.

Stone's fluency in English, his patience and intelligence, and his knowledge of the past made him an ideal interpreter and, Steward said, an "invaluable informant." His age—midforties—normally would have barred him from the role of cultural informant about the past. But his close attention to the stories his grandfather told allowed him to speak for a man who lived only in memory. Stone so surpassed his other informants that Steward later called him "a native ethnographer of sorts."[46]

Mary was also friendly, "all smiles," as Steward put it, despite a painful case of rheumatism that made moving difficult. She wore a long gingham skirt, loosely gathered at the waist, a long-sleeved cotton blouse, and sturdy shoes. Her dark hair and her face, weathered but not deeply creased, belied her age. She sat quietly and waited for him to begin. He decided to ask Mary to tell him the story of her life, but she repeated the same word, meaning "nothing, nothing." She seemed to think that nothing notable had happened, he later complained; but perhaps she had not learned to view her past as a narrative, or a sequence of noteworthy events. With Tom's help he managed to learn enough to write a short sketch of her life. He recorded a far longer biography of Tom Stone's paternal grandfather, Panatubiji, who raised him. Panatubiji died in 1911, when Stone was twenty years old.[47]

Steward spent two days asking Mary Harry questions about Fish Lake Valley, where she spent so much of her early life. Land divided by the California-Nevada border and occupied by ranches had once been home only to her people and Shoshones. Mary gave him one of the most detailed pictures of how people had lived in a specific place.

6. Mary Harry, May 1935 (Photo by Julian H. Steward, courtesy of University of Illinois Archives)

She remembered a hundred people in that large valley during a period that Steward judged to be about 1870. Of the eight permanent village sites, six stood near streams that flowed down from the White Mountains, and the other two at springs in the mountains at the eastern end of the valley. Each village had from one to four households or, as Steward termed them, *families* or *camps*. Their size varied, but six was about the average number of people in a camp, comprised of kin who shared shelter and their daily food.[48]

Fish Lake Valley, far less fertile than the Owens Valley, supported fewer people, and they had to walk much farther to find food. The valley's Paiute and Shoshone families spent much of the year living in these villages, but they had to leave them seasonally to gather seeds in summer and pine nuts in fall. Villages were permanent as sites, but again in contrast to the Owens Valley, their populations were very fluid. People did not stay put, not even from one year to the next. They moved to other valleys to live near kin, and they might return to Fish Lake Valley years later, as Mary and Captain Harry did early in their marriage.[49]

The people of Fish Lake Valley, Steward finally concluded, were so scattered that they rarely cooperated as a group. In their arid land, sources of food and water were limited and scattered, and that affected how they lived. They did not qualify as "a true band," Steward later wrote in *Basin-Plateau*. "Chieftainship was tenuous," he explained, "and people in certain villages seem to have cooperated as often with Lida [Valley] or Deep Springs Valley people as with Fish Lake Valley neighbors."[50]

Although Mary could remember the people who lived in the valley when she was young, and she could recall how they were related to each other, she had forgotten the names of many. They had been dead for so many years, and no mention had been made of them. She still knew the names of all the villages, but ranchers had occupied most of the sites, drawn to the nearby streams and springs. The Patterson

7. Fish Lake Valley, 1935. (Photo by Julian H. Steward, courtesy of University of Illinois Archives)

ranch, the Moline ranch, the McNett ranch, and others stood near the very water sources where her people had located their villages.[51] Ranchers usually purchased or otherwise obtained water rights when they gained legal title to land.

As Steward put it in *Basin-Plateau*, Paiutes and Shoshones were "gradually forced off the native economy" when grazing livestock destroyed their hunting and gathering grounds. Some families went to live on reservations. Others, he said, "attached themselves to ranches and towns." Since those ranches and towns often stood at or near the sites of their own camps and villages, it could also be said that American settlers had attached themselves to Paiute and Shoshone villages, taking land and water. In the Owens Valley they even took over some of the irrigation canals that Paiutes had constructed. Before settlers arrived and planted crops, Paiutes in the valley had routinely irrigated fields of wild grasses and then harvested the seeds in summer.[52]

Near the end of his week with Tom Stone and Mary Harry, Steward finally completed a culture element list for Kroeber's project. "Exceedingly painful work," he noted. He expressed doubt about the accuracy of the results: "With lack of comprehension of questions & knowledge of answers, prob. ⅓ or more answers are unreliable." The trait list covered everything from hunting practices to religious beliefs.

Steward would always consider the entire project misguided. Lacking any clear question or hypothesis or theoretical direction, so far as he could see, it amounted to a virtual fishing expedition. The project cast a wide net, but to what end? It was not at all evident to him what big fish Kroeber and his associates hoped to catch. In letters to Kroeber, once his teacher and now his patron as he searched for employment, Steward repeatedly expressed his qualms, but he did so politely. He understood Kroeber's professional stature and power, his ability to help—or not to help.[53]

Julian and Jane took time off during the weekend to spend time with friends from Deep Springs. One of the teachers, along with his wife and another teacher, drove to Keogh's Hot Springs on Saturday night, joining them "for dinner and dance," Jane recorded. The next day she and Julian drove to Glacier Lodge on a mountain slope near Big Pine, where he painted a picture of the landscape. His deep attachment to the Sierra Nevada dated from his student days at Deep Springs, and he had warm memories of mountaineering adventures with his friends. Although he lacked formal training in art, his strong visual sense and a gift for representing line and color in nature expressed themselves in drawings and small paintings.[54]

Before leaving the mountains that day, they planned a hiking trip in the High Sierra during July, when the wildflowers reached peak bloom in the mountains and heat reached a peak on the valley floors.[55] It would offer a break from fieldwork and the best escape from the simmering desert. Their descent into Death Valley in early spring had given them a taste of the soaring temperatures they would face in summer, even at higher elevations, and especially in the Nevada desert. In those days air conditioners remained a rare, mostly eastern luxury; and evaporative coolers, called swamp coolers in the West, were several years away from mass production. The only relief from heat came from cold water, fans, shade, sunset—or, better yet, a trip to the mountains.

The recent and welcome news that Julian had just been awarded a research fellowship, starting in a few months, assured them of a live-lihood for another year. It gave them reason to feel optimistic about the near future. The fellowship would also allow him to extend re-search to Utah. With light hearts they made plans to finish the field-work in California and move on to Nevada in a few days.

The only remaining task was to find an informant from Deep Springs Valley. They drove to Bishop to look for a man named Peter Sport, a native of the valley and probably recommended by Mary Harry and Tom Stone. Bishop, the largest town in the Owens Valley, was home to the largest community of Paiutes. Many lived at Bishop Colony, which had gained official status as a reservation about twenty years earlier. Steward had spent most of his time in Bishop and Big Pine during summer fieldwork in the late 1920s, and through working with Tom Stone he had just learned more about the people who lived in the northern part of the valley. As he knew, hamlets and towns now stood in the very areas where Paiute villages were long located, near the limited sources of water. Several villages had occupied the area that later took the name Bishop, after an early settler.[56]

They never found Peter Sport, who had lived in the Owens Valley for many years, both at Big Pine, where his mother came from, and at Bishop. At some point his family had moved from Deep Springs Val-ley to Big Pine, and Peter married there. In the 1920s he worked as a farm hand and lived with his wife, Minnie. By 1930, when he was in his midseventies and she was in her late sixties, they were no longer able to work. But they had recently sold a piece of land south of Big Pine to the City of Los Angeles, land they may have acquired by homesteading.

The funds, which were placed in trust, must have provided some income. Unlike most of their Paiute neighbors, they were classified in a report as *Independent* rather than *Government Ward*.[57]

Peter Sport's father, known as Sport, was from Deep Springs Valley, and his father's brother, a man named Joe Bowers, had once been leader of the people who lived there. During the wars with the Americans, Bowers spent long spells away, "dealing with white men," Steward later wrote. His cousin Big Mouth Tom served in his stead, organizing festivals and rabbit drives in Deep Springs Valley and Fish Lake Valley. Sometime after the wars with the Americans ended, Joe Bowers took a job as an army scout.[58]

Instead of working with Peter Sport as he had planned, Steward happened to run into a Paiute man in Bishop who remembered him from his student days. He did not recognize the man at first. Deep Springs Johnny, as John Alston was known at the ranch, was about seventy years old and had aged very visibly in the fifteen years since Steward left the valley to attend college. He and his wife smiled so pleasantly that Steward felt encouraged to ask if he could work with him that day and record what he remembered of the valley and its people.[59]

Alston agreed, and his daughter, Lizzie Bacoch, served as interpreter. A tall woman with a broad smile, she was in her forties and lived with her parents, a daughter, and three sons in Laws, a hamlet near Bishop. Her husband—or former husband—was away, working at a mine in Nevada, a hundred and twenty miles from Bishop and due east of Death Valley. Steward later praised her as "intelligent" and listed her as an informant, not simply an interpreter. An official report of the time stated approvingly of the family, "Ambitious Indians."[60]

The family offered hospitality that day, along with a lesson in culinary adaptation, when they gave Jane and Julian a sample of ground, roasted wheat mixed with wild seeds. The women had gathered the seeds and then mixed this native fare with wheat: a grain that the settlers brought with them and cultivated and that quickly became more plentiful than the seeds. The native grasses, the source of the seeds, had literally lost ground to farm fields and pastures. Later, when most of the farmers left the valley, sagebrush and other shrubs came to dominate land where native grasses had once thrived.

Julian understood that, but what most impressed Jane was that the wild seeds provided extra food. Years later she remembered that by harvesting the native plants and by hunting, Paiutes and Shoshones increased their food security during the lean years of the Depression. The old ways helped them survive even in the twentieth century. People also made creative and practical use of the new and the nonnative. That day the family extended their welcome to an unexpected visitor who had arrived in Bishop after an absence of years—and they exchanged some old knowledge and goods, using the new medium of exchange, cash. Before leaving, Steward bought a basket and, for a museum collection, a pair of moccasins.[61]

Alston, as Steward may already have known, was the son of Big Mouth Tom. Captain Harry, who succeeded Alston's father as talker in Deep Springs Valley, was his mother's brother. Both men were leaders of a type that Steward termed a *chief* and a *headman*. He sometimes used the terms interchangeably in *Basin-Plateau* but concluded that *chief* "usually connotes extensive authority," exceeding that of headman. Later anthropologists, including some of Steward's students, drew sharp distinctions between different types of leaders. Influenced in part by his ideas about sociopolitical groups in *Basin-Plateau* and other works, they identified different types of leadership in different types of groups. To those later generations, chiefs had far more power; headmen, who led by example and persuasion, had less.[62]

Recalling the valley during what Steward judged to be the 1870s, Alston named five households, or camps. They had a total population of twenty-three. Steward had already seen archaeological evidence that convinced him that the largest cluster of camps, a winter village, had stood near the springs at one end of Deep Springs Valley. Besides providing drinking water, the springs fed a small salt lake.[63]

Alston told him where people had harvested seeds and pine nuts and how they had hunted animals, ranging from deer, antelope, and mountain sheep to rabbits and ducks. His answers about food areas suggested to Steward that the Paiutes who lived in Deep Springs Valley did not claim ownership of these areas. He later remarked in *Basin-Plateau* that his informant for the valley viewed the practices of the Owens Valley Paiutes, who had claimed and enforced exclusive rights to certain tracts, as "strange and selfish."[64] The people who lived in Deep Springs Valley evidently viewed the land as a common.

Steward finally concluded that they had not formed a band after all, despite his expectations. ("To Bishop," he had written in his journal, "to get Peter Sport and the Deep Springs band.") Although they cooperated in rabbit drives and perhaps festivals, and in other ways, their unity was "incomplete," he later said in print. They often married people from other valleys, visited other areas for festivals and rabbit drives, and did not own hunting and seed areas.[65]

Only the Owens Valley Paiutes had achieved true bands, as Steward defined them, and they were not the patrilineal bands that he sought. He planned to continue his search in new territory, the deserts of Nevada.

PART 2. Nevada, 1935

4. Coyote's Country

AFTER SOME QUIET DAYS at Deep Springs, where Julian worked on his field notes and made repairs to the car, he and Jane left for Nevada in late May. He hoped to find Shoshone elders in western Nevada who could tell him more about Death Valley country, adding to what he had learned from George and Mamie Gregory at Olancha. The California-Nevada border divided the Western Shoshone people of the region, but held little meaning for them. They had their own geography of the high desert, with names and boundaries that differed from those shown on the U.S. Geological Survey maps that Julian studied so carefully.[1]

He and Jane drove forty miles east toward Lida, Nevada. Famed as the first mining town complete with saloon in the region, Lida had boomed in the 1870s. It soon faded, then briefly revived in 1905, when it boasted a population of six hundred people, a newspaper, and a dozen saloons. Thirty years later it stood almost empty, a lonely place of weathered wood buildings with broken casements and sagging roofs.[2]

After passing Lida, they turned south. Their route, which skirted the border, offered a better road—and despite the scorching heat, greater safety and comfort—than a direct route through Death Valley. From his years at Deep Springs Julian knew that motorists who ventured into Death Valley during the hottest months risked their lives. Temperatures soared, sometimes rising above 130 degrees Fahrenheit; and travelers who ran out of water or who lost their way or had any other misadventure in that vast arid zone often died there. The valley's name gave fair warning.

A journey of a hundred miles took Jane and Julian from Deep Springs Valley to the town of Beatty, Nevada. They drove past bare hills and through open desert where sagebrush, along with a scattering of Joshua trees, claimed the valley floor. Nevada, standing in the rain shadow of the Sierra Nevada, was America's most arid state, and they were passing through one of the driest parts of that dry land. Despite its great size, the state also had one of the smallest populations—only ninety-one thousand people—and a population density of fewer than one person per square mile. Compared to neighboring California, it looked like a lonely land.[3]

Beatty, with a population of about two hundred, was due east of Death Valley and just six miles from the California-Nevada border. It stood at the south end of Oasis Valley on the banks of the elusive Amargosa River. The river flowed largely underground, emerging now and again as a small ribbon of water or in seeps, but withholding most of its water. Minerals sometimes colored the water nearly red and turned it poisonous to animals. The nearby Amargosa Desert stretched for forty miles almost without surface water and edible plants.[4]

In Beatty they looked up a town resident, recommended as a contact by a friend in Utah. He in turn gave them a letter of introduction to "a real, 100%, red Indian, a gentleman," Steward later said, mockingly. They located the man, who turned out to have only one Indian grandparent—and Cherokee at that. In the language of the time, he was "¾ white." More to the point, he had not grown up Shoshone, a detail that had escaped the notice of Steward's contact in Beatty.

Although his cultural ancestry disqualified him as an informant, he did give Steward the name of someone who might help him: a man named Albert Howell who lived at Ash Meadows in Amargosa Valley. Howell, while not Shoshone, was the child of a Southern Paiute woman and had grown up among her people. His father was African American.[5]

Julian and Jane left Beatty and drove south to Ash Meadows, where dozens of springs and seeps had once supported an expansive oasis, with carpets of native grasses and other edible wild plants. Overgrazing by livestock and years of extravagant irrigation had damaged the fragile ecology of the wetlands. A green land turned brown. Many of the native plants vanished, and many of the birds left. Groves of mesquite and ash trees had flourished near the wetlands, and Julian saw that some screw-bean mesquite trees still grew at Ash Meadows. The bean pods, pounded into meal, had long provided a good source of food for people. He took a photograph of the trees, to use in print as an illustration.[6]

Howell lived with his wife and her sister, both Southern Paiutes. When Jane and Julian arrived, only the sister-in-law was present, but she left as soon as she spotted them. They tracked her down so that they could ask Howell's whereabouts, but she kept her back turned to them, continued washing a piece of clothing, and did not reply to Julian's questions. He persisted, although she said nothing and laughed quietly. Finally, in exasperation, he said it was too bad that he could not find Howell because he wanted to work with him.

As he and Jane walked away, Howell's sister-in-law jumped up and "streaked across a field," Julian wrote, "with me in pursuit, & we found him planting." Howell's wife did not speak English, and his sister-in-law, Annie Tecopa, perhaps understood only a few words, among them "work." A rare chance to earn money had sent her racing to tell Albert, who spoke English and could talk to these white people.[7]

Howell, slightly built and mild in manner, agreed to work with Steward the next day. Steward learned that he came from Las Vegas, an ancestral home of Southern Paiutes who now lived in a colony on the outskirts of the city. The springs at Las Vegas had always attracted people to that place, including Southern Paiutes and, later, ranchers.

Once a drowsy desert outpost, Las Vegas was booming, not from mining but from another kind of gambling, at gaming tables in casinos. Just four years earlier, Nevada, in keeping with its strike-it-rich history, had legalized gambling. No other state allowed it.[8]

Albert Howell was the son of John Howell, the first African American to settle in Oasis Valley, in the vicinity of Beatty. He arrived there to try his hand at ranching in 1895. Born in North Carolina, John Howell had made his way more than two thousand miles west to Nevada by the time he was in his thirties. He was working as a teamster in the mining camps of Eldorado Canyon, south of Las Vegas, when an 1880 census taker recorded his name, estimated his date of birth in the 1840s, and categorized him as *mulatto*. Twenty years later, a census taker listed him as *white*, and his children as *½ Ind.*[9]

Albert Howell had the reputation of being "very smart because he can read, write, and vote," Steward noted. American Indians had only gained the right to vote in federal elections a decade earlier, in 1924. Howell was apparently one of the few who exercised it in that part of Nevada. Then in his midsixties, his ability to read English and to write was unusual among Paiute men his age. Growing up with an English-speaking parent had offered an advantage in that respect. His younger brothers and sister were also literate. Very likely their father, given his origins, had understood deeply the value of literacy and the right to vote.[10]

Howell's wife, Mary, was Southern Paiute and also in her midsixties. She came from nearby Pahrump Valley, midway between Ash Meadows and Las Vegas. Census takers usually termed her *full blood Paiute*, and her husband *mixed blood Paiute*. According to Steward, Albert and Mary Howell did not hold legal title to the land they lived on, "a once ambitious ranch," he recorded in his journal. Albert planted "mostly native crops," he added, meaning plants domesticated in the Americas, not those brought from other parts of the world.[11]

As he would learn from the Howells, Southern Paiutes living in

Pahrump Valley before the American conquest had cultivated small plots of corn, squash, beans, and sunflowers. They planted seeds in small plots of moist soil near streams and irrigated them. This provided only a portion of their food supply. By necessity they also gathered seeds and hunted, covering a large territory.[12] Albert Howell planted the same crops but departed from past practice of Southern Paiutes by plowing the land and keeping animals. His father had brought this way of living on the land to Nevada. It was a legacy of an earlier life in the American South.

Howell and his wife owned some pigs and chickens as well as three horses whose prominent ribcages revealed their chronic hunger with painful clarity. They also had an old and very hungry dog, as Jane and Julian found when they camped in the Howell's yard that night. Besides putting up with the pigs as neighbors, they had to fend off the dog while they prepared and ate dinner. Deaf, blind, and diseased, the dog did not respond to threats, Julian grumbled, thus posing "a constant menace to our grub department."[13]

They went to bed as the light faded and woke up at 5:30 the next morning in the gray half-light of dawn. By 7 a.m. Steward set to work with Howell. He asked, and Howell answered, questions about bands all morning. "Painfully procured fragmentary infor. on Paiute band— Kelly's 'Las Vegas [band]' that covers half the U.S.," Steward wrote at the end of the day. A sentence that began with a tone of fatigue ended in a wisecrack.[14]

Just a year earlier Isabel Kelly had beat Steward into print when she published an article titled "Southern Paiute Bands." Worse, the article had appeared in the leading journal, the *American Anthropologist*. Formerly fellow students at Berkeley, she and Steward were now fellow competitors. Neither one had steady work, like many Americans during this time. Several years of anxious searching had not yielded a prized and full-time position in anthropology at a museum or university.[15] They were trying to establish themselves in a profession that had few jobs to offer and that demanded original ideas and findings—and theirs conflicted.

Based on differences in dialect, Kelly divided Southern Paiutes into fifteen groups, or bands. That was generally in keeping with the approach of Kroeber and many others who drew cultural boundaries along linguistic lines. Her ideas also took precedence because they had already reached print. Steward mocked them privately in the journal entry. A few years later he called them into question in *Basin-Plateau*.[16]

Steward would eventually conclude that the Southern Paiutes of this region did *not* form bands before the entry of Americans. The only shared activity was an annual festival, the last of which had been held around the turn of the century, after American conquest. But in the period between contact and conquest, the loss of wild foods—which spelled starvation—led Southern Paiutes to band together. In order to get food, they raided settlers, whose grazing livestock ate the native grasses. The use of horses helped them travel widely and communicate over large areas. After conquest, many went to live on reservations, unlike the Howells who lived independently.[17]

During the afternoon that day, Steward worked with them on kinship terms. Terminology associated with patrilineal kinship systems could be encouraging evidence of a patrilineal band, but he had not yet found that type of terminology. Mary Howell answered some of his questions, her husband interpreting. Although Steward thought her "well informed," he reported that he "got nowhere." Moving on to the trait list, he had greater success, finally calling it quits for the day after seven wearing hours.[18]

He took a walk below the ranch to look for potsherds, fragments of pottery that might mark the sites of old villages. Fed up for the moment with asking and listening, he welcomed the more soothing work of looking for surface sites. A little archaeology, in solitude, could help him shed frustration with the day's work. Finding sites would also help to verify what Albert and Mary Howell had told him about where people once lived.

Looking at open land that stretched far into the distance had a calming effect as well. The arid reaches of the Amargosa Desert held special appeal because of the intensity of light and color. "Different from the Sierra flanked Owens Valley, this country has real charm," he wrote. "Desert without end, virtually no water, but shining with color."[19]

He and Jane went to bed with the sun and woke up with the sun the next morning. On that second day, he worked only on the trait list—or "the damned trait list," as he called it. Mary Howell answered most of the questions, but reluctantly, he thought. Her replies came slowly and through the filter of an interpreter, Albert. They worked for about eight hours in the open air, where gusts of wind scattered Julian's papers, blew dust in his eyes, and carried away Albert's words. Everything about the day—the constant wind, Mary's perceived reluctance, the tedium of waiting while questions and answers were translated from English into Southern Paiute, and back, and above all, his dislike of the task—made a long day even more tiring.[20]

Steward finished the trait list the next morning and paid Albert Howell $7.00 for nineteen hours, instead of the standard $5.00 or so for his time. The extra money provided some compensation for his wife's work and the means to buy extra food. Steward could see that the Howells lived on the edge of hunger, their problems made worse by age and infirmity. Raising pigs and chickens helped them survive, he wrote, but Albert "broke his leg and his wife is old so that existence is a struggle."[21]

Before leaving the Howells, he took a photograph of Albert standing beside the house. He was wearing jeans and a freshly laundered and starched cotton shirt. It had been carefully pressed with an iron heated on the wood stove. His canvas hat had a narrow brim, and he angled it to shield his eyes from the strong sunlight. A full beard,

8. Albert Howell, May 1935. (Photo by Julian H. Steward, courtesy of University of Illinois Archives)

which he wore short and neatly trimmed, revealed that he had some non-Indian ancestry.[22]

If Steward asked Mary Howell to pose for a picture, she must have refused. His cryptic comments suggest that she felt relieved to see the strangers go, even though she and Albert had earned precious cash by answering the man's questions. Some of the questions may have struck her as odd or confusing or intrusive, or perhaps the man's persistence wore on her. Sometimes she explained as best she could, and then he asked her to explain again. It was all a routine part of serving as a cultural informant, as she may or may not have known. The process, at any rate, was culturally alien.

Julian and Jane left the Howells' ranch at noon and followed directions to a camp nearby in Ash Meadows. They were looking for Mary Scott, an old woman who spoke some English. Julian had been led to believe that she was Shoshone and perhaps from Death Valley. They soon located the place where she lived with a young grandson in what struck them as complete poverty. Jane and Julian counted the remnants of eleven derelict cars scattered in the area around her camp as they searched for her.

They found her at work, Julian wrote, "in a 'garden' some distance away, where she had hobbled—God knows how—and sat feebly chopping at a bush with a broken tire spring." He estimated her age as eighty, but a census taker recorded 1863 as her date of birth, suggesting that she was in her early seventies. She occupied the uncommon—for a woman—category of *farmer*, instead of the usual *laundress* or *none*. A notation in the records stated, "currently at work on own farm." To Julian, the Howells' more extensive fields qualified as a farm, however hardscrabble. The small patches of ground where Mary scratched the soil and dropped the seeds of native plants such as corn and squash barely amounted to a garden in his view.[23]

Government rations, which she received once a month, added to the food she grew and gathered. But the portions probably sufficed only as condiments, not daily fare. According to an exposé in the *Los Angeles Times*, published ten years earlier, two elderly Paiute women in Big Pine, California, received the following skimpy rations: "Four cups of flour, two cups of rice, about three pounds of sugar, a couple of handfuls of macaroni, two small cans of baking powder, and a piece of bacon the size of your hand." The indignant reporter added, "This ration was given these two old women to last them a month!" As the superintendent of Bishop Agency explained, he had no more to give them. "'It is simply a question of my giving a few enough [food] or giving all of them a little. I do the latter.'"[24]

There is not much reason to think that rations increased during the hard years of the Depression, or that Mary Scott fared any better. But she seemed as hungry for company, and a rare chance to earn some money, as she was for food on the day that Julian and Jane visited. She passed up lunch—if she had food on hand—to talk to them for several hours. They sat in the open air while Julian asked her a long series of questions.

Talking about her early life to these strangers who had suddenly appeared at her camp called up memories from fifty and sixty years in the past. She told them that she had married a soldier as a young woman, but they showed little interest in that or any other details about life after American settlement. The questions about how her people had once lived confused her, and she struggled to find the words in English to answer.

Julian quickly learned that Mary was just "¼ Shoshone" and had grown up among Southern Paiutes at Ash Meadows. He also decided that her halting English limited her usefulness as a cultural informant. Since his questions about bands yielded very little, he considered what else he could learn from her. Finally he asked for a list of Southern Paiute words. He also recorded several stories, noting that they were Shoshone (at his request) and difficult to follow because she spoke so little English.[25]

One earthy tale from Death Valley featured Coyote as the father of people in the region. Steward would hear variants of this story from other elders.

The Origin of People

One day, Coyote went out to hunt rabbits. While he was hunting, he saw a large naked woman in the distance. This excited him. He said to himself, "Whew, I have never seen a woman like that. I will follow her . . ."

Coyote did follow her, and later left her, carrying away a basketry water jug filled with tiny babies, his children. As she had instructed, he scattered the babies, first in Saline Valley and Death Valley where they grew into very handsome people, and then in other places. The last of the babies, the dregs, grew into ugly people, distant neighbors who were not Shoshones. They had lice in their hair and sores on their eyes.[26]

A story that remained untold that day linked Mary and Jane, but neither knew that, or the full story. Forty years earlier, long before Jane's birth, Mary had shown some unusual rocks to her cousin, a prospector, who recognized them as gold float. She received no real compensation for taking him to the place in the Black Mountains where she found the rocks. For the promise of $4,000, he showed the site to two men from a mining camp; they staked a claim and, without paying him, later sold the claim for the Confidence Mine to investors from Salt Lake City. The investors included Hugh J. Cannon, one of Jane's many uncles.

Mary's cousin never collected the $4,000 he was owed by the Confidence Mining Company, an all-too-common experience for an Indian

9. Beatty, Nevada, in the early 1930s (Exchange Club on the right). (Courtesy of Nevada Historical Society)

prospector. He came to a bad end fifteen years later, murdered by his brother-in-law, a white rancher from Kentucky and allegedly a former cattle rustler. The Confidence Mine never amounted to much, and its unpaid accounts led some to speak of the *Lost* Confidence Mining Company. In the end Hugh Cannon managed to recoup some of the money he had invested.[27]

Jane knew nothing of these complex and long-ago business dealings, or of her improbable connection to this old woman living at the edge of the Amargosa Desert. But when Julian and Jane left Ash Meadows, after spending four hours there, he paid Mary $1.50, not the usual rate of $1.00. Her disability, her circumstances, and her age triggered a flash of sympathy. She "hobbled," as he noticed, because she had badly injured her back a few years earlier when she fell ten feet from a pinyon tree while collecting pine nuts.

Her pleasure at earning the money was unmistakable: "Left her at 4, delighted to see $1.50 in hard cash," Julian recorded. It was more than she ever received for the peculiar rocks she picked up in the

Black Mountains, which had provided some profit to unknown people in other places.[28]

Discouraged by the day's work, which had produced no details about bands or Shoshones around Death Valley, Julian and Jane left Ash Meadows and drove north to Beatty. They stopped for a drink at the Exchange Club where, unexpectedly, an Englishman from Cornwall presided over the bar. The end of Prohibition two years earlier, in 1933, had spelled the end of speakeasies and bootleg liquor and the return of saloons and brand-name alcohol.

The Exchange Club, a venerable institution in Beatty, featured a long bar of ornately carved dark wood. Behind it stretched an equally long beveled mirror that let customers watch their backs—carefully. Julian and Jane surveyed the scene as they drank their beer. They saw some "sporting ladies," as Julian put it, and, as he said more directly, several "drunks [who] staggered in and out." He summed up their observations two days later in just one sentence of a long typewritten letter to Kroeber. "Now we are at Beatty, one of Nevada's gems," he wrote, "where the main hotel consists of brothel, old time saloon and restaurant and where, in spite of the extremely small population, people get themselves shot, poisoned, blown up or wrecked every few days."[29]

Since Julian had other prospects in the area, he and Jane decided to stay at a private auto camp in Beatty. The comfort of a cabin promised to lighten the burdens of fieldwork—such as the need to defend their food from hungry dogs when they camped. Even renting an auto cabin presented some complication that day, leading Julian to complain later that the man in charge was an "idiot."[30]

His luck turned and his mood lifted the next morning when he located a Shoshone elder from Death Valley. Then in his midseventies, Bill Doc had lived at Scotty's Camp in Grapevine Canyon a few years earlier, the place where Steward met his first informants, Wilbur

Patterson and John Hunter. They probably gave Steward his name. In 1930, at the age of seventy, Bill Doc had still been employed. Census takers listed him as *laborer at private estate, currently working*. At the time, and for five years previously, he had worked at Scotty's Castle, helping to construct the improbable Moorish mansion in the desert. Construction halted when the owner suffered financial reverses from the onset of the Depression.[31]

Sometime in the early 1930s Bill Doc and his family left Grapevine Canyon on the California side of the border. They moved across the desert to Beatty, on the Nevada side, and may have lived at an Indian camp that stood east of the railroad tracks and along the river. The railroad sometimes had jobs to offer. Some fifteen families, mostly Shoshones, occupied makeshift shelters shaded by leafy cottonwood trees that lined the banks of the river. In summer, when the remorseless heat invaded even deep shade, many of them went to cooler camps in the mountains.[32] In late May, with the heat at a low simmer, Steward found Bill Doc and his family still living somewhere on the outskirts of Beatty.

The family had moved back and forth between the California and Nevada sides of Death Valley over the years. Some of Bill Doc's children were born in Nevada. His people had covered such a large territory during the early years of his life that he could give an account not only of Death Valley but also of the region around Beatty and the Belted Mountains to the east.[33]

Bill Doc and five or six others lived in what Jane described as "a tiny brush wickiup." The assortment of relatives included two of his daughters, one widowed and one single, a nine-year-old granddaughter, and a six-year-old grandson. His wife, Tina Doc, was in her mid-sixties. A skilled basket maker, she sold baskets of great artistry to collectors and received modest payment.[34]

Baskets had not yet gained a strong place in the art market. *Art,* as collectors defined it, was perhaps an alien concept to her, but *market* was not. Like Mamie Gregory and other basket makers of that time and place, Tina Doc made baskets with the old materials and techniques and began to create new designs for those she sold. By the time she died many years later, she was recognized as one of the last Panamint Shoshone women who knew the technique of twined basketry. Still later, collectors paid thousands of dollars for some of her baskets.[35]

Julian spent five hours with Bill on that first day. They worked steadily until a dust storm blew up in the early afternoon, damaging the shelter and disrupting their work outside. The powerful wind blew dust into their eyes and threatened to carry away Julian's papers. He and Bill moved to the side of an old wagon to find shelter from the buffeting wind. They finally gave up two hours later, planning to continue the next day when the wind might have died down. "The man is a good informant," Jane noted that evening in a journal entry, "probably the best yet."[36]

When they returned the following morning to see Bill Doc, Jane noticed that the damaged brush shelter had undergone repair. She saw two women working inside, surrounded by piles of bedding and boxes. A ketchup bottle that sat in the middle of the floor caught her eye. It held a few purple wildflowers, a token of outdoor beauty taken inside.

Over the course of three days, Julian spent as much time with Bill Doc as he had spent with the Howells, but he learned far more. The pleasure of fieldwork returned, and he felt more optimistic about his project. With Bill's help he could fill in many of the gaps that had remained in his knowledge of Death Valley country, even after the several days he spent questioning George and Mamie Gregory. He and Bill sat outside in the wearing heat and sunlight for long hours at a time, and Julian asked the full range of questions that could help him understand band structure.

He learned that Bill grew up in Grapevine Canyon, the son of a man named Doc, a shaman. Besides his role as a healer, Bill's father also served as leader of the people living in the area. Doc had two wives who were sisters. Steward recorded this as an instance of polygyny, plural marriage of a type that anthropologists termed *sororal polygyny*. As he was to find in the course of fieldwork, marrying sisters was an accepted practice not only among Panamint Shoshones but also among native people in many other parts of the Great Basin.

Doc's family spent winters at Grapevine Canyon but left in the spring, when the stored food ran short. Bill had vivid memories from childhood of crying for food during the early spring. His people often went to the western side of the Grapevine Mountains to gather seeds in the spring, or elsewhere in Death Valley in April to collect seeds and berries. In June and July they picked mesquite pods at yet another place. After removing the seeds, they ground the bean pulp into flour, which was easy to carry or, if they had a surplus, to cache until they returned for it on another trip.[37]

They harvested pine nuts in the fall in the Grapevine Mountains, where families usually picked on the same tracts from year to year. Since they did not claim exclusive rights to the plots, Steward concluded that they did not own them. Doc, as leader, announced when the pine nuts were ripe, and people then went to the mountains to harvest them. He also directed rabbit drives. The word for leader, which Steward termed *chief*, meant "talker" or "big talker," Bill Doc said.[38]

After the entry of Americans who brought grazing livestock into the region, life changed suddenly as the ecology changed. Spurred by the sharp decline in wild plants and game, a few people began to produce some of their food. They grew the same plants and used the same techniques as the neighboring Southern Paiute. As early as 1870 Bill Doc's father, grandfather, and uncle cultivated acres of land in Grapevine Canyon. Men and women shared the work of planting and irrigating, using digging sticks before shovels were introduced.

"Plots were family owned," Steward later wrote. "This conformed to the principle of use ownership and conflicted with no native patterns." He had evidently learned from Bill Doc that the people who put their labor into growing food held exclusive rights to the food they produced. He concluded that they owned the plots. This conclusion was in accord with a long tradition of European and American legal thinking, a way of thinking that came easily to him. Steward, the son of a lawyer, had briefly considered a career in law before choosing anthropology instead.[39]

By 1890 visitors to Death Valley country saw more evidence of farming, but it never grew very important. People ate most of the food as it ripened, finishing it by the end of summer, so it did nothing to help them through the winters. More to the point, the need to earn money often drew them away from their land, and the scheduled nature of wage work interfered with the different schedule demanded by farming.

During the mining boom in nearby Rhyolite, Nevada, in 1906, as Steward noted in *Basin-Plateau*, Shoshones from Death Valley left their small farms to earn money by hauling wood for the mines. Thirty years later, in the mid-1930s, some farming continued, although, he explained, "odd jobs offered by the white man relegate it to a secondary place."[40] Earning money to buy food and other necessities took precedence over farming.

On the evening of that second day, Julian and Jane drove to Rhyolite, a boomtown turned ghost town. Thirty years earlier it had suddenly sprung to life in the desert, its population surging to eight or ten thousand following the discovery of gold. Large buildings, some made of brick, sprouted in the midst of the sagebrush. Banks and churches and an opera house shared ground with gambling houses, dance halls, and more than fifty saloons. Miners, entrepreneurs, investors, and other gamblers from all over the United States and beyond disembarked at the new railroad station.[41]

Shoshone and Paiute men had not only hauled wood for the mines;

some, like Mary Scott's cousin, tried their luck at prospecting. They knew the land far better than any of the new arrivals, but few of the Indian prospectors gained much from their knowledge and labor. Double-dealing in the mining camps was not confined to the gambling houses. It almost guaranteed that the newcomers, who knew how to read and write and get financial backing, would profit, not the Indian prospectors.

Bill Doc's half brother, known as Johnny Shoshone, had found a site in the early 1900s that over time yielded more than $2 million, but he had little to show for it. Although the famous mine, known as the Montgomery Johnny, shared his name, mine owner Bob Montgomery shared almost none of the profits. Unlike Mary Scott's cousin, whose downward spiral ended in a violent and early death, Johnny Shoshone lived a long life. Besides receiving a few dollars from Bob Montgomery now and then, he earned money posing for snapshots taken by tourists in Death Valley.[42]

When the mines played out, most of the people left Rhyolite, and the town fell into disrepair. Surveying this scene of collapse, Jane decided that the shells of two-and three-story buildings looked pretentious even without roofs and floors. Some of the adobe and frame shacks that once housed workers still stood, but "in the last stages of decay," she remarked. "Now only a few miners amid all that ruin." Aside from the stubbornly hopeful miners, the odd site also attracted curious visitors, spillover tourists from nearby Death Valley National Monument. Some of the visitors lingered, and the railroad station had been converted to a casino.[43]

Unlike this place of ruin, abandoned as soon as the mineral wealth ran out, the desert around it shone with beauty that endured. In the deep silence, as dusk gathered, Jane and Julian admired the shifting hues of purple and rose and blue. "Minerals color the hills," she wrote, "[and the] desert stretches out to the south and east. Spectacular in the evening shadows."[44]

On the following day Steward spent seven grueling but productive hours with Bill Doc. He finished a trait list and ended by recording some stories. One of them told about the origins of people, and it varied only in details from the version he had heard from Mary Scott. Coyote figured in the stories that Bill Doc told that day, and in most that Steward heard as he traveled through Coyote's country. In nearly all of the tales, no matter the perils and problems the supremely adaptable Coyote emerged as a survivor. And even if he did die in one story, he appeared alive and well in the next.[45]

Steward took the next day off to work on his field notes and type some letters, and he stayed inside the cabin.[46] Writing at a table in a sheltered place offered a welcome change from days of open-air fieldwork in heat and high wind and dust. The glare of sun on white paper, and the sorties of wind on pages of precious notes, interfered with the main task: asking questions and listening carefully, following up with other questions to clarify or amplify what Bill Doc told him, and recording what he learned.

The next morning Steward located his last informant in the area, an elder named Tom Stewart. Like Bill Doc's family and the Howells, Tom Stewart lived independently, not on a reservation. Bishop Agency could not enumerate all of the people termed *Scattered Indians* in each census. They had a habit of moving, not only within their ancestral territory but sometimes outside it to find wage work. The agency's 1920 census had listed Stewart as *widower*, born in 1871, noting *can't locate*. By 1925 he was living in Death Valley for months at a time while he worked at Scotty's Castle. His employment there ended in 1931, as did Bill Doc's.[47]

Steward found him living somewhere near Beatty, and they set to work immediately. He spent nearly three days with Stewart, learning about Western Shoshones who had lived in the area of Beatty and the Belted Mountains. Although perhaps younger than Steward judged him ("born ca. 1865," he estimated), Tom Stewart proved an excellent informant. Steward commended him as "cooperative, well informed, intelligent and careful; one of the best informants; English fair." The only distraction from fieldwork during these three days was a baseball game in town. Steward took a few hours off to watch a team from Death Valley Junction, about fifty miles away, defeat the home team.[48]

Tom Stewart provided a detailed census of the people who lived in the Beatty region of his boyhood, during the late 1870s. He remembered the sites of six winter camps in the vicinity of Beatty and eight along the southern end of the Belted Mountains. Stewart had spent winters at the mouth of Beatty Wash on the Amargosa River, at the place where his father was born. He lived with his parents and a brother and sister, and near his father's two sisters, their husbands, and their children. The sisters had married two brothers from Gold Mountain.

Stewart's father—and his father before him—served as talker, or leader, of the people who lived at the six winter sites, directing rabbit drives and festivals until he died. No one succeeded Stewart's father as talker because the communal hunting and the festivals came to an end in the area around Beatty, as elsewhere in the Great Basin. The reasons for this may have been complex, but they included the simple fact that wage-paying work interfered with taking part in a weeklong or monthlong festival or rabbit drive.

Wage work had quickly become necessary for survival. It followed a daily schedule and could not easily be interrupted and then resumed. Leaving a job usually meant losing a job. In a land of limited and scattered resources, wage work became the scarcest and most scattered of all. It often dictated where people lived, and increasingly it also dictated how they lived. It was not compatible with some of the old ways.

The ecological crisis brought about by ranching and mining may have been especially severe for Western Shoshones living around Beatty because they depended so heavily on wild plants for food. They gathered greens and Joshua tree buds in early spring, seeds in summer, and pine nuts in the fall. Men hunted mountain sheep during summer in the mountains, and rabbits in communal drives during the fall; but game was scarce in this region, and water very limited. The mountains were too low to have streams fed by snowmelt, and few springs existed.[49]

American settlers who entered the area established ranches around springs that were sites of some winter camps. Grazing livestock ate the wild grasses, churned up the thin soil with their hooves, and fouled the water. A lucrative market for beef—to feed the many people drawn to nearby mining camps or living in more distant places—drove changes in the fragile ecology of the high desert.[50]

Tom Stewart gave Julian Steward one of the richest accounts of a local area—and a vast one, covering more than a thousand square miles where people foraged for food. Steward eventually concluded that the Western Shoshones of Beatty and of the Belted Mountains had formed two independent, named groups, each with a leader who organized rabbit drives and festivals. Each group "approximated a band," he later wrote, but did not comprise either composite or patrilineal bands as he defined them. They did not claim and enforce exclusive rights to food areas, leading him to conclude that they did not own land; and they did not have rigid social boundaries. The Beatty people often cooperated with those of the Belted Mountains, and—as Steward already knew from George Hanson and Bill Doc—they also had links to Death Valley. They sometimes gathered pine nuts and took part in rabbit drives and festivals there.[51]

Besides asking questions about bands, Steward also worked with Tom Stewart on a trait list, which they finished on their last day. He and Jane packed and prepared to leave Beatty the next morning, planning to return to Deep Springs by way of Gold Point and Tule

Canyon, both on the Nevada side of the border. They had agreed to take along Bill Doc's fourteen-year-old granddaughter, Alice Kennedy, as a passenger. She wanted to visit her father's parents who lived in Tule Canyon. Julian hoped to enlist Alice's paternal grandfather as a cultural informant for the area around Lida Valley.[52]

Gold Point, a boomtown gone bust, had recently revived. Mining promised to bring another wave of prosperity. Small frame buildings with false fronts, which lined Main Street, stood open for business once again—an incongruous hub of commerce in an open space of sagebrush plain and sky. The town lay along a sandy track about ten miles from the road that led to Lida and the California border and then continued on to Deep Springs. Alice thought that her grandparents lived only three miles from Gold Point, but the true distance, as Julian and Jane discovered hours later, was sixteen grueling miles over a rutted trail. On their arrival they learned that her grandfather did not come from Lida Valley. He came from Death Valley, "which we had covered," Jane recorded with dismay, "so was no use as informant."[53]

Alice, although born in Nevada, had also lived in California. Her parents moved back and forth, from Beatty and Oasis Valley in Nevada to Grapevine Canyon in Death Valley. In 1930 she lived in the canyon, at Scotty's Camp, with her parents and two brothers. A census taker listed both Alice's father and her teenage brother as *laborer, at private estate, currently working.* Like Bill Doc and Tom Stewart, they helped construct Scotty's Castle. Everyone in the family could speak English, but none of them had learned to read and write. Unlike Paiutes of the Owens Valley, they lived in an area so remote that it had no school.[54]

Julian and Jane left Alice with her grandparents and backtracked the sixteen bone-jarring miles to Gold Point. A thin veil of dust lifted from the narrow trail and tagged along behind the car until they reached the road. "We drove on past mines," Jane wrote, "Julian panning his first gold during our lunch stop." Although they had left Beatty soon after daybreak, they did not reach Deep Springs until late afternoon because of the fruitless detour to Tule Canyon. They found a stack of letters and telegrams awaiting them, conveying both good news and bad.

Julian's research fellowship for the next year had been reduced from twelve months to ten, with a matching decrease in the stipend. Kroeber, who already knew about this cost-cutting measure, had written to offer more funds for field expenses, to help make up for the loss. A colleague at the Smithsonian Institution in Washington DC had sent a telegram urging Julian to apply for a position as ethnologist with the Bureau of Indian Affairs. "Sent them all telegrams to straighten it out," Jane said in summary.[55]

They spent a few days putting their camping gear in order, cleaning the car of dust and grime, and doing the laundry and other chores. Reworking field notes always took time, and seeing friends at Deep Springs was always a pleasure. They drove to Bishop and Independence one day and had visitors the next. Their stay stretched out to nearly two weeks.[56]

In mid-June they left for Nevada. Their plan called for spending the next six weeks there and then returning to California in early August for a break, a hike in the High Sierra.[57] Instead of traveling through Lida Valley again they turned near the border in the opposite direction and drove through Fish Lake Valley, Mary Harry's old home. Steward still hoped to find an elder who could tell him about the people of Lida Valley before American settlement. He knew only a few details, provided by Mary Harry, and had taken the detour to Tule Canyon on the last trip in the mistaken belief that he would learn more from Alice Kennedy's grandfather. Her grandfather had nothing to tell him except perhaps the name of someone who might help, a Western Shoshone man named John Shakespeare.

The people who lived in the Lida Valley region before American settlement were mainly Western Shoshones, Steward later wrote. They had links with Northern Paiutes in nearby Fish Lake Valley and Western Shoshones who lived at Gold Mountain and elsewhere in the area. Intermarriage among these Paiutes and Shoshones was common. The parentage of Mary's late husband, and her own marriage, illustrated that. Captain Harry's father, a Shoshone from Lida Valley, or perhaps Tule Canyon, married a Paiute woman from Fish Lake Valley. Captain Harry's first wife, who died before he was thirty, was Shoshone. Mary, his second wife, was Paiute.[58]

As Steward had seen on past trips, Lida Valley was narrow and unusually green, with dense stands of pinyon trees in the mountains. In contrast the open desert to the north, east, and west had few sources of water, and the low mountains bordering the desert did not reach the elevation where pinyon trees grew. Pine nuts, a mainstay of the food supply in Lida Valley and other places, were not available there. "The population was so sparse," Steward said, "that there are few informants today who know anything about it."[59]

One of those few, John Shakespeare, lived miles north of Lida and east of Fish Lake Valley, in Clayton Valley near the Silver Peak Range. Cow Camp, where he made his home, was remote even by the standards of western Nevada. His former home, lonely Lida, seemed heavily trafficked by comparison, as did Fish Lake Valley with its few ranches.

Steward judged John Shakespeare, a sturdy man with white hair and a weathered look, to be in his eighties. Census takers thought he was in his seventies. A census of Indians in western Nevada categorized him as *full blood Paiute*. Federal census takers termed him *full blood Shoshone*. Perhaps this reflected the frequent intermarriage in the region. His occupation, according to a federal census, was *caring for horses*.[60]

At Cow Camp he lived with his wife, Ella; one of his daughters and

10. John Shakespeare (*second from left*) and family with Jane Steward, June
1935. (Photo by Julian H. Steward, courtesy of University of Illinois Archives)

her husband, a white man called Flint; and some small children. Indians had long lived at the site. The area was so far from a town, and a
school, that no one in the family—except perhaps Flint—knew how
to read or write, but everyone could speak English. Jane and Julian
camped out behind the one-room cabin and lean-to where the family lived. Julian had "uncharitable thoughts," Jane said, about Flint's
cattle business. He did not own a ranch, which might suggest a business more akin to cattle rustling than to cattle raising.[61]

Finding John Shakespeare knowledgeable and intelligent, Steward
worked with him for several days, "getting data on Lida band," he
noted in a journal entry. Despite suspicions about Flint, he wanted to
work with his father-in-law, and he showed a friendly demeanor toward
the whole family, his standard policy. Ella Shakespeare also served as
an informant, answering some of his questions about basketry for the

trait list. One day he took a photograph of Jane sitting in the shade of a ramada with John and Ella's family, and another snapshot of John standing next to a wagon.[62]

Steward's questions about the Lida band yielded a partial list of the former camps and villages in the area and details about the places where people had gathered food in the past. They hunted deer, mountain sheep, pronghorn antelope, and smaller game in the mountains, gathered seeds in Tule Canyon and berries in Clayton Valley, and sometimes collected pine nuts with Paiutes from Pigeon Spring in Fish Lake Valley. If they had to look farther afield for pine nuts, they went forty miles south to the Grapevine Mountains, bordering Death Valley, or traveled even farther eastward to the Kawich Mountains. The introduction of horses in the nineteenth century helped them make these long journeys. John Shakespeare, part of the first generation to grow up around horses, had spent his life working with them, probably as a ranch hand.[63]

He recalled that people from Lida Valley and the area had often visited nearby Pigeon Spring in Fish Lake Valley for festivals. Pigeon Spring was only about ten miles away from Lida: that is, only ten miles from a camp at a spring, a site later occupied by the mining town named Lida. Big Mouth Tom or Captain Harry usually directed the festivals that drew people from such widely scattered places.

Steward eventually decided that bands had *not* existed in the sparsely inhabited country in and around Lida Valley. Practically speaking, every household—the basic residential unit that he usually termed a *family* or *camp*—was independent in a political sense. As he put it, "each family was the political unit." This would prove to be one of the most unexpected and unusual—and years later, controversial—discoveries of his fieldwork. He believed that for ecological reasons no political entity larger than the household, or camp, existed. The scattered and severely limited supply of food and water dictated a small and scattered population, preventing unity as a band. This was true, he concluded, not only in Lida Valley but also throughout much of Nevada and in the Death Valley country of California.[64]

Jane and Julian moved on a few days later to Tonopah, a mining town and the seat of Nevada's largest county. Nye County covered eighteen thousand square miles, an area larger than some eastern states, and Tonopah qualified as a desert metropolis with a population of more than two thousand. Driving along the main street, they passed stores, saloons, and the once elegant Mizpah Hotel, which shared the name of the famous silver mine. The Mizpah mine had proved to be one of the richest on record in Nevada. It was rumored that Jim Butler, the man who staked the claim, had learned of the site from Shoshones, and perhaps from one of the greatest Indian prospectors, Tom Fisherman. Unlike Butler, Fisherman earned little in fortune or fame from his skill at prospecting. He died in Tonopah after falling down a mineshaft.[65]

John Shakespeare had probably given Julian and Jane the name of John Best, a Western Shoshone elder and a resident of Tonopah. He was sixty-seven years old and lived with his wife, Susie, and three grown children who were not married. Best's mother came from Lida Valley, his father from the Kawich Mountains, and he knew about the people of both regions. Before moving to Tonopah, he and his wife and children had lived for many years near Lida.[66]

Julian and Jane spent a few hours with Best on the day they arrived in Tonopah, and he clarified some points about Lida Valley that had puzzled Julian. Either John Shakespeare had not understood or known how to answer some of his questions, or Julian had not understood the answers—or perhaps more questions had come to mind after he left. In any case, he wanted to crosscheck and extend what he had learned from his informant at Cow Camp. While open-ended questions often yielded new findings, sometimes they created confusion as well. As he already knew from experience, trying to resolve the confusion was a vital part of ethnographic fieldwork. It could also open fresh lines of inquiry.

The yes/no, or present/absent, format of the trait lists reinforced this lesson every time he labored on a list. He rarely discovered anything new and complex from the work. He largely recorded the presence and absence of specific traits that had already been reported somewhere in print. Open-ended questions, and the answers, told him much more. Asking those questions was the best way for him to learn about unknown or unfamiliar matters and the past. Sometimes it led him to answers for questions he had not even thought to ask. It offered the most promising path to discovery, a major aim of fieldwork.

He planned to continue the work on the following day, but when he and Jane went back the next morning John Best refused to answer any more questions, saying that he had to go to Lida. Despite the informant fee and their interest, he chose not to continue. "Who knows why?" Jane wondered. "This finished our story in Tonopah as far as Indians went," she added. Her overriding impression of their informant—"He seemed scornful of Indians"—may explain why he decided not to tell these visitors anything more about how Western Shoshones had lived in the past. Perhaps it seemed to compare badly to the way he now lived in Tonopah, or perhaps he did not want it recorded for another reason. Many Americans held "uncivilized" ways of life in contempt, especially those based on hunting and gathering.

With time to spare that day, and a county courthouse in town, Julian and Jane decided to get married again. The legal status of their 1933 marriage in Mexico remained uncertain. They put on their city clothes, went to the Nye County Courthouse to get a marriage license, and within a half hour were married again—this time by a judge with oversized mustachios, "a pompous old boy" as Jane described him.

In a celebratory mood, they had a drink in town and then set off on the next leg of the journey, in search of Western Shoshone elders from central Nevada.[67]

5. The People's Land

IN THE WILTING HEAT of late June, Julian and Jane drove to Schurz, Nevada, the trading post and administrative center of the Walker River Reservation. Just before reaching Schurz they skirted Walker Lake, thirty miles long and as blue as the sky.

At Schurz, a hamlet shaded by tall cottonwood trees, they left an arid and open landscape and entered a small oasis created by the waters of the Walker River. They stopped first to see the superintendent of the reservation, which was home to hundreds of people. Most were Northern Paiutes who made a living by raising livestock. Some Western Shoshones lived there as well. The houses that Jane and Julian saw were built of squared-off logs and had low slanting roofs and few windows.[1]

The superintendent was away, but they discovered that C. Hart Merriam was visiting. Merriam, eighty years old and still active, was a physician who had long ago given up the practice of medicine to devote himself to the study of natural history. In the nineteenth century natural history spanned geology and biology and included what became the new field of anthropology. Merriam had joined the ranks of government scientists, for many years directing the Division of Biological Survey.[2]

His early research interests centered on mammalogy and ornithology, and he also ventured into the new science of ecology. On a scientific expedition to the West in 1889, he carried out a biological survey of a mountainous region on the Colorado Plateau, mapping how animals were distributed. The biodiversity that he and his fellow scientists found there led to later publications on the concept of *life zones*. As he explained, temperature and climate changed with increasing elevation: temperature decreased and precipitation increased. The hot and dry lower slopes were home to different plant and animal communities than the windswept peaks and points in between. The succession of plants and animals changed in a patterned way as Merriam's expedition proceeded up and down the mountains. In a report published in 1890 he and a colleague named six life zones, each with a dominant species of plant that served as indicator.[3]

That work, a landmark in ecology, opened the door to further study of life zones. A few years after meeting Merriam, Steward cited some of the latest research by other scientists in *Basin-Plateau*. He included a map of the region's life zones and remarked that each zone "predetermined to a large degree not only population distribution but seasonal movements." In other words, life zones, and the different sources of food found in each of them, explained where native people of the Great Basin had lived and when and why they moved from one place to another.

In the fall, for example, as Steward learned again and again from elders, they had moved up to an elevation between 5,000 and 7,000 feet to harvest pine nuts. This was the Upper Sonoran zone, he wrote (borrowing Merriam's term), defined as the pinyon-juniper belt in the Great Basin. Pinyon and juniper trees served as the indictors. Winter villages, he noted, often stood at the lower reaches of this zone.[4]

By the time he began fieldwork, Steward had come to think that ecology in general, and the concept of life zones in particular, could explain the distribution of not only plants and animals but also people on the land. This idea surfaced sometime in the mid-1930s, before meeting Merriam at the Walker River Reservation. A month earlier he had written to a zoologist he knew at the University of Utah, asking him to recommend a book on animals of the Great Basin. "I should like specifically to get something on the life zones and distribution of the larger animals," he said, explaining that his study was "essentially an ecological one."[5]

Besides some mutual interests, Merriam and Steward had mutual acquaintances, ranging from Kroeber in Berkeley to George and Mamie Gregory in Olancha. After leaving his post with the federal government, Merriam had spent many years carrying out research with California Indians. A few years earlier on a visit to Olancha, he had taken some photographs, including one of Mamie Gregory holding a basket.[6]

Unable to find a cabin to borrow at headquarters or to rent in Schurz, Julian and Jane left the reservation and drove to Yerington, about twenty-five miles away. They spent the night there and the next morning headed for Carson City, the state capital. Julian hoped to find some serviceable maps of northern and central Nevada. He needed detailed maps for his upcoming work with Western Shoshone elders at the Walker River Reservation and elsewhere, who came from that remote region.[7]

Finding nothing of use in Carson City, they drove thirty miles to Reno and looked there, again with no luck. They spent that night and the following day and night in the city. Julian tried to draw his own map of an area in central Nevada not covered by his U.S. Geological Survey maps. They also bought new tires for the car. Driving long distances had worn down the tread; and car tires, then made with canvas casings, did not stand up well to hard wear on rough desert roads.

Reno also offered a few hours of distraction that took their minds off fieldwork and bad roads. They went to see a movie on a Saturday night, and they observed the novelties of nightlife and the fast life around the casinos: "gambling & tarts, etc.," Jane summarized. A chasm, of culture and nature, separated the world they entered in downtown Reno from the one they had left in the high desert: the blinking neon lights and clamor of the city's crowded casino district, the strong steady light and blanketing silence of an open, spacious land.[8]

They returned to the Walker River Reservation to work with a Western Shoshone elder, Jennie Kawich, identified as "daughter-in-law of Old Kawich." Although many of the elders at the reservation were Northern Paiutes, Steward chose not to work with any of them. He did not distinguish sharply between the Owens Valley Paiutes in eastern California and Northern Paiutes in Nevada, despite linguistic differences. He had already published on Paiutes who had once lived in composite bands.[9] Time was short, and Western Shoshones perhaps offered better prospects for discovering patrilineal bands.

By Steward's estimate Jennie Kawich was about sixty or sixty-five years old. She married a man from the Kawich Mountains area, he later explained, but "spent most of her life among white people." "Very amiable and cooperative but information is poor and much was sheer guess," he added. If she was born in 1870 or 1875, as he thought, she was too young to have firsthand memories of the period before American settlement—the era that Steward referred to as "native times," in contrast to postsettlement or "post-Caucasian times." A census taker, however, recorded Jennie Kawich's date of birth as about 1857. If that date was correct, she was in her late seventies when Steward met her. She lived with her daughter and son-in-law and seven young grandchildren.[10]

Steward worked with her for two days, although he greatly preferred men as informants. Men, he believed, could tell him more about hunting and the political organization of bands. They could tell him what they had directly observed as hunters and what they remembered about leaders and about conflicts between groups, which Steward termed *warfare*. In line with his behaviorist thinking, as well as what seemed to be good science, he preferred direct observation as evidence. Women, he assumed, had few observations to report (although they did take part in communal hunts of rabbits and antelope, and some had experience of warfare—as captives if not as combatants).[11]

Like many anthropologists of the time, and Americans in general, Steward associated women with domestic life and men with the world of politics and economy. American women had only gained the same voting rights as men fifteen years earlier, after centuries of exclusion from a direct role in politics. In the labor market they were still excluded from most occupations. Decades would pass before some anthropologists began to question dualistic ideas about women and men, including notions of firmly bounded, gendered sectors: private and public, domestic and political. Those categories often said more about observers and their own social experiences than about the fluid social worlds that some encountered in fieldwork.

Steward decided that day to work with Jennie Kawich because she spoke English; because she willingly, if hesitantly, answered his questions; and, more to the point, because she was the only elder he found at the Walker River Reservation who could tell him about Big Smoky Valley (or Great Smoky Valley) and Monitor Valley in central Nevada. Doubting much of what he learned from her, he later said simply, "Fragments of information suggest that Great Smoky Valley Shoshoni were like other Nevada Shoshoni in all important features." He did not elaborate, and he provided just a sketch of that long valley and the adjacent Monitor Valley. There was no ownership of seed areas, he concluded. As he put it, the people who lived around Hot Springs in Big Smoky Valley "gathered seeds in their own valley" and in the nearby ranges "where they pleased."[12]

Jennie Kawich recalled that a man named Captain Jack directed a fall festival and a rabbit drive in Big Smoky Valley. In Monitor Valley, around the mining town of Belmont, the director was Old Joe. Bill Kawich, who succeeded him as leader, was her late husband. His father, Jennie's father-in-law "Old Kawich," was probably the man

identified in official records as Kai'-wits, a leader from the Kawich
Mountains who lived around Belmont in the 1870s.[13]

Settled in the 1860s after the discovery of silver, Belmont soon had a
population of two thousand, an imposing brick courthouse, a school,
and rival newspapers. Jennie Kawich's contact with white people may
have come from living in Belmont. Many Western Shoshones went
there to find work during the boom times. John Shakespeare lived in
the area as a child but returned to his birthplace in Lida Valley at the
age of fifteen, perhaps during the town's first decline in 1876. When
John Muir passed through with a government surveying party in 1878,
mining had not yet revived, but he gave little notice to the town and
its people. He and his companions had just spent two desperate days
and nights in the desert after running out of water. They nearly died
in the searing August heat.[14]

Belmont's fortunes, and population, rose and fell and rose again.
By 1935 the town had boomed, busted, brightened, dimmed, and finally died.

Still in pursuit of maps and with other errands in mind, Jane and Julian decided to take time off and drive to Berkeley. Their route skirted
Lake Tahoe, which straddled the California-Nevada border and, as
Julian knew, formed part of the ancestral territory of Washoe Indians. Washoes shared some cultural features with their Northern Paiute neighbors, but they were not Numic speakers and they lived in the
well-watered Sierra Nevada region. He excluded them from his study,
perhaps as much for environmental as for linguistic reasons.

The dark green land looked strikingly different from the desert
they had just left. Mountain streams that fed the large freshwater lake,
its water a deep cobalt blue, had long provided Washoes with fish,
a steady source of food. They lost access to the fish and many other
wild foods after the discovery in the late 1850s of high-grade silver

ore near Virginia City, Nevada. The famed Comstock Lode was just twenty-five miles away from the lake.

Within two years twenty thousand miners and entrepreneurs rushed into the area, hoping to make a fortune in mining or to profit in other ways. Commercial fishermen began taking thousands of tons of trout from Lake Tahoe each year, to sell in Virginia City and other settlements. Groves of pinyon trees disappeared as forests were clear-cut to meet the relentless demand for mine timbers and for fuel.

The story of American settlement, and the costs to native people and their land and wildlife, followed a course for Washoes similar to that for Paiutes and Shoshones. The gold and silver mines around Virginia City had largely played out by the 1880s, but the savage search for wealth had reduced Washoes to poverty and despoiled their homeland. Ranchers and other settlers took legal title of the land, and many Washoe men took the only jobs they could find, as ranch hands.[15]

In Berkeley Julian and Jane visited her brother, Grant, a new resident. After studying anthropology with Julian at the University of Utah, Grant had worked briefly in archaeology. Julian found a job for him as a member of a crew in Zion National Park, and when that work ended, Grant moved to Berkeley. He hoped to live near Jane and Julian, find steady employment, and take courses in anthropology. "He looked up to Julian," Jane remembered about her closest brother. But because of Julian's own quest for employment, and fieldwork, they had soon departed, leaving Grant to fend for himself.[16]

On this return trip to Berkeley they saw an array of old friends and colleagues in anthropology. A frantic spell of socializing immersed them in a familiar world, wholly apart from the one they had just left in the desert of western Nevada. Julian had known most of these friends for ten years, and he identified closely with them as fellow professionals. Many shared his Anglo-American and middle-class origins, and they also shared an unusual education, in the new discipline of anthropology.

His relations with them contrasted in every respect with the experience of fieldwork, and his fleeting contact with elders whose experiences and way of life diverged so sharply from his own.[17]

The ongoing search for maps led to San Francisco, where they found nothing useful but did happen to see one of Julian's friends from his student days at Deep Springs. The three quickly decided to make a pack trip together to the High Sierra in just two weeks. The weeklong trip would take them into the mountains during peak wildflower season and away from the desert's heat.

Then Julian and Jane boarded a ferry to cross San Francisco Bay to Marin County. The Golden Gate Bridge was still under construction, and they saw it looming in the distance. In Marin County they stopped to visit Julian's mother and sister. Grace and Marion Steward shared a cottage in Mill Valley, a quiet village at the foot of Mount Tamalpais. Like many Californians, and Julian himself, they were émigrés from the East but had lived in the state for more than fifteen years while Julian pursued his education and career in other places.

Marion, as he and Jane learned, was still unemployed but had good prospects of temporary work on a state relief project. She had endured some harrowing years of marginal employment, and unemployment, while the Depression dragged on. Despite an uneven relationship with her mother, she sometimes lived with Grace and provided her support. Marion's mood fluctuated as circumstances went from bad to worse to better; and now, Jane noted, "Her spirits [are] good & outlook very reasonable."[18]

The next morning Julian and Jane left Mill Valley and drove north through the gentle landscape of Marin County. The golden grasses of summer, punctuated with stands of dark green trees, covered low hills. An hour or two later, after crossing a county line, they reached the Kroebers' country house in the hills above St. Helena in Napa Valley. The old house and a barn stood on forty acres of land, mostly pasture or brush and with views of wooded hills and the valley. They stopped to visit for a few hours, which gave Julian time to discuss his fieldwork with Kroeber. Then they headed back to Nevada, driving toward Carson City and the high desert beyond it. On the second day they reached Fallon, a county seat with two thousand people about forty miles north of the Walker River Reservation.[19]

Steward found some Western Shoshone informants living on the Fallon Reservation, on the outskirts of town. Although most of the people who lived there were Northern Paiutes, Western Shoshones from central Nevada had moved to the reservation in the early years of the twentieth century. In some cases Paiute friends—men from Fallon who worked with them in the mines of central Nevada—had encouraged them to move there.[20]

Steward started work with two men, a father and son. Albert Hicks, the son, was in his midforties, married, and the father of seven young children. He had arrived at the reservation as a young child, spoke English fluently, and could interpret what his father said. Steward thought Pat Hicks was in his sixties, which qualified him by age to serve as a cultural informant. He spent just one day with the two men, asking questions about Little Smoky Valley, their birthplace in central Nevada. Pat Hicks seemed so reluctant to answer questions that Steward finally gave up in the afternoon.[21]

The next day, July 3, Julian and Jane drove back to the Walker River Reservation to see the Fourth of July celebration. They had made plans to attend months earlier, hoping to see some native games and dances. The scheduled events that evening included a movie and a dance. They went to see the movie, passing time until the people attending a boxing match in Yerington returned to the reservation. Then at last the dance began. Jane reported that eight or nine young people began shuffling around a pole in the dark. She and Julian, mystified by the event, could see nothing other than dust rising when car lights occasionally shone on the scene. A man sang, and the meaning of the song also remained obscure to them as outsiders who did not understand his language. They noticed people playing American card games by lamplight in a cabin, but having no interest in nonnative games they gave in to fatigue at 1 a.m. and decided to go to sleep.[22]

Too tired to look for lodging in Yerington, they drove behind the trading post and threw their bedroll on the ground—"& climbed in, clothes and all," Jane added with mild exasperation. When they woke up the next morning, they were surprised to find themselves just fifty feet from unexpected neighbors who had decided to sleep in the same place. They had made camp quietly in the middle of the night.

With no activities planned that morning, Julian and Jane decided to visit Jennie Kawich. As they sat outside in still air and under open sky, a cloud of gnats and mosquitoes descended on them. This feature of outdoor life, like the sun's glare and the rising heat, tried the patience of Jennie Kawich's visitors that day. They had "the house habit," to borrow a phrase from John Muir, and were used to spending much of the day as well as night indoors. Jane looked forward to the shelter of an auto cabin when they returned to Fallon.[23]

She and Julian may have gone to see Jennie Kawich that morning to collect a few stories. He later included three that she told him in *Some Western Shoshoni Myths*, although he described them as "poorly remembered and very synoptic." The account she gave of her people's origin was much shorter than Bill Doc's and it included Wolf, Coyote's older brother. As usual, Wolf acted in a responsible and serious way, unlike the curious and impetuous Coyote. The contrast in the stories was never between good and evil but instead between wisdom and foolishness, foresight and improvidence, attentiveness and carelessness.[24]

The Origin of People

Wolf had a big water jug. He said to his brother Coyote, "Coyote, don't touch or open this jug. Be careful!" Then Wolf went away.

Coyote said, "What is the matter with my brother? What is in that jug? Why did he tell me not to open it? I am going to open it." Coyote pulled out the stopper.

Many people came out and flew away. He replaced the stopper while a few remained. The good ones had come out and had flown away like flies.

Wolf told Coyote they were going to move. He told Coyote to carry the big jug. They went to Smoky Valley. Wolf did not know that Coyote had opened the jug. He thought all the people were still in. When they came to Smoky Valley, Wolf said, "Open that jug!" Just a few Indians came out. They are the Shoshoni.

Wolf and Coyote also figured in a tale of death that Jennie Kawich told. Short and to the point, it left some listeners wincing.

The Origin of Death
Wolf said, "When people die they must die twice." Coyote said, "That isn't right. I don't want people to die twice. They must die once and be buried."

Wolf bewitched Coyote's boy and wished that he would die. Coyote knew that he had done this. The boy died. Coyote went to Wolf crying. He said, "Oh brother, you said when people died they should get up and die again. When will my boy get up?" Wolf said, "Don't you remember saying they should die only once?"[25]

Later that day Jane and Julian witnessed a Fourth of July celebration that seemed a world apart from Coyote and Wolf, and a familiar part of their own world. The afternoon events included a barbecue and parade, two all-American events that happened to have origins outside of North America. Eight men on horseback, including one who carried an American flag, led the parade. A car followed the mounted riders, pulling a trailer of local dignitaries who sat under a big orange and black umbrella. Other cars followed the first one, every operable car on the reservation according to Jane. She was bemused to see some cars break rank as drivers stopped to get ice-cream cones, a staple of Fourth of July celebrations.[26]

The afternoon races reminded her of those she had often seen in Salt Lake City: "three-legged, sack, children, etc.," she recorded. Blind boxing, with the opponents wearing blindfolds, also entertained the crowd. And then at last came the hand game, a native game of chance that Jane had never seen. This one pitted a team of men against a team of women. Players on one team concealed a plain bone and a marked bone in their hands; the opponents had to guess the position of the plain bone. The game lasted only fifteen minutes and the men won.[27]

Races and games occupied just a fraction of the time that day, violating Jane's notion of good scheduling, and the tedium of waiting wore her down. From her cultural perspective, most of the afternoon was wasted as she and Julian waited, with mounting impatience, for each event. She noticed the Indians "waiting very amiably, gossiping & just sitting for the most part"—but they likely experienced this differently, not as "waiting."[28]

"Waiting" was part of the world of work schedules, clocks, and appointments made to the minute, a world where "time is money," time is "short," and time can be "wasted." That was the world Jane and Julian came from, where the clock did dominate daily life and a sense of time scarcity dominated consciousness. To be in a place where time was not tightly scheduled or treated as scarce produced a slight impatience, even mild anxiety.

Jane and Julian returned to Fallon after the last event of the Fourth of July celebration. Whatever he had learned did not find its way directly into print, although it may have reinforced Julian's belief that only remnants of the old times remained in 1935: the hand game, the songs and dances, the stories, the languages. As it happened, those held little interest for him because of his behaviorist leanings. He focused

on what could be observed, on the external world of objects and behavior. He did not study the symbolic and expressive—the songs and
stories and languages, which had survived—in any depth.[29]

Like many Americans of the time, he saw assimilation underway:
in this instance, in the form of the Fourth of July parade and most of
the games. As an anthropologist he also saw what he termed *deculturation*, the loss of many of the old ways. He seemed to regard both
types of changes as inevitable.[30]

Julian planned to work next with a Western Shoshone man named
George J. Johnnie and two elders, his mother and stepfather. They
could tell him about a large region that encompassed three valleys in
central Nevada: the Reese River, Ione, and Smith Creek valleys. Having
no detailed maps would complicate the task of identifying sites from
a distance of hundreds of miles. The U.S. Geological Survey map of
the Tonopah quadrangle, the best map he had found, covered only
the southern portions of the Reese River and Ione valleys.[31]

George Johnnie, who agreed to serve as interpreter, was thirty-
nine years old. He lived with his wife, Inez, and young son at the
Fallon Reservation. But when Julian contacted him the next morning, George told him that "the old people" wanted to trap ground
squirrels that day. Hunting, as well as gathering, still provided some
food for families.

The regulation of hunting by the state, which limited what and
when and where they could hunt, had resulted from the sharp decline
in wildlife after American settlement. Nevada law required a license to
hunt. It also strictly defined the seasons for most game animals, if not
for ground squirrels. This scheduling, as well as the other restrictions
and the fees, conflicted with customary hunting practices of Shoshones, and with need. They could not always afford the fee for a license,
and they often needed wild game for food, not just in season.[32]

Reluctant to waste time—as his own cultural experience led him to

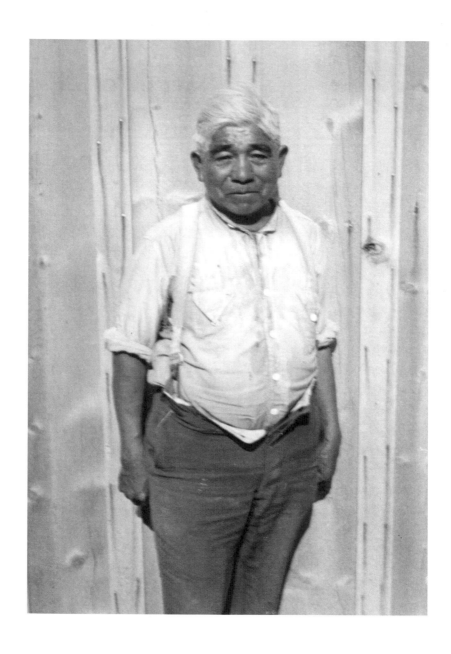

11. Tom Horn, July 1935. (Photo by Julian H. Steward, courtesy of University of Illinois Archives.)

construe such delays—Julian found another elder, a very friendly man named Tom Horn. White-haired and slightly stout, he was dressed that day in a long-sleeved cotton work shirt and a pair of suspenders that held his pants aloft. He greeted the two strangers and agreed at once to work with Julian. "He was an amusing old codger," Jane wrote, "full of curiosity about what the whites called things & how they did things." The interviewing turned reciprocal as he answered Julian's questions and then posed some of his own. This incongruity, as they saw it, of the questioner being questioned, struck Jane and Julian as funny.

To Jane, at the age of twenty-six, Tom Horn was an old man. According to a census he was sixty-one. Julian judged him to be at least sixty and no more than sixty-five years old, born around 1870 at the earliest, when mining in central Nevada was already booming. He spoke "passable English," Julian said. Better yet, he proved to be "intelligent, conscientious, and exceptionally amiable," valued qualities in a cultural informant. A widower, he lived with two unmarried daughters. The older daughter died that year at the age of twenty-nine.[33]

Tom Horn told them what he remembered about Smith Creek Valley, probably during the 1880s. He said that the Reese River, Ione, and Smith Creek valleys—and territory as far north as the Humboldt River—were united under a leader named Tu-tu-wa. Steward later concluded that the crisis of American settlement had led to that political unity. In earlier times, he suggested, the three valleys had probably formed separate, although not completely independent, districts, like other valleys in the region. Most of the people in Ione Valley were Shoshone, but some Paiutes lived there and had intermarried, and Smith Creek Valley was largely Paiute.[34]

Unlike areas farther south, these three valleys had a greater proportion of roots and berries to seeds, with the exception of pine nuts. Those were abundant and formed a staple of the diet. People did not have to go far to find food, allowing a more sedentary way of life.

Tom Horn and his other informants for the region also told Steward about a practice he had not encountered previously. People in the three valleys had sown wild seeds, a practice that extended throughout north-central Nevada.

They recalled burning the brush in certain areas of the hills near their winter villages and broadcasting several species of wild seeds. Both the men and women of a village took part in planting. By Steward's definition of property ownership, they owned the plots of sowed wild seeds because they held exclusive rights to harvest the seeds, and they defended those rights. In Smith Creek Valley, Tom Horn said, any trespasser was shot.

"Ownership of sowed plots," Steward later summarized, "accords with the Shoshoni principle that there are property rights only in things on which work has been done." (This principle applied generally to objects of manufacture, giving the maker the rights to use or share or dispose of the object.) As stated by Steward, it implied that people held no property rights to land where they habitually hunted and gathered. And if they did not own a territory, by his definition, they did not constitute a patrilineal band. He decided, in any case, perhaps based on what he learned about the size of the planted plots, that the sowed wild seeds had probably not supplied a major portion of food.[35]

In the Reese River and Ione valleys, as Steward would learn from the Johnnie family, villages also claimed specific tracts of pinyon trees. These ranged from a hundred to two hundred acres in size and were bounded by known natural landmarks. The tracts' defined boundaries, and the claims to use, suggested to him that the people of the Reese River and Ione valleys owned them. The people of Smith Creek Valley did not make such claims, and by his definition did not own the pinyon groves where they usually harvested pine nuts.

Rabbit drives, held around the time of pine nut collecting and during festivals, lasted for five days. People from Ione Valley sometimes went to the Reese River or Smith Creek valleys for drives. A man named Wagon Jack directed those communal hunts in Smith Creek Valley. Tom Horn recalled that Wagon Jack also had skill as a rainmaker. "He told us about Wagon Jack asking the 'Old Man,' i.e., God, for rain," Jane reported. "'Why,' says Tom, 'he talks to Him like on a telephone & He sends down rain.'" The rainmaker had recently said that, for a reward, he could end an ongoing drought in Nevada.[36]

Horn also told them a Coyote story and another memorable story about a man with Coyote-like wits. Eagle feathers, as he and other elders explained, were prized for arrows and for use in ritual. A man once climbed up some dangerous cliffs to a nest, Horn said, and then spent weeks stranded there. He survived by eating some of the rabbits that the eagles brought to the nest to feed their young. As time passed he grew very thin. Finally, when the young eagles were nearly grown, he grabbed two of them by their legs. They carried him slowly to the ground where he made a soft landing.[37]

That ended Steward's work with Tom Horn, and Julian spent the next days with George Johnnie and his stepfather, Joe Frank ("born ca. 1870 or 1875 in Ione Valley"). Besides completing a trait list, he also recorded a long list of named sites, both camps and villages. They worked indoors, where "Old Frank," according to Jane, seemed to be dozing most of the time—"but he answers all right," she added. He proved a good informant: "Information fairly extensive and reliable" was the verdict.

One day he stretched out on the floor, lying so far under a table that they could hardly see or hear him. "Today he is lying on the work bench, an old auto seat under his head, propped up, partially, by a tool box," Jane wrote. This struck her as an odd posture for working, as she and Julian defined their activity. Joe Frank may have had a different definition of what he was doing for the stranger who carried papers and wrote on them, and who spoke English at great length with his stepson.[38]

Steward also worked with George's mother, Maggie Johnnie, whom he found "fairly cooperative and well informed." Like Joe Frank, she came from Ione Valley. Although Steward thought that both she and Joe Frank were sixty or sixty-five, census takers recorded her date of birth as 1880. If the date was correct, she was just fifty-five, and more knowledgeable than Steward would have expected for a woman of that age.[39]

With her son George interpreting, Maggie Johnnie served as an informant for the trait lists for the Reese River and Ione valleys, and she also answered other questions. She told him that her people harvested pine nuts on the western slope of the Shoshone Mountains and in the Paradise Mountains. Although Steward concluded that they owned the pinyon tracts, he learned that they did not use weapons to defend their claims. Instead, trespassers were attacked only with words—and in one memorable case with rain. Tu-tu-wa's brother, "a weather shaman," had driven trespassers from his land by producing a rainstorm with hail.[40]

Steward later judged these claims of exclusive rights to use natural resources so unusual for Western Shoshones that he tried to account for them. "Ownership of seed territory is contrary to Shoshoni custom," he asserted in *Basin-Plateau*. Although he usually avoided diffusion as an explanation, he suggested that such a practice might have come from their Paiute neighbors. Or perhaps ecology explained it. He favored that view and thought it made sense of claims by Owens Valley Paiutes to specific tracts of land. In the three Nevada valleys, he reasoned, ownership "may have developed from the fact that the population here was denser, more stable, and able to get all essential foods within a small radius of the village, so that habitual use led to ownership."[41] In any case, survival in these three valleys—as in the Owens Valley—did not depend on holding food resources and land in common, unlike many other places where Western Shoshones lived.

On a hot day in mid-July Julian and Jane left Fallon and drove a hundred miles due east to Austin. They took the Lincoln Highway across central Nevada. Famous as the first coast-to-coast highway for automobiles and a popular route for tourists, the highway ran for more than three thousand miles directly between New York City and San Francisco. By the 1930s long stretches were paved, but not in remote parts of the West. In much of Nevada motorists traveled on a narrow roadway with a graveled surface. Still, it looked like a smooth broad boulevard compared to the dusty rutted tracks that here and there met the Lincoln Highway. The tracks dwindled and then disappeared in the distance, on the way to somewhere else.[42]

Their route took them through basin and range: across a broad valley, up to a low pass in a mountain range, down into another valley, up to a pass, and down, along a roller-coaster ribbon of road. Nevada could claim hundreds of mountain ranges, exceeding any other place of its size in the Americas. The narrow highway pointed straight ahead to a horizon where sky always met mountain. As Julian and Jane drove down into each valley, they saw wide sweeps of open country to north and south and a blue sky filled with billowing clouds.

The road passed by the Reese River Valley, just twelve miles wide but more than a hundred miles long. The Reese River, fed by water from the bordering Toiyabe and Shoshone mountains, flowed north toward the Humboldt River. In the 1930s the running water no longer reached its destination, dying instead in a sandy flat. Deforestation, decreased rainfall, and intensive use of the water for irrigation had so reduced the flow that a dry channel reached for miles north toward the Humboldt River.[43]

A few hours and many mountain ranges after leaving Fallon, they reached Austin, a boomtown of the 1860s. As county seat, it had managed to hold on to a population of five hundred long after mining, and fortune, if not fame, had declined. Among the relics of a cosmopolitan past, the International Hotel still welcomed visitors. Three old churches and the courthouse from its early days also stood among the houses on the town's few streets. Austin struck Jane as "the most picturesque of its kind as it straggles down the canyon." It sat in the hollow of Toyaibe Canyon, where the high walls dotted with prospect holes gave vivid evidence of its mining past.[44]

They stopped briefly on the outskirts of Austin, at a reservation for about one hundred and fifty Western Shoshones. Wagon Jack, who was in his nineties by the 1930s, lived there for years with his grandson and other relatives. Like Tom Horn, he came from Smith Creek Valley; later in life he worked at a ranch west of Austin. Steward must have inquired after him at the reservation. In *Basin-Plateau* he cited Jack just once as an informant.[45]

From Austin Julian and Jane turned south and drove through Big Smoky Valley along a rutted dirt road, "Nevada's worst," Jane summarized. They were headed toward Round Mountain, where they hoped to find an elder who could tell them about the past in that valley. After driving just ten miles Julian stopped near a large grove of pinyon trees, the site of some old camps. He picked up arrow points and blades of flint and later made sketches of them, illustrations for the trait lists.[46]

Despite the slow speed of the car, a defense against potholes, the tires kicked up towering clouds of dust. After sixty jarring miles they reached Round Mountain where, Jane said, "we found Rutabaga Bob and every other Indian working." Many of the men who worked at the Round Mountain Mining Company were Indians. Census takers listed Rutabaga Bob, who was seventy years old in 1935, as *miner, at placer camp, currently working.*

The name came from his father who long ago had taken produce from his garden to sell in Belmont, perhaps during the town's first boom. Although he had lived his early life mainly as a hunter, after miners and other settlers arrived he turned to gardening as well. Like other Western Shoshones, he worked hard to adapt to the loss of food lands and to the new market economy. Whites called him Rutabaga.

The son became Rutabaga Bob—or Rutabegger Bobb as a census taker recorded the name in 1930. At that time he lived at Round Mountain with his wife, Lucy; his elderly mother; and three children. His two younger children were still attending school. Earlier, in the 1920s, he had lived on the Walker River Reservation, and Steward probably first heard of him there from Jennie Kawich.[47]

Steady work at the mine paid him more than he could earn in a day or two as Steward's informant. Since no other man was available, the trail ended there for Julian and Jane. They gave up the search for a cultural informant for Big Smoky Valley, an elder who might add to what Jennie Kawich recalled. Little Smoky Valley remained just as hazy. Pat Hicks had revealed very little of what he remembered about the valley's past and how his people lived there.

Despite sixty wasted miles of hard travel, they shifted course without regret and happily headed toward Deep Springs, one hundred and fifty miles away. They had an appointment to keep with friends: a hiking trip in the High Sierra and a complete break from fieldwork and from high summer in the desert.

Their sojourn in the Sierra Nevada lasted nearly a week and took them into the high country of sky-blue lakes and lush meadows filled with blooming wildflowers. One day it rained, and the rain turned to hail, a novelty after three dry months in the desert. In the mountains they saw water, or its transforming effects, wherever they looked. Instead of carrying water as they did in the desert, they took it from the lakes and streams.

Pack burros bore the heavy burden of the camping gear and supplies. Still, the strenuous hiking challenged Jane and perhaps the others as well. The high altitude—above eleven thousand feet at one pass—and a habit of smoking cigarettes left her panting as she climbed. Years later Jane recalled her status as a novice hiker and the sense that she was being tested. She thought she passed the test, but she did not care to repeat it and never did.

When they descended from the High Sierra, they camped at a site that showed signs of escalating tourism and careless visitors. "This place, while lovely, is much more accessible," Jane recorded in the journal, "& tin cans and campers' debris all over [the] place."[48]

In late July Jane and Julian left the summer-green mountains of the Sierra Nevada in California and returned to the open and arid lands of central Nevada. They headed east toward Railroad Valley, where they hoped to find Western Shoshone elders who could tell them more about the remote country of central and eastern Nevada. At Tonopah they turned onto a road that ran toward Ely, Nevada. Few people traveled on that lonely road, which crossed miles of unfenced open range.

Their route took them past many of the valleys—Big Smoky, Monitor, Little Smoky, and others—that Steward had learned about from Western Shoshone elders at reservations in western Nevada. Many of the elders at the Walker River Reservation and Fallon Reservation lived hundreds of miles away from the valleys that they regarded as home. Those places, which they knew deeply, formed part of Newe Sogobia, the People's Land: the homeland of Newe, as Western Shoshones called themselves. The same country looked barren and bone dry that day to two travelers who did not call it home and who had just left the alpine lakes and meadows of the High Sierra. Billowing clouds swept across the desert sky, carrying a cargo of rain to faraway places.[49]

When they arrived at Duckwater, a place they knew only as a name on the map, they saw little more than a ranch house. It stood near a dirt road that ran through Railroad Valley, stretching more than eighty miles from north to south. The ranch was one of a dozen or more owned by settlers and supported by the waters of Duckwater

Creek. Western Shoshones had lived around the site, which they called by a name meaning Red Top Grass, for generations. Some still lived nearby. Others had gone to distant reservations but would return after 1940, when the federal government bought ranchland to set up a reservation at Duckwater.[50]

Despite the car's new tires, purchased in Reno just a month earlier, the wear and tear from rough roads resulted that day in a flat tire. It took time for Julian to change it, but they still reached Duckwater before dark and managed to locate an informant. "After scouring 10 miles of creek," Jane recorded, "we found Barney Hicks." They discovered that he was the younger brother of Pat Hicks, their recent and reluctant informant in Fallon. Julian made plans to work on a trait list with him the next day.[51]

That evening they camped under cottonwood trees by the creek. The nearest auto cabin was hours away, in Ely. After days of strenuous hiking in the High Sierra, Jane welcomed this quiet pause on level ground, even if camping held little appeal. Their simple dinner consisted of the usual fare. Most of the food came out of cans, a steady diet of corned beef or sardines or tuna and canned vegetables that they warmed over a campfire. Years later Jane recalled that bread dried out in just a day, and that potatoes and carrots survived the desert heat for only two or three days before spoiling. Coffee, brewed over the fire cowboy-style, always tasted strong and reviving.[52]

As the sun sank in the west, light played across the mountains that enclosed the valley on the east. Shadows crept up the mountain slope, pushing against an ebbing band of bright sunlight. After a long and wearing day, night fell.

Jane and Julian spent the next day with Barney Hicks. He was about sixty years old, and his weathered face, more than his lean frame, showed his age. He wore a light canvas hat with a narrow brim; his shirt and

12. Barney Hicks, July 1935. (Photo by Julian H. Steward, courtesy of University of Illinois Archives)

pants were made of sturdy thick cotton that stood up to hard wear. Julian learned far more about Little Smoky Valley from him than he had from his older brother Pat in Fallon. Little Smoky Valley lay west of Duckwater, across the aptly named Pancake Range, which in places seemed more mesa than mountain. The brothers had grown up near

Morey, an old station on the stagecoach route that ran through the valley from Eureka in the north to Warm Springs in the south.[53]

Eureka's name told its history. Dozens of mines yielded lead, silver, and gold in the 1870s, producing enormous wealth for the owners and investors. The smelters produced something else: clouds of toxic black smoke that killed desert plants and was harmful for people to breathe. Pinyon trees, cut down by the tens of thousands, provided the charcoal that fed the smelters. The industrial appetite for pinyon trees, known locally as "Reese River lumber," continued until the mines played out in the 1880s. By the late 1870s, it was said, pinyon forests no longer stood within as much as a fifty-mile radius of Eureka—or Austin, seventy miles to the west.[54]

The few mines near Morey, in contrast, never amounted to much, although mining went on for years. By the early 1870s the population had grown large enough to merit a post office, but it closed soon after the turn of the century. In 1935 Morey was just a memory, another ghost town in a landscape of lost dreams.[55]

Barney Hicks, born in the mid-1870s by Steward's estimate, lived far from the boomtowns of Austin and Eureka and grew up on the margins of mining in Nevada. Steward found him "well informed and extremely conscientious." Unlike his older brother, he spoke English with fair fluency, understood Steward's questions, and gave careful answers. Hicks had lived at the Fallon Reservation for years before moving back to the region where he grew up and where his ancestors had lived. He drew on memories of Little Smoky Valley around 1880.[56]

He recalled nine villages and camps, as well as details about the people who lived in them. His paternal grandfather's camp was located about four miles from Morey. His grandfather lived there with three wives and ten children. Barney's father, one of the ten children, was the child of a wife who came from the Kawich Mountains to the south.[57]

The grandfather was a talker, the leader who directed festivals in

Little Smoky Valley. His grandsons, Barney and Pat Hicks, remembered him well as a man of influence who spoke persuasively and acted decisively. Steward later wrote that Pat Hicks "boasted that his grandfather traveled widely, seducing men's wives and, if necessary, killing the men." Barney Hicks explained that when a woman's family objected to her marrying a certain man, the man and his friends might try to abduct her, sometimes resorting to violence. Perhaps he spoke with his grandfather in mind.[58]

Other men also told Steward stories that he termed *marriage by abduction*. That common term—for what in some parts of the world qualified as captivity (or enslavement) of women—later disappeared from the vocabulary of anthropology. Whether the cases that Steward recorded always involved unwilling women is not clear. He used the word "philandering," not only "courting," to sum up what elders told him about the conduct of some men and women at festivals.[59] This might raise a question about whether women, married or not, were sometimes "abducted" willingly and with advance notice. As he would later learn, an unwilling woman, unimpressed by her captor, could walk back home. She voted with her feet as it were.[60]

The people who lived in Little Smoky Valley had contact with those in other valleys of the region, attending their festivals and communal hunts of rabbits and pronghorn antelope. They sometimes met people from Railroad Valley in the Pancake Range while collecting pine nuts, although those mountains were so arid and low that few pinyon trees grew there. Little Smoky Valley supplied them with most of the other seeds that they gathered. In years of good harvest they sometimes sowed surplus wild seeds in plots near their villages—like the people in several valleys to the west, as Steward had already heard.[61]

After working with Barney Hicks for a day and camping for two nights by Duckwater Creek, Jane and Julian packed their camping gear and left. They drove sixty miles northeast to the town of Ely in Steptoe

Valley, not far from the Nevada-Utah border. They went in search of Western Shoshone elders from Railroad Valley and other places in eastern Nevada. The road took them across rolling terrain where mountain ranges formed the horizon in every direction. Cloud shadows moved across the open land, and now and then across the road. For a few moments the punishing heat eased and the strong light dimmed—and then they drove out of the shadow and back into the sun.

Ely, a county seat with a population of three thousand, offered a range of services, from hotels and stores to restaurants and casinos. They passed the six-story Hotel Nevada, which towered over other buildings in town. It was a new addition to Ely, where copper mining remained strong. Their strict budget did not permit a room in a hotel—certainly not the Hotel Nevada—and rarely allowed a meal in a restaurant. It barely covered the many expenses of field research.[62]

Jane always remembered the amount of funding from the research grants: "Only eighteen hundred dollars!" she exclaimed. It seemed a small sum of money for six months of fieldwork, especially more than fifty years later, but during the Depression years many people lived on far less. Still, the expenses added up. Besides the cost of food and lodging, they had high transportation costs. The gasoline for their long journeys was expensive, as were the new tires and other replacement parts for the car. They also spent hundreds of dollars on informant fees. Now and then, they splurged on a steak dinner in town; but in Nevada's ranch country, she explained, steak sold for a bargain price.[63]

In Ely they rented a cabin at an auto camp, put on their city clothes, and did their routine town chores. These ranged from washing their other clothing and sorting out the camping gear to stocking up on food and catching up on the national news. Then they drove to the Ely Colony, a small enclave on the outskirts of town, to look for informants.[64]

The town of Ely, located along Duck Creek in the broad and arid

Steptoe Valley, got its start as a mining camp in the 1860s and later prospered from copper mining and ranching in the region. Western Shoshones had long lived at that site on Duck Creek and elsewhere in the valley. The ecological effects of mining, as well as ranching, put an end to the foraging economy almost at once. Wildlife declined. Settlers cut down pinyons and other trees for fuel and mine timbers, and the supply of pine nuts dwindled. Grazing sheep and cattle destroyed stands of wild seed plants, especially sand bunch grass. Wild game dwindled, from overhunting by the flood of settlers and from habitat loss.

Ranches quickly occupied much of the land in Steptoe Valley. American ranchers were drawn there by the natural meadows of wild grass, soon overgrazed; by the tracts of lands that the federal government opened for settlement; and, as elsewhere, by the nearby market for beef in booming mining camps.[65]

So many miners and workers from so many places found their way to Ely that Western Shoshones at once became an ethnic minority. In the 1930s the town still had a diverse population. White residents formed a majority, but small numbers of African Americans, Japanese, Chinese, and Mexicans also lived in Ely—along with fewer than one hundred and fifty Western Shoshones.[66]

Elders at the Ely Colony had survived despite the complete transformation of their former world and of their way of life. They had lived and moved freely before American settlement. They had rarely known hunger. Now they occupied a small piece of land on the margins of a town and a place at the bottom of the class hierarchy. Towns and social classes and poverty had not existed in the past. Newcomers, who had brought about so many changes, also claimed exclusive rights to their homeland, amounting to far more than ten thousand square miles. Railroad Valley alone encompassed more than two thousand square miles.

"The Ely group," as Jane called these cultural informants, consisted of three men and three women who grew up in Steptoe Valley and elsewhere in the vast region that became eastern Nevada. In time they had all gone to live in Ely, no doubt with a deep sense of loss. The Ely Colony, which stood on just ten acres of land, had been established four years earlier, in 1931, by the federal government. At that time the elders and their families were already living in small houses at the site.[67]

Two of the elders had memories that reached back to the years before American conquest and settlement. The oldest among the six was Jennie Washburn, born about 1845. At the age of ninety she still looked sturdy and stood straight. Frank Stick, born after 1850, was in his early eighties. Census takers listed him with two names, Frank Stick and Horse Stick, classifying the second as *male Indian name*. He was Jennie Washburn's husband. They lived with her nephew, Harry Johnny, who was in his sixties and a widower, and his son who was about twenty-one years old.[68]

The other informants included a married couple whose names Jane and Julian mistakenly recorded as John and Annie Roddy; the surname was Riley. John Riley was in his midsixties, and his wife was younger. They lived with their sixteen-year-old son. A woman identified, also mistakenly, as Maggie Cotton was most likely Aggie Stanton. Stanton, in her midsixties, lived with her sister-in-law, Mary; Mary's son Albert; and three grandchildren. In recent years the family had lost two of its men: first Harry, Mary's husband and Aggie's brother; and then one of Mary's sons. The son had died just a year earlier, at the age of about forty. Harry Stanton had been a leader on land rights issues, and a surviving son, Albert, assumed that role in the 1930s.[69]

Harry Johnny, who acted as the group's leader, insisted on interpreting for the others, even those who also spoke English as a second language. "The strange thing is that we must use Harry as interpreter," Jane said, "when, in most cases, he speaks less understandably than the [other] informants." The whole group, she and Julian soon decided, had a "grievance against whites." A few acres in Ely did not compensate for the loss of thousands of square miles of homeland.

As Jane and Julian learned, Harry Johnny knew how to read English, and he owned books about the treaties that the federal government had made with Western Shoshones and then broken. (They thought that he could not write, but he reportedly wrote letters to a friend on another reservation.) As he told his two visitors that day, he believed his people would one day receive money to compensate for the lands taken from them.[70]

He may have thought that talking to these visitors could advance the fight for justice since the man planned to write about Shoshones. There might be advantage in explaining carefully where their ancestors had lived in a sprawling territory of mountains and valleys. Ranchers claimed part of it as private property. The federal government held and managed as public land most of what remained.

Johnny and the other elders, Jane reported, had recently voted against the Wheeler-Howard Act, also known as the Indian Reorganization Act. She referred to legislation passed a year earlier, and originally proposed by John Collier. Collier, a nationally known reformer, became commissioner of Indian Affairs under Pres. Franklin D. Roosevelt. As commissioner he tried to turn federal Indian policy in a new direction, promoting cultural pluralism rather than assimilation.

Collier believed that Indian cultural survival depended on retaining shared lands, reservations. He endorsed consolidating Indian land holdings and promoting Indian self-government by creating tribal governments and courts. The legislation he proposed was meant to end the ongoing breakup and loss of their lands. Under the allotment system, the Dawes Act of 1887, reservation land once held in common continued to be privatized. Individuals received small allotments as private property, which could be sold, and often were in times of need, leaving them landless.[71]

The act that passed was not the bill that Collier supported. The original plan called for repeal of the Dawes Act and return of the so-called surplus lands. Those lands had been taken from Indians, with the claim that they did not "use" or "need" or "own" them—hence the word "surplus." The federal government opened those lands for settlement.

The plan of returning them met strong opposition. Too much land had been allotted, opponents said, and too many settlers now lived on the surplus lands. Businesses with leasing rights on reservations also fought the provisions to consolidate lands, and conservatives who believed in assimilation attacked any measures that promoted cultural pluralism. The important provisions about land were finally eliminated from the bill as too controversial or unworkable.

The congressional act that finally passed created Indian tribal governments with both rights and duties in relation to the U.S. federal government. It gave tribes one year to hold referenda and decide whether to adopt constitutions and set up tribal councils. It did nothing to reform land policies and practices.[72]

When elections took place in 1935 more than two-thirds of the tribes accepted the provisions of the act. Just a month earlier Harry Johnny and his group, still intent on receiving land or compensation, had voted against it.[73]

Over the next ten days Steward spent long hours asking questions about how people had once lived in the valleys of the region. Jennie Washburn came from Railroad Valley. Aggie Stanton, born at Duck-water and nearly thirty years younger than Washburn, had memories of the valley only after mining and ranching began. Harry Johnny, whose birthplace was near Washburn's, was even younger than Stanton, but his grandmother had lived in the valley before settlement.[74] What they told Steward added to the few details that Barney Hicks had already given him. Their memories yielded a composite portrait of a place before and soon after American settlement.

Jennie Washburn had much to tell about her old home, but she seemed ill at ease in the role of cultural informant, perhaps because the experience was new and completely alien. She appeared to be embarrassed rather than unwilling to answer questions about where she had once lived. By means of patient and persistent inquiry, Steward learned that her home was on the west side of a tall mountain that became known as Mount Hamilton. The place where she spent winters with her parents and seven brothers and sisters had a name that meant Water Dries Up in Summer. Her family often stayed there for months at a time along with her father's brother and his family. The two brothers came from that place, and her mother came from the Kawich Mountains. In the late 1860s the area near their home became the site of a mining town named Hamilton.

Jennie Washburn was already in her twenties when Hamilton boomed. Previously, if pine nuts were very plentiful in the fall and her family had large caches, they remained in the mountains near their food supply and melted snow for water. No doubt their pine nut collecting ended soon after Hamilton came to life as a mining camp. In a matter of months, ten thousand people arrived to mine and smelt ore for silver, with the usual effects on the pinyon groves and wild game.[75]

She remembered that before American settlement, her people went to the hills for seeds in spring. They walked at night when days were too hot, carrying water in the basketry jugs that women made. Sometimes they went as far as Duckwater, sixty-five miles from their winter village, to attend a festival held there in May. In the fall men burned brush, and in the spring they sowed wild seeds. She recalled that people from other places might be given permission to gather on the sowed plots, and they might be given seeds if they were in need. Her family went to Duckwater in the fall for another festival, and then left to gather pine nuts.

Because the creek made Duckwater a place more fertile than most in the valley, people sometimes traveled on foot from distant places to gather seeds there in June. People who lived at Duckwater rarely needed to travel far except to collect pine nuts and to take part in rabbit drives in the fall. They attended the drives at a place near Blue Eagle Springs, about fifteen miles away. An old man whose name meant Big Talk directed them, and dozens of men took part. In the spring, communal hunts for pronghorn antelope were held in a low pass at the northern end of Railroad Valley.

After the introduction of horses, people from more distant places began to attend festivals at Duckwater. Even Kawich—Jennie Kawich's father-in-law, who was leader of Western Shoshones in the Kawich Mountains—sometimes attended those gatherings and talked. The Duckwater festivals, as Steward learned, had continued well into the twentieth century, after ceasing elsewhere.[76]

On one of the days that they spent with Jennie Washburn and the other elders, Jane and Julian went with them to gather seeds of a wild grass called *wai*. They drove away from town, following directions to a place where stands of the grass still grew. *Wai* seeds had long provided a staple food for Shoshones and Paiutes throughout the Great Basin—until livestock brought in by American settlers fed on *wai* and other wild grasses harvested for seeds. The elders said that sheep had destroyed *wai* in the mountains south of Ely, where it once thrived.[77]

Against the odds some small stands survived in Steptoe Valley or, more likely, an adjacent valley. Years later Jane still recalled the exhausting work and heat on the day in late July when they collected seeds. Most of the elders wore hats with wide brims to protect against the stabbing sun. Jennie Washburn wore a scarf pulled low over her

13. Jennie Washburn, July 1935. (Photo by Julian H. Steward, courtesy of University of Illinois Archives)

forehead and a long-sleeved dress of printed cotton that reached her ankles.

Julian took several photographs of Washburn at the task of winnowing the seeds. In the background, others sat on the ground threshing the grasses; the car stood at a distance, and far beyond it, a low spine of mountains. That day he and Jane saw the old ways in practice, as participant observers who helped gather wild grasses. The Ely elders showed unexpected endurance, pushing on in the rising heat, working intently for long hours in the open.[78]

On another day Annie Riley and Harry Johnny answered questions about Steptoe Valley and its people in the past. Annie Riley, who was in her late forties, had tousled black hair that she wore short and parted in the middle. Strands brushed against her dark eyes and high cheekbones. Because she was so young, she drew mostly on memories of what her grandfather had told her about the past. He was probably born around the same time as Jennie Washburn, in the 1830s or 1840s. Steward treated him as another posthumous informant. A ghostly figure, like Tom Stone's grandfather Panatubiji, he too spoke through a grandchild. Annie Riley's memories of his memories yielded a partial list of villages in the valley around the time of contact, with few details about the people who lived in them.

There were six remembered villages, the largest at Ely. The people of Steptoe Valley—unlike those living in some of the valleys to the west—did not sow wild seeds. Besides the seeds and pine nuts they gathered, they ate rabbits, deer, and pronghorn antelope taken in communal hunts. Annie Riley's grandfather also told her—as she told Steward—that just before contact a few families began to grow corn, a type of blue pumpkin, and large white beans. The plants came from the south, he said. This led Steward to conclude that these domesticated plants had diffused from Southern Paiutes. The garden plots at Ely, as Harry Johnny remembered, were irrigated.[79]

"English fair; knowledge limited," Steward later remarked about

14. Annie Riley, July 1935. (Photo by Julian H. Steward, courtesy of University of Illinois Archives)

Annie Riley. He spent a frustrating day working on a trait list with her, but finally gave up because the number of blank spaces and question marks rivaled the number of answers. He must have prompted her at some point, or even repeatedly as the long hours passed. Perhaps he asked a leading question, such as, "People lived near the creek, didn't they?" Whatever the specific question, it provoked a sharp reply that he recorded. "If you know, why do you ask me?" she demanded.[80]

John Riley, gray haired and fifteen or twenty years older than his wife, told Steward what he recalled about four other valleys in eastern Nevada and in Utah. Cave Valley, the smallest, lay to the south of Ely. Spring Valley, located across the Spring Mountains, was east of Ely. Antelope Valley stretched out near the Nevada-Utah border, and Snake Valley straddled the border. A state line cut across an area of thousands of square miles where people had long lived without boundaries that excluded others. They traveled to other valleys and intermarried with people there.

John Riley, born about 1870, remembered where people lived in those valleys when he was a young man, which Steward took to mean around 1885. Steward learned that the people were mainly Western Shoshones, but mixed with Southern Paiutes in the southern tips of Spring and Snake valleys. Some Shoshones in Snake Valley could speak Paiute and took part in their neighbors' festivals. Relations between Western Shoshones and Southern Paiutes were recalled as "entirely amicable," Steward wrote. The same was true of Cave Valley, where a few Shoshone families lived. They intermarried with Southern Paiutes, allowed them access to pine nut areas, enjoyed reciprocal access, and lived in peace with them.[81]

During his time in Ely, Steward drove to Spring Valley, John Riley's old home, to see it firsthand and look for the sites of old camps. The Snake Range marked its eastern edge. As he drove through the valley, Steward noticed that the unusually tall mountains rose far above the pinyon-juniper belt, which rarely reached past seven thousand feet. Mount Wheeler, many miles to the south, had a summit above thirteen thousand feet. That placed it in the Arctic-alpine life zone: a zone extending from eleven thousand feet upward and "unimportant to man except as it supports animal species," Steward noted. Mount Wheeler qualified as the highest peak in the Snake Range and one of

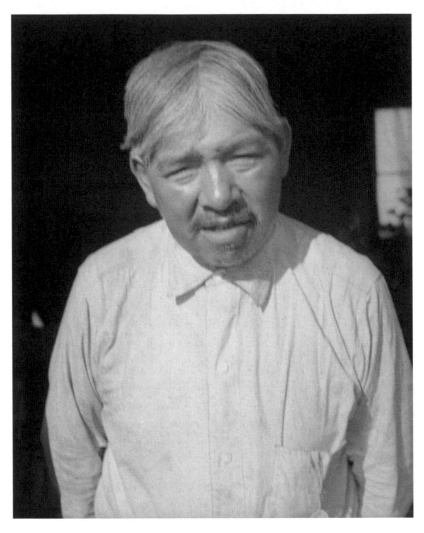

15. John Riley, July 1935. (Photo by Julian H. Steward, courtesy of University of Illinois Archives)

the highest in Nevada. He took a photograph that day of the valley floor and the mountains rising in the distance.[82]

Hundreds of springs and the many perennial streams in the Snake Range provided water for Spring Valley on its western side and for Snake Valley on its eastern side. Most of the large streams originated as springs high in the mountains, and they flowed down thousands of feet to the valley floors.[83] The fertility of the two valleys permitted unusually dense populations: by Steward's estimate, about one person to six square miles. The more arid Nevada valleys, in contrast, had much lower population densities. His estimate for nearby Antelope Valley was one person to eleven square miles; and for the Kawich Mountains, just one person to about twenty square miles. In California's Owens Valley, which had become his point of reference for a favored place, the population density was about one person to 2.5 square miles before American settlers arrived.[84]

Diamond Valley, northwest of Ely, was not a fertile area except around the Roberts Mountains, which reached heights above ten thousand feet. When he questioned Frank Stick about the valley, Steward learned that a winter village of at least six camps had once stood at the foot of the Roberts Mountains, at the place "where there are four sloughs." In that arid landscape four spots of soft muddy ground served as a landmark. Some of the richest pine nut areas were located on the western slopes of the Roberts Mountains. Frank Stick told Steward that no one claimed exclusive rights to pine nut groves—neither families nor villages. "Outsiders were welcome and even encouraged to come when the crop was good," Steward reported.[85]

In years of scarcity the people walked as far west as the vicinity of Austin, where they gathered pine nuts and took part in festivals. Frank Stick remembered that if stored foods ran short in spring, some people might weaken and die. The success of the pine nut harvest could spell the difference between life and death. A talker in Diamond Valley, who directed pine nut gathering and announced when other seeds were ripe, prayed for good harvests to Coyote, known as "the father of the people."[86]

Up to this point Steward had heard about many cases of plural marriage: specifically, polygyny, and especially sororal polygyny. Some Shoshones in eastern Nevada also told him about plural marriages that qualified as polyandry. Frank Stick said that his mother had two husbands at the same time, one of them a talker. He claimed the talker as his father but could not explain why, Steward later wrote.

Steward wondered aloud, in print, if he simply preferred to think that his father was a talker. But perhaps Frank Stick, and Harry Johnny as interpreter, could not easily explain the reason in English, or in a way that their visitor could readily understand. Or perhaps they chose not to explain fully, a choice that was theirs as the keepers of cultural knowledge and collective memory. They could decide what to tell him and what not to tell him. At Fallon, Pat Hicks had evidently decided not to tell him very much, leading Steward to search for another elder.[87]

The instance of polyandry he heard about from Frank Stick was of two brothers, co-husbands who shared a wife. Harry Johnny explained that his grandmother, who had lived in Railroad Valley, also had two husbands who were brothers. Steward used a standard term, *fraternal polyandry*, for those cases. He would later hear of other instances elsewhere in the Great Basin that involved unrelated men, not brothers.[88]

Polyandry, a rare practice worldwide, had not previously been reported for Western Shoshones. Steward believed that he had discovered a new case, a contribution to the knowledge base of anthropology. Within months he used what he had learned in fieldwork to write a short article on the subject. It soon appeared in the *American Anthropologist*.[89]

Finding polyandry qualified as an unexpected discovery, as did the practice of sowing wild seeds. The patrilineal band, which he still expected to find, continued to elude him.

6. River from Snow Mountain

AFTER TEN WEARING days of work Jane and Julian left Ely, Nevada, in early August to spend a week in Salt Lake City, two hundred and fifty miles away. Julian needed more maps, and he had plant specimens that he hoped to have identified at the University of Utah. They headed northeast, still traveling on the Lincoln Highway as they left Nevada and entered Utah. The narrow paved road took them through the heart of the Great Salt Lake Desert and across miles of salt flats that glared white in the hard sunlight.[1]

In Salt Lake City they stayed with Jane's sister, Libby, who lived in the Avenues, near downtown and Temple Square. Jane's family had lived in that neighborhood for most of her life. Her father, in a varied career as a business owner and newspaper editor, sometimes worked in office buildings near Temple Square. Months earlier, he and his wife had left for London, to serve a mission there at the request of the Mormon church.[2]

Jane and Julian spent some time visiting with Libby and her new husband, Frank. Otherwise, they were busy, Jane reported, "getting maps, having botanical specimens identified, doing errands, and drinking sloe gin fizzes with Stan at Maxie's." They searched for maps to use on their upcoming trip to northeastern Nevada, where they hoped to find more Western Shoshone elders to serve as cultural informants. They also looked up Walter Cottam, a plant ecologist at the University of Utah. Julian had written to him a few months earlier with questions about life zones and the distribution of plants in the Great Basin.[3]

Cottam agreed to look at the specimens, most of them edible wild plants known to the Nevada elders, and to identify the plants by their scientific names. Many of the wild grasses, which provided generous supplies of seeds, were notoriously difficult to identify—according to botanists, not to Paiute and Shoshone women with a lifetime of experience in collecting them. Other grasses were distinctive. The seed heads of *wai* had a delicate and lacy look. Cottam, a trained and experienced botanist, easily identified *wai* as *Oryzopsis hymenoides*, commonly known as sand bunch grass or Indian rice grass.[4]

He had joined the faculty of the University of Utah shortly after Steward. At the University of Chicago he had studied with Henry C. Cowles, often credited as the first professional ecologist in the United States and as the founder of the new field of plant ecology. Cottam, one of many students trained by Cowles, belonged to the first generation of professional American ecologists. He would come to be regarded as one of Cowles's most successful students.[5]

By 1926, when Cottam received his PhD, one of Cowles's other students had just published on the ecology of Salt Lake Valley and nearby canyons, pointing out some effects of settlement. "The native vegetation of the entire region has been greatly modified by the activities of civilization," she wrote. Those "activities of civilization" ranged from overgrazing the land to farming and irrigating it. Cottam would spend his career documenting those changes to the land and native vegetation.[6]

Cottam and Steward met sometime during the year before Steward left the University of Utah, and they soon discovered that they shared broad interests. Both carefully read the journals of explorers—John C. Frémont, John Wesley Powell, and others—to learn about the Great Basin before and shortly after American settlement. Cottam wanted to know about the native vegetation, Steward, about the native people who gathered some of those native plants. As a child growing up in southern Utah, Cottam had seen firsthand how overgrazing and deforestation damaged the land. As a trained ecologist, he tried to document and understand scientifically the environmental changes and destruction that took place so quickly after settlement.

Cottam always remembered that when the U.S. Forest Service began to manage land near his home in southern Utah, respected ranchers laughed at the college students who took part in research. The students set up protected plots of land, counted blades of grass, and kept careful records. He later realized that this work formed the crucial first step in a research program on range and watershed problems. The knowledge gained through years of painstaking labor, Cottam wrote, helped to save the skeptical ranchers from economic ruin, and their communities from more of the devastating floods that resulted from deforestation.[7]

In 1929, shortly before he met Steward, he published an article in the new journal *Ecology* that documented severe damage to a once-lush natural meadow near his childhood home. In just twenty years following settlement, overgrazing had turned a place of green grass and freshwater springs into a site of complete desolation.[8] By 1935, when he and Steward crossed paths again, massive dust storms caused by overgrazing and drought had just taken place in the Great Basin, as on the Great Plains. This ecological disaster spurred him to lead a study on the amount of desert land needed to support grazing cattle. The result for the study area—one square mile per head of cattle—cannot have pleased local ranchers. Throughout his long career, Cottam would remain a fierce defender of the environment, even in the face of pressure to stay silent.[9]

Steward, unlike Cottam, had far more interest in what existed before American settlement than in what happened afterward. Years earlier, as a graduate student, he had begun to think about the relationship between people and environment. Influenced at first by behaviorism in psychology and by some courses in geography, he would eventually choose a new name for his new approach. In *Basin-Plateau* he used the term *human ecology*, which an archaeologist named Lyndon Hargrave had also used in print. Steward had met Hargrave in Arizona a few years earlier. Twenty years after fieldwork in the Great Basin, and after trying out other names, he finally settled on *cultural ecology*, a term that he could claim as solely his own.[10]

He never said that Cottam or Hargrave—or behaviorists or geographers—had influenced his ideas. Perhaps he did not think that he had learned much from colleagues about the relation between organism and environment—the focus of both behaviorist psychology and ecology. (To ecologists and Steward, the term *environment* specifically meant the natural world; to behaviorists it had the more general meaning of anything external to the organism.) Or perhaps, like most of his colleagues, he wanted his ideas to be appreciated as original, not dismissed as derivative.[11]

In 1935, early in his career and in the midst of fieldwork, Steward already understood that his profession valued original ideas and discoveries. He would also learn over time how hard it was to get a hearing for new ideas. Senior scholars—including his teachers, Kroeber and Lowie—had invested years of labor and thought in other approaches. They generally resisted or ignored new ones.

For twenty years he would also fight the stigmatizing label of "environmental determinism," which detractors flung his way. "Attention to the role of ecology," he insisted, "is neither environmental determinism nor economic determinism." But he may have opened himself to the charge by using the phrase "ecological determinants" in the closing pages of *Basin-Plateau*.[12]

When he and Jane left Salt Lake City for northeastern Nevada in mid-August, they traveled again on the two-lane road that did double duty in Utah as part of the Lincoln Highway and the Victory Highway. It took them back through the blistering heat of the nearly waterless

Great Salt Lake Desert. For fifty miles the road ran almost arrow straight. The air shimmered, and mirages appeared suddenly and then vanished from the blinding whiteness of the salt flats and the dark surface of the paved road. The vacant blue sky held no promise of rain. A few miles from the Utah-Nevada border, they saw the Silver Island Mountains in the distance. The blue-gray mass of rock seemed to rise out of a white sea of salt known as the Bonneville Salt Flats.

In Nevada the road split, and the Lincoln Highway turned southwest. They stayed on the Victory Highway, the newer road and another major route across Nevada to California. It continued due west, following part of the old California Trail along the Humboldt River. As Jane recorded, they stopped first on the outskirts of Wells, Nevada, about sixty miles west of the state border. Finding no elder among the Western Shoshones who lived there, they went on to Elko. It offered good prospects, as they knew. They already had a lead, probably given to them by Harry Johnny before they left Ely.[13]

Elko, population four thousand, served as the seat and the commercial and shipping center of Elko County, which proudly claimed to cover an area the size of several New England states combined. With more than seventeen thousand square miles within its borders, it was an oversized county in what easterners saw as an oversized land. Elko County qualified as cowboy country. It offered glimpses of the Old West and claimed pride of place as the center of ranching in the Great Basin.[14]

The town of Elko sprawled along the banks of the Humboldt River at an elevation of five thousand feet. Its main street featured buildings from the late nineteenth century, some with classic western false fronts. A few casinos and two hotels that catered to well-heeled travelers and cattlemen, the Commercial Hotel and the Stockmen's Hotel, stood among stores and other businesses in downtown Elko. Railroad tracks ran through the center of town, dividing it in half. The stockyards—literally located on the other side of the tracks, toward the southeast—received tens of thousands of cattle and sheep each year. They were shipped in railroad cars to points east and west.[15]

American settlers began moving into the area in the 1860s, and ranches soon occupied most of the vast high desert in the Humboldt country around Elko. Trappers had preceded settlers and had hunted out beavers by the time the ranchers arrived. Beaver pelts fetched high prices in the 1830s. Beaver felt hats were high fashion for men in the East and in Europe, until top hats made of silk finally superseded them.[16]

Western Shoshones who lived near the river thereby lost one of their food sources to competition among trappers, market forces, and men's fashion in faraway places. Worse soon followed. They lived at many sites along the Humboldt River, Nevada's longest river and the main water source of their region, including the area that grew into the town of Elko. Because of the water, and the bordering meadows of grass that could sustain grazing livestock on a long overland trek, the Humboldt River route bore heavy traffic in the mid-nineteenth century. American explorers and legions of miners and settlers followed it to California in the 1840s and 1850s.[17]

The Humboldt Valley had long been one of the most fertile lands occupied by Western Shoshones, but that soon changed. Tens of thousands of people, along with their grazing oxen, horses, mules, cattle, and sheep, crossed the valley on the California Trail, which ran along the river. The overlanders hunted wild game, depleting the supply. Their livestock ate the wild grasses and trampled the turf to a hard surface; and they may have passed on Old World diseases to game animals that Shoshones hunted.[18]

American explorers and travelers from the east thought that Shoshones lived in complete hunger and want. Steward had read their accounts and later included excerpts in *Basin-Plateau*, remarking that most descriptions by outsiders centered on the "poverty" of

Shoshones.[19] They visibly did not possess what many of the travelers and settlers valued and hoped to acquire in the West: herds of live-stock, tilled fields, substantial houses, and large holdings of private land, which the owners could one day sell for profit.

Perhaps few of the Americans in the 1850s and 1860s fully realized that the Shoshones' hunger had grown chronic, even severe, because of the newcomers' actions. People had lived on that land in a sustain-able way, by foraging, for generations. Years of excessive trapping and hunting, and of trailing untold thousands of grazing animals along the Humboldt River, had nearly ruined their hunting and gathering grounds. Then the food producers—ranchers and other settlers—arrived in overwhelming numbers, and stayed. Their way of living on the land dealt the deathblow to the foraging life.

In Elko Steward visited the Western Shoshone colony that stood on a hill on the north side of town. The Elko Colony, covering just thirty acres, was home to about one hundred and fifty people, a small mi-nority among the largely white population of the town. Steward went there to meet a man named Bill Gibson, an associate of the Ely Col-ony leader, Harry Johnny.[20]

Gibson, who was in his late fifties, lived with his wife, Alice, and several children and stepchildren. Census takers appraised his house as more valuable than those of his neighbors, and they listed his oc-cupation as *contractor, cement*, noting that he was self-employed. Ev-eryone in his household could speak English, and most of the chil-dren knew how to read and write, as was common in towns. His oldest stepdaughter, who was not literate, worked as a laundress.[21]

Beyond his skills as a contractor, Gibson also had some powers as a healer. He usually received instructions in dreams about how to heal. After visiting the patient and singing, he learned from animal spirits how to proceed. His powers had begun to decline in recent years, the result of some disturbing experiences. One of his sons was dreaming of otters and "other good animals," perhaps a sign that he, the son, was gaining powers.[22]

During a week in Elko, Steward spent several days questioning Gibson and working with him on a trait list. Since his firsthand memories stretched back only to the 1880s, Gibson also drew on secondhand memories of the Humboldt country before American conquest and settlement. Those memories came from his parents and grandparents, who in years past had told him what they remembered. They served, posthumously, as ghost informants.

The work went well except for repeated interruptions during the week. Several telegrams reached Steward, one with a tentative offer of a research position at the Smithsonian's Bureau of American Ethnology, and another with a firm offer of a teaching position at the University of New Mexico. He went to the Western Union office to send a telegram to Washington DC inquiring about the research position, which carried a higher salary. Then he waited anxiously for a reply, but it did not arrive immediately.[23]

"The death of Will Rogers & Wiley Post delayed our receiving message," Jane noted tersely. The two men had died in an airplane crash in Alaska a day earlier. Post was a famous aviator but Rogers was a national icon. Part Cherokee, former cowboy, and a native of Oklahoma, his career had progressed from lasso artist to actor, humorist, and political commentator. ("I don't make jokes. I just watch the government and report the facts.") The high volume of telegraph traffic carrying news about Rogers and Post had delayed the Stewards' telegram. Jane felt on edge as she waited for it, hoping it would lead to a rooted life in a city when she and Julian left their wandering life in the desert.

Deciding to take a chance on the research position at the Smithsonian, they sent a telegram to the president of the University of New Mexico, declining his offer. Nevada may have put them in a gambling

16. Bill Gibson, August 1935. (Photo by Julian H. Steward, courtesy of University of Illinois Archives)

mood, but the stakes were too high for them to rest easy with that decision. Feeling upset and tired, they did not work that day. They lost another day when a young woman who lived at the Elko Colony collapsed and nearly died. No one wanted to answer questions about the past in the midst of that current crisis.[24]

During the rest of their time in Elko they worked with Gibson. He was a thoughtful-looking man with deep-set eyes and sculpted features. His thick dark hair, cropped short, showed gray at the temples. Jane found him friendly and said that the white residents of Elko regarded him highly. Gibson's business must have brought him into regular contact with them; no doubt they were his major customers.

His keen sense of history—"the first of its kind we have found," Jane noted—also impressed her.[25]

Gibson may have acquired this awareness of his people's history on his own, after attending the Stewart Indian School in Carson City, Nevada, in the 1890s. Off-reservation boarding schools for Indian children, set up in the late nineteenth century, purposely promoted assimilation in both language and culture. Children were forbidden to speak their own languages; fluency in English was an intended goal of their education. The schools discouraged any strong sense of native identity and history, but Gibson's experience at the Stewart Indian School may have produced a result opposite to the one intended. In any case, after he returned to his home in northeastern Nevada, he emerged as one of the leading advocates of Western Shoshone treaty rights. He argued that Shoshones had not lost title to their lands. The Treaty of Ruby Valley, an 1863 treaty with the federal government, recognized them as rightful owners of territory in the Great Basin.[26]

Gibson provided some of Steward's material on the Humboldt country. Like Harry Johnny in Ely, he may have thought that he could advance his people's case for treaty rights by talking to this white man who was going to write about them. Those writings could document that the ancestors of his people had lived throughout a vast area around the Humboldt River, occupying land now held by ranchers and others. Fence lines divided territory that had always been open to his people, and crossing those lines to walk or hunt or gather food on ancestral lands qualified as trespass.

On his last morning with Steward, according to the day's journal entry, Gibson gave "a clear picture of surrounding bands which are much smaller than others in less fertile localities." Later, and in print, Steward explained that the foraging areas in this region were rather small, and that people generally did not have to walk as far to find food. More rainfall, the many perennial streams, and the diverse landscape made the Humboldt country more favorable than most territories occupied by Western Shoshones—until a flood of overlanders, and then settlers, degraded their hunting and gathering grounds.

Besides hunting, people also fished, either as individuals or in groups. Communal fishing sometimes involved the use of stone dams, an unusual feature in Steward's experience. He drove thirteen miles west of Elko one day to photograph a stone dam on the Humboldt River. According to Steward, Gibson denied that anyone claimed exclusive rights to fishing places; but perhaps Gibson, or Steward, referred to places without dams.

Steward later said that people did claim rights to places where they built dams. As he put it, generalizing about all Nevada Shoshones, "the principle of property ownership was simple: things to which human effort had been applied were owned by the person or persons who had worked on them." (It seems doubtful that twenty words could fully represent concepts of property held by people living in so many, and in such different, places.) In any case, memory of fishing techniques and fishing places was hazy, as Steward conceded, because irrigation by settlers had reduced the Humboldt River to a mere trickle decades earlier.[27]

Despite the greater fertility of this area, Gibson told Steward that his grandmother had to walk twenty or thirty miles south of Elko to gather pine nuts on the western slope of the Ruby Mountains in the fall. Pine nuts were not available near Elko. She and others who went there "gathered where they pleased," Steward later wrote. The erratic nature of the food supply also meant that families often had to move to different places and associate with different people from one year to the next. Communal hunts and festivals thus did not bring together—or as Steward later phrased it, "did not always unite"—the same people. "In short," he later concluded in *Basin-Plateau*, "there was no band organization."[28]

On their last afternoon with Gibson, Jane and Julian listened to a long story, "Cottontail Shoots the Sun." It took hours to record. The story told how Cottontail Rabbit killed the Sun because it scorched the ground with its heat. Then he threw a part of it back into the sky, creating a new sun that shone less fiercely. Gibson called this saga *the* Shoshone classic "that explained everything," the "'bible'" of the Western Shoshones.[29]

Afterward they discussed another idea about the sun. "He told us," Jane said, "[that] some of his white friends had said that the earth moved around the sun." For twelve years he had faithfully kept records of sunrise in order to investigate that idea.[30]

In mid-August Julian and Jane left Elko and returned to California where he underwent a medical examination, as required for employment with the federal government. "Julian's impatience" with this formality, Jane recorded, led him to keep the medical appointment before receiving the forms that told what tests the examination should include. "By some miracle, they were the right ones," she added. Afterward, he filled out the sundry forms needed for an appointment to the federal service.

The Bureau of American Ethnology had not yet provided final confirmation of the position, but receiving the forms encouraged them. It gave Jane hope that in a matter of months they could proudly claim a fixed address and a regular income. They packed the books and few belongings that they had left in storage and took them to the wharf for shipment to the East Coast. In Berkeley they visited Jane's brother and old friends in a rush, "an average of 3 social encounters a day," Jane reported.[31]

Moving to Washington DC would limit their future contact with Berkeley friends to letters and to hurried conversations at conferences. The high cost of traveling across the continent, whether by train or by car, prohibited casual visits; and the expense of long-distance telephone calls made those a last resort, strictly for emergencies.

They took advantage of this last chance to say hello and then good-bye to friends.

In early September they left Berkeley and spent two days on the long drive back to northeastern Nevada. Between Reno and Elko they drove on the Victory Highway, crossing miles of salt flats and sagebrush plains. The salt flats had the look of dirty snow at the end of winter, an odd sight on a meltingly hot day near the end of summer. Sometimes a dust devil came into view, a furious swirl of sand and dust moving along the valley floor in the distance.

Railroad tracks ran parallel to the highway for miles. Somewhere along a lonely stretch of road Jane glimpsed a sight that would remain in her mind's eye for the rest of her life. She saw a freight train headed toward California, and a long line of men huddled on top of the freight cars—tiny figures dwarfed by the dimensions of land and sky. They had no shelter from sun or heat or wind as they crossed open desert beneath a blank sky for hundreds of miles. Down on their luck, like millions of Americans in 1935, they were riding the rails west to the land of hope.[32]

Back in Elko Jane and Julian collected mail that the post office had held for them. The General Delivery address was one of a series of temporary addresses that they had used during the past four months of fieldwork. Among the letters, Julian found final notification of the research position at the Bureau of American Ethnology. "That is settled," Jane recorded with satisfaction in their journal that evening.

She wrote to her parents on the same day to tell them about Julian's new job and about his turning down the offer from the University of New Mexico, which paid less and required full-time teaching. "The Smithsonian job will be research and field work," she explained. "It will seem grand," she said, "to get a salary for doing things we have scraped and sacrificed to do. Virtue is its own reward, nicht wahr?"

"If you don't hear from me for about a month," she added, "you will know that I am in Ruby Valley or Owyhee or somewhere else and working my head off." Transcribing and typing stories, helping with the trait lists, and dealing with such practical matters as cooking took hours at night—to say nothing of the time spent by Julian's side each day as he questioned elders.[33]

They mailed the letter and made plans to leave Elko the next morning, headed toward the Ruby Mountains and the namesake valley. Bill Gibson had probably suggested a man named Ruby Valley Johnson as an informant. He told Steward a memorable story about Johnson's father, a story probably first told to Gibson by his mother. She was from the area around Elko, and Johnson's father, who wished to have her as his wife, abducted her. Refusing to stay with him because "she did not like him," she made the long walk from Ruby Valley back to Elko. She knew the way from traveling to the mountains in the fall to harvest pine nuts. The massive range, a landmark always in view, guided her home.

The case of Gibson's mother was not unique. "When a woman so abducted did not like her new spouse she ran away to return home," Steward later wrote. The element of choice in the matter suggests that the outcome of abduction hinged on persuasion rather than force, just as leadership depended on persuasive "talking," not coercion.[34]

When asked if Western Shoshone women ever had more than one husband at a time, Gibson had strongly denied that practice. He expressed surprise when Steward recounted cases of polyandry from valleys to the south—although Gibson had known the talker who was a polyandrous husband of Frank Stick's mother, the man whom Stick claimed as his father.[35] Steward would hear more about polyandry in Ruby Valley.

After one night in Elko Julian and Jane left for Ruby Valley, planning to camp at a ranch. The valley's distance from Elko made it impossible to stay in an auto cabin in town. A faculty member at the

University of Utah had given them the name of the Neff family, local ranchers; Mrs. Neff was his sister. Their ranch was one of many in
Ruby Valley. After the mid-1860s so many farmers and ranchers settled there that the federal government reneged on a plan to survey
land for a reservation in the valley.[36]

As Jane and Julian drove south from Elko, they saw the Ruby Mountains rising in the distance. Peaks that reached above eleven thousand
feet, capped with snow for much of the year, made the Rubies one
of the highest mountain ranges in the Great Basin. Western Shoshones called the range Snow Mountain. It resembled the Sierra Nevada
but on a far smaller scale.

Streams fed by snowmelt filled two large lakes in the valley, and
the south fork of the Humboldt River flowed out from Snow Mountain. Compared to most other areas of eastern Nevada, the valley had
abundant water and food. Predictably, it had a much higher population density than those other areas in the years before the American
conquest: perhaps one person for every 2.8 miles. This figure, which
approached that of the Owens Valley before settlement, attested to
the fertility of the land at the foot of Snow Mountain.[37]

The very features that made Ruby Valley desirable to Western Shoshones also attracted American settlers, and those settlers owed a large
debt to the peacemaking efforts of a man named Temoke. Bill Gibson had already told Steward the story of Chief Temoke, the leader
of Western Shoshones in Ruby Valley and the surrounding region
in the 1860s. As a young man, Temoke and his people had foraged
over a large area, hunting as far north as Jarbidge, rugged and mountainous country near what later became the Nevada-Idaho border.
They walked more than a hundred miles to reach Jarbidge. They also
hunted in Ruby Valley.

During one spring in the 1850s, when Temoke was probably in
his twenties, he happened to see three strangers while he was trapping sage grouse in the valley. They greeted him with raised hands,

motioning to ask for directions to a trail. These were the first white men Temoke had ever seen, and he was frightened, perhaps by their strange appearance—they had long beards—or perhaps simply because of their number. He was alone that day. He directed them to a mountain pass, and they gave him food and chewing tobacco as a reward, promising to leave more for him at a certain place on their return. Temoke told others about meeting these "dog face people," and when the men made good on their promise of food and tobacco a few months later, he took that as a sign of friendship. Among his people, gifts of food signaled goodwill.

Temoke had no authority at the time, but as the years passed his influence grew. He was intelligent, good humored, and known to many because of his travels throughout Western Shoshone territory. During the same period, a stage line came into use that passed through Steptoe Valley. Armed conflict soon broke out between American settlers and the Western Shoshones who were alarmed by the flood of intruders and by the changes to their land.

Temoke, who had maintained good relations with Americans, helped to keep the peace between them and his own people. The wars ended in 1862, and in the following year, Temoke and eleven other men signed the Treaty of Ruby Valley. It promised some compensation for land. The treaty also guaranteed reservations in the valley so that Western Shoshones could live there and support themselves as the government wished: by raising cattle and farming. Although land set aside for reservations in Ruby Valley was never surveyed, Temoke refused to leave. "'If you move my country,'" he reportedly said, "'I go too.'" The valley stayed put and so did Temoke. He remained in Ruby Valley until his death in 1891, Gibson said, with many friends among the settlers.[38]

A few years later in print, Steward called Gibson's story about Temoke "one Indian's version, not an objective chronicle." In his view and in keeping with behaviorism, only a detached and impartial observer, an outsider, could provide an objective account. Such an account consisted strictly of facts, details about observable places, people, and events. That ruled out any interpretation of Temoke's motives or of the meaning of past events to Western Shoshones—matters that were not visible to an observer.

Steward did concede that the terms of the 1863 treaty had gone unfulfilled. "It is only in recent years," he added, "that various self-appointed leaders have assumed this task [of trying to enforce treaty rights]." Bill Gibson, like Harry Johnny, worked actively for the cause; but both were elected, not self-appointed, leaders. Just a few years earlier, in 1932, they had been elected to an eight-member Shoshone treaty council in Elko, to promote treaty rights.[39]

The Western Shoshone population of Ruby Valley, which Steward estimated at more than four hundred before contact, had fallen to fewer than seventy several years before his visit. Some people had left in the nineteenth century for reservations, but others, besides Chief Temoke, refused to leave. Instead, they adapted culturally to the new world in their old homeland. They grew some of their food and also earned money to buy food; and they continued to forage, hunting ducks and deer and gathering pine nuts. The Carson Agency, which had jurisdiction over Ruby Valley Shoshones, categorized them in the 1934 census as *scattered Indians*. Sometimes the term used by the government was *homeless Indians*—but from their own point of view they were neither scattered nor homeless. They lived together in their homeland although others claimed to own it.[40]

In Ruby Valley Steward worked intensively with Ruby Valley Johnson and another man named Billy Mose.[41] Mamie Moore, Johnson's daughter, interpreted. Steward thought she was fifty, but a census put her age at forty-two. She had chiseled, strong features and thick black hair that she wore short and parted in the middle. Besides interpreting,

17. Mamie Moore, September 1935. (Photo by Julian H. Steward, courtesy of University of Illinois Archives)

Moore also served as an informant about childbirth, puberty, and menstrual practices for a trait list.[42]

She drew on memories of her own puberty ceremony, which involved staying alone in a hut for a month. As she recalled, her aunt came to the hut early each morning to wake her, and then returned home. That was around the turn of the twentieth century, decades after settlers arrived in Ruby Valley. Some of the old ways had continued.

18. Ruby Valley Johnson, September 1935. (Photo by Julian H. Steward, courtesy of University of Illinois Archives)

She may not have told Steward that the old practice of retreat during menstruation had also persisted into the twentieth century. Anthropologists came to term this *menstrual seclusion*. He likely did not inquire about current practice, in part because of his interest in the previous century and the time before settlement. He did note that dwellings and other structures built in the past included a type that the trait list classified as *menstrual houses*.

In truth, Steward dutifully recorded information on these aspects of female life only because they appeared as categories on the trait lists. They seemed to have nothing to do with band structure or hunting or men's other economic activities, and thus held no interest for him. Most of the answers that he recorded came from male informants. This was not an uncommon practice at the time.[43]

Moore's father, Ruby Valley Johnson, was a widower in his mid-seventies according to census takers. Steward thought he was older and quite "feeble." He estimated an age of eighty. Johnson had thick white hair, combed straight back from a broad forehead. White stubble covered his chin. His eyes had the permanent squint that came from a long life spent outdoors in sharp sunlight.

Billy Mose, with a date of birth recorded as "ca. 1848," may have been nearly ninety years old, not just eighty, as Steward thought. He was the son of Mose, one of the men who signed the Treaty of Ruby Valley in 1863. He told Steward what he recalled of some of his father's memories. Mose, long dead, thus served as a ghost informant.[44]

Billy Mose's father was the source of such observations as this one: that he, Mose, had once seen a few bison near the Butte Mountains, midway between Ruby Valley and Steptoe Valley. As Steward later wrote, the Great Basin did not provide "the optimum bison environment." Elders did tell him, however, that several generations earlier some bison had ranged along the Humboldt River and around Steptoe Valley.[45]

As Billy Mose told Steward, he and his father were born in Egan Canyon, south of Ruby Valley. Although they lived mainly in the canyon, Billy Mose's family spent time hunting in Ruby Valley, both because of family ties—Ruby Valley was his mother's birthplace—and because of the good hunting. Many mountain sheep lived in the Ruby Mountains. He remembered that the people of that valley, who did not have an antelope shaman, hunted pronghorn antelope communally in or around Butte Valley and Long Valley. An old woman was the antelope shaman in Butte Valley, according to Billy Mose; this was the only instance Steward recorded of a woman directing the hunts, although he did learn of other women who were shamans. It offered just one example of a marked flexibility in social practices that he would record, generally without comment, among Western Shoshones. Marriage practices offered other examples.[46]

Ruby Valley Johnson, like Billy Mose, recalled men who had more than one wife at a time; and they agreed that women in such polygynous marriages were sometimes, but not always, sisters. The two men also agreed that men who shared a wife were not always brothers or, in at least one case, even related to each other. Billy Mose had heard of instances of polyandry from places beyond Ruby Valley, including Elko. He was at least thirty years older than Bill Gibson, who denied the past practice of polyandry—suggesting that collective memory of these plural unions may already have faded. Perhaps only the oldest people still remembered the women who once had multiple husbands.[47]

Steward spent about a week in Ruby Valley, producing a trait list and recording kinship terminology, a list of core vocabulary, and his own material on bands. Ruby Valley shared some environmental features with the Owens Valley, where Steward thought Paiutes had lived in composite bands, a result of the ecology in his view. The Shoshones of Ruby Valley may have traveled farther to hunt, to judge from Temoke's trips to Jarbidge. In any case, he concluded that they had *not* lived in bands. He did not believe that they had claimed exclusive use of clearly bounded tracts of land before American settlement. By his definition, they had not owned land—an essential feature of bands as he conceived of them.

Steward later told Lowie that his informants in Ruby Valley were a "cooperative and kindly bunch." Working with those friendly elders came as a relief after the ten edgy days in Ely. But of course his

19. Ruby Valley Johnson's grandson, September 1935. (Photo by Julian H. Steward, courtesy of University of Illinois Archives)

Ruby Valley informants still lived in their beloved homeland, in sight of Snow Mountain—unlike elders exiled to the Ely Colony and to the social and economic margins of the town. In Ruby Valley his informants' memories were not primarily of loss.

Before leaving, Steward took a few photographs of Mamie Moore and Ruby Valley Johnson. He persuaded Johnson's grandson—Moore's adopted son, who was ten years old—to pose for one picture. The boy wore striped overalls and a cotton shirt buttoned to the neck. He stood facing the sun and looked shyly at the tall stranger with the camera.[48]

On their return to Elko Jane and Julian stopped at the post office to pick up mail sent to their General Delivery address. Jane found a letter from her sister, who had been having marital problems since her wedding. She had married after Jane, but at the much younger age of nineteen. Jane was nearly twenty-five when she and Julian married and went to live in Berkeley. Just six months earlier Libby had abruptly left Salt Lake City to visit them there. Unhappy with her husband's volatile temper, she wondered whether to return to him. She told her mother, "J and J are frankly skeptical about its working out permanently and I have just a little worry about it myself, but I feel I won't have much to lose by giving things another chance." Her mother advised against that.[49]

Libby went back, but her husband's temper, as well as other problems, did not improve. In her letter to Jane she alluded to divorce. Since their parents were so far away, Jane decided to go to Utah at once, to help her sister as best she could. After checking the railroad schedule, she boarded a train for Salt Lake City at the small station in the center of town. She and Julian planned to meet at the station in ten days, when she returned from Utah.

Julian also left Elko, driving about a hundred miles north to Owyhee, near the Nevada-Idaho border. The paved road turned to a gravel and dirt track after about twenty-five miles. It took him through one of the most isolated and sparsely populated parts of the West. In that remote country he traveled on a road nearly without turnoffs, and through open range.[50]

Owyhee, headquarters of the Duck Valley Reservation, stood at the northern end of the Bull Run Mountains. More than five hundred Western Shoshones and Northern Paiutes lived there. Many of them raised livestock and farmed land along the Owyhee River, a tributary of the Snake River. Some of the Shoshones had ties to Ruby Valley and the Humboldt country, and Steward hoped to learn more about both areas.[51]

In the decade following the 1863 Treaty of Ruby Valley, Western Shoshones in east-central Nevada had waited in vain for the promised reservation in Ruby Valley. Along with Chief Temoke, many of them quietly resisted efforts by the federal government to relocate them to southern Nevada, Idaho, or Utah. Their attachment to ancestral land remained strong, and they stated a wish "'to live in our own dear Mountains and valleys as we have done in times gone.'"[52]

In 1877 the federal government set aside land in Duck Valley, straddling the Nevada-Idaho border, and established the first permanent reservation for Western Shoshones. The remote valley was suitable for agriculture, distant from—and thus protected from—white settlements, and within the ancestral hunting and gathering grounds of one group of Western Shoshones. Some people from the region around Ruby Valley finally agreed to move there, while Temoke and others resolutely remained on home ground.[53]

Steward set to work with four elders at Owyhee, praising them at once to Lowie as "extraordinarily willing . . . and my interpreter the best yet." Tom Premo, his interpreter, was about forty years old, married, and the father of eight children. He had attended a boarding school for Indian children in Pennsylvania, where the students were required to speak English. Passing through seven grades of formal education at the Carlisle Indian Industrial School had given him fluency in English and familiarity with the dominant culture. This resulted in the skills that made him an "exceptional interpreter," as Steward called him, and later helped him as a leader on the reservation. He had to deal with government officials, which required speaking their language and serving as a cultural mediator between them and his people.[54]

Those skills came at a great cost. More than twenty years after his death, one of his daughters remembered what he told her about going to Carlisle. He had not gone willingly. He and other children were taken forcibly from their families and sent far away to the east, to an unknown place called Pennsylvania. "'As they were being hauled away in a buggy their mothers ran behind them, crying,'" his daughter said. "'They did this because they didn't want them to leave.'"

Another daughter has said that her mother also "had a tremendous wealth of knowledge and understanding of her own culture." In the course of a long life Anna Premo "shared this knowledge," she explained, "not only with her family but also with anthropologists," including Steward. He made no note of Anna Premo's name, listing only her husband as an outstanding interpreter and as an incidental informant. Tom Premo offered a few details—learned from his mother and grandfather, ghost informants—about Shoshones who had lived near the North Fork of the Humboldt River.[55]

Steward found people from the far-flung reaches of the Basin-Plateau region living at the Duck Valley Reservation. They included Western Shoshones from Nevada, Northern Shoshones from Idaho, and Northern Paiutes from Nevada and Oregon. "I will have about two weeks here," he told Lowie, "& expect to get a great deal."[56]

A Western Shoshone elder, born at Battle Mountain near the confluence of the Reese and Humboldt rivers, proved to be one of his best informants. Johnnie Pronto was seventy-seven years old, a widower, and a shaman. He lived with his daughter, her husband, and their son. Steward, who judged Pronto to be older, in his eighties, conceded that he was "particularly good on [the subject of] shamanism."[57]

Pronto reported that animal spirits came in dreams. Each came in a separate dream to give shamans instructions on healing. The spirits included Bear, who gave strength; Coyote, who gave intelligence;

Magpie, who helped the shaman see hidden objects; and Woodpecker, who offered the power to find disease by tapping on the patient's body. There were many other spirits as well, including Eagle and Deer.

Steward carefully recorded what he learned from Pronto about shamans and their powers, later publishing it as part of a trait list. Pronto spoke of white doctors as "now more effective" in curing disease than Indian healers, Steward wrote without offering any details. He said nothing more about religion because for reasons of theoretical approach as well as personal conviction he had no interest in the topic. As he said in print, tabulating traits did not add up to a cultural account of religion—but he always left that task to others.[58]

He questioned Pronto closely about where his people had lived in the area around Battle Mountain. Americans began to settle there in the 1860s, when Pronto was about five or ten years old. They established the town of Battle Mountain, as well as ranches and mines throughout the region. Steward had passed the town and seen that country several times in the course of recent trips across northern Nevada, from Reno to Elko and back again.[59]

As the Humboldt River flowed west from Elko it cut through mountain gorges, emerging into a broad plain around Battle Mountain. Western Shoshones lived as far west as Iron Point, beyond which Northern Paiutes lived. Pronto remembered that Shoshones and Paiutes intermarried and that they also cooperated in pronghorn antelope hunts under the direction of a Paiute antelope shaman. At times they came into conflict over the abduction of women.

Pronto's family lived along a stretch of the river up to Iron Point. Although some foods were abundant, the local supply of pine nuts was not; and in the fall his people walked as far as eighty miles south, toward Austin, to gather pine nuts. Pine nuts were more abundant in central Nevada than in the north, and northerners were not kept from gathering them. During the time of Chief Tu-tu-wa they sometimes took part in the festival he directed near Austin. They did not spend the winter there but returned home carrying their harvest of nuts. Sometimes they walked the same distance north to get salmon from the headwaters of the Owyhee River or other tributaries of the Snake River in Idaho.[60]

Steward learned about cases of polygyny, usually with sisters as co-wives, as well as polyandry, which always involved brothers as temporary co-husbands. A woman married the older brother, and then, if she liked a younger brother, "took him into the household" as a second husband. The younger brother hoped eventually to marry another woman, preferably one of her sisters. If a woman's husband died, she often married his brother; if a man's wife died, he often married her sister. As Steward put it, the levirate and sororate, while not required, were preferred.[61]

A Northern Paiute elder named Charley Thacker provided him with some other details about the Battle Mountain region and also about Winnemucca, an area to the west. Thacker's family came from a place south of the site that became the town of Winnemucca. The town bore the name of a Paiute leader famous as a peacemaker. Winnemucca's daughter, Sarah, was briefly married to Thacker's brother. She had earlier learned to read and write English, and her book, *Life among the Piutes: Their Wrongs and Claims*, was published in the early 1880s. The first book by an Indian woman to reach print, it made a strong case for Northern Paiute land rights, but to little effect. Steward sometimes cited *Life among the Piutes* as a historical source.[62]

Thacker, then in his eighties, was in poor health. His wife, Nellie, was in her midsixties according to census takers. They identified her as ½ *Paiute*, ½ *white*, and their son as ¾ *Paiute* since Charley, his father, was *full Paiute*. In some cases the reservation censuses contained calculations expressed in sixteenths. These reflected an intense interest in "blood," or biological ancestry, based on then prevailing ideas about race and racial mixture. The census did not note that the

Thackers shared a sense of cultural identity as Northern Paiute—only that their biological ancestry differed by degrees.[63]

Steward learned so few details about the Winnemucca region from Thacker that he wondered about his reliability as an informant. "Very cooperative; English good; knowledge limited," he remarked. Thacker had grown up "mostly among white people," he explained. As a young man he had served as an army scout. That no doubt explained why he spoke English so well and why Steward did not need an interpreter to work with him. Thacker had lived on the reservation for forty-five years, and Steward suggested that his long contact with Shoshones there "may have confused him on some matters." Perhaps Thacker's poor health also had some effect, but Steward did not mention it.[64]

He worked on a trait list—"incomplete but probably reliable so far as it goes"—and recorded a story about Coyote and Wolf.[65]

The Ice Barrier

Coyote and Wolf went to the north to fight. Many people went with them. Coyote had been to Snake River alone [before this]. He gathered the people and went back there. Ice had formed ahead of them, and it reached all the way to the sky. The people could not cross it. It was too thick to break. A Raven flew up and struck the ice and cracked it [when he came down]. Coyote said, "These small people can't get across the ice." Another Raven flew up and cracked the ice again. Coyote said, "Try again, try again." Raven flew up again and broke the ice. The people ran across. They ran across. Coyote was the last person over.

Another elder, Frank Smith, provided only a few details. "Information somewhat limited; English poor," Steward noted. He thought Smith was eighty years old, but census takers listed his age at about seventy. Smith, who was Western Shoshone, had lived at Austin as a child. If he was born in 1865, not in 1855 as Steward estimated, he lived there after mining began, not before. That may explain why he had so little to say about the time before settlement. He had spent most of his life, more than fifty years, at the Duck Valley Reservation.[66]

Steward's last informant at Owyhee, Charley Tom, came from the Snake River country, Coyote's destination in the story. Tom, who was Western Shoshone and sixty-one years old, lived with his wife, Annie, and a son who was about twenty. He had spent most his life, some forty-five years, at the reservation. With Premo interpreting, Steward worked with him for several days. The time proved productive, yielding a trait list as well as answers to Steward's questions about bands. He gave Charley Tom high marks: "well informed, cooperative, very conscientious and one of the best informants but needs interpreter."[67]

Tom told him that the people in the Snake River country north of Owyhee had lived mainly by fishing and by gathering seeds and roots. Some lived along the river below the site that later became the town of Twin Falls, Idaho, and they called themselves by a name that meant Salmon Eaters. Their neighbors, the Nez Perces, had horses; but most of the Salmon Eaters, the Western Shoshones along the lower Snake River, did not. They lived in a place without much good pasture for horses. Lacking horses, they rarely went south to collect pine nuts. The closest source was hundreds of miles away, too far to walk and then return with the harvested nuts.

Tom provided no evidence of patrilineal bands or land-owning bands as Steward defined them. Married couples made their own decisions about where to live; patrilocal residence was not a rule. People did not claim exclusive rights to fishing places. Camps and villages remained small because of the limited supply of food, and people shifted between them. What Tom said suggested flexibility in social practices and social relations, not rigid rules or male-centered groups. He had never heard of a woman among the Salmon Eaters having more than one husband at a time, but he did not think that other people would have disapproved.[68]

After spending more than a week at Owyhee, Steward drove back to Elko to meet his wife at the train station. They returned to Owyhee for a few more days, where "[we] finished the fieldwork for the 1935 season," Jane recorded. In late September the days were often mild and sunny but nights edged toward cold. They stayed in a small stone cabin at headquarters, courtesy of the reservation superintendent.

Superintendent McNeilly may also have done Steward the favor of recommending Tom Premo and one or two of the men who proved to be such outstanding informants at the Duck Valley Reservation. That marked a departure from Steward's usual way of finding informants. Up to that point he had located nearly all of them through referral by elders; they gave him the names of elders in other places. Having that personal connection turned him from a complete stranger into an acquaintance of a kinsman or friend. Those connections, as well as the offer of a wage, had usually allowed him to set to work immediately with a new informant in a new place—and to cover a great deal of ground quickly.[69]

Steward was due at the Bureau of American Ethnology in Washington DC in mid-October 1935 to begin work, at the rank of senior ethnologist. But before making the long trip east, the bureau had a task for him that required a trip west. With his wife he drove nearly four hundred miles to Pendleton, Oregon, crossing the plateau region of southern Idaho and the remote high desert in eastern Oregon. Since he had never traveled through this country, the trip presented a valuable opportunity for observation: he saw the land that he had just heard about from an elder. Days earlier, Charley Tom had told Steward about the Snake River country in southern Idaho.

The work in Oregon took time but, like the road trip, qualified as a learning experience. The bureau had asked Steward to examine a private collection of thousands of photographic glass plates from John Wesley Powell's 1870s scientific expeditions in the Great Basin and the Southwest. Jane assisted in this "dirty & tiresome job," as she called it. For Julian it provided another opportunity for observation, offering many glimpses of native people and landscapes from an earlier time. They finished the work on October 1.[70]

Julian was due to begin work just two weeks later on the other side of the continent. Leaving Pendleton behind, he and Jane drove nearly six hundred miles across Oregon and Idaho to northern Utah. The trees lining the streets in Salt Lake City, like those on the lower slopes of the mountains, still wore their best fall foliage, shining gold and copper and bronze. In the midst of all that light, they discovered Jane's sister still in a dark mood. "Found Lib's divorce not yet accomplished," Jane summarized, "but consoled her & the family as best we could."

Libby took comfort in Jane's happy prospects. "J & J left for Washington tonight," she told her parents in a letter, "and while I hated to see them go, they'll soon be established in their own home & I'm thrilled for them." Leaving Utah and then the Rocky Mountains behind, Jane and Julian headed east over rolling plains, toward the Mississippi River and beyond. They had a journey of two thousand miles on two-lane roads to complete in a week.[71]

Just when they would return to the West remained unclear, but they were finished with Nevada, a place of ghost towns and ghost informants. Steward had not yet found evidence of the patrilineal band, despite a wide-ranging quest. He planned to continue the search in new territory, in Idaho and Utah, sometime in the future.

He probably never knew that he had collected the memories of two elders, his last informants in Nevada, in the final year of each man's life. He planned to return to the Duck Valley Reservation, but never did. Charley Thacker died in mid-September, 1936. The cause of death was recorded as *chronic nephritis,* an incurable disease of the kidneys. Johnnie Pronto died two weeks later, the cause of death *unknown; no physician called.*[72]

PART 3. Idaho and Utah, 1936

7. Basin and Plateau

IN LATE JUNE 1936 Julian and Jane left the crowded streets and steamy heat of Washington DC for the open reaches of the West. As temperatures edged up in summer, the smothering weight of humid heat pressed down. The thick air settled indoors, where even the whirring fans could not stir it. Leaving behind high summer in the city and work that promised to pull Julian into political quicksand, they headed two thousand miles west, to the drylands of Utah and southern Idaho.

Over the last six bruising months in the city, Steward had tried to find his way through the federal bureaucracy, a place of long hallways and closed doors that protected entrenched alliances. The air was heavy with politics—but he would always prefer the clear, dry air of science. He saw science and politics, like science and religion, as completely separate. Identifying far more as a government scientist than as a civil servant, he did not quickly make allies among the bureaucrats, especially at the Bureau of Indian Affairs (BIA) where the doors had swung open but would soon slam shut.

When the firm offer of a position with the Bureau of American Ethnology (BAE) had reached him in Nevada a year earlier, he accepted it with mixed feelings. He looked forward to a research position with the Smithsonian Institution. He did not look forward to returning to Washington, where he had spent the first fifteen years of his life. Only the prospect of working in peace on his own research, having time to think and write about ecology and hunters, had drawn him back to the East.

But just months after he arrived, the BAE assigned him to the Bureau of Indian Affairs as a temporary consultant in applied anthropology. He was to assist in applied research on American Indians. The work life that he had imagined—centering on basic research, "pure" research of his own choosing—suddenly shifted shape. He left the Smithsonian Institution and the BAE, where his colleagues included two friends, both strong allies. The Bureau of Indian Affairs, which was part of the U.S. Department of the Interior, qualified as foreign turf in the federal bureaucracy. Worse, the BIA director, John Collier, was promoting new policies that Steward thought misguided. He did not hide his views, and his new superiors did not hide their displeasure.

As summer approached, Steward planned his escape from the East and from rising tensions with the BIA. Arriving in the open spaces of the West always felt like a homecoming, despite Washington DC's status as his birthplace and now his official place of residence. His own father had enjoyed a long and successful career in the federal service, at the U.S. Patent Office. In a sense Steward had entered the family business when he accepted a position with the federal government. But he did not feel at home in Washington, and in a matter of months he had fallen ill. Jane summarized her husband's emotional state ("Disgusted with BIA") and his physical symptoms ("nausea, weakness, dizziness") in two short sentences of sympathy.[1]

The prospect of spending much of the summer on his own research, which had been interrupted by work demands and illness, lifted his spirits. He had an assignment in Utah for the BIA—and generous funding. He saw the trip as an opportunity to continue the fieldwork that he had begun the previous year in California and Nevada. His ambitious plan called for extending his field research to Idaho and Utah, thus completing his study of an immense arid region: the Great Basin and fringes of the Columbia and Colorado plateaus.

John Wesley Powell had explored a large part of that country, by river or on horseback, sixty years earlier. But no anthropologist in Steward's time had taken on this region, or another of its size in the United States, for fieldwork. The Great Basin covered more than two hundred thousand square miles, and Steward had already seen much of it. Now he intended to see the rest, and more of the Columbia Plateau, which bordered it. He planned to drive to the Fort Hall Reservation in Idaho and to visit other reservations and other sites in Utah.[2]

"I should be able to get about three months of continuous field work in," he told Kroeber optimistically, as he was about to leave for the West. Kroeber, who knew about the travails with the BIA and applied anthropology, had already sent encouraging words. "Congratulations at being back at science," he said. *Science* clearly meant basic research to Kroeber. He did not see much promise, professionally speaking, in applied research.[3]

Jane, who was three months pregnant with their first child, went along with her husband's plans, but from a sense of duty rather than her former sense of adventure. Unlike him, she left Washington with a twinge of regret, even as she returned to her own birthplace in the West. She and Julian had just given up their apartment in the city, on Belmont Road. Expensive and cramped, it seemed far too small for the rent they paid. Before leaving for the summer, they signed a lease for a much larger apartment in the new suburbs across the Potomac River, in Arlington, Virginia. They would need more room for a family of three. But now, with most of their possessions in storage except for the camping gear, Jane once again faced months of travel and a series of temporary addresses.[4]

Her goal of having a home, instead of an itinerary and a map, still seemed elusive. The man she had married belonged to a little-known and wandering tribe called anthropologists. They used the term *fieldwork* for their esoteric way of studying the world, a word always spoken in a serious tone, affirming its importance—to them, if not to the many people who did not understand exactly what fieldwork was. Fieldwork seemed to require dislocation and difficulty. Just when she had grown used to the comforts of settled life in a city, she found herself uprooted again.

Her life with Julian continued to have a seminomadic quality, although, happily, he now held the status of a midlevel federal employee, with the benefits of an office, a regular salary, and a group of highly educated men as colleagues. Two of the men, Dunc and Matt, even qualified as good friends. William Duncan Strong, an archaeologist, had been one of Julian's classmates, and briefly his roommate, in Berkeley. Matthew Stirling, the head of the BAE, was a native of Berkeley and also a graduate of the University of California.[5]

No longer newlyweds but now a comfortably married couple, Jane and Julian fit in well with his colleagues and their wives. Jane, always outgoing and friendly, looked forward to social occasions with them. She and Julian valued the feeling of acceptance, of belonging to the social world of respected Smithsonian scientists. They both appreciated a memorable pronouncement on her suitability as a wife. The endorsement came from Julian's most famous colleague at the Smithsonian, the physical anthropologist Aleš Hrdlička. He told Julian that she was "a fine, sensible woman—no flapper."[6]

Hrdlička, although born in Bohemia, was no bohemian. Then in his midsixties, and socially conservative, he held uncompromising views on the place of women: they belonged in the home. Ashley Montague, a fellow physical anthropologist, recalled that Hrdlička had a "strong antipathy to women in science" and avoided any contact with them at professional meetings. Jane, a full-time housewife when she met Hrdlička, clearly passed muster as Julian's wife, to her great satisfaction.[7]

When they arrived in Salt Lake City at the end of June, the sky was a bright western-blue and the air hot and dry. Wildflowers spread across the lower slopes of the nearby Wasatch Mountains while broad swaths of snow still covered the rocky peaks. The Oquirrh Mountains at the south end of Great Salt Lake showed only lingering traces of the past winter. In Temple Square, the heart of the city, the carved spires of the Mormon Temple soared high above other buildings, shining white in the strong sunlight.

Jane, born and bred in the city, had deep family roots there and an extended family that included dozens of aunts and uncles and hundreds of cousins, descendants of her paternal grandfather, George Q. Cannon. English by birth and an early convert to the Mormon faith, he achieved great prominence in the church. He was among the earliest Mormons to settle in the land they called Deseret, a name taken from the Book of Mormon. That vast territory stretched from the Rocky Mountains across the Great Basin to Southern California.

Cannon arrived just two months after Brigham Young and the first party of settlers reached Salt Lake Valley in July 1847. They formed the leading edge of an exodus from the midwestern prairie to the western desert, following the assassination in 1844 of their prophet, Joseph Smith. His revelations, and rumors that he had more than one wife— as well as the political threat posed by his thousands of followers, who voted as a bloc—had alarmed and angered many people. They considered the revelations blasphemous and marriage to more than one woman immoral. Smith's angry opponents included the mob of men who attacked and murdered him in Carthage, Illinois.[8]

Cannon, like legions of later settlers, made the trip west as part of a wagon train. On the last day of that long trip, he emerged from the narrow green corridor—soon to be called Emigration Canyon— that cut through the Wasatch Mountains. A broad valley spread out below him, a pale brown land dotted with green that bordered the shining waters of Great Salt Lake. Exactly eighty-five years later, one of Cannon's many granddaughters would have a picnic in a canyon with a man she found impossibly handsome and would soon marry.

As Jane recalled, she and Julian drove to a nearby place in the mountains: "probably Emigration Canyon," she mused, although she could not say with certainty so many years later.[9]

When she met Julian—a new faculty member, the sole anthropologist at the University of Utah, and still married to his first wife—she did not know what anthropology was, and she did not foresee that he would have to leave the university. Julian considered himself separated from his wife, but his wife thought otherwise, and so did the university president. "I'm afraid there was a scandal," Jane said ruefully, with a small shrug, more than fifty years later. She and Julian did marry—and nearly a year before Julian's first wife finally completed divorce proceedings. That delay had led Julian to seek a divorce in Mexico, where he and Jane then married—and then married again at the courthouse in Tonopah, Nevada, two years later.[10]

Jane's father, Joseph J. Cannon, was the son of George Q., as Jane fondly referred to her well-known grandfather. Although George Q. died seven years before her birth in 1908, he remained a presence in the lives of his many descendants. He had six plural wives and more than thirty children borne by five of the wives: hence Jane's countless cousins. Joseph grew up on the Cannon Farm, a compound on the outskirts of the city where most of the wives lived. Each had her own house and lived with her own children.[11]

Joseph did not see his father on a daily basis both because George Q. visited his wives in turn and traveled extensively for the church—and because he spent time underground, as a fugitive from federal marshals during the antipolygamy raids of the late 1880s. "Wanted" posters featuring George Q. Cannon's portrait and the promise of a large reward for his capture circulated widely after the federal government issued warrants for the arrest of one of the most prominent polygamists in Utah Territory.[12] (*Polygamy* is defined by anthropologists, and by most dictionaries, as "plural marriage," whether it involves multiple husbands or wives. But *polygamy* would remain the term of common usage for polygyny, marriage to more than one wife at a time; and that practice, although illegal and not sanctioned by the Mormon church, would persist into the twenty-first century in Utah and neighboring states.[13])

Cannon finally surrendered in 1888, and Joseph, a schoolboy at the time, remembered visiting him in jail. A photograph taken of George Q. and some fellow polygamists—respected members of a church that regarded them as "prisoners for conscience' sake," not as felons—shows sober-faced men in prison stripes posing for a formal portrait. He was finally released after serving five months in the Utah Penitentiary.[14]

What United States federal law defined as bigamy, and criminal, church doctrine defined as holy, a path to the highest degree of salvation. By the time Joseph married, however, the church had changed its position on polygamy. That shift finally allowed Utah Territory to gain entry into the Union as the state of Utah in 1896, after many failed attempts, and years after its neighbors, Nevada and Idaho, gained statehood.[15]

Joseph's first wife, Jane's mother, died unexpectedly and left him with three small children. Jane, the middle child, was just four years old. Years later she remembered the sudden loss of her mother as traumatic. The family had recently moved from the Cannon Farm, her birthplace, and they moved again, joining Jane's grandmother and two aunts who lived in the center of Salt Lake City. Joseph remarried about a year later. His second wife, Ramona Wilcox Cannon, known as Mona, cared for the three children. She also bore four others.[16]

Jane spoke of her with respect as an educated woman who taught now and then at the university—and who not only possessed knowledge but also gained wisdom over the years.[17] Later in life, years after Jane married, Mona wrote an advice column for the *Deseret News* under a pen name, dispensing good counsel to the lovelorn and others in distress. (A young man wrote, "I am a returned missionary in love with four girls, and I don't know which one I love best." He was expected to marry soon, and he asked which of the four candidates would make the best wife. She replied gently, "Dear Confused: Of course you are not in love at all—yet.")[18]

As Jane recalled, Mona also helped *her* when her relationship with Julian finally came to Joseph's attention. He had assumed editorship of the *Deseret News*—a position that his own father had once held—after a few years of public service in the Utah Legislature and a long career in business. The new position only increased his prominence in public life. His daughter's relationship with a still-married faculty member at the university threatened the respected place that he and his family occupied in their community.

Mona quickly persuaded her husband that the best course of action was to help their daughter marry the man she loved, not to fight the inevitable. Opposition would only divide the family and provide more grist for the rumor mill. They reluctantly accepted their daughter's decision to leave Salt Lake City, following Julian to California. She stayed in San Francisco for a few months, close to two of her aunts, and found temporary work; Julian was nearby, in Berkeley. When he returned to Utah for two final terms of teaching, she moved to Los Angeles, where an uncle and aunt and other relatives lived.[19]

Mona and four of the children joined her there that summer. Detecting an opportunity in the problem, Mona had decided to use the time to study creative writing at UCLA or the University of Southern California. She took a class and worked on a novel and some short stories. Jane had found work as a secretary and was waiting for Julian to obtain a divorce. He had moved to Los Angeles himself after finishing his last term at the University of Utah in June.

Joseph wrote often to Mona, reporting in one letter that Julian's wife had apparently not yet begun divorce proceedings. "I had hoped that it would move on," he remarked, "and leave the two free to do what they wish. You have said so little about them that I wonder how things are going." "Tell Jane to write to me," he added. Libby replied to one of her father's many letters, explaining, "Mother is rushing her head off doing her novel and other writing, but she would have me tell you that she loves you dearly and can't wait to get home to you." Then she teased, "This is the first time I have ever written a love letter—by proxy."[20]

Three years later, when Jane and Julian arrived in Utah in the summer of 1936, Joseph and Mona were living in London, in the second year of a mission in England. Joseph had left the *Deseret News*, accepting a position as president of the British Mission. It offered a chance to serve his church and also to distance himself from rumors about his older daughter and her new husband that continued to circulate. Jane had earlier tried to assure him that "there probably hasn't been as much talk as we have thought," enclosing a letter from a friend in Salt Lake City. He wrote, "It appears that there has been surprisingly little gossip here about your affairs." Perhaps belying that, a former friend of Julian's recorded in his journal what he had heard. The details, all hearsay, included Julian's intention "to marry Jane Cannon when the divorce is final." "So the rumors," he concluded, "were true after all . . ."[21]

Libby's divorce, which came just two years after Jane's marriage, had added to Joseph's strain. And then his son Grant refused to go on a mission, despite Joseph's urging and contrary to the church's expectation of young men. Telling his father, "This is one of the hardest letters I have ever had to write," Grant declared himself an atheist. (Years later he became a Quaker.)[22]

If Joseph and Mona held out any hope that Julian would convert after marrying Jane, they were disappointed. Julian always remained a convinced nonbeliever. Jane let her ties with the church lapse even before she married, but she maintained warm relations with her immediate family. They had not only supported her steadfastly but had also accepted her husband.

Julian felt welcomed into the Cannon family. Confiding in Joseph a few years later that his own father had "played a very marginal and negative role" in his life, he added, "it is a real satisfaction to have someone I can call 'Dad.'"[23]

After the long and tiring trip from Washington DC Julian decided to put off work for a few days. He still did not feel well, and fieldwork meant more driving, first to the Fort Hall Reservation in Idaho, a long day's journey. Instead, he and Jane settled down to a few days of "loafing," as she recorded. They also visited her relatives. Some of Jane's aunts and uncles lived in the Avenues, while other members of the family were now scattered across the continent and across an ocean: from Berkeley, California, where Grant still lived; to New York City, where Jane's oldest brother worked; to London, where Libby had gone for a long visit with their parents and younger brothers.[24]

In just two years there had been an exodus from Salt Lake City by many of the people in their former social world. Even Julian's ex-wife had left the university, accepting a series of professional positions that finally took her to the East. In the meantime a few new faculty members had arrived, although academic positions remained scarce during these Depression years. The English Department had a young instructor named Wallace Stegner who would teach at his alma mater for a few years before leaving for Harvard University and finally settling at Stanford University. Stegner, later a Pulitzer Prize–winning writer and a respected commentator on western lands, would introduce the arid West to a large audience of readers. His books included one about John Wesley Powell, *Beyond the Hundredth Meridian*, and other classics such as *Mormon Country*.[25]

By the summer of 1936 the worst period of the Depression in Utah had passed, although no one would know that for years. The photographer Dorothea Lange visited the state just three months before Steward arrived and just days after taking what became the iconic photograph of the Great Depression, *Migrant Mother*. The federal government sent her to Utah to document conditions in mining towns. She found poverty and hardship in those remote places although the rate of unemployment in the state had actually fallen, to 10 percent in 1936 after setting a record high of 35 percent in 1932.[26]

Foreclosures had reached a crisis point in the same period in the early 1930s. During Steward's last term at the university, in 1933, a riot broke out in Salt Lake City when people tried to stop the sale of property confiscated by the county for tax delinquency. Police used clubs and tear gas to try to disperse the crowd. Then the sheriff called out the city's firefighters to turn a fire hose on protesters. The story headlined in newspapers from coast to coast.[27]

Three years later, when Julian and Jane left Salt Lake City for field-work, Utah's largest city was calm but simmering in the fierce July heat. Temperatures reached record-setting highs that summer, a product of drought and dust bowl conditions. In a time before air conditioners and evaporative coolers, driving up into the nearby mountains still offered the best relief from the daily heat. Some residents of the city owned small plots of land in Emigration Canyon, where higher elevation brought lower temperatures. They stayed in small cottages or camped out during part of the summer or spent time at Pinecrest, a small resort. Most people remained at home in the city, where they looked for shade or sat near a fan and waited for nightfall.

Steward well remembered the rugged canyons near the city, a solace to anyone who, like him, preferred open space to any cityscape. A few months after leaving the University of Utah, he remarked in a letter to a colleague, "perhaps you are keeping cool in one of those beautiful canyons." "There," he added with feeling, "is something I hated to leave!" In some of the canyons, even in midsummer, small patches of snow hid in high rocky crevices; and tall spruces circled alpine meadows, dark shapes looming against the bright emerald green. Those images lingered.[28]

But now, with no time for excursions and no spare money for a room at a mountain resort, Julian and Jane set out for the field. On the first day they drove just thirty-five miles north to Ogden. With a population of forty thousand, it qualified as the most cosmopolitan city in Utah. The transcontinental railroad passed through Ogden, carrying passengers east and west. It had brought small numbers of African Americans and immigrants—Chinese, Italians, Greeks, and Mexicans, among others—to live and work there. Unlike many places in Utah in the 1930s, the population was mainly but not entirely white.

Ogden was also known for its notorious Twenty-fifth Street, near the Union Pacific Railroad station, where many things were for sale with no questions asked. A former New Yorker who worked there a few years later recalled, "At that time you could do anything on Twenty-fifth Street that you did in New York City. Anything. It was a pretty rough street." Just blocks away stood neat houses and churches and a park.[29]

Intending to stay in Ogden for only a day or two, Julian and Jane stopped to see one of his old friends, Maurice Howe, and his wife, Lucie. They lived in a two-story brick house on a quiet street near downtown and within view of the Wasatch Mountains. Julian and Maurice had trekked across the red rock country of southern Utah in the early 1930s. More recently Maurice, a staff writer for the *Ogden Standard Examiner,* had been appointed director of the Federal Writers' Project in Utah. It was a new work-relief program, part of the Works Progress Administration. Julian agreed to serve as a consultant for one of the projects, a guide to Utah compiled by a team of writers. The book, published five years later, listed "Dr. Julian H. Steward, Bureau of American Ethnology, Washington DC" as one of the scientists and other experts consulted.[30]

In Ogden Jane and Julian consulted a physician, Dr. Maximillian Seidner. Jane, who reported feeling well in the early stages of pregnancy, was in good health according to Dr. Seidner. But Julian had

20. Sun Dance, Fort Hall Reservation, July 1936. (Photo by Julian H. Steward, courtesy of University of Illinois Archives)

an appendectomy a week later, then rested for two weeks. "Convalesced at Mrs. Howe's pleasantly," Jane recorded. There she and Julian weathered Utah's hottest month in some comfort, despite the record-breaking heat.[31]

In late July they finally said good-bye to their friends. Driving through the shaded streets of Ogden, they passed rows of neat bungalows bordered by green lawns and gardens. On the outskirts of the city, farm fields and pastures spread out in the distance. Then the terrain abruptly took on the familiar look of high desert, with patches of pale silver-green sagebrush strewn across a brown land.[32]

They drove sixty-five miles north to the Utah-Idaho border and continued on to Pocatello, a small city in southeastern Idaho. Julian planned to begin work at the nearby Fort Hall Reservation, but they found the annual Sun Dance in progress. He had no real interest in the ceremony, which was new to Fort Hall. And in any case another anthropologist, who had preceded him two years earlier at Fort Hall, had recently described it in print.[33]

After watching casually and taking some photographs, he and Jane returned to Ogden because he felt ill and had no appetite. He consulted Dr. Seidner again, "who assured him he was okay," Jane noted. She observed that his appetite had begun to improve and he was gaining weight.

"Was it couvade?" she teased, showing off her new knowledge of anthropology. The term *couvade*, as she had recently learned, referred to practices by men that simulate their wives' experiences of pregnancy or childbirth. Anthropologists found it in remote places, mostly among people she had never heard of and never expected to meet. The vocabulary of anthropology had a new relevance to her own life, but fieldwork had lost its novelty and adventure.[34]

Their travels that summer, unlike those of the previous one in California and Nevada, took her back to known, and even tiresomely familiar, places and landscapes in Utah. They drove on paved roads, past fenced fields, and through sleepy hamlets. The long days spent listening to questions and answers—first in English, and then in translation in Shoshone or Bannock, and back again—added to the tedium. Her journal entries for the summer dwindled to a few desultory sentences, mostly about personal matters. These ranged from Julian's health to the approaching birth of their first child and their living arrangements in the fall.

Jane and Julian left Ogden at the beginning of August and returned to Idaho, traveling one hundred and thirty miles to Pocatello. The Sun Dance had ended, and Julian found so many willing and knowledgeable informants at the Fort Hall Reservation that they stayed in Idaho for the next five weeks. As he later reported to Matt Stirling, he had unexpectedly discovered "a mine of information" at Fort Hall.[35]

Generous funding for the summer's work—from the BIA, the BAE, and Kroeber—along with more than a month of hospitality in Salt Lake City and Ogden, meant that they did not have to camp at Fort Hall as an economy measure. The proximity of a city also removed any need for roughing it. Jane, now five months pregnant, gladly renounced bedroll and tent. They rented an auto cabin in Pocatello, just ten miles from the Fort Hall Reservation, and drove back and forth each day. Pocatello, unlike the reservation, offered all of the amenities that defined modern life for them: restaurants and stores, motion picture theaters and newspapers, auto camps and hotels—to say nothing of electricity and plumbing.

Due to the vagaries of history the Fort Hall Reservation bore the name of a wealthy Bostonian, Henry Hall, who never set foot in the West. He helped to finance the trip that led to the building of an early trading post, and then a fort, by the banks of the twisting Snake River. The trading post later prospered as a supply station on the Oregon Trail. Over the years a steady stream of wagon trains on their way west to Oregon stopped at the trading post to buy provisions.[36]

The city of Pocatello, in contrast, a largely white community and county seat, took the name of a leader of Northwestern Shoshones, Chief Pocatello. At the Fort Hall Reservation he was remembered for resisting the entry of Americans into Shoshone country. Elsewhere, many remembered him as an Indian leader who finally surrendered peacefully and was friendly to whites.[37]

The settlement that bore Pocatello's name began as a railway junction on reservation land that was ceded to the Union Pacific Railroad. It grew slowly until the turn of the twentieth century, when the government opened so-called surplus lands of the Fort Hall Reservation for settlement. Pocatello grew quickly as settlers poured in, and it soon reached the size of a small city.[38]

The reservation had a far smaller population, just eighteen hundred people. Unlike the nearby and newly arrived settlers, some of the reservation's residents did not live there voluntarily and did not regard it as home. They came from an immense area, divided by borders recently drawn and called by new names, taken from Numic languages or Spanish or unknown in origin: Utah, Nevada, and Idaho.[39]

21. Adolph Pavitse, August 1936. (Photo by Julian H. Steward, courtesy of University of Illinois Archives)

At Fort Hall Steward hired a young Shoshone man to serve as his interpreter. Adolph Pavitse appeared for work early in the morning, in the cool hours before the sun launched its daily assault. He wore a cardigan sweater, a shirt, and dress pants with a leather belt. His black hair, cut short in barbershop style, was trimmed well above his ears.

Pavitse, who was twenty-seven years old and unmarried, spoke English fluently. He had attended the Carlisle Indian Industrial School in Pennsylvania. Steward's memories of his excellent interpreter at the Duck Valley Reservation, Tom Premo, who had attended the same school, may have led him to seek out Pavitse.[40]

They set to work with a Northern Shoshone elder, James Pegoga. Then in his early eighties, and long married to his wife, Lucy, who was in her seventies, Pegoga had lived at Fort Hall for thirty years. Like many of the people on the reservation, he and his family came from a different and distant place. His homeland lay hundreds of miles north.[41]

James and Lucy Pegoga had once lived at a smaller reservation located in the Lemhi Valley, south of the Salmon River and west of the Bitterroot Range. They raised children there and left that home in their beloved green valley only because the reservation closed in 1907, opening the land for homesteading by non-Indians. Along with more than four hundred other people, James and Lucy Pegoga walked south to the Fort Hall Reservation, nearly two hundred miles away. Three young daughters—Julia, Cora, and baby Martha—made the long journey with their parents.

Cora later told her own daughter what she remembered of the forced march to Fort Hall. A woman went into labor during their journey, she said, and bled to death. This happened somewhere along the Big Lost River. The body was wrapped in a blanket, put on the back of a horse, and taken away for burial by the men. Then the long journey south continued.[42]

The Lemhi Shoshones did not go willingly to the Fort Hall Reservation. They went peacefully but not quietly; ranchers could hear them weeping as they left their home in the Lemhi Valley and walked south to an arid and alien place.[43] It bore no resemblance to their homeland in the Salmon River country, a sheltered valley blessed with the flowing water of the Lemhi River. American settlers had begun to move into the valley in the mid-nineteenth century. By the early twentieth century they occupied nearly all of the land, including what had once been the Lemhi Reservation.

Because of Steward's interest in the time before contact and American settlement, this part of his informant's life story—and the valley's recent history—seemed beside the point. He wanted to learn about how they had lived in the distant past. He would say almost nothing in his book about how political events of the nineteenth and early twentieth centuries, including loss of their lands, had affected Northern Shoshones, or how they had adapted to the change.[44]

Pegoga told Steward that he had once lived in the mountains above the Lemhi Valley. During his boyhood in the 1850s and 1860s, people still lived there in small and isolated villages, although far more lived in larger groups along the Lemhi River. The mountain people were known by a name that meant Sheep Eaters, and the valley people by a name meaning Salmon Eaters. Lewis and Clark's Corps of Discovery visited the valley in 1805, fifty years before Pegoga's birth. Steward drew on their journals and the records of other explorers, along with what Pegoga told him, to reconstruct a way of life that had vanished from the valley after conquest in the nineteenth century.

Since he had read the journals of Lewis and Clark, Steward probably knew that Sacajawea was a Salmon Eater. Ignored by generations of historians, by the late twentieth century she would occupy a place in national memory as a member of the Lewis and Clark Expedition. With her help they reached the Lemhi Valley and got the horses and food that they needed in order to continue travel and exploration. These events, and her role in them, had no direct bearing on Steward's interests, and he made no mention of them.[45]

He spent at least a full week questioning Pegoga, one of his longest spells with any one elder. Besides compiling a lengthy trait list for Kroeber, he asked questions about ecology and band structure. This resulted in one of the most detailed accounts of a specific place and people in *Basin-Plateau*, virtually all of it provided by Pegoga. As Steward soon saw, and later said in print, the contrasts between Shoshones who lived in the mountains and those in the valleys held "great importance" for his ecological study. Although near neighbors, they had lived in very different environments—and that explained why, he believed, they had lived in such different ways.[46] Each had adapted to a specific place and set of environmental conditions. His thinking ran counter to that of the time. According to the tenets of diffusionist theory, proximity and contact produced cultural similarity.

Pegoga told Steward that people in the mountains had gathered seeds and roots, fished for salmon, and hunted deer and mountain sheep: hence their name, Sheep Eaters. Pronghorn antelope, he said, were always scarce, and there were no bison. Steward concluded that their way of life, if austere, had allowed them to avoid nearly all contact with "the white man." He used the common term of the day. Singular and generic, it obscured the array of explorers, trappers, soldiers, merchants, miners, farmers, ranchers, Mormon missionaries, and other settlers who had flooded into the Lemhi Valley in the nineteenth century. The valley's name came from the Book of Mormon.[47]

The Sheep Eaters' isolation meant that their old way of life continued long into the nineteenth century, increasing both their importance and the value of Pegoga's memories for Steward. The men in Lewis and Clark's Corps of Discovery, and many of the Americans who followed, saw only the Salmon Eaters, the people of the valley. The Sheep Eaters, Pegoga said, did finally move down to the Lemhi Valley because of the promise of rations.[48] They had long experience in surviving seasonal shortages of food, suggesting that they may have needed rations because ecological changes in the valley affected their supply of food as well.

Unlike their mountain neighbors and most of the people who lived in the Great Basin, sometime in the eighteenth century the Salmon Eaters in the Lemhi Valley acquired horses. If salmon had once sustained them, as implied by their name, they increasingly depended on bison. Ranging widely on horseback in search of food, they rode south and east to hunt bison. They went to the Snake River and to the nearby Salmon River and its tributaries to take salmon, other fish, and lampreys. They traveled west to Camas Prairie to trade hides and also to collect seeds and roots to preserve and store for the long winter.

Camas Prairie, treated as a common by native people, covered a sprawling plateau surrounded by mountains and rugged canyons. It was home to vast stands of camas, a lily with vivid blue flowers and a sweet-tasting bulb. When the camas bloomed, an annual spectacle, the prairie appeared from a distance as a shining blue lake. After wading among the lilies to harvest the bulbs, women roasted them and then ground the roasted bulbs into flour. This vital staple helped sustain their families during the winter. (Later, when American settlers brought herds of livestock to the prairie, the animals ate the camas, destroying an ancient and reliable source of food for native people. This triggered a war between settlers and Indians. Farmers eventually destroyed most of the camas fields by planting wheat and other crops.)[49]

After bison were hunted to extinction in the south—by 1840, Steward said, drawing on explorer John C. Frémont's account of his journeys—families who wanted to hunt bison had to cross the steep Bitterroot Mountains to the east. Entering Crow territory, they put themselves at risk of attack, especially by roving parties of Blackfeet and others. Those very circumstances had led to Sacajawea's capture in the 1790s by Hidatsa raiders and her eventual meeting, years later and far east of her homeland, with Lewis and Clark.[50]

The Salmon Eaters took fast horses to ride while running down the bison, and they followed the herds all summer. In the fall the families returned to the Lemhi Valley carrying hides, some meant for trade, as well as dried meat to eat during the winter. They lived on the stored seeds and roots and meat, along with the meat of any deer or pronghorn antelope they killed.[51] Pegoga gave Steward long lists of the names of plants and animals that provided food, such as *winigo* and *payump*. Pavitse could not always provide English names.

Pegoga also told Steward where people had once lived in the valley and mountains and how many people had lived in each place. By Steward's calculations, before American settlement some two hundred families, or twelve hundred people, had lived in an area of about twenty-seven thousand square miles. This suggested a very low population density like that of most areas to the south, in the Great Basin: about one person for every twenty-two square miles.

The Lemhi Valley had a lush look in spring and summer, especially along the narrow river. But Steward concluded that it could not support the far higher population densities that he had discovered in the more fertile Owens Valley in California and Ruby Valley in Nevada. Despite the river and streams and stands of green trees, what Pegoga told him about the people and the place suggested a limited supply of wild game and edible plants. Pegoga's memories of that northern land spanned fifty years. Even in the best of times, Steward later wrote, "foods were not plentiful."[52]

Unlike the Sheep Eaters, who lived in the protective isolation of the mountains and without need of strong leaders, the Salmon Eaters in the valley had to contend with raids by enemies, especially by Blackfeet. In 1805, when Lewis and Clark visited, they learned of several leaders, and they noted that every man kept a horse picketed at night. Later in the nineteenth century the people of the Lemhi Valley united under one leader, Chief Tendoy, to fight against enemies. Steward eventually decided that they had formed "a loose band" and sometimes went to war under the leadership of "a true chief." Warfare, he suggested, had the important effect of unifying them. The Salmon Eaters of Lemhi Valley did not, however, constitute a patrilineal band. He found no evidence of patrilineal kinship or the other identifying traits.[53]

During their five weeks in Idaho, Julian and Jane also spent time on the road, crisscrossing the area while Julian looked for surface sites. He found the site of an old winter village near American Falls, about twenty miles from the reservation. From the outset of fieldwork he had tried to locate old camps and villages, guided by U.S. Geological Survey maps and by landmarks that elders recalled. Instead of depending solely on what informants told him, he preferred to observe the old habitation sites directly if they were easily accessible.

As he had learned of each one, he had added it to a map. He also included "subsistence areas," indicating the places where people foraged for seeds, pine nuts, or other foods. Six densely drawn maps, based on his own observations and the memories of dozens of Paiute and Shoshone elders, later appeared in *Basin-Plateau*. American Falls and the nearby site of a winter village appeared on his map of Idaho.[54]

He could easily see that southeastern Idaho, like the land just across the border in northeastern Utah, formed an extension of the Great Basin. Arid, flat, and covered with sagebrush, it stretched out for miles in every direction, with only an occasional range of low mountains rising along the distant horizon. The land to the north—the Lemhi Shoshones' homeland in central Idaho—belonged to a different natural region, the Columbia Plateau. Water from the Lemhi and Salmon rivers flowed into the Snake River and finally reached the Columbia River. Steward had spent time ten years earlier, as a graduate student, working at an archaeological site on that river, along the Oregon-Washington border. He recalled its breadth as well as the high winds that whipped up waves as the water coursed swiftly toward its final destination, the Pacific Ocean.[55]

The land west of Fort Hall—that is, south-central and southwestern Idaho—also formed part of the Columbia Plateau. He and Jane had driven across it during the previous summer on their trip to Pendleton, Oregon. As he would learn from elders at Fort Hall, people near the borders of the Basin and Plateau had moved back and forth in search of food, trade goods, even husbands and wives.[56]

Steward's search for the patrilineal band had led him also from the Basin to the Plateau. So had his goal of including all Shoshones of those regions, no matter how far flung, in his ambitious ecological study. As he now knew from experience, not just from studying books and maps, the Shoshone homelands covered an immense area: east from Death Valley in California, across much of Nevada and Utah, and north to Idaho and even Wyoming.

While he found no evidence of the patrilineal band among Northern Shoshones, he did discover something else of note. The horse was a food-getting tool in one environment and a resource—that is, food—in another. As he later wrote, the horse "revolutionized" the Northern Shoshone economy "by making it possible to use new methods of hunting." This yielded more food and hides and allowed people to live in larger groups. In contrast, Shoshones who lived in the most arid part of the Great Basin regarded horses as food. In such places without large game animals, horses offered no help in hunting, and they grazed on grasses that women harvested for seeds.

In the framework of cultural ecology, which Steward was beginning to develop, people adapted differently to environments with and without large game. They treated horses as technology in the former environment and as a resource in the latter. He thought that using horses as a food-getting tool had brought about many changes, from how labor was organized to the size of groups. Steward's comments on the horse foreshadowed one of the core ideas of cultural ecology as a theory: that the interplay of technology, natural resources, and labor shapes social and political structures—and shapes the course of cultural change.[57]

As he had learned from elders, the people known to outsiders as the horse Shoshone, or mounted Shoshone, had lived in a way that differed from that of the so-called foot Shoshone of the Great Basin.

In Steward's view these cultural differences resulted from adapting to different environments—not from, say, the diffusion of varied cultural traits from other places. Shoshones shared ancestry, but over time they had diverged culturally as they adapted to local environments of the Basin and Plateau.

In the meantime, as Steward drove across the Fort Hall reservation he saw that some people still kept horses. Years earlier, cars and trucks had also found a home on the range, on reservations as well as on ranches. People from Fort Hall drove to other parts of Idaho and to northern Utah to seek seasonal work in farm fields and to visit family and friends on other reservations.[58]

Five other elders—two women Steward never named, and three men—served as cultural informants during the following weeks at Fort Hall. Steward worked intensively with the men and paid them the standard informant fees. The youngest, Silver Ballard, was in his midsixties. He was a Shoshone from the Fort Hall region. Steward spent about a week with him, again with the able assistance of Adolph Pavitse.[59] Ballard and a Bannock elder named Whitehorse, who came from the same area, provided much of what Steward learned about the people who had lived in that part of the Snake River country before the Fort Hall Reservation was established in the 1860s.[60]

Whitehorse was in his midseventies and a widower according to the census. Steward estimated his age at eighty-four and said Whitehorse "claimed to have been a young man when the Fort Hall agency was founded in 1862." The word "claimed" suggested some doubt about this. If Whitehorse was in fact a young man in 1862, the estimated age of eighty-four made sense. But if census takers were correct, Whitehorse was only about two years old at that time.

There was also some confusion about whether he was a widower, as stated in the census, or married. Steward mentioned, without naming, two women whom he identified as Whitehorse's wife and his sister-in-law. The sister-in-law served as a cultural informant, along with White-horse, when he recorded a trait list. Whitehorse's wife, a Shoshone from the Snake River country in western Idaho, told him what she knew about an antelope hunt. The details came from her grandfather, an antelope shaman of long ago, and another ghost informant.

Despite confusion about some details of Whitehorse's personal identity, he proved to be an excellent informant. Steward spent about a week questioning him, assisted by Adolph Pavitse as interpreter. They worked at Whitehorse's camp. Steward saw that two tents standing near some small trees served as shelter during the hot months. With the flaps pulled up during the day, the tents were open to the breeze; and at night, even with the flaps pulled down, they were cooler than a log house—or a stuffy auto cabin, for that matter.[61]

Whitehorse told a story that Steward had already heard from Western Shoshone elder Tom Horn in Fallon, Nevada; but this telling featured a sinister twist. It seems that a man who wanted to capture some young eagles for their feathers needed help climbing down the cliffs to a nest. A friend went with him and held a rope while he descended. Then he removed the rope and went away, planning to take the man's widow as his wife. The stranded husband survived by eating food brought to the nest for the young eagles. Finally, when they were full grown, he took hold of their legs, and they flew him from the nest to the ground.[62]

The story ended there, with nothing more said about the treacherous friend and what he should or should not have done, or about revenge. Survival seemed to be the point. The act of betrayal was treated as a precipitating circumstance, an unexpected event. In his encounter with the unexpected—call it life, or the world—the man was resourceful. He survived by using his wits, Coyote-like.

Whitehorse thought that his people, the Northern Paiute–speaking Bannock, had come from the west, but he did not know when they had arrived around Fort Hall. Steward recorded a short vocabulary, which convinced him that Bannocks and Northern Paiutes had once formed a single group. He eventually concluded that Bannocks had lived in the Fort Hall region "since prehistoric times" and before acquiring horses. Beyond a difference in language, he found little that culturally distinguished Bannocks from Shoshones around Fort Hall. As he learned from Whitehorse and Silver Ballard, their people had a history of close contact. They made joint hunting and fishing expeditions on horseback, spent winters together, and took their horses to lush pastures around the Snake River.[63]

Like the Salmon Eaters or Northern Shoshones of the Lemhi Valley, the Bannocks and Shoshones who lived in country around Fort Hall hunted bison and traveled west to Camas Prairie to trade and to collect roots and seeds. Whitehorse named some of the plants, including camas, the most important. *Kuiyu* was called tobacco root in English. Others, such as *pasiago* and *yamp*, did not have English names. He remembered that a few families stayed around Camas Prairie all summer, but that most headed east in late summer to hunt bison.[64]

Until the mid-1830s they hunted in the Snake River region where Fort Hall was built. But by 1840 bison had vanished from all of the country that one day would fall within the borders of Idaho. They had disappeared even earlier from lands to the south that came to comprise northern Utah. "No doubt the sage-covered plains were not their optimum environment," Steward later wrote, "so that the arrival of trappers and the acquisition of fire arms and horses by Indians was sufficient to exterminate them." Trappers had begun streaming into the area in the 1820s, hoping to grow wealthy by selling beaver pelts. They also hunted bison, a major source of their own food; and their hunting reduced the number of elk, moose, and deer.[65]

After 1840, and perhaps earlier, Steward said, Bannocks and Northern Shoshones from around Fort Hall made long trips across the Rocky Mountains to the high plains to hunt bison. Sometimes they went in company with Flatheads, Nez Perces, and Northern Shoshones from the Lemhi Valley and elsewhere. Acquiring horses not only permitted these long journeys in search of food but also changed the politics of the Bannocks' and Shoshones' world. Their horses attracted the unwelcome attention of enemies who lived east of the Rocky Mountains. When they traveled, safety depended on moving in large and organized groups.

Gradually, scattered families and villages began to form a band, Steward suggested. Warfare encouraged "band solidarity," he wrote. Still, judging from what Whitehorse and Ballard told him, it seemed that "the Shoshoni-Bannock band" of the Fort Hall region never achieved great unity. "A larger band afforded greater security against the predatory Blackfeet," he explained, but leadership remained rather decentralized.

Even after Fort Hall became the main winter headquarters, small groups with different leaders often left on their own quests for food or on other ventures. Political leadership was never so centralized that all members of the band could be forced to act together, as a unit. In fact, as Whitehorse and Ballard recalled, the Bannocks and the Shoshones of Fort Hall each had a leader, although the two men sometimes cooperated.[66]

The two elders agreed that the leaders had little importance or influence until sometime after bison became extinct. When problems arose with "the white man," especially about land, band chiefs and councils grew more important. Older men formed a council, which advised the chief. But as Steward learned, councils had no special name, and anyone could attend the meetings. A general social equality prevailed, as throughout most of the Great Basin.

Despite their close association and many similarities, Bannocks differed from Shoshones in carrying out frequent raids against whites. Whitehorse recalled the names of several Bannock leaders, including a band chief and a war chief during the time when he was young. Ballard said that his father, Jimmy, had represented Fort Hall Shoshones in dealings with whites. Jim Ballard, also known as Sheme, strongly opposed land allotment and any further ceding of reservation land.[67]

Born in 1873, Silver Ballard had no firsthand knowledge, no personal memories, of life before the reservation. His father, who was probably born in the 1840s, may have served as a ghost informant for those earlier times. But Silver Ballard had witnessed the transformation of the land, and of the way of life of his people, after large-scale settlement. Fences, roads, and railroad tracks soon divided what had once been open country.

The Sun Dance ceremony, which Steward had glimpsed a month earlier at Fort Hall, was new to the reservation according to Ballard. It originated among Plains Indians to the east, and he dated its introduction at Fort Hall to about 1900. Because it did not date back to the time before settlement, and because Steward had no real interest in religion and ceremony, he said little about it in print. Limiting his comments to a sentence or two, he noted that another anthropologist had mistakenly said that the Sun Dance was old at Fort Hall.[68]

His interpreter was too young to remember a time without the annual Sun Dance. Born in about 1909, Adolph Pavitse lived in a world far different from the one that the elders recalled. He belonged to the twentieth century: to a world in which the reservation held less than half of its original territory and only a fraction of the land his ancestors once occupied; to a world in which he and his people belonged to a small ethnic minority. They lived on a virtual island, surrounded by people from all parts of the United States and beyond who had settled on the Snake River plain, as farmers and ranchers and city-dwellers.

Evenings in Pocatello: heat ebbed, night fell, and lights blinked on across the small city. Inside their small housekeeping cabin at an auto camp, Jane and Julian ate a simple dinner. Then Julian worked on his notes and the trait lists, caught up on correspondence, or read. Jane helped as needed, typing the lists or assisting in other ways. The grinding labor of producing the trait lists—from long hours of questioning and listening to elders to time spent in transcribing notes and typing—seemed to have no end. Sometimes she took a break and used the typewriter to write a letter to her parents.

One night as they were reading, Jane reported to her father, a man knocked on the door of their cabin and invited them to "a Mormon meeting" held on the lawn. "A quartet sang two numbers, they had two speakers, prayers," she said, "and the whole group sang 'We Thank Thee O God for a Prophet' and then went away." She did not tell her father, who was busy overseeing missionaries in England, that this was her closest brush with organized religion since leaving Utah four years earlier.[69]

Jane typed long letters to her family, and Julian sent short dispatches about fieldwork to colleagues. To Kroeber he mentioned learning about a recent predecessor at the Fort Hall Reservation. E. Adamson Hoebel, the anthropologist who mistook the Sun Dance for an old ceremony at Fort Hall, had spent a summer doing fieldwork there two years earlier. "Which made me wish there were some way of getting out a[n] annual list of field work done & field work planned," Julian remarked, "so that people's trails would not cross so often."

Like explorers, and perhaps most anthropologists, his goal was discovery and staking a claim of priority. He always aimed to enter new territory in his research, to go there first—hence his idea, which he told Kroeber, of publishing an annual list of fieldwork in the *American Anthropologist*. "I think I'll mention it to Leslie," he added. Leslie Spier served as editor in 1936.[70]

Julian and Jane traveled back and forth each day across cultural boundaries and, by means of Julian's questions and the elders' memories, across time. But back in Pocatello at the end of the day, they entered a completely Anglo-American space and gave their attention to life in present tense. The concerns of that life ranged from professional issues to housekeeping matters to current events.

With access to newspapers and magazines, they followed the national and international news. During those first weeks of August 1936, the Summer Olympics, held in Berlin, garnered front-page stories in newspapers as well as airtime on the radio. As Julian later told a BAE colleague who attended the Games, he and Jane had followed the coverage as best they could during fieldwork.

Hitler wanted to showcase Aryan racial superiority to a world audience, and he hoped that German athletes would dominate the Berlin Games. Instead, an African American track star from Ohio, Jesse Owens, captured world attention. He set new records and won four gold medals.[71]

During his last days at the Fort Hall Reservation, Steward worked with an elder called Grouse Creek Jack, his oldest informant. Jack had a weathered face framed by a shock of white hair. His English first name came from a name given to his distant birthplace, Grouse Creek, in northwestern Utah. The state boundary that eventually divided Utah and Nevada, years after his birth, lay a few miles to the west.

Jack was probably born about 1840, before any border of a western state was drawn. Steward thought he might be a centenarian, noting his claim to be 105 years old. Census takers put his age at ninety-five. Lacking any birth records, that too was a guess.[72]

Whatever his birth date and birth name, Grouse Creek Jack, like many Shoshones and Paiutes, adopted or accepted an English name for his dealings with white settlers, employers, and census takers. He was also known as Pugahjunip Jack. He was still a child when the first Mormons reached Salt Lake Valley in the late 1840s. Mormon ranchers settled around Grouse Creek in the 1870s, displacing any Shoshones who had remained there. As a young man Jack met Brigham Young. Along with some other Shoshones he was baptized as a Mormon.[73]

22. Grouse Creek Jack and his wife, August 1936. (Photo by Julian H. Steward, courtesy of University of Illinois Archives)

After his first wife died at a young age, Jack married her sister. The sororate was customary. The name of his second wife appeared in early records as Angapompy, translated as Red Hair. She and Jack had several children. The family moved often, living in various places in Utah, including Salt Lake City, and shifting from one reservation to another in Idaho and Utah.

For most of his adult life, Jack worked as a laborer. He helped to build the Mormon temple in Logan, Utah, in the late 1870s and early 1880s. As late as the 1920s, when he was in his eighties or perhaps ninety, he had the vigor to hunt and trap animals. Along with one or two of his sons, he sometimes traveled to country he had known as a child, to hunt or trap or collect pine nuts.[74]

In the mid-1930s when Steward met him, he still lived with his second wife, named in some records only as Mrs. Grouse Creek Jack and in others as Jennie Angapomba Jack. Steward took a photograph of the couple seated on the ground under a shelter, their backs to the camera.[75]

Steward spent four days with Jack, asking him questions about how his people had lived in Grouse Creek country. He had little need of an interpreter's help. "In spite of his age, his mind was alert," Steward remarked. His English, he added, was "adequate."[76]

Jack told him that the Shoshones who lived around Grouse Creek were called Pine-nut Eaters. They occupied the northernmost part of the pine nut belt, while near neighbors to the north lived beyond it. About two hundred people lived in Grouse Creek country, finding their food in an area of some 4,700 square miles. The low population density resembled that of many parts of the Great Basin, with about one person for every twenty-three square miles.[77]

The man who became the most famous native of that region, Chief Pocatello, was the son of a woman from Grouse Creek. He had once been a leader of families who lived to the east. He later became leader of the Bannock Creek Shoshones, or Jackrabbit Eaters as they were sometimes called, to the north. Many elders at the Fort Hall Reservation had firsthand memories of him since he had died just fifty years earlier, while living there. Jack was already middle-aged at the time.[78]

Jack's father, a contemporary of Chief Pocatello, came from a distant place to the west. His people were known as Groundhog Eaters and lived around the Boise River, a tributary of the Snake River, in the plateau region that eventually became southwestern Idaho. But families who traveled south in search of pine nuts took the name of Pine-nut Eaters. Jack's father took that name as well when he married a woman from Grouse Creek and remained there. Steward worked long hours with Jack on a census and learned that, like Jack's father, some of the other people of Grouse Creek had moved in, or moved away, in order to marry.[79]

By the time Steward met him in 1936, Jack lived far from home, but not because of marriage. Like many of his people he and his wife had moved to the reservation as exiles from Grouse Creek country. They joined Bannock Creek Shoshones who occupied Bannock Creek Valley, about twenty miles west of Pocatello in an isolated corner of the Fort Hall Reservation. Steward learned that Bannock Creek Shoshones had occupied territory that extended from the creek and valley to the northern shore of the Great Salt Lake, hundreds of miles to the south.

The people of this great region eventually came to form one band under Chief Pocatello, although they did not always live together. During summer they usually scattered widely, with small groups of families heading in different directions, and on foot. Some went eastward to the Malad River, a tributary of the Snake River, or further east to Bear Lake. Others went west, following the Snake River to a point "beyond Twin Falls," Steward recorded, "perhaps to Camas Prairie."

After acquiring horses they came into conflict with the wagon trains traveling west on the California Trail. The trail crossed their territory, and the steady stream of travelers with grazing livestock damaged their hunting and gathering grounds. Steward thought that during this period Chief Pocatello's influence came to extend over the entire territory of the Jackrabbit Eaters and beyond, to the west. "These people were eventually admitted to the Fort Hall Reservation," he later wrote, "where Pocatello seems to have been a personality of some importance."[80]

The bland wording overlooked a complex process of change, environmental and political. The degradation and loss of their land led to the exile of Grouse Creek Jack and his family. Along with most of the Pine-nut Eaters, they left their ancestral territory. By the 1930s virtually no Indians remained as full-time residents in Grouse Creek country. Its population was almost exclusively white and Mormon. The land claimed by ranchers (call them the Beef Eaters) had once been Shoshone hunting and gathering grounds. The effects of livestock grazing—first by the animals that overlanders brought through, and then by herds that ranchers brought in—had long ago made it impossible for Shoshones to live as foragers. Edible wild plants declined, as did game animals due to habitat loss.[81]

Steward spent three days working with Jack on a trait list, just half the time he had spent with Whitehorse and his sister-in-law. He hurried to finish it, anxious to move on to five more field sites in the short time that remained. All of the sites were in Utah, but they were separated by hundreds of miles.

When Steward left the Fort Hall Reservation in early September he had the name of a man who, like Jack, remembered the time before American settlement. He was still alive ninety years later—and despite a smallpox epidemic that reportedly swept through Washakie, his community in northern Utah, that summer of 1936. Steward decided to bypass him for the moment, head farther south in Utah, and return when the smallpox had completely abated.[82]

8. Land of the Utes

ON THEIR RETURN to Utah Julian and Jane stopped briefly in Ogden to see their friends, the Howes. The next day they left Salt Lake City and drove due south, skirting the base of the Wasatch Mountains as they entered Utah Valley, passed Provo, and headed for the Kanosh Reservation where some Pahvant Utes lived. It was an easy day's journey over paved roads and through the heart of Mormon country.

They drove through a landscape of memories. Jane had attended college in Provo, briefly and unhappily, in the late 1920s. She had already studied for two years at the University of Utah in Salt Lake City—a public university that her father considered "too worldly"—when he enrolled her at Brigham Young University in Provo. He hoped that she would meet, and marry, a young Mormon man who had completed a mission for the church. There were many candidates at BYU, a Mormon institution; but Jane found Provo "too provincial," and she did not share her father's vision for her life. The onset of the Great Depression gave her a good reason to withdraw from college and look for paying work in Salt Lake City.[1]

Julian had different memories of the area around Provo, the most recent, of skiing in Provo Canyon five years earlier. He and his first wife had gone there with one of their students, Kilton Stewart. Kilton's younger brother, Omer, had also been one of Julian's students at the University of Utah. Omer began graduate study in anthropology a few years later at Berkeley, where he worked closely with Kroeber. During that very summer, in 1936, he was in Nevada working with Northern Paiutes on trait lists.[2]

Kilton and Omer had spent summers during childhood at a homestead ranch in Provo Canyon. The Stewart family still owned the property, but they were not living there when Julian visited. More than twenty feet of snow usually fell in the canyon each year, and that one proved no exception. The snow lay so deep that Julian and his companions entered the family's house through a second-story window, skiing directly up to it.[3]

Now, in early September, as he drove past Mount Timpanogos, which loomed above Provo Canyon, he could see no sign of white, not even on the crest of the mountain. The last traces had vanished in the melting heat of summer, and the first snows had yet to fall. The mountain, one of Utah's most famous landmarks, attracted many summer visitors, drawn there by glacier lakes and waterfalls and fields of wildflowers. Stands of the flowers, still in bloom, lingered on the upper slopes, but he and Jane bypassed Mount Timpanogos and a feast of color in the high country.

The Wasatch Range, sentinel of the eastern edge of the Great Basin, held no warm memories, unlike the Sierra Nevada of the western edge. His three years in Utah were marred by what he recalled of an unhappy marriage that suddenly fell apart and threatened to destroy his career. Those years did not compare to the three he remembered from his student days in Deep Springs Valley, near the foot of the Sierra.

Trying to make up for lost time, Steward gave complete attention to the work at hand. His illness and the surgery in July had cost him a full month. Unlike the previous summer, when he had interrupted fieldwork to take a pack trip into the High Sierra with his wife and friends, nothing distracted him now. Excursions and adventures in the wild belonged to the past. The contours of his life had changed in ways that affected fieldwork.

He and Jane felt pressed for time because, strictly speaking, he was on assignment for the BIA—and he had not yet begun that work. Jane planned to leave Utah in just three weeks, and the idea of remaining in the West for a month or two after she left held no appeal. He no longer had the freedom to spend as much time as he wished following his own interests in the field, in company with Jane, for as long as the meager funds permitted. He had traded independence, and an utter lack of security, for assignments, schedules, deadlines—as well as a regular paycheck and impending parenthood.

The physical challenges of outdoor adventure—and fieldwork—had also grown more daunting in just one year. Months of stress, heavy smoking, and work at a desk in Washington had left him feeling sick and tired. Having to cover so much ground in so little time added to the strain. And Jane, who always preferred city sidewalks to mountain trails, and who was in the last trimester of her first pregnancy, did not encourage even a short walk in the wild.

They drove on, through what had once been a valley of the Utes and was now called Utah Valley. The road skirted Utah Lake, where the water glinted silver in the sun. They could see the other shore only as a faint line in the distance. Mount Timpanogos bore the name of a band of Ute Indians who long lived beside the lake, where Spanish explorers met them in the eighteenth century. Early in the nineteenth century, trappers traveling north from Taos entered their territory, including a French Canadian, Etienne Provost. His name later became affixed to a new settlement, Provo, which grew up on the eastern side of the big lake.[4]

Beginning at mid-century Mormon settlers quickly spread out in the fertile areas along the western front of the Wasatch Range, "preempting Indian village sites and food areas," Steward wrote. Brigham Young had almost immediately begun to send colonies of settlers to the fertile valleys north and south of Salt Lake City, wherever rivers and streams allowed irrigation. He created a planned economy and a settlement of a type and on a scale unique in the American West. It would one day bring him a reputation as the preeminent colonizer of that region.[5]

Settlers in valleys to the south not only built villages in the favorable places where Utes lived, close to water. They also took lands where Utes found their food, and removed fish from Utah Lake by the ton. The newcomers' farming, fishing, ranching, and building practices had devastating effects on hunting and gathering grounds in these valleys and the nearby mountains. The Utes, and their lake, bore the brunt of settlement almost immediately.

Utah Lake, which covered one hundred and fifty square miles, was one of the largest bodies of fresh water west of the Mississippi River. Early explorers told of seeing geese, ducks, beavers, and otters, as well as fish so abundant that they could be caught by hand. Soon after settlement, commercial fishing began. Fishermen used nets up to five hundred yards long, harvesting as much as three thousand pounds of trout per haul. Taking water from the lake, and from the rivers that fed the lake, to use for irrigation, destroyed the fragile habitats of wildlife. Most of the native fish were driven to extinction.[6]

Settlers cut down trees to clear fields and pastures and used the wood for building houses and for fuel. They put up fences and laid out roads. They hunted game animals to eat, and they killed other animals that preyed on their livestock or ate their crops. They domesticated Utah Valley and the others, and in the process they destroyed much of the wildlife, both plant and animal. For Utes, this brought about an ecological crisis. Using language that qualified as litany in *Basin-Plateau*, Steward observed that the settlers soon "decimated supplies of native foods" in Ute country.[7]

Grazing livestock, and overgrazing in particular, accounted for some of the most dramatic changes in valley ecology. Sheep and cattle stripped the land of the native plants that Utes ate, as well as plants that sustained many of the animals they hunted. Within thirty years of settlement the number of sheep in Utah Territory reached 230,000, and cattle, 91,000—and those numbers had multiplied many times over by the time Steward began his research in 1936. The number of sheep had peaked at nearly four million in 1900, and then declined. By 1931 more than two million sheep grazed on land in Utah, along with more than 340,000 head of cattle. Sixty percent of Utah's range-land was overgrazed by the millions of sheep and cattle, and it became badly eroded as a result. When rain came, it washed away soil that had lost the anchoring roots of grasses and other plants.[8]

The valleys lining the Wasatch Front, the western face of the Wasatch Mountains, had attracted the earliest and the largest number of settlers in Utah Territory. The region received less than fifteen inches of rainfall a year—more than most areas of the Great Basin, but about five inches short of the minimum for dry land farming. Other water came from snowmelt, which cascaded down the mountains in spring and summer. This gift of water allowed Mormon settlers to practice agriculture as they had in the East and Midwest, with one defining difference: they dug irrigation canals to direct needed water to their fields.[9]

Small villages and towns soon appeared at intervals in the valleys along the entire length of the mountains. Each had a church at the center and streets lined with trees, so often Lombardy poplars that they came to be called "Mormon trees."[10] Fields of grain, fruit orchards, and gardens covered land that just a few generations earlier, and for many generations, had allowed a hunting and gathering way of life. This was the landscape that Julian and Jane saw as they drove south through the valleys of the Utes. Unlike the Owens Valley, where Paiutes had managed to remain in their homeland, Utes had long ago left Utah Valley, forced to move to a distant reservation.

The conversion of the Wasatch valleys to farmland was rapid, and unlike the case of California's Owens Valley, it was lasting. A year earlier, in their first weeks of fieldwork, Jane and Julian had seen that some parts of the Owens Valley had the look of high desert before settlement, although the tall stands of wild grasses had not returned. By 1935 the orchards and fields and pastures that Julian remembered from his student days at Deep Springs had vanished, along with most of the water. The Wasatch valleys, in contrast, kept much of their water; and even during the worst years of the Great Depression and drought, many farmers and ranchers kept their land—sometimes with help from the church and from relief agencies, public and private.[11]

What Steward saw along the Wasatch Front and on maps in 1936 offered slight guidance about the past, from how the land had looked a century earlier to how Utes lived on it. The settlers had not only physically altered the valleys, with fenced fields and villages and irrigation canals and roads. They had also rewritten the landscape, founding settlements with names such as Nephi and Lehi, drawn from the Book of Mormon, and using biblical names for some features of the landscape.[12]

The maps showed Mount Nebo, the southernmost mountain in the Wasatch Range and the tallest at an elevation of almost twelve thousand feet. The Jordan River, as shown on the maps, ran north from Utah Lake, a freshwater lake, to the Great Salt Lake—just as the Jordan River of the Bible ran from the freshwater Sea of Galilee to the saline Dead Sea. Utah's Mount Nebo, like the original, was the highest mountain east of a ribbon of water called the Jordan River.[13]

English names prevailed—American Fork, Fillmore, Beaver—while Ute and Paiute names were rare. A snow-capped range that Utes called by a word meaning White, or White Mountain, recorded by early settlers as Tushar, did keep that name. One of its tallest peaks became Mount Belnap. Some places in Utah—Ogden, Fremont Canyon, Mount Powell—bore the names of nineteenth-century trappers and explorers, or names given by explorers. Others honored church leaders: Brigham City, Heber City, Cannonville. Although Utah Lake, Utah Valley, and the Wasatch Mountains carried names of Ute origin,

Utes themselves had almost vanished from that western part of their homeland.[14]

With the destruction of their food supply soon after settlement, Utes had gone hungry. They had no choice but to ask settlers for food or take it—or starve. Taking livestock, Utes believed, compensated for the loss of game animals. It also spared greater damage by livestock to their gathering grounds. Brigham Young, as church president and as the territory's first superintendent of Indians, advised his people to give food to Indians. He famously said, and often repeated, that it was less expensive to feed them than to fight them. "Besides being the cheapest," he explained, "it is far easier, and exercises a better influence, to feed and clothe than to fight them." To judge from the many accounts of hungry Indians, the settlers—whose primary concern was their own supply of food and their own survival—did not always heed his advice.[15]

Simmering conflict finally led to armed conflict in the 1850s and 1860s, when some formidable Ute leaders—including Wakara and Black Hawk—gained influence. The Utes, superb horsemen, were the lords of the mountains and valleys, and their warriors won many battles, both before and after settlement. But in the face of a relentless flood of settlers, they finally lost the wars. In the 1860s nearly all of the survivors were forced to go to a reservation, and settlers soon occupied their lands. "The distant mountains were a constant reminder to their minds and hearts of their ancestral homes—places now vanishing beneath the fence and plow," a Ute spiritual leader said in the twenty-first century.[16]

By the 1930s most of the descendants lived in exile far from Utah Lake, on the Uintah and Ouray Reservation hundreds of miles northeast, across the mountains. Steward had made two short trips there in the early 1930s. He planned to return once again before leaving Utah, in search of an elder to serve as a cultural informant. In the meantime, he hoped to find a good informant at Kanosh where a few Utes remained, having evaded exile to the distant reservation.[17]

His original plan, of spending nearly a year studying Utes with the support of a fellowship, had long since been scrapped. Given new practical constraints, including limited time, he was willing to settle for just a week or two with two good informants.[18]

As he and Jane drove south, they passed through Fillmore, a place of note in Jane's personal geography. Her grandfather, George Q. Cannon, married her grandmother, Sarah Jane Jenne, in the 1850s in Fillmore. Jane was the namesake of her grandmother. As a child, Sarah Jane walked more than a thousand miles with her family and other Mormon emigrants, crossing plains and mountains on the journey from Illinois to Great Salt Lake Valley in Deseret.

When she was eighteen, she met her future husband in Brigham Young's office in the village of Fillmore, the first capital of Utah Territory. Young served not only as head of the church and as superintendent of Indians but also as the first territorial governor. (Pres. Millard Fillmore appointed him governor—hence, the name of the new territorial capital, given in his honor.) Sarah Jane Jenne became Cannon's second, plural wife. Jane's father, Joseph, was their fifth child of seven.[19]

About fifteen miles south of Fillmore Jane and Julian reached the village of Kanosh, which Julian knew well. He had excavated a nearby archaeological site a few years earlier while still a faculty member at the University of Utah. Heavy snow finally put an end to the work, although it had not discouraged visitors to the site. During the last days, Steward later reported, the crew shoveled "'more snow than dirt.'"

Hired in 1930 to replace an archaeologist, he worked at prehistoric sites throughout the state during his three years at the university. The first report on his work at Kanosh had already been published under

23. Julian Steward (*center*) and visitors to Kanosh archaeological site, November 1930. (Photo by Frank A. Beckwith, courtesy of the Beckwith family)

the auspices of the University of Utah. The second report appeared in print that very year, 1936, under a different imprint. That was a result of the unhappy departure from Utah and lingering tension with the president of the university.[20]

Kanosh had seen little change in the years since Steward's last visit. The quiet Mormon village consisted of a church, houses, and tree-lined streets, with a few shops on the main street. Perhaps its most unusual feature was the name, Ute rather than English. Originally called Corn Creek by settlers, it later took the name of a Ute chief who died in the 1880s. He was remembered as a "friendly" chief, like a few others whose names were adopted by new settlements.[21]

Chief Kanosh, a leader of Pahvant Utes, lived in the area until the late nineteenth century. After coming into conflict with settlers, he decided that his people would gain more by living in peace than by fighting the newcomers, whose numbers kept growing. He became not only a Mormon convert but also an ally of Brigham Young. Chief Kanosh had already married several times—which did not trouble

Young, who had dozens of wives—when the two men strengthened their alliance in an age-old manner. A strategic marriage, of Chief Kanosh to Young's foster daughter, made the men affinal relatives. Young became the father-in-law of Chief Kanosh.[22]

The foster daughter and new wife was a young woman who was thought to be Ute or Bannock in origin. Known as Sally, she was raised by one of Young's plural wives, Clara Decker Young. Sally spent nearly half of her life in the imposing structure called Lion House, where some of Brigham Young's many wives and children lived. Built of adobe and stucco, with a front entrance guarded by a seated lion carved from stone, the house stood near the Tabernacle and not far from the commercial district. The furnishings included wooden tables and chairs and carved bedsteads and carpets. The only objects Sally may have recognized from the earliest years of her life were the large baskets used for laundry in Lion House. Indians traded them to Young's household—tellingly, in exchange for food.

Unlike the other children, Sally was not taught to read and write. While the others slept in rooms upstairs, she slept in the basement, near the kitchen. She worked there "with the other maids," one of Young's birth daughters recalled. The kitchen staff devoted long hours to preparing meals for the fifty members of Young's family who sat down to eat three times a day in Lion House. Another daughter remembered the breads and delicacies that Sally made and her kindness to children.[23]

In a photograph taken when Sally was about thirty, she has a serious and dignified look. Her dark hair is bound up behind her head in the manner of the time for an Anglo-American, not Ute or Bannock, woman. Seated in a chair for a formal portrait, she is wearing a long dress with a full skirt and a prim white collar. She appears anchored in place by the weight of the stiff, dark fabric.[24]

As a city-bred woman, when she married Chief Kanosh she entered exile. Her home for the next ten years, until her death, was a

24. Sally Kanosh, ca. 1870. (Used by permission, Utah State Historical Society, all rights reserved)

hamlet many miles south of Salt Lake City, a journey of several days by wagon or horse. She arrived there wearing an expensive black silk dress. At first she and her husband stayed at the nearby Ute camp, but they soon moved to Kanosh where they lived in a small log house and attended church every Sunday.[25]

About a mile north of the village of Kanosh, at the end of a dirt road and at the foot of a mountain in the Pahvant Range, Julian and Jane drove into the Kanosh Reservation. With a stated population of just twenty-three, it consisted of a few small houses. Julian had some work to do there for the BIA, but he also wanted to find an informant who could tell him about Pahvant Utes who had once lived in far greater numbers in that area. He and Jane arrived on September 10 and were disappointed by what they found. "Very few (approx. 24) Indians left here, all young," Jane noted cryptically in their journal, one of just three sentences she recorded about that summer's fieldwork. "I leave for Washington the end of this month," she added with detectable relief.[26]

Despite the limited prospects, Steward told Stirling in a letter that he would see what he could learn there. He typed the letter on BAE stationery, using the typewriter he had brought on the trip. "Now it is Kanosh, Utah, trying to wring a few drops of"—and reaching the end of that line, he hit the carriage return on the typewriter and began typing a new line—"information from an almost extinct band of Pahvant Utes." Stirling was both a friend and Steward's supervisor, and the letter served as an informal report to headquarters.

Although most of the people were too young to serve Steward's purposes, a recent census had recorded two widowers over sixty and a widow who was seventy. But he chose to work with a man who was just forty-four, his youngest informant that summer. The man was about the same age as Tom Stone, Steward's prized informant of the previous year in the Owens Valley. Stone, who had listened carefully to the stories and memories of his grandfather and other elders, spoke good English and was willing to tell Steward what he knew. Since he had proved as knowledgeable as some people twice his age, Steward had good reason to think that he might once again learn a great deal from a fairly young man.[27]

His Kanosh informant shared some of Stone's qualities, but unlike Stone, as Steward soon learned, he was not native to the region where he now lived. Although married to a Ute woman from the Kanosh Reservation, he was Southern Paiute by origin. He came from the Kaibab Reservation in northern Arizona, nearly two hundred miles away. Steward recorded his name as Joe Pikavich and later referred to him in print as Joe Pihavits, but most people knew him as Joe Pikyavit.[28]

He and his wife, Emily, a pretty woman in her twenties, lived with their two small sons. Emily's mother, Martha Sobrequin, was the seventy-year-old widow named in the census. She remembered Chief Kanosh, who died in the early 1880s when she was a young girl, and she must have known Sally Kanosh as well. She might have been a better prospect for answering Steward's questions about the past, but perhaps she did not want to answer questions or spoke little English. He preferred to work with men in any case, and he may have thought that Martha Sobrequin would have little to say about hunting and about band structure.[29]

The Kanosh Reservation community seemed to regard Pikyavit as a leader and spokesman, and Pikyavit presented himself to Steward as someone with extensive knowledge about his wife's people. A large man, powerfully built, he had a strong presence. He spoke quietly, chose his words carefully, and was used to explaining Indian ways to curious white people. Steward was not the first to question him.

Years earlier, Frank Beckwith, editor of the local newspaper, the *Millard County Chronicle,* had sought out Joe and his younger brother, Ted. He thought they might be able to explain the meaning of some

25. Joe Pikyavit, late 1930s. (Photo by Frank A. Beckwith, courtesy of the Beckwith family)

petroglyphs—pictures and symbols carved on rocks—that he had seen in Clear Creek Canyon, not far from Delta, Utah, where Beckwith lived. Fifty miles separated Delta and Kanosh, but from that first encounter, and extending into the 1940s, Beckwith and Joe Pikyavit met often for wide-ranging conversations. They covered "every conceivable topic," Beckwith later recalled, although a few of his questions did remain unanswered. "That for Indian, not for white man, Beckwith," he remembered hearing more than once. Beckwith came to have high regard for Pikyavit as "a man of character, kind, thoughtful, and the best teacher among the Indians" that he ever met.[30]

Steward had no doubt heard of Pikyavit previously, through Beckwith. He met Beckwith in 1930, when he excavated at Kanosh and at a site near Delta. Beckwith wrote an article for the newspaper and also published one by Steward about the excavation at Kanosh. Steward may also have known about Pikyavit from a mutual acquaintance, Charles Kelly. The short-tempered Kelly, who did not suffer fools gladly and who met them wherever he went, earned a living as a printer in Salt Lake City. He regarded writing as his vocation and had already published the first of many books on historical topics.[31]

Six years earlier, soon after Steward arrived at the University of Utah, Kelly had shown him a promising archaeological site. "It proved to be better than we expected," Kelly later wrote, "and has added some valuable scientific information to the story of ancient man." Nearly two years later they made a river trip together, exploring and searching for archaeological sites in Glen Canyon along the Colorado River. Three other men joined them, and the trip did not go well.[32]

After the disappointing expedition through Glen Canyon, Kelly avoided Steward. He vowed not to take part in any future ventures, or misadventures, with the professional archaeologist. "So far I have shown Steward every site he has excavated. Hereafter I will do my own excavating and keep the specimens myself," Kelly decided irritably. The trip had left him with ill feelings about his companions on the recent river trip. "Beckwith is still a better desert rat than any of them," he added.[33]

Kelly often explored remote parts of the desert with his friend, and the two men sometimes searched for petroglyphs. Unlike Beckwith, he had doubts about Pikyavit's interpretation of the petroglyphs in Clear Creek Canyon: in other words, about his reliability as an informant in that specific instance. Kelly did not believe that the petroglyphs illustrated a particular legend, as Pikyavit told Beckwith. He thought that the legend Pikyavit told was authentic; he only doubted that it had any direct connection with the site in Clear Creek Canyon.[34]

Pikyavit, as Beckwith knew, made a strong family claim to the role of cultural guide. It was something of a family tradition. He told Beckwith that his grandfather had served as guide for Jacob Hamblin, an early Mormon explorer and missionary to Indians. Brigham Young sent Hamblin south in the early 1850s to a remote part of Utah Territory along the Colorado River, and Hamblin was among the first to understand fully that grazing livestock destroyed the Indians' gathering grounds.

"The great number of animals brought into the country by the settlers," he later recalled, "soon devoured most of the vegetation that had produced nutritious seeds." At harvest time Southern Paiutes found that cattle had destroyed almost everything. "With, perhaps, their children crying for food, only the poor consolation was left them of gathering around their camp fires and talking over their grievances," Hamblin continued. "I have many times been sorely grieved to see the Indians with their little ones, glaring upon a table spread with food, and trying to get our people to understand their circumstances, without being able to do so." Their complaints of hunger often fell on deaf ears, despite Brigham Young's advice to feed the famished Indians.[35]

According to Pikyavit, his grandfather was with Hamblin when they met a man the Southern Paiutes called "One-Arm." That was explorer John Wesley Powell, who had lost part of an arm in a Civil War battle. Pikyavit said that Hamblin and his grandfather escorted Powell to Kanab, a remote Mormon outpost along the Utah-Arizona border, when Powell left the Colorado River near the end of his second river journey, in 1872. His grandfather, he recalled, was known as Jake because of his close association with Jacob Hamblin.[36]

The chance to earn money must have encouraged Pikyavit to answer Steward's questions, just as his own grandfather had received compensation for guiding and helping Hamblin. There were few opportunities to earn money around Kanosh Reservation in the best of times, and times were hard in 1936. At one point during the Depression years, more than half of the county's residents received government relief, a figure more than double the national average. A high rate of foreclosure had left nearly a third of the county's real estate in the hands of banks or other firms.[37]

Some men at the Kanosh Reservation found work on WPA relief projects, although they had lower priority in hiring than other county residents. ("Indian opportunity is extra," Beckwith remarked pointedly.) Some of the women took in laundry. No one had work that qualified as steady, and the average household income in 1936 was only about $200.[38]

The people of the Kanosh Reservation adapted to the new and challenging conditions, often by means of the old ways. Some earned money by using traditional skills: collecting pine nuts and selling any surplus, or hunting deer and tanning the hides, some for trade. Men hunted. Women did much of the time-consuming work of turning rough hide into buckskin, and the buckskin into gloves, moccasins, and garments. Emily Pikyavit tanned hides, no doubt having learned the method from her mother. Beckwith remembered seeing her mother, Martha Sobrequin, at work one day, "rickety specs on nose, busy snipping with scissors [the] patterns out of buckskins to make gloves for sale."[39]

The white residents of the county prized the gloves, and they also used buckskin for shoelaces and saddle string. Hopi Indians, hundreds of miles south in Arizona, valued the buckskin as well. Joe Pikyavit told of taking it to them for trade and returning home with silver jewelry and sometimes with Navajo blankets, which he then sold to whites.[40]

As a result of their enterprise, people at the Kanosh Reservation made ends meet. They grew some of their food and purchased some, but cash was always scarce—so Pikyavit seized the chance to answer Steward's questions about the past in exchange for a daily wage. It may have helped that Steward knew Frank Beckwith and appeared to share some of Beckwith's interests. Steward soon doubted Pikyavit's expertise about Pahvant Utes; but, lacking another candidate for the job of cultural informant, he worked with him for several days. He asked questions about the Pahvant Ute and Southern Paiute past and recorded two trait lists for Kroeber.[41]

Pikyavit told Steward that Pahvant Utes were known as Water People. They lived west of the Pahvant Range, in the desert around a lake that settlers later called Sevier Lake. In winter they occupied six villages. The Water People ranged far west of the lake, almost to the area that later became the Utah-Nevada border. "This territory was owned by the band," Steward concluded, "and defended against trespass by other Ute, Paiute, and Gosiute." Within the band, he learned, villages and families did not hold exclusive rights to food areas.[42]

Pahvant Utes hunted deer in the mountains and waterfowl along the Sevier River, where they also fished. They gathered pine nuts, berries, and roots, traveling west through the desert to a particular mountain range to collect pine nuts. On the western side of the mountains (later named the House Range), mile after mile of winding limestone cliffs formed a nearly vertical wall, a pale palisade in the desert. Pikyavit knew the area well. He often went to the mountains in the fall with companions to collect pine nuts. They drove there in his Model-T Ford.[43]

A Spanish explorer who encountered Pahvant Utes in the eighteenth century recorded that they spoke the same language as the Utes around Utah Lake—and that they had Spanish features. (Chief Kanosh, a descendant, had the telltale facial hair of a European ancestor. A photograph taken later in life shows him wearing an ample walrus mustache.) Like the Utes who lived around Utah Lake, the Pahvant Utes around Sevier Lake already had horses when Mormon settlers entered their lands in the mid-nineteenth century.[44]

By 1936, when Steward traveled through the region, Sevier Lake—like Owens Lake in California—was a dry and shallow basin of sand. Its name memorialized the lost water. Settlers took so much for irrigation, diverting water from rivers that emptied into the lake, that the lake went dry before the turn of the twentieth century. Along with the river water and fish, Pahvant Utes lost the waterfowl that had once lived at the lake and at smaller playa lakes, which also dried up. Only now and then, when water was more abundant than usual, did any still manage to reach Sevier Lake. The meager and erratic supply could not sustain life.

Joe and Emily Pikyavit had no memories of the living lake. Like most people at the Kanosh Reservation, they were too young to have seen the clear waters or walked along a reed-lined shore, twenty-five miles in length. The reeds, ducks, and other birds had all vanished.[45]

Steward soon gave up on his quest for "a few drops of information" about the Water People. He paid for several days' work and left Kanosh feeling discouraged and thwarted. He doubted the value of the two trait lists he recorded, and they never appeared in print. Suspecting that they were "probably worthless," he invited Kroeber to "throw them out." The overlap between the two lists led Steward to suppose that he had been given answers about Southern Paiutes to questions about Pahvant Utes. In frustration, he wondered aloud in a letter to Kroeber whether his Kanosh informant had tried to deceive him. That had never happened before, he said.[46]

Later, and in print, he simply remarked that the informant seemed unable or unwilling to make distinctions between Pahvant Utes and Southern Paiutes. As a result, he said, the information he recorded was "too unreliable to distinguish Ute from Southern Paiute," and of limited use. The source of the problem, Steward suggested, came from white men in the area around Kanosh who treated Pikyavit as an authority on "Ute lore," not knowing of his Southern Paiute origin. The confusion, however, ran deeper.[47]

Beckwith, who knew that Pikyavit came from the Kaibab Reservation in northern Arizona, referred to him and to his parents as "Ute." Census takers listed Pikyavit as "full Paiute" and an enrolled member of the Kaibab Reservation, and his wife as "full Ute" and an enrolled member of the Kanosh Reservation. A census of the Kanosh Reservation taken around the time when Steward visited listed many of the people as "full Paiute" or "mixed Paiute." Over time, Southern Paiutes from other places had moved there, and some, like Joe Pikyavit, had married Utes.

A few years after Steward met Pikyavit and questioned his ability to distinguish Pahvant Ute from Southern Paiute traits, the Kanosh Reservation changed its name and legal status. It identified as Paiute and received a corporate charter as the Kanosh Band of Paiute Indians of the Kanosh Reservation. Pahvant Utes shared both Ute and Paiute cultural features, and intermarriage may have led over time to more emphasis on Paiute heritage at the Kanosh Reservation. (Another interpretation holds that the name change, perhaps a defensive maneuver, allowed Utes to stay at the Kanosh Reservation, avoiding exile to the distant Uintah and Ouray Reservation.)[48]

The cultural differences between Utes and Paiutes, as understood by at least one man at the Kanosh Reservation, were not so marked as Steward expected. Pikyavit did not make sharp distinctions between Ute and Southern Paiute cultural *traits*, although those cultural *identities* remained distinct. During his grandfather's time, Utes and Southern Paiutes were sworn enemies. Utes, who had horses, raided Southern Paiutes, who did not. They carried off women and children to the slave markets of the Southwest.[49]

Born just forty years after his grandfather met Jacob Hamblin, Pikyavit lived in a world with scant likeness to the one his grandfather had known. The open sky and massive mountains endured, but the stands of waving wild grasses that once covered the valley around his birthplace, the Kaibab Reservation, remained only in memory. Ranchers had settled on the land, with the usual results for the tall grasses and the Paiutes' gathering grounds.[50]

Unlike his grandfather, Pikyavit belonged to a colonized people, an American Indian minority. He lived on a small reservation with just over twenty other Paiutes and Utes, located in a county with a non-Indian population of ten thousand.[51] Visiting kin at other reservations required driving long distances in his Model-T Ford. He also traded goods and enjoyed friendships with other people whose ancestors were enemies of his ancestors.

On those journeys he passed by immense stretches of territory now claimed and occupied by the descendants of the recent immigrants. They had arrived by the tens of thousands, in a powerful surge, just decades earlier. His own people lived on small islands scattered in a sea of people of European descent and Mormon faith whose close-knit communities centered on the church.

Pikyavit, along with his wife and some of their relatives, eventually chose to be baptized as a Mormon. Years earlier he had wondered about one theological point that troubled him. He questioned the idea that his darker skin—the skin color of Lamanites, as Mormons called American Indians—signified a curse. (The name and belief about skin color came from the Book of Mormon, a scriptural history revealed to the Mormon prophet, Joseph Smith. It identifies American Indians as descendants of ancient Hebrews.) The idea of a curse hurt him, but later, after reading the Book of Mormon with his wife, Emily, he called it the "'Best book [he] ever read.'"[52]

Beckwith recorded this with little comment. As a Gentile, the term for any non-Mormon, he always held the status of outsider in the community where he published the county newspaper for many years. "'I live here as practically a lone gentile in a Mormon town,' he once told a friend, 'tolerated but not loved by my Mormon neighbors.'"[53]

Despite feeling discouraged and irritated when he left Kanosh, Steward planned to resume his research on Utes as soon as he had completed other fieldwork in northern Utah, at Washakie. He and his wife went there directly. A few weeks later, the day after Jane left for Washington, he typed a hasty letter to Kroeber. The letter said he was sending seven trait lists by express mail and then departing immediately for Whiterocks, Utah, and the Uintah and Ouray Reservation. He hoped to find an elder who could tell him about the Utes of Utah Lake.[54]

The trip to the reservation took Steward across the Wasatch Mountains and into the Uinta Basin, the high country south of the Uinta Mountains. Its elevation, above five thousand feet, brought long winters and severe cold. The aridity—less than ten inches of precipitation each year—also made it far less desirable to farmers than the valleys along the Wasatch Front. That explained the placement of the reservation. By the time Steward visited the Uintah and Ouray Reservation in the 1930s it had shrunk, as had the Fort Hall Reservation and others, because again and again land was taken away.[55]

This was a return visit to the reservation for Steward. Five years earlier, in 1931, he had attended the annual Bear Dance there. He returned a year later with his first wife, Dorothy Nyswander, an educational psychologist who trained at Berkeley with the famous neobehaviorist Edward Chase Tolman. They spent two and a half weeks on collaborative research, a pilot study that never had the intended follow-up because their marriage suddenly ended.[56]

The memory of that short project might have stirred other recollections, including Dorothy's skeptical comments about Julian's research methods. "Just *one* old man?" she asked him more than once, challenging an approach that she thought depended too much on the words and memories of a single informant. She was proud of her rigorous training in the laboratories of Berkeley's Department of Psychology and of her skill as a self-described "rat-runner." Her training and experience convinced her that research had to meet the highest standard to qualify as scientific.[57]

That standard included multiple testing or repeated experiments to replicate results, something impossible to achieve without tests or outside the controlled setting of the laboratory. In the field, researchers could not exert control and manipulate variables—nor did they wish to do so. Cultural anthropologists tried to understand something about human life as it is, or as it once was, by going out into the world, not by working in a laboratory.

Years later Dorothy Nyswander conceded that she never saw the value of research outside the laboratory, or its difficulties, until she tried it herself. Her lasting memory of the pilot study at the Ute reservation centered on the physical hardships: "It was *hard work*," she said. But the most memorable experience came later, while working in New York City as an educational researcher. She was threatened during an interview in a private home, and she vividly recalled losing one of her shoes in her haste to get away.[58]

Whiterocks and the Uintah and Ouray Reservation held other memories for Steward, beyond those of his former wife. He met Jane Cannon there for the first time, briefly, at the 1931 Bear Dance, which she attended as something of a lark with friends from Salt Lake City. The dance, held each March by Ute Indians, celebrated the coming of spring. His student, Kilton Stewart, happened to see her at White-rocks; and he introduced his former flame, Jane Cannon, to his professor, Julian Steward. They met again in 1932, the second meeting also arranged by Kilton. And they married a year later.[59]

Steward stayed for just one day at the reservation on this trip, spending a few frustrating hours with an informant. As he later told Kroeber, "I made a trip to the Uintah Basin in Utah, hoping to get just the right informant from around Utah Lake but had no success." He quickly discovered that many Utes who lived on the reservation, and whose homelands had covered a vast area of Colorado and Utah and northern New Mexico, did not identify themselves with named bands of the past. "Their consciousness of former band affiliation," he later explained, "appears to have been overshadowed by present reservation divisions."[60]

A year later, when Kilton Stewart's younger brother Omer visited the reservation, he questioned three elders who did identify as Timpanogots, or Utah Lake Utes. His main informant for a trait list was an old woman, Karoomp Longhair, also known as Kate Longhair. She insisted that she knew more about the "'real old way'" than the other two informants who as young men had gone to Wyoming and Colorado. They had not spent as much time at home, she explained, talking to the old people.[61]

Steward left the Uintah and Ouray Reservation in late September, as he had earlier left Kanosh, feeling frustrated by an informant he regarded as unreliable. Later, in contrast to his usual practice in *Basin-Plateau*, he did not draw heavily on the memories of elders to reconstruct the Utes' way of life. He made slight use of what Joe Pikyavit told him about Pahvant Utes. Even his observations of Ute country required an unusually large dose of inference. The density of Mormon settlement and the intensity of farming and grazing had transformed

Ute lands and destroyed the Pahvants' lake. As he stated tersely, "Little information was obtained through field work among the Ute."[62]

In the end Steward depended primarily on written sources and gave more attention than usual to the years during and just after contact and conquest. The earliest published works obviously dated from that time. The authors included dozens of American and European men who entered the region in the eighteenth and nineteenth centuries as explorers, trappers and traders, or early Mormon settlers. They later wrote about what they saw in the land of the Utes.

Powell and the others recorded those memories in books and reports that university libraries catalogued and kept. Years before he began writing *Basin-Plateau*, Steward had spent long days in the libraries of the University of California and the University of Utah, searching for early firsthand accounts of the Great Basin. It was in part a legacy of his training in anthropology in the 1920s, when students wrote dissertations based on research in the library rather than in the field.[63]

He had thumbed slowly through the small cards that numbered in the hundreds in every narrow wooden drawer of the card catalog. Each card held the library record of a book or report or other publication. An identifying number, based on the Dewey Decimal System, helped to locate the place where the work was shelved in the library stacks.

Since many of the reports could not be borrowed, and photocopy machines did not yet exist, he spent long hours sitting in a wooden chair at a table, reading and taking notes in longhand. Typewriters were not permitted. The clack of typewriter keys—punctuated by the jingle of a bell whenever the carriage return was struck—would have disturbed the quiet. Signs posted in libraries requested silence, and silence, or muffled whispers, prevailed.

His days of work in the deathly hush of reading rooms amounted to a diligent search for another type of ghost informant. They had transmitted their memories in writing to "intellectual descendants," rather than orally, to genealogical descendants. Lacking Ute informants to question about earlier times, Steward turned to explorers of the American West. They counted among his professional ancestors, his tribesmen, and they also served as his guides. By reading their journals, letters, and reports he hoped to find answers to questions that he could not directly ask the long-dead authors. He thought that they might shed light on the question of Ute bands and reveal something about the effects of warfare on band structure.

What those explorers and the settlers remembered seeing may have differed sharply from what Steward would have heard from a Ute elder. But because he had failed to find "just the right informant," as he put it, he listened to dozens of authors instead. Their voices spoke beyond the grave about what they had once seen as outsiders in Ute country.

In *Basin-Plateau* Steward listed two pages of names as sources for Utes. It was the single case in which his time in the library may have exceeded his time in the field, at the two reservations in Utah in 1936.[64]

Based on what he had read and what he had seen of Ute country, Steward finally concluded that before contact Western Utes, those living west of the Wasatch and Pahvant mountains, resembled Western Shoshones. They had lacked bands, by his definition. After contact, he suggested, and specifically after the introduction of the horse and the escalation in warfare, these Utes developed bands. "Data on Ute bands are inadequate," he wrote, "but suggest a pattern like that of Northern Shoshoni."[65] Ute bands did not qualify as patrilineal bands.

9. Trails West

IN MID-SEPTEMBER—just two weeks before Jane departed for Washington and Julian left the Uintah and Ouray Reservation—they left Kanosh and drove two hundred and fifty miles north. They could see the first signs of fall scattered across the mountain slopes. Small patches of red showed where mountain maples, soon to shrug off their leaves, had begun to prepare for winter. Scrub oaks and other stragglers still wore their summer greens, and stands of wild sunflowers still blazed yellow along the roadside.

They were headed for a place called Washakie. Like Pocatello, Idaho, and Kanosh, Utah, it bore the name of a man who was regarded by settlers as a peacemaker, a "friendly" chief, and by his own people as a respected leader. A few miles south of the Utah-Idaho border Julian and Jane turned west toward the village of Portage. They followed a dusty and rutted track from Portage to Washakie, a cluster of small wooden and log houses. About a hundred Northwestern Shoshones lived there, in a broad and arid valley bordered by low mountains on the west.[1]

A few days earlier Steward had reported to Stirling at BAE headquarters that he had "a fine old Shoshoni lined up" at Washakie. Grouse Creek Jack, his oldest informant at Fort Hall, had once lived there. He probably gave Steward the name of Ray Diamond Womenup, also known to census takers and in other records as Wo-ne-ip, Diamond, Diamond Wo-ne-ip, Ray Diamond, Ray Diamond Woe-mup, and Old Diamond.[2]

Steward later estimated Diamond's age at "more than eighty" and said that he had "joined the Mormon church and moved to Washakie, where he has lived to this day." But census takers listed him as a centenarian (at least one fellow Shoshone thought he was younger), church records for Washakie did not include his name, and he was not living there when some censuses were taken. Adding to the confusion, the 1930 federal census recorded Diamond's occupation as *mail carrier, government*, yet it also listed him as unable to speak English or to read and write. According to someone who knew him well, he did learn to read; and contrary to Steward's surmise, he never joined a church.[3]

Diamond wore his age well, whether he was in his eighties or a hundred years old. Despite many discrepancies about his recorded name and some other matters of identity, Diamond knew who he was and clearly remembered the place he came from: a region north of Great Salt Lake, shown on maps as Promontory Point and the Promontory Mountains. He also remembered how his people had lived there before settlers arrived in Utah in the late 1840s. The people of that region were known as Seed Eaters, and Chief Sagwitch was their leader. Some of them later went to Washakie to live as farmers and Mormon converts. Steward reported that Shoshones at the Fort Hall Reservation called them by a name meaning Mormon Children.[4]

Diamond was old enough to have known Chief Washakie, whose name was later taken by the community. The famous Shoshone leader had a long association with Brigham Young from the time when he first visited Young in Great Salt Lake City, as it was then known. Chief Washakie wanted to establish trade relations with the settlers and to negotiate peace with some Ute enemies who had just left the city. Like many who recorded their memories of him, one of Young's daughters remembered Chief Washakie as "a fine-looking, powerfully built man of commanding and dignified carriage." She considered him a proven friend of her father. Their relationship eventually led to the founding of what was called the Washakie Indian Farm in the early 1880s, a few years after Young's death.[5]

Twenty-seven years earlier, in 1854, Young had sent the first in a series of letters to "Wash-e-kik" to advise that his people take up farming. "I love the Shoshones," he wrote to Chief Washakie in one of those letters, "and therefore wish to tell you and your people some of my ideas which I think will be for your good." He pointed out that living in small and scattered groups exposed them to attacks by their enemies, and that depending entirely on hunting and fishing for their food raised the risk of hunger, even starvation. "Moreover the game is continually getting scarce," he said in another letter, "which makes it more and more difficult for you to get a living." He did not mention gathering as a source of food or acknowledge the major cause of hunger: settlement by thousands of people with herds of grazing livestock, which had greatly reduced the supply of both edible plants and wild game. But as a former superintendent of Indian Affairs for Utah Territory, he undoubtedly understood these effects of settlement. Jacob Hamblin understood, and he reported regularly from Southern Paiute country.

"Now I would like to see your people collect into large bands," Young continued, "and begin to cultivate the earth that you may not starve, when you are unfortunate in hunting." He recommended a good location for farming and offered to send some men to assist them in getting started. The letter was signed, "Your Friend & Brother, Brigham Young."[6]

Six months later he wrote another letter, again urging them to "make locations on good land and raise grain and stock and live in houses and quit rambling about so much." This had been his standard counsel and goal for all Indians under his jurisdiction as superintendent of Indian Affairs, and also as president of his church. According to church teachings, American Indians, a fallen remnant of Israel, must be helped to achieve a civilized way of life. Settling in one place and farming represented the road to uplift and improvement, and the church intended to help them find suitable land.

Many years passed before this finally happened, and then largely at the prompting of Chief Sagwitch and another prominent Shoshone, his cousin. His name was recorded as Egippetche or Ejupitchee, and translated as Wolf. Also known as Ejupa Moemberg, John Moemberg, and John Meombers, he lived in Cache Valley. As a result of those efforts, several hundred Northwestern Shoshones finally moved in the early 1880s to the place named for Chief Washakie. Their number included Chief Sagwitch, Ray Diamond, and other survivors of a massacre twenty years earlier.[7]

At the Fort Hall Reservation Steward had learned that there were few descendants of the hundreds of Shoshones and Bannocks from the Bannock Creek region who died by the Bear River in 1863. In print he called this the Bear River Massacre, not the Battle of Bear River, as it was then commonly known among non-Indians. When he and Jane drove past the town of Preston, Idaho, a historical marker already stood at the site of the massacre, a few miles north of the town. It commemorated what some historians and anthropologists would later call one of the worst massacres of American Indians in U.S. history.[8]

The tall stone monument stood beside the road Julian and Jane took through Cache Valley, which crossed the Idaho-Utah border. Erected just four years earlier, in 1932, the monument represented a joint project of a lineage society, the Daughters of the Utah Pioneers, together with a landmarks association and the local council of the Boy Scouts of America. The inscription announced, "THE BATTLE OF BEAR RIVER was fought in this vicinity, January 29, 1863." On that bitterly cold day, Col. Patrick E. Connor led three hundred men in an attack at dawn against a camp where some of the men, women, and children were still sleeping.[9]

He led the soldiers, according to the marker, "against Bannock and Shoshone Indians guilty of hostile attacks on emigrants and settlers, engaged about 500 Indians, of whom 250 to 300 were killed or incapacitated, including about 90 combatant women and children."

An eyewitness account put the number of dead at 280, but the number may have been higher. "Chiefs Bear Hunter, Sagwitch, and Lehi were reported killed. 175 horses and much stolen property were recovered. 70 lodges were burned."[10]

Far fewer soldiers died. The twenty-three casualties included men killed that day and others who did not survive their wounds.

More Indian men, women, and children perished in the Bear River Massacre than died nearly thirty years later at the infamous Wounded Knee Massacre in South Dakota. In the East, where the Civil War was raging, the violence at Bear River went nearly unnoticed. A weekly newspaper in Utah Territory noted the events under the headlines, "The Fight with the Indians," and "The Battle of Bear River." Both reports appeared in the back pages of the newspaper.[11]

The site that Connor and his men attacked was a winter village, hence the lodges and the presence of so many women and children. Contrary to wording on the 1932 monument, they were not combatants; they did not go to battle. And contrary to reports, Chief Sagwitch did not die that day. "Only about fifteen of the warriors are supposed to have escaped," one newspaper account stated, after listing Chief Sagwitch among the dead. He was in fact one of the few men who survived the attack.[12]

The people who moved to Washakie in the early 1880s lived at a distance from the old Oregon Trail and other trails west, which had brought a flood of outsiders through their country. But a new trail—the transcontinental railroad, completed twelve years earlier, in 1869—passed by just forty miles to the south.

Construction began in January 1863, the very month and year of the Bear River Massacre. Six years later, two lines of rails, from east and west, finally converged at Promontory Summit, in the homeland of the Seed Eaters. A cross-country trip that had once taken six months by wagon had been reduced to less than a week by train. Multitudes of travelers crossed the continent, and some stopped in Utah Territory to settle. The railroad also carried in army troops and supplies, to deal with Indians who opposed settlement of their lands.

Promontory Summit would remain in national memory as the place where the final spike was driven, joining the rails and connecting a continent.[13] The Promontory Mountains, a low spine of peninsula that stretched south to Great Salt Lake, held different memories for Seed Eaters. Ray Diamond and Chief Sagwitch were already middle-aged when railroad tracks crossed the land where they had spent decades of their lives. They remembered a place inhabited only by their own people, before American settlement and the intrusion of the national thoroughfare.

Chief Sagwitch converted to the Mormon faith in the mid-1870s, when he was in his fifties. He worked on the Logan Temple with his sons and Grouse Creek Jack, along with many other volunteers who gave their labor. The temple, designed in a modified Gothic style, was constructed from massive blocks of limestone that workers quarried in a nearby canyon and transported to the building site. The completed Logan Temple, an imposing five-story structure that stood on a hill, could be seen from a distance of miles in Cache Valley.[14]

A few years later Chief Sagwitch died near Washakie. He was Ray Diamond's uncle, his mother's brother. By the mid-1930s Diamond and his cousin Yeager Timbimboo, who was Sagwitch's son, were apparently the sole remaining survivors of the Bear River Massacre at Washakie. Diamond had escaped the mayhem, and certain death, by swimming across the icy waters of the Bear River and finding shelter in the hills. Timbimboo, just fifteen years old at the time, narrowly survived by following his grandmother's directions and lying down among the bodies strewn on the frozen ground. A soldier, detecting life, raised his rifle to shoot the boy, then lowered it; raised and lowered it again; raised and lowered it a third time. In the end, he walked away.

Both Diamond and Timbimboo told and retold the story of the massacre for the rest of their very long lives. Steward probably heard the story from Diamond. That may well explain his use of the word *massacre* in print, not *battle* as on the historical marker in Cache Valley and in many books.[15]

In Diamond's memory the Promontory Point people, or Seed Eaters, comprised four winter villages. In *Basin-Plateau* Steward identified their leader, Chief Sagwitch, as "Segwitc," the "father of Yegai Timbimbu, an old man now living at Washakie." When Steward visited, Yeager Timbimboo was in his late eighties, a longtime resident, and one of the oldest.[16]

Fifty years after the founding, the number of people living at Washakie had dwindled to about a hundred. Some of the former residents lived at the Wind River Reservation, more than three hundred miles away in western Wyoming, where Chief Washakie spent the last years of his life. Others, including Grouse Creek Jack and his wife, moved to the Fort Hall Reservation in Idaho, about ninety miles away. Still others left to look for work in Utah towns. Although Brigham Young had urged Shoshones to gather together, in Mormon fashion, over the years many of the people of Washakie had scattered in all directions, in Utah, Wyoming, Idaho, and beyond.[17]

Even in the generally prosperous years of the 1920s, those who remained at Washakie worked very hard to make a living. Willie Ottogary, who grew up at Washakie and later wrote hundreds of news columns about his people for county newspapers, reported on how they earned a living. In some cases they used new skills, acquired after they moved to Washakie. They produced some of their food—by farming and by raising sheep and cattle—and sold any surplus. Some men and women worked for wages seasonally as farm laborers in nearby sugar beet fields, thinning the beets in spring and harvesting them in the fall. Sometimes they traveled to Idaho to harvest potatoes or to shear sheep.[18]

They also used old knowledge and skills in new and creative ways to earn money in a twentieth-century economy. They cut trees to sell, as cedar posts during most of the year and as Christmas trees near year's end. At least one woman sewed buckskin gloves and sold them. Drawing on a long tradition of trading, a man took several horses and cows to a nearby town and traded them for a Buick. "I expect he made a good trade," Ottogary commented. Knowledge of horses and a tradition of racing also brought income: cash prizes that winners took home from horse races held at fairs. Ottogary mentioned a "very nice race track" at Washakie where hopeful racers were training their horses. "We have some good horses here now," he added.[19]

A few young men capitalized on their athletic skills to earn money. In an early column, Ottogary told readers about a wrestling match in a nearby town that pitted the butcher, touted as the best, against a man from Washakie. The butcher lost. By the 1920s some men had taken up boxing, entering matches as far away as Salt Lake City. Ottogary reported on their wins and losses, and also on double-dealing outside the ring. Kid Davis, he said, had reneged on a contract made the "old Indian custom way," by word of honor, not in writing.[20]

People also earned money by hunting rabbits—as of old, but for new gain. The rabbit population had soared after settlers arrived and began to cultivate large tracts of land. The farmers killed coyotes—a major predator of rabbits—to keep them from killing any livestock. Then the rabbits, in swelling numbers, ate farmers' crops and created other nuisances for them. When the county began to offer a bounty for rabbits, requiring hunters to turn in pelts as evidence of success, the people of Washakie drew on old skills as rabbit hunters to earn money and also put food on the table. They held rabbit drives during the winter, sometimes killing thousands in a season, and then collected hundreds of dollars in bounties.[21]

Some men tried to provide for their families by hunting deer. The herds had increased after settlers eradicated wolves and grizzly bears, but by the 1930s the state was managing deer and other game. Even before that time it had regulated hunting. When a man from Washakie was arrested, evidently for some infraction of state hunting regulations, Ottogary complained. The wild game, he insisted to his readers, belonged to American Indians. An old treaty gave his people the right to hunt in any season.[22]

Less than a century after settlement little remained of large game. Bison were long gone, and the number of elk greatly reduced. Mountain sheep had disappeared from northern Utah by 1930, and grizzly bears survived only in distant and wild places.[23]

Ottogary died in the late 1920s, and times grew harder in most places during the Depression years of the 1930s. The stranger who arrived at Washakie in September 1936—in search of answers to questions about the past—thus represented an income-earning opportunity. He and his very friendly wife knew Grouse Creek Jack and other relatives and friends, not only at Fort Hall but also at reservations in Nevada. That changed their status from complete strangers to visitors who shared some mutual acquaintances. Two men and a woman agreed to answer Steward's questions, willing to share some of their knowledge and memories in exchange for a daily wage.

One was the elder with many recorded names: Old Diamond, as Steward called Ray Diamond.[24] The other man was middle-aged. Diamond may have spoken English, but at a level of fluency that led Steward to hire the second man as interpreter. Seth Eagle, also known as Seth Eagle Pubigee, was in his fifties. Diamond was a widower, but Eagle lived with his wife, Ivy Woonsook Eagle (Pubigee), and their two youngest children, both daughters. The couple had older children as well; and Ivy, also known as Ivy Pojennie, had another daughter from an earlier marriage to a son of Grouse Creek Jack. Like most people at Washakie—besides Diamond and a few others—the family

26. Seth Eagle (*on left*) at Washakie. (Used by permission, Utah State Historical Society, all rights reserved)

was Mormon, each of them a baptized member of the Church of Jesus Christ of Latter-day Saints.[25]

Seth Eagle, born at Washakie in the early years of its settlement, was listed as *wheat farmer* in some records, and as *farm laborer* in others. Like many people at Washakie, he farmed and also worked for wages. Steward learned that he was a shaman as well. Besides acting as interpreter, he provided information on shamanism, part of a trait list compiled for Kroeber. Since Steward viewed that material as largely peripheral to his own interest in bands and ecology, he said very little about it in *Basin-Plateau*. Only antelope shamans, who directed hunts, seemed directly relevant.[26]

Eagle told Steward that he came from a family line of shamans. His predecessors included his father, from Washakie's Wyoming band of Eastern Shoshones, and his father's father; and also his mother, mother's father, and mother's grandfather, all from Nevada. One of his daughters, he reported, was in the process of becoming a shaman before she died; and his fourth wife (probably Ivy Pojennie) also had powers. Despite tension with the church about shamanism, the couple continued their practice, which included curing through recovery of lost souls.

Eagle told Steward this story: His wife had once lost consciousness and gone rigid for half an hour while looking for the lost soul of a boy who had fallen ill. In order to help her, Eagle's soul left his body and went to a green and fertile place where berries and other foods were always ripe (tellingly, where there was always good food to gather— not where green fields needed plowing). He found the boy's soul and persuaded it to return. Then Eagle regained consciousness, revived his wife, and restored the soul to the boy's head. The boy quickly recovered from his illness.[27]

Among his powers, Eagle could also save lives by curing snake-bites. He told Steward about a time when he cured a horse that a snake had bitten on the nose. After making a cut on the horse's nose and above each of its eyes, he sucked out the blood—and got a handsome reward from the grateful owner of the horse. Intrusion of a foreign object into the body, as Steward noted, was thought to be one of the main causes of disease or even death; sucking was one way to remove it and bring about a cure. Soul loss was the other main cause of serious illness.

Eagle said that he had even cured himself after a snake bit him. Once, at a circus, he heard a man bet that no one could handle his collection of snakes, which included an impressively large and irritable rattlesnake. Eagle took the bet, with a wager worth several months' earnings. He handled all of the snakes and happily collected his winnings. The rattlesnake did bite him, but by rubbing a little of his own saliva on the wound, he explained, he made the bite harmless.[28]

Steward spent nearly six days with Eagle. During four of those days he worked with Diamond, Eagle interpreting. He learned that Seed Eaters, the people who lived around Promontory Point, had traveled as far as Grouse Creek, a hundred miles away, to collect pine nuts. Families without horses sometimes made four or five trips on foot to carry the nuts home.

Through his previous work as an archaeologist, Steward knew that bison had once lived in that area north of Great Salt Lake. He had excavated a cave at Promontory Point in 1930 and 1931. (Coincidentally, Diamond's birthplace was a nearby cave, and his date of birth exactly a century earlier, 1830, according to most records.)[29] Diamond recalled that bison had ranged along the lower reaches of the Bear River. He told Steward that some of his people had horses, and they joined Chief Washakie and his band of Eastern Shoshones for bison hunts.

They had also hunted pronghorn antelope, deer, rabbits, and waterfowl. "Communal duck drives were held under the direction of Segwitc," Steward reported, "in the marshes around Bear River Bay, which abounded in waterfowl." People took trout and other fish from the Bear River, sometimes using nets.

Shoshones called the river by a name that referred to the color of the water. One of the early fur trappers in the region, impressed by the number of bears—brown and black and grizzly—gave the river its English name. Grizzly bears, along with bison and most other large game, had soon disappeared from the area. The trappers hunted bison, elk, and bear, and the early settlers killed grizzly bears and wolves to protect their cattle and sheep.[30] Those predators had turned to livestock when wild prey declined.

Diamond told Steward that people from the region around Promontory Point traveled as far east as Cache Valley, sixty or seventy miles away, to search for food. His mother was living with the people of that valley when she bore a daughter, Diamond's half sister. Rachel Perdash, whose date of birth was listed as 1846 in some records and 1858 in others, also lived at Washakie. She was a widow. She had lost not only her husband but also her children years earlier. Steward worked with her for a day and a half, again assisted by Eagle, to fill out what he had just learned from her brother about Cache Valley. She was

27. Rachel Perdash. (Courtesy of Utah State University, Special Collections and Archives)

Steward's sole female informant in Utah, and one of the few women he ever paid an informant fee.[31]

Rachel Perdash was born just before the first Mormon settlers reached the Salt Lake Valley or, if the later birth date is correct, just after Mormons first tried to settle Cache Valley—but at least twenty years after trappers entered her homeland. "This fertile valley," Steward wrote, "was long the center of trapping operations by the white man and, as early as 1826, the site of an annual rendezvous of Indians and trappers." Their presence, he continued, disrupted the way of life of Cache Valley Shoshones from the start.

The first trappers may have entered the valley in 1818, part of the steady stream of mountain men who made their way west in the years after the Lewis and Clark Expedition crossed the Rocky Mountains. Jim Bridger, Peter Skene Ogden, and Jedediah Smith were among the many explorers and trappers—most of them Anglo-American, British, or French-Canadian—who passed through, or spent months at a time, in Cache Valley. In later years James Beckwourth, the famous African-American trapper, sometimes got credit for naming the valley.[32]

Beckwourth, a Virginian born into slavery, had headed west to a life of adventure and freedom in "the Indian country," as he later recounted in a best-selling book. The name Cache Valley memorialized the trappers' custom of caching furs, tools, and supplies in storage pits or other secure places. Shoshones called the valley by a name that meant Willow River. Early trappers called it Willow Valley.[33]

Some of the mountain men kept journals, as the explorers Lewis and Clark did; others, including Beckwourth, later drew on memory to tell of their journeys. Steward read books and reports by explorers and trappers to reconstruct how Cache Valley looked in the first half of the nineteenth century and to learn who lived there. They served as ghost informants, guides who told what they had seen of the land and the native people. He had no archaeological evidence from Cache

Valley to guide him, unlike some other areas in Utah—such as Kanosh and Promontory Point—where he had excavated sites.

Early visitors to that valley, mountain men and Mormons alike, praised the beauty of the green expanse framed by white-peaked mountains. More to the point, they remarked on the lush grass, plentiful water, and abundant game. Those very resources led settlers to enter the valley in the mid-1850s, seeking pasture for a herd of more than three thousand head of cattle. The severe cold and deep snow of Cache Valley in winter killed most of the herd and delayed settlement, but only for a few years. Thousands of Mormon settlers from points to the east, including Europe, continued to pour into Utah Territory, gathering in Zion as they said. By 1860 more than 2,600 people lived in Cache Valley.[34]

Rachel Perdash, despite having reached her eighties or nineties, began life after trappers entered Cache Valley. The old times that Steward wanted to document had already ended. Still, her memories, and her half brother's, helped him learn about the Cache Valley band. Called by a name that meant Fish Eaters, they also hunted bison, rabbits, and mountain sheep. Diamond thought that just twelve families had formed this band, but Steward later concluded that the population had once been far larger, before the Bear River Massacre of 1863 greatly reduced their numbers.[35]

The Cache Valley band had once foraged along the Bear River, led by Bear Hunter and Lehi, who later died in the 1863 massacre. They also traveled to Bear Lake, a large and deep freshwater lake, vivid in color. It shone turquoise on bright days, and it teemed with trout and whitefish. The Cache Valley people went there, some fifty miles to the east, on horseback. At Bear Lake they met Shoshones from distant places, including the territory that became Wyoming.[36]

Rachel Perdash left Cache Valley to live at Washakie, thirty miles to the west; but she returned to her old home at least once late in life, about ten years before she met Steward. She visited Cache Valley with a companion, another elderly widow from Washakie. Ottogary mentioned in one of his newspaper columns in 1925 that she and Mrs. Hightop Joshua had recently returned from "motoring over there."

Like Rachel Perdash, Hitope Joshua, also known as Hightop and Hitope Ankegee, was a relative of Chief Sagwitch. She is remembered for her attempt to save his life in the mid-1880s, when he and a small number of Northwestern Shoshones went to live in the aptly named Rough Canyon, west of Washakie. They took refuge there to protect Bishop Isaac Zundel, a white church official, one of many polygamists pursued by federal authorities in the antipolygamy raids of the time. The same raids—against white polygamists, not Shoshone men with more than one wife—led to the imprisonment of George Q. Cannon, Jane's grandfather.[37]

Living conditions in Rough Canyon were so difficult that Sagwitch fell gravely ill. Hitope, who had given birth just two weeks earlier, took her tiny infant with her when she hurried to Washakie to find his sons. Sagwitch died while they were carrying him back. He was buried in a marked grave at Washakie, following Mormon practice and in a departure from Shoshone custom.[38]

When she and Rachel Perdash visited Cache Valley forty years later, in 1925, it scarcely looked like the land of Rachel's childhood. A small city named Logan stood at the site of her birth. Fenced pastures, irrigated fields, and orchards; villages and towns with houses, churches, and schools; two-lane roads and sturdy bridges—all filled the once open land. Most was privately owned. Grazing livestock had degraded the valley's rich grasslands, creating shrubland where wild grasses had flourished. Perhaps two hundred Shoshones had once lived in a place inhabited by more than twenty-seven thousand people when Perdash visited.[39]

Writing later about the Cache Valley Shoshones, Steward named "OD and his sister"—that is, Old Diamond and Rachel Perdash—as his informants, but cited Diamond as the source of specific details.

What he learned from Rachel Perdash, or about her, remained opaque. He did not question other elders, including Hitope Joshua and Yeager Timbimboo. Both of them were Mormon converts who had completed missions for the Mormon church, and Steward may have decided that they were too "assimilated" for his purposes.

Hitope Joshua and her husband had once gone to the Wind River Reservation in Wyoming as missionaries. They traveled hundreds of miles there on horseback.[40]

With just days remaining until Jane's departure for Washington DC, Julian and Jane left Washakie and returned to Salt Lake City. The city of 150,000 occupied part of a broad valley bordering Great Salt Lake. Exactly who had lived there before settlement remained open to question. Archaeology, and the firsthand accounts of nineteenth-century trappers and explorers that Steward consulted, offered little help. As he noted, "surprisingly little information" was available about the people who lived in the valley before Mormons arrived.

Diamond had told Steward that Utes lived at the place where the settlers built their city. Some explorers' accounts suggested, in contrast, that Goshutes and other Shoshones had lived there. According to a Ute tradition, it was neutral territory. According to Mormon tradition, the first settlers to reach the valley in July 1847 found it unoccupied. The people who lived there in some seasons had evidently already left for other hunting and gathering grounds that summer, although a few of them soon returned. "Two Utah Indians came to camp, & traded away two ponies for a rifle & musket," one of the settlers wrote, just five days after the first party of Mormons arrived in the valley.[41]

In 1936 anyone who drove along the broad city streets—past shady green parks and rows of bungalows with hedges and flower gardens and lawns, and through the busy downtown district—found it hard to visualize Salt Lake Valley before settlement. Some of the first Mormon women to reach the valley, after the hard journey across plains and mountains, recalled it as a barren waste. One of the men, who later served as president of his church, may have felt a surge of hope when he saw the creeks that flowed out from canyons in the mountains, still snowcapped in the middle of summer. He called the valley "'the grandest & most sublime'" scenery on earth. Another man reported high stands of grass, six feet tall in some places and ten to twelve feet in others. "After wading thro' thick grass for some distance," he recorded, "we found a place bare enough for a camping ground, the grass being only knee deep, but very thick; we camped on the banks of a beautiful little Stream which was surrounded by very tall grass."[42]

Settlers entered Salt Lake Valley by the thousands during the first year, bringing hunger and disease to the native people who camped there in winter and other seasons. The settlers' livestock—horses, mules, oxen, cattle, sheep, goats, pigs, chickens, geese, and more—ate the grasses and other native plants. The crushing numbers of people, and the nine thousand animals they brought with them, soon burdened the fragile ecology of an arid land. Within a year overgrazing in Salt Lake Valley led settlers to seek new pasture and to take livestock to other valleys.[43]

The newcomers also brought diseases. In 1850 dozens of people who belonged to Wanship's and Goship's bands sought healing at a mineral spring just a mile or two from the heart of the new settlement, named Great Salt Lake City.[44] The area around the spring was an established campsite. Warm, crystalline water flowed from the spring to fill several nearby shallow pools. People immersed themselves there in the sulfurous healing warmth.

Brigham Young and some companions saw the pools only days after reaching the valley in July 1847, and the settlers soon began to use them as well. One of those early settlers recalled that in March 1850, "A great number of Indians came to the warm springs suffering from measles." "It was a new disease to them," he explained, "and they didn't know how to cure it or where they got it." They immersed themselves in the warm waters of the pools, a traditional curing practice, but to no avail. Wanship and Goship were reportedly among those who died and who were buried in a mass grave.[45]

Eight months later, in November 1850, the settlers opened a large bathhouse at the site to serve residents of the quickly growing city. More than six thousand people already lived in the city and valley. It quickly became established practice in Utah Territory, as elsewhere in the Great Basin, for settlers to appropriate the rare and precious water sources of that dry country: springs, streams, rivers, lakes. They did that with a certain sense of entitlement, in the belief that they were "reclaiming the waste," bringing civilization to a wild and unproductive land—and in their view, to wild and unproductive native people who "wandered" or "rambled" on the land. Like nearly all Americans of his time, Brigham Young spoke for civilization and against wild lands as wasteland. He exhorted the settlers to "improve upon, and make beautiful everything around you. . . . Build cities, adorn your habitations, make gardens, orchards, and vineyards." They took most of the water for those tasks.[46]

The bathhouse at Warm Springs went through many incarnations over the years. In the 1920s the city commissioned a new structure for the site. Jane and Julian drove past the white Mission-style building with a red tile roof when they left Salt Lake City on the way north, to Ogden. An architectural firm owned by one of Jane's innumerable Cannon cousins had designed the latest building.[47]

A plaque had been placed at the site ten years earlier by a lineage society, the Daughters of the American Revolution. It memorialized Jim Bridger, Jedediah Smith, and Etienne Provost as some of the first white men to visit the area. There was no mention of Indians who had lived and died at the site. No trace of their former presence remained visible to residents of Salt Lake Valley, aside from a few place names. A village in a nearby valley took the name of Wanship, recalled as "a friendly Shoshone Indian chief."[48]

The ecological and cultural transformation of the valley had been swift and thorough. The first settlers had launched a campaign against the wild, putting an end to a foraging way of life in that place. The men immediately set to work plowing the land, sowing seeds, and diverting water for irrigation. They tore up sagebrush not only to clear the land but also to use as fuel.

According to the first settlers' memories, as reported by one of Brigham Young's daughters, they found only one tree growing in the valley. As in most arid places, trees did not naturally take root at a distance from water, but cottonwoods and willows did line the banks of the Jordan River and creeks. Mere traces of green dismayed the easterners, who came from wooded lands. The newcomers could not conceive of nonnative trees as thirsty intruders in sagebrush country, and they quickly began to plant a great variety, for ornament and shade and fruit. A grove of locust trees soon stood near the bathhouse at Warm Springs.[49]

They also systematically killed any wild animals that preyed on their animals or crops, a repetition of organized hunts carried out a century earlier by farmers in the East. In the first winter two teams of a hundred men each competed in hunting. Brigham Young reported that they killed seven hundred wolves and foxes and two wolverines in the valley and vicinity. The first number probably included "prairie wolves," another name for coyotes. The hunters killed smaller predators as well: twenty weasels and skunks, five hundred owls, hawks, and magpies, and a thousand ravens. Shoshones had not hunted these animals for food, as Steward learned from elders, and they had no other reason to kill them.[50]

When he and Jane drove through the city in 1936, few Indians lived and worked there, but many Shoshones, including the people of Washakie, visited. Some of those baptized as Mormons attended the church's General Conference, held twice yearly in spring and fall. Others sought medical care in case of a serious illness, or bought goods available only there. They came and went, fleeting visitors to the city in the big valley.[51]

Jane boarded a train at the Union Pacific Railroad station in downtown Salt Lake City in late September 1936. Her departure for Washington, just ten weeks before she was due to give birth, represented a quiet victory. Julian had urged her to remain in Utah for the birth so that he could keep on with fieldwork through December. As he had told Kroeber two months earlier, "we might stay out here until the child is born, which would give me a couple of extra months for work and consequently more [trait] lists."

With great tact, Jane listed some reasons against this plan in their journal. In the first place, their lease for the apartment in Arlington, Virginia, began on October 1; and, "more important, Seidner is leaving for London to be gone all fall." She did not search for a substitute for Dr. Seidner in Ogden or Salt Lake City. With her parents far away in London, and her favorite physician on his way there for advanced medical study, prolonging the stay in Utah seemed pointless.[52]

In truth, she felt neglected. Libby's marital problems, other family concerns, and the pressing demands of work at the British Mission had occupied nearly all of Joseph and Mona's attention for more than a year. They had not written to her for months. Mona's sister, Claire, heard a plaintive report from Jane during a visit in Salt Lake City that summer. "By the way," she told Mona, "Jane feels a little hurt that you have not acknowledged her news about the little Steward—or Stewardess." "Perhaps you have by now," Claire added, "but her appeal was more or less pathetic when she was visiting us." "Now for goodness' sake, don't pass that on to her!" she urged. "Just write a happy letter showing lots of interest in *her*."

Joseph, distracted by work and by concerns about his five younger children, put off writing for months. A letter he received earlier that summer from Jane and Julian did not provoke a quick reply, or perhaps any reply. It contained Julian's withering critique of Mormon scripture in light of scientific evidence about American prehistory. ("You asked for a frank statement," Jane reminded her father.) Months later Joseph did finally write, and perhaps recalling Claire's advice he told Jane, "We are extremely anxious about the Great Event."[53]

Only a year earlier Jane had sent long letters to her parents filled with details about the journeys with Julian. She had entered into fieldwork with great energy, treating it as high adventure and a mission for science. In her first letter from the field she reported, "The work is pleasant—and the prospect of getting data on these comparatively unknown people is making the trip so important." But circumstances had changed, and now the consuming demands of fieldwork wore on her.

Months of travel—from the cross-country trip in high summer; to the days spent driving in stifling heat to and from reservations, where she listened for hours on end, or did not listen, to countless questions and answers about what the elders remembered; to say nothing of nights spent in a series of dreary auto cabins—had only strengthened her wish for a rooted life.

Just two years earlier she had told Mona breezily, "I'll probably be a grandmother before I have a house where I'll stay put for more than 6 months." In the interval, she and Julian had lived in three apartments, one house, and a room in a residential hotel. They had stayed with an array of friends and relatives across the United States, from Berkeley to Washington DC, in the course of their travels. They had camped in the desert at sites scattered across five states. They had checked into and out of auto cabins in a blur of little hamlets and towns. The nomadic life had lost its appeal. She settled into the sanctuary of the train compartment, pleased by the prospect of a new apartment with a long lease, and of the comforts of domesticity that awaited her at journey's end.

Even her husband looked forward to that change in their lives once he yielded to the realities of marriage and parenthood, which in this instance meant ending fieldwork two months sooner than he wished. Putting the best face on his early return to the East—and expressing a truth about his unsettled life of the past several years—he remarked to Stirling, "And, oh boy, to think of having an apartment already contracted for when we get back. Never had such a luxury before."[54]

10. Trail's End

STEWARD LEFT SALT LAKE CITY the day after his wife boarded the train for Washington. His original plan called for spending a week at the Uintah and Ouray Reservation, then driving west to Skull Valley and Deep Creek Valley to find Goshute informants. With less than three weeks to finish his own field research, he needed to complete one piece of work as well for the BAE in western Nevada. It added up to nearly two thousand extra miles of travel but provided a chance to circle back through southern Nevada, where he hoped to find a Southern Paiute elder to serve as his last informant. And he still needed to visit one or two reservations in Utah in order to write a report for the BIA. Time was running short.[1]

When his work at the Uintah and Ouray Reservation did not go well, he set aside his first plan and left after just one day. Hoping to put his waning time in the field to better use, he reversed course and drove back across the Wasatch Mountains, where groves of quaking aspens gleamed bright gold in the sunlight. The shimmering silver-green trees of summer now wore the rich colors of autumn. Stands of mountain maples shone copper and bronze, lighting up the slopes and heralding the coming cold.

Descending from fall flamboyance in the mountains to a dry plain, Steward continued on toward Skull Valley in Utah's west desert. The highway passed between the southern shore of Great Salt Lake and the northern end of the Oquirrh Mountains. John Muir had walked in those mountains sixty years earlier, during the summer of 1877.

Steward drove by the northern slope where Muir had climbed toward the crest, a place that he would not have recognized in 1936.

Muir recorded seeing thick stands of spruce and quaking aspens and fields of wild lilies. "The whole mountain-side was aglow" with lilies in full bloom, he said, from an elevation of "fifty-five hundred feet to the very edge of the snow" near the peak. As he climbed he noticed tracks of deer and wild sheep that lived in the high country. An arresting scene—of mountains and wildflowers and shining colors—lingered in his mind's eye. "[A]mong my memories of this strange land," Muir wrote, "that Oquirrh mountain, with its golden lilies, will ever rise in clear relief."

By 1936 that scene was no more than an old memory recorded in the pages of a book. Muir had died twenty-two years earlier, some said from a broken heart, a witness to the devastation inflicted on the Sierra Nevada and other western lands. On the northern slope of the Oquirrh Mountains, the lily fields and trees that he admired and wrote about lovingly, had vanished.[2]

Walter Cottam believed that a smelter built at the foot of the slope around the turn of the century explained the loss of life and erosion on the mountain. The trees and other plants were probably all dead by 1920, he said, killed by toxic fumes from the smelter. When heavy rain fell on the bare land, it cut gullies that deepened over time. Cottam began to take students in his ecology courses to the site, to see the ruin. He ignored No Trespassing signs posted by a mining company that owned the land and smelter. For Cottam, the importance of this lesson in ecology for his students took precedence over property rights that had allowed the destruction.[3]

As Steward passed through Garfield, the company town where the smelter stood, the usual pall of blue-gray smoke hung over it. The smelter, a sprawling structure of steel and sheet-iron, produced blister copper from ore, which was then shipped to refineries in other states. The ore came from an enormous open-pit mine in a canyon to the south.[4]

A mile or two from Garfield, he drove past waste from the smelting process. The molten slag, carried away from the smelter and dumped there, formed high mounds. At night the glow of molten rock was visible for miles—a sad successor to the glowing lilies of the Oquirrhs.[5]

Skull Valley's resonant English name captured the bare-as-bones look of the land. The name Goshutes, which Steward learned meant Dust Utes, was both apt and misleading. Dust storms did sweep across the open and empty terrain of the nearby salt desert, but the people, Steward soon concluded, were Shoshones, not Utes. Their name had confused many explorers and settlers and, later, anthropologists as well. Some twenty-five years earlier, in print, Kroeber had alluded to the Goshute language as Shoshone, but their cultural and linguistic identity remained a source of confusion in the 1930s, as Steward noted in *Basin-Plateau*.[6]

Explorers and others called them Go-Sha-Utes, Goships, Gosh-Uta, Go-Shute, Goshoots, and Gosiutes. Their territory stretched south of Great Salt Lake in the most arid part of western Utah and included a fringe of eastern Nevada. Steward had seen the northern portion of it during the previous summer, on trips between Salt Lake City and Elko, Nevada, when he crossed the Great Salt Lake Desert.[7]

The northern part attracted few settlers, but land to the south proved more hospitable. As early as 1849, two years after the first Mormons arrived in Salt Lake Valley, settlers moved into an adjacent valley, on the other side of the Oquirrh Mountains and in a favorable part of Goshute territory. Wild grasses, water, and timber were reportedly abundant there. The settlers built houses, surrounded by a wall to protect them from attack by Indians, and called their new home Tooele. Their horses, oxen, cattle, and sheep grazed on lands where Goshutes collected wild plants and hunted. Within a decade of settlement, a thousand people had settled in Tooele Valley. The few Goshutes could no longer find enough food for themselves and their children by foraging there.[8]

During those same years, thousands of overlanders, headed for the goldfields in California or Nevada's Comstock Lode, also entered Goshute country on the way west. A young Samuel Clemens—better known by his later pen name, Mark Twain—crossed it in 1861. Years later he recalled the people and the land in *Roughing It*, a chronicle of that journey and his sojourn in the West. When he passed through Goshute country, he was on his way to Nevada. After failing as a miner, he would launch a writing career, making his debut as a reporter for the *Virginia City Territorial Enterprise*.

Because of his fame, Twain's comments on Goshutes endured in the public mind. Taken at face value, they were a first, and his worst, piece of reporting. In truth, his book was a strange hybrid, part memoir and travelogue and part tall tale. An irreverent and unsparing humor—his hallmark as a writer—surfaced on nearly every page. No one escaped his barbs, including the author himself. But in chapter XIX the humor qualified as cruel wit, in light of the desperate state of Goshutes in his time—not merely judged by the standard of another time.

Although he had only glimpses of them, he accurately described "Goshoots" as "hungry, always hungry." But he apparently did not know, as generations of his readers would not know, that the people he scorned as food scavengers were near starvation. Few outsiders, perhaps including most settlers, fully understood that their own presence and actions had ruined Goshute hunting and gathering grounds. This ecological crisis for Goshutes brought about their hunger and desperation. Many settlers, and Twain as well, complained instead about the nuisance of their "begging." Some Goshutes asked for food instead of quietly starving.

The Pony Express and Overland Stage had added to the damage

by building stations at intervals across their territory and next to the few water sources. The stations provided respite for riders and travelers. Goshutes had thus been displaced from their most vital resources, food and water, not only by settlers but also by a steady flow of transients. The latter included the well-fed Twain and fellow passengers. Just before reaching Goshute country, the travelers had spent a few days enjoying city comforts. Twain recalled his pleasure at eating "a fine supper of the freshest meats and fowls and vegetables—a great variety and as great abundance." In his own words, "we left Great Salt Lake City hearty and well fed and happy."[9]

The hungry Goshutes did not partake in such fine suppers. When foraging failed and asking for food proved futile, they tried taking food ("stealing" or "raiding"). That began soon after settlers arrived and disrupted the ecology of their desert land. Goshutes finally resorted to direct attacks, meant to drive out the intruders, although they had no warrior tradition. As Steward pointed out many years later, "they were not aboriginally inclined to war . . . and could readily escape into the deserts and mountains." Pahvant Utes may have led them in some attacks. Twain complained of a recent assault on a stagecoach that had resulted in the driver's death.[10]

To stop the escalating violence, a new superintendent of Indian Affairs in Utah Territory—Brigham Young's replacement in that position—decided to establish Indian farms. Some Goshutes resisted at first, but then agreed to try farming. They faced a stark choice: grow food or starve. So willing was one group to try that, even before getting any tools or instruction, they managed to turn up the stubborn soil with sticks and to plant seeds of wheat on forty acres of land. Some men also found paid work as laborers for white farmers and ranchers. That became a common practice throughout the Great Basin, and it persisted, as Steward saw during his boyhood years in Deep Springs Valley and on his first trips through the Owens Valley.[11]

In early October 1936, when he visited the Skull Valley reservation, a few people still eked out a living by farming. That even thirty-nine Goshutes, the total number of residents, lived on ancestral land was surprising. In the 1860s, starting before the signing of treaties, there had been efforts in Utah Territory to remove Goshutes as well as other Shoshones and Utes from their homelands: at first, to send them east to the Uinta Basin; and later, north to the Fort Hall Reservation in Idaho; or a thousand miles southeast to Indian Territory, soon to become Oklahoma. Goshutes steadfastly refused to leave their native lands, and they adapted to the new and radically changed conditions of life in order to stay and to survive. The federal government finally established a small reservation in Skull Valley in the early years of the twentieth century, and later enlarged it.[12]

In contrast, the outsiders who moved in often moved on. Discouraged by a hard life in a hard land, they did not long remain in a place they found so alien. When Steward left the highway to drive into Skull Valley, the rutted road took him past the abandoned site of Iosepa. A colony of native Hawaiians and other Polynesians, converts to the Mormon faith, had once lived there on thirteen hundred acres of land provided by the church. The settlement was called Iosepa, Hawaiian for Joseph, in honor of Joseph Smith. Steward undoubtedly knew about Iosepa. His wife's grandfather, George Q. Cannon, had served as one of the first Mormon missionaries to Hawaii, where he translated the Book of Mormon into Hawaiian.[13]

The colonists had moved to Utah to be near a temple, but they struggled in Skull Valley. The contrasts between their tropical homeland and Utah's west desert—with palm trees replaced by sagebrush, soft Hawaiian air by dry gusting wind, green taro by struggling stands of pale wheat—made adjusting to life at Iosepa difficult. They well recalled the gentle climate and steady warmth of their island home. Skull Valley offered singeing heat and sun-baked soil in summer. In winter, dustings of snow on sagebrush left the desert floor clothed in sparkling frozen lace.

Some of the Hawaiians remained in their adopted home for more than twenty years, but they never fully adapted to the desert. In 1917 nearly all of them returned to Hawaii where construction of a temple was underway on the island of Oahu. They left Skull Valley to the Goshutes with no regrets. The two groups had lived amiably but not intimately as neighbors. Goshutes reportedly attended luaus as guests, and sometimes a Goshute named Frank Moody invited men from Iosepa to hunt with him in the mountains. They may once have hunted wild game in Hawaii or Samoa, but any skills as fishermen that they brought to Skull Valley went largely to waste in that parched land, and any appetite for seafood went unsatisfied. There was reportedly no intermarriage between Goshutes and the Mormon Polynesians, who left few traces behind when they disappeared from the desert.[14]

As Steward already knew, the people of Skull Valley had deeper and more enduring ties with kin and friends at Washakie and the Uintah and Ouray Reservation. He looked up a man named George Moody as soon as he arrived, no doubt having heard of him at Washakie or the Uintah and Ouray Reservation. Moody was a familiar visitor in both places. Seth Eagle and Ray Diamond probably recommended him as an informant for Skull Valley, and Steward set to work with him immediately.

Moody, whom he also called Mudiak in print, was a widower. His wife and one of his daughters had died years earlier, but a surviving daughter was about thirty years old and married. She lived two hundred miles away at the Uintah and Ouray Reservation, and he went there often to visit her. As Steward learned, intermarriage between Goshutes and neighboring Utes was not uncommon. "They intermarried somewhat with Ute to the east," he later wrote, adding that "it made Gosiute no less Shoshoni." After most Utes went to the reservation in the Uinta Basin, some of the people of Skull Valley who had ties with Utes traveled there each year to visit.[15]

Moody sometimes went to the Fort Hall Reservation in Idaho as well as to Washakie. Ottogary occasionally mentioned him in his newspaper columns, along with visitors from other reservations. As Ottogary reported in one column, Moody had stayed with him for about two weeks in January. He had traveled to Idaho a month earlier on a "land matter," and expected to return there soon on the "same business." "His home is in Skull Valley," Ottogary explained to readers, "and he will return home some time next month." Other people whom he mentioned by name paid visits to Washakie while working seasonally as farm hands nearby, and for a range of other reasons.[16]

Steward, like most outsiders who traveled through Goshute country in Utah's west desert, saw it as among the most desolate in the entire Great Basin. "The Gosiute habitat," he later wrote, "is one of the least favorable in the entire Shoshoni area." Such an arid and "exceptionally unproductive" place, as he called it, supported few people. "The population was probably sparser," Steward said, "than in any other part of the Shoshonean area of the same size."

Based on what he learned from Moody, he estimated a population density just one-tenth or less of the density of Nevada's Ruby Valley and California's Owens Valley. As he neared the end of fieldwork, those valleys retained their standing as two of the most fertile and densely populated in the Great Basin. "It is probable," he said, "that, including the Great Salt Lake Desert, there was not over one person to 30 or 40 square miles" in Goshute country. And unlike neighboring Utes and the Northern Shoshones, but in common with neighboring Western Shoshones, Goshutes had lived in a land that could not easily support horses along with people. They had traveled on foot in the past.[17]

The forbidding Great Salt Lake Desert stretched out to the west of Skull Valley. It qualified as Utah's version of the Amargosa Desert at its worst, or Badwater, the notorious but far smaller region that Steward had seen in Death Valley. He summed up the desert in one sentence of precise and harrowing detail: "a level plain of alkali and

pure salt, 20 to 40 miles broad, more than 100 miles long, and per-
fectly level, which supports no vegetation and has no fresh water."
(Twain preferred metaphor: "Imagine a vast waveless ocean, stricken
dead and turned to ash," he wrote.) Travelers who crossed that waterless plain on foot or by wagon had done so at the risk of their lives.
Both Steward and Twain had heard tales about the ill-fated Donner
party and others.[18]

Moody, like other Goshutes, knew exactly where to find water in
his own country, although settlers had claimed much of it. Here and
there in the Oquirrh and Cedar mountains, springs seeped out of
the earth and fed small streams. No rivers ran through their country, and far less rain fell than in the Wasatch valleys to the east. That
made Skull Valley and land directly west perhaps *the* most arid inhabited place that Steward visited in his fieldwork.

When he passed through in 1936 the damaging effects of settlement no doubt contributed to what most outsiders viewed as the valley's bleak look. Goshutes, still strongly attached to their home, saw
it differently. However desolate the land appeared to travelers, they
had known how to support themselves there, as Moody explained in
detail to Steward.[19]

He told a story that featured not Coyote but Sinav, a name that
Steward did not translate. The story ended with some revealing words
about Goshutes.

The Origin of People
Two women, a mother and her daughter, lived on an island in
Great Salt Lake. . . .

Sinav and Coyote lived in Skull Valley. After the girl had killed all
the men in the world, she came to get Coyote. Sinav told her that
there was [no such person as] Coyote. Sinav went with the woman
toward her home. It was very hot and they had no water. After a
while the woman wanted to rest under a tree, but Sinav knew better
[than to let her stop]. He said, "No, we must go on." They went

on to Great Salt Lake. The woman walked across on the water to the island. Sinav stayed near the shore, standing in the water. The girl's mother said to her, "Why don't you bring him over?" The girl made a path of earth through the water. Sinav walked over to the island, the water closing in behind him all the way . . .

For several days Sinav hunted and brought in two deer each day. Each night he visited the women. Each woman bore a baby daily and put it in a large basketry jug. The jug became larger each day.

Finally the older woman told Sinav to go South and take the jug with him. . . . At first, as he walked along, the jug was light and easy to carry. It became heavier. After a while, he had to set it down. . . .

Sinav heard a buzzing noise like a bee inside the jug. He wanted to look. When he began to open it, men jumped out and made a lot of dust. They knocked him over and ran away. . . . They were Shoshoni, Ute, Paiute, and other tribes. The last man to come out was all covered with dust. He was the Gosiute. He is tougher than other people; he is bulletproof.[20]

Although Steward thought Moody was seventy-six, born about 1860, census takers listed his date of birth as the early 1870s and gave his age as sixty-three. If they were correct, Moody was born nearly twenty-five years after the first Mormon settlers arrived in Tooele Valley, which explains why he had no firsthand knowledge about Goshutes who had once lived there. They were almost immediately displaced by settlers and grazing livestock.

Eighty years later, those Goshutes might not have recognized their home. Tooele Valley, as an explorer described it and an early settler remembered it, had once looked like fertile grassland. Stands of high waving grass spread across the valley. The first cattle brought there to graze sometimes disappeared from the view of their keepers, lost in tall grass.

Steward, like most people in the 1930s, did not understand the scale of damage done in a very short time by settlement. It had completely changed the look of the land he saw around him. Even Walter Cottam did not reach that understanding of Tooele Valley until about ten years later. He gave a public lecture then with the controversial title, "Is Utah Sahara Bound?"[21]

By the 1930s years of overgrazing had turned Tooele Valley into what newspapers called "Central Utah's 'dust bowl.'" The abundant tall grasses had not only declined quickly after settlement, but by 1930 nearly all of the natural forage, including shrubs, had vanished. Transient herds of livestock that passed through the valley—en route from winter pasture to summer pasture and back again—had grazed the land to dust. Wind had blown away inches of soil, and the valley floor, no longer level, had a surface marked by hummocks and pits. In the severe dust storms of 1934 and 1935, sheep and cattle died from breathing the dust. The recurrent storms so discouraged people that many spoke of moving to other places. At least one rancher simply abandoned his ranch.

The U.S. Soil Conservation Service soon launched one of the largest land restoration projects of the time. The goal was to reclaim tens of thousands of acres of bare land in Tooele Valley that had turned to dust. The strategy, which was showing some signs of success when Steward drove by, was to help hardy weeds such as tumbleweed and salt brush to take root, thereby anchoring the soil. The next step was to sow grass seed.[22]

Skull Valley may have shown slightly less wear and tear than Tooele Valley since not so many people lived there, and it had less to offer by way of pasture. But a few ranchers had settled in the valley at an early date, and others brought in large herds of sheep, numbering in the thousands, to winter each year in the valley. At least one ranch, as Steward was to learn from Moody, occupied a site where Goshutes had once lived in a named village. The ranch also claimed one of the valley's few springs.[23]

Moody had come to Skull Valley at a young age from his birth-place in eastern Nevada, in Goshute country around the Deep Creek Mountains. He grew up in Skull Valley and spent most of his later life there. Since he had no firsthand memories of that valley or Tooele Valley before settlement, he drew on those of his maternal grandfather, another ghost informant. Moody spoke English so fluently that Steward did not need to hire an interpreter.[24]

Moody told Steward about several sites in the valley or nearby where his people had once lived, including some on the western slope of the Cedar Mountains, and one near the place where the Hawaiians later settled, at Iosepa. Another site was a cave at the northern end of the Skull Valley Mountains. Steward found it a short distance from the highway, but when he entered the cave he saw little evidence of Goshute occupation. He reported only "a single muller," a pestle used for grinding seeds.[25]

He learned from Moody that families gathered seeds from areas along the streams and in the mountains; few edible plants grew in the arid valleys. Skull Valley Goshutes went south, or more than a hundred miles west to the Deep Creek Mountains, to collect pine nuts, a crucial part of their food supply. Families agreed before they went to harvest pine nuts that each would pick in a defined area.[26] They appear to have treated the mountains as a common.

"There was no ownership of seed or pine-nut areas," Steward later wrote, "even Ute being permitted to gather in Gosiute country."[27] Of course, some Utes had ties through marriage, which may explain why they gathered food there. The word *permitted* also suggests that Goshutes may have claimed a right to decide who used their gathering grounds. Whatever the case, the concept of ownership that Steward had taken into the field had not changed in many months of field-work with people who did *not* enforce a rigid set of exclusionary rights to natural resources.

Instead of rethinking that concept of ownership—by asking about, and taking account of, Goshute beliefs and concepts—he concluded that they did not own the land where they gathered plants. He still gave attention only to the external and observable. He had learned that Goshutes did not exclude others, which was an observable practice. He did not care how Moody might have explained that practice from a Goshute point of view. That could not be observed. And in Steward's view, and by the tenets of behaviorism, that disqualified it as a subject for scientific investigation.

Besides traveling west for pine nuts, Goshutes from Skull Valley had also walked more than fifty miles east to a narrow green canyon in the Wasatch Mountains for deer and pronghorn antelope drives. Mormon settlers named it Mill Creek Canyon within a month of arriving in Salt Lake Valley in 1847. The clear, cold water of the creek filled small pools and spilled over rocks as it ran west, where it joined the Jordan River. Water-driven gristmills set up in the canyon to grind grain soon ruined it as a Gosiute hunting ground. Years later it became a favorite picnicking place for residents of Salt Lake City.[28]

In their valleys to the west Goshutes routinely found only small game such as rodents and rabbits. One early settler and scout recounted how women hunted ground squirrels—or, as some might prefer to say about women, how they gathered ground squirrels. They diverted water into the squirrels' holes by means of small ditches, killing dozens of the rodents in short order as they fled from their underground home. Along with the crickets and grasshoppers that Goshutes collected, the ground squirrels provided a far more reliable supply of food than deer and pronghorn antelope.[29]

The first settlers in Salt Lake Valley regarded it as a calamity and plague when multitudes of large black crickets descended on their fields, consuming the crops. For Goshutes, the arrival of crickets presented a splendid opportunity. They gathered them in baskets, dried them, and feasted on cricket cakes. Sun dried and roasted, the insect silage could last for months. Ground up, it resembled coarse meal.[30]

Although Goshutes kindly demonstrated how to make the nutritious cricket cakes, the famished settlers refused to eat them. Instead, they tried to exterminate the crickets and to quell their hunger by eating wild greens, sego lily bulbs, and other plants that they had learned about from Goshutes. Some resorted to eating the wolves (or perhaps coyotes) and hawks they killed as vermin, fending off starvation with those remnants of the wild.[31]

Goshutes did not regard those animals as vermin or, in general, as food. Hawk, Wolf, and Coyote figured in some of their origin stories:

> It was Hawk who made the Deep Creek Mountains. Hawk was angry. It must have been because someone was fooling around with his wife. He flew up high, then dashed himself against the mountain (Mt. Wheeler) and broke it all up. It made all these mountains.[32]

After spending three days with Moody, Steward left Skull Valley. His destination—the Deep Creek Mountains and a second, larger Goshute reservation—was about a hundred and fifty miles away. He headed there on a dirt road that crossed the desert from Skull Valley to the Utah-Nevada border. His route took him through open land along the edge of the Great Salt Lake Desert, south of a site featured just days earlier in the national and international news. The racers, reporters, and spectators who had materialized at the Bonneville Salt Flats in late September had already disappeared from that land of mirage by early October.

Steward had passed the Bonneville Salt Flats many times, on trips to and from Salt Lake City along the highway that crossed the middle of the Great Salt Lake Desert. The salt flats, an open stretch of shimmering white bordered by the austere Silver Island Mountains, covered a hundred square miles and had a crust as hard as concrete. Goshutes had not likely found any food or water in that place, but in the twentieth century the Bonneville Salt Flats attracted auto racers who saw a natural racecourse with commercial potential.[33]

A few days earlier a racer named Ab Jenkins had set eight land speed records. He was a hometown boy, from Salt Lake City, trying to overturn records set there in the previous years by world-famous British racers Malcolm Campbell and John Cobb. Driving a Duesenberg Special, dubbed the *Mormon Meteor*, Jenkins set a new endurance record of over 170 miles an hour. *The New York Times* and newspapers around the world reported his triumph. Three years later Salt Lake City's most celebrated citizen was elected mayor.[34]

As Steward neared the Utah-Nevada border, traveling at a fraction of racing speed, he turned off the dirt road and onto an even rougher track. With clouds of dust still in pursuit, he drove toward the reservation. Ibapah Peak, rising more than twelve thousand feet above sea level and more than seven thousand feet above the valley floor, stood as a sentinel of the Deep Creek Mountains. Its granite face shone white even when the snow melted away in summer. Green trees covered its flanks.

Nearby valleys where large stands of wild grasses once grew had met the usual fate after settlement. Ranchers prospered for a time by raising sheep. Outside herds also wintered in the Deep Creek country. After spending the summer months grazing high in the mountains of Idaho and Utah, they were trailed hundreds of miles to Utah's west desert, where winters were less severe. The wild grasses soon declined, but the sheep continued to arrive in numbers, grazing on any forage they could find.

Just two years earlier, in 1934, federal legislation in the form of the Taylor Grazing Act had finally brought an end to unrestricted grazing on public lands. It became illegal to move tramp herds—those that grazed entirely on public range—from place to place. Much of the land bore the marks of overgrazing: the patches of bare ground, eroded stream banks, and shrubs where grasses had once grown all signaled a decline in biodiversity. Overgrazing, together with drought, had produced the blinding dust storms of the early 1930s.[35]

When Steward arrived at the Goshute Reservation, he found that about a hundred and fifty people lived there, on land that straddled a state line. Most of it lay on the Utah side, with a smaller portion in Nevada, but for Goshutes the more meaningful border separated their recently acquired reservation from the surrounding land held by farmers and ranchers. The reservation had been established only about twenty years earlier. Steward saw that many of the people lived in log houses, as on other reservations, and he passed the small school that children attended.[36]

Despite years of effort by missionaries—beginning with those sent in the nineteenth century, and including Willie Ottogary in the next— there were far fewer Mormon converts at Deep Creek than at Washakie. Ottogary and fellow missionaries had also visited the Skull Valley Reservation, with limited success. By the 1930s peyote ceremonies took place at the Deep Creek Reservation, Uintah-Ouray Reservation, Fort Hall Reservation, and others. About half of the Goshutes at Deep Creek reportedly attended the ceremonies in which peyote, a mildly hallucinogenic plant, was treated as sacramental.[37]

Before Steward left Skull Valley, Moody had probably given him the name of Frank Bonamont, a Goshute elder and lifelong resident of the Deep Creek country. Then in his midseventies, Bonamont looked younger than his years. Underestimating his age, Steward described him as "a man of about sixty or seventy, who has always lived at Deep Creek where he was born." Like Moody, Bonamont spoke English so fluently that there was no need for an interpreter.

He lived with his wife, Minnie, who was in her fifties, and three of their children. A thirty-three-year-old son sometimes worked as a sheepherder for one of the white ranchers in the area. None of their children had learned to read or write except perhaps the youngest daughter, who was seven years old and enrolled in school. The day school that she attended had not existed when the older children were her age. Every member of the family could speak English. Census takers listed Frank Bonamont's occupation as *farmer*.[38]

Bonamont told Steward that his people collected pine nuts, an important staple, in the Deep Creek Mountains, at the southern end of their valley. They did not have to cache the harvested nuts or carry them far to take them home. As Steward knew in advance, by reading Ralph Chamberlin's publications, Goshutes had used about a hundred species of wild plants for food, medicine, or other purposes. In a rare show of feeling in print, Steward praised Chamberlin's very thorough and helpful studies as "splendid."[39]

Chamberlin, a zoologist, was a senior professor and chairman of the departments of Botany and Zoology during Steward's time at the University of Utah. The two men shared some interests as well as an alma mater: Chamberlin earned a doctorate at Cornell, where Steward later majored in zoology and geology as an undergraduate. Both of them had experienced conflicts between science and religion. Years earlier Chamberlin had resigned from the faculty of Brigham Young University because of controversy about teaching evolution. "'I have an obligation to the students,' he said at the time, 'and I'll teach them what I honestly believe can be supported by the evidence.'"

Chamberlin had helped Steward in a variety of ways, even after he left the University of Utah. At one point he interceded with the president about a publication matter, involving an archaeological report that Steward had written. At the outset of fieldwork in 1935, Steward had contacted him once again. He inquired about Chamberlin's research materials on Goshutes.[40]

Many years earlier Chamberlin had worked with Goshute elders in Skull Valley. He may have had some contact with others as well, in Deep Creek country where he had personal ties. Later, after earning a PhD, he published detailed studies of Goshute ethnobotany: their knowledge of wild plants, including how they used those plants for food, medicine, and other purposes. He remarked that Goshute plant names often had to do with habitat, "the ecological relations seeming most obtrusive in their minds."[41]

Nearly fifty years after meeting Goshute elders, who taught him part of what they knew, Chamberlin called them with admiration, "thoroughly good naturalists in a real sense of the term." That endorsement came from a professional biologist who had spent a long career in teaching and research. He recalled the depth and breadth of the elders' knowledge. "They knew the habits and activities of the animals great and small, and they knew the plants in form and color, texture and taste, and according to season and habitat," he explained.

By the early years of the twentieth century those knowledgeable elders, as he noted, were already "fast passing away." Young people knew far less about the natural world, a world that had in any case been transformed by settlement. Two of those young people would serve thirty-five years later as Steward's informants. In terms of ecological knowledge, George Moody and Frank Bonamont probably could not match the elders who had instructed Chamberlin. That made his research on Goshute ethnobotany all the more valuable to Steward.[42]

The German scientist Ernst Haeckel, born about the same time as those earlier elders, coined the term *ecology*. He named something previously unnamed but not unknown in science—or outside of science. Hunter-gatherers, including the Goshute elders, were the original ecologists.[43]

The people of Deep Creek country, as Steward learned, had not only collected but also sown wild seeds. They shared that practice with some Western Shoshones in Nevada, but not, he noted, with Goshutes of Skull Valley. Deep Creek Goshutes burned off brush in the fall and then sowed seeds of *tui*, a plant he could not identify. He speculated that it was a root or "possibly *Urtica*" (nettle). "There was no native horticulture of domesticated plants," he added. In other words, Goshutes did not cultivate corn or beans or squash or other plants domesticated in the Americas.[44] But their previous experience with wild seeds, as well as their acute hunger after settlers arrived, may explain why—before receiving any tools and instructions—some of them planted wheat.

Chamberlin's publications spared Steward the task of asking about plants and recording a long list of plant names. It gave him more time to ask Moody and Bonamont questions about hunting, a topic of far greater interest to him. He learned that besides hunting deer, people in Deep Creek country held rabbit drives in the winter. Communal antelope drives, which could yield two dozen of the animals, took place in a valley about twenty miles away. These were rare events. It took years for the population of pronghorn antelope to recover and to make the work worthwhile. Many men and women cooperated to build a corral and drive the antelope into it. Even in Deep Creek Valley, which Steward called "a comparatively fertile oasis," game animals were limited, and crickets and grasshoppers provided a mainstay.[45]

Here, as elsewhere in the Great Basin, Steward found great flexibility in a range of cultural practices. Married couples in the past had resided with the wife's family for a year or so, "as a kind of bride service," Steward explained. Decisions about where to live after the first year "depended upon circumstances," he added. He learned of instances of polygyny, often sororal, and one case of polyandry: a woman in Skull Valley who had lived conjugally with two half brothers.

Steward spent at least three days with Bonamont, but left with some questions about his reliability as a cultural informant for Deep Creek country. Bonamont had always lived there, but he had associated with people "from a hundred miles in all directions," Steward said. They came from many locales to live on the reservation. It seemed likely, he concluded, that some traits from other places had ended up on the Deep Creek Goshute trait list.[46]

When he wrote to Kroeber a month later, Steward reported having greater luck with Goshutes in Skull Valley and Deep Creek Valley than with Utes in the Uinta Basin. His work had yielded two trait lists for Kroeber and material for his own ecological project. He had found no evidence of patrilineal bands in these sparsely populated places—in fact, no evidence of bands at all as he defined them. Instead, "the family was the sovereign unit," he said. The final verdict from his research in Skull Valley and Deep Creek Valley was that Goshutes (or Goshute Western Shoshones) were "indistinguishable" from other Western Shoshones in language as well as in culture. As he told Kroeber, "They are, incidentally, thorough-going Shoshoni in language."[47]

Steward apparently did not take time to photograph Goshute country or Moody and Bonamont. He may have put away his camera because he had already taken many photographs in Utah during fieldwork in the early 1930s.[48]

When Steward left the remote Deep Creek country, it was pine nut season. He and Jane had planned the previous year to join Shoshones for the harvest in the fall. "We want to go up to the mountains to pick pine nuts with some of them," Jane told her father then. But life took an unexpected turn, and they left for Washington DC in October 1935. A year later, alone and with other tasks to complete farther west, Steward did not linger to take part in the harvest. What he had learned about it from elders, and from at least one old report, would have to suffice.[49]

He headed four hundred miles west to Fallon, Nevada, traveling on the Lincoln Highway. The BAE wanted him to investigate some caves near Fallon, and, as he complained to Kroeber, what looked like one inch on a map at headquarters in Washington added up to hundreds of highway miles in Utah and Nevada. But he did have the pleasure of fall weather on this trip across the Nevada desert, in contrast to his trips of the previous year. Cool air rushed in the open windows as he drove through a desert ablaze with stands of rabbitbrush in autumn bloom. Thick clusters of yellow-gold flowers lighted up the pale brown land, giving it the look of a spacious sand garden.[50]

Pressed for time, he passed up a return trip north to Elko and then on to the Duck Valley Reservation where he had worked the previous summer. Before leaving Washington, he had told Kroeber that he planned to go there again. The few days he had spent on the trait lists were "all too short," he remarked. "Especially," he added, "I hope to get a lot of material on society and religion at Owyhee that I did not have time for last year."

More details about religion would contribute to Kroeber's trait lists, not to Steward's own project. But he knew that there was still much for him to learn from Johnnie Pronto, the shaman. Steward had broken off fieldwork in 1935 not because he was finished but because he had run out of time. He was due in Washington to take up his new position; and before leaving for the East he had to make a trip to Pendleton, Oregon, for the BAE.[51]

A year later, once again on BAE business and short of time, he continued to drive west toward Austin and Fallon, instead of turning north toward the Duck Valley Reservation, hundreds of miles away. If Steward by chance knew that Pronto had been sick—and that another elder and informant at the reservation, Charley Thacker, had died in mid-September—he had probably heard it at Washakie. Letters arrived there from other reservations, including Duck Valley, carrying all manner of news, from the dates of upcoming festivals to reports of illness and death.[52]

Steward probably did not know—and may never have known—that Pronto had died just days earlier. Many other elders also died within a few years of his fieldwork, including the centenarians Ray Diamond and Grouse Creek Jack. At the Fort Hall Reservation, Silver Ballard died only six months after meeting Steward; and Adolph Pavitse, the capable interpreter, died at the age of just thirty-one. Jane Steward remembered Tom Stone as nearly the only informant her husband had contact with after his fieldwork ended. Eleven years separated them in age, not decades as in the case of the elders. He saw Stone again on a later trip through the Owens Valley, and the two men exchanged letters now and then over the years.[53]

If Steward had turned north that day, he would have passed the small town of Carlin, Nevada, just months earlier the site of a war against crickets. Mormon crickets—so named because the Utah settlers first reported them—had appeared in record numbers during the summer of 1936 in parts of Nevada, Utah, and Idaho. They moved along the ground in waves reportedly up to twelve miles wide and twenty miles long, eating everything green in their path from wild plants to crops. The federal government had responded with a WPA project, employing workers to erect low metal barriers and dig trenches directly in front. The wingless crickets, stopped in their tracks by the barriers, filled the trenches. Workers killed them by firing guns loaded with sodium arsenite dust. At Carlin, the barriers and trenches reportedly surrounded the entire township, forming a wall and sandy moat to protect houses and the water supply from invasion.

Scientists could not explain why the hordes of crickets appeared in some years and not in others. "The problem is receiving increasing study, however, by numerous scientists," one reporter wrote, "who contend that termites, ants, mosquitoes, locusts and crickets will some day fight a battle to the death with civilization, and that civilization will be wiped out unless the situation is met with stronger measures than have yet been perfected."

In just a few years, those stronger measures would include DDT and a host of other toxic pesticides—setting the stage for Rachel Carson's *Silent Spring*. Her questions about how synthetic pesticides affect ecology and human health helped to ignite the environmental movement of the late twentieth century. Decades after WPA workers sprayed sodium arsenite on crickets in 1936, it was categorized as acutely toxic, a human carcinogen, and a suspected endocrine disruptor.[54]

When he reached Fallon, Steward hired a guide to take him into the caves. As soon as he completed his task for the BAE, he left for Las Vegas, hoping to find a Southern Paiute informant for the "Las Vegas band." A good informant could help him crosscheck and extend what he had learned a year earlier about Pahrump and Las Vegas from Albert and Mary Howell.[55] As he traveled south the elevation dropped and the temperature rose. At Las Vegas, almost two thousand feet lower than Fallon, the October sky was a brilliant blue. The autumn air, released from summer's grip, had settled into mild warmth.

The springs and the abundant wild grasses at Las Vegas had long attracted Paiute Indians and others to that oasis in a desiccated land. The apt Spanish name meant The Meadows or The Grasslands. As Steward knew from reading explorers' accounts, in the previous century the visitors to Las Vegas included Utes on their way to raid Spanish missions in California. (Chief Kanosh's Ute father had crossed that country; his mother, who was not Ute, lived at a mission in Southern California where he was born.) In the 1850s Mormon settlers arrived at Las Vegas, sent by Brigham Young to establish a colony in that hinterland; but they soon returned to the eastern Great Basin, the heart of Mormon country.[56]

By the time Steward reached Las Vegas in October 1936, the once remote desert outpost had grown into a small boomtown. New casinos attracted hopeful visitors by the thousands. Construction of nearby Boulder Dam (later known as Hoover Dam) also brought thousands of hopeful construction workers and their families to southern Nevada during the Depression years. Once again, outsiders arrived en masse, with an unsustainable way of living in the desert. It had long supported only small numbers of people who lived by hunting and gathering and horticulture.[57]

The dam, widely viewed as a marvel of modern technology, even the eighth wonder of the world, reached completion shortly before Steward arrived in Las Vegas. Given the importance of water as a key resource in his ecological study, Boulder Dam held interest. The towering dam—and the nearby city in the desert that began to import its water and energy—would offer new illustration of one of Steward's central ideas: that the interplay of technology and natural resources directly affects population size and density. He had seen that first, and in reverse, in the Owens Valley, where a technological feat allowed Los Angeles to import water from a distance. That had led to the *loss* of much of the valley's water and population.

Southern Paiutes who lived in a colony at Las Vegas and at the nearby Moapa River Reservation formed a tiny minority in 1936. They numbered fewer than two hundred people in contrast to the city's population of more than six thousand. Steward hired a Southern Paiute man as an informant, but learned so little that he gave up after one day. He drove across the border into southwestern Utah, where he hastily visited Indian reservations for the BIA, and then returned to Salt Lake City.[58]

His fieldwork had drawn to a close, despite a few opaque spaces in his survey of the region. He had not found helpful informants in some places. He had not located an elder in Idaho or Utah who could tell him about Wyoming Shoshones, and he never took the time to drive hundreds of miles to the Wind River Reservation in Wyoming. Far more disappointing and puzzling, he had found no trace of the patrilineal band. Despite surveying a vast area, he had drawn a complete blank. That, as well as practical concerns, argued against continuing the search in the Great Basin.[59]

Deep snow covered the peaks of the Wasatch Mountains, a harbinger and a warning. October was a fickle month in northern Utah. Each early-autumn lull of blue sky and mild air soon gave way to a spell of steady rain spilling from a pearl-gray sky. Now and then clouds the color of wet slate brought not only driving rain but also sleet in the valleys and snow in the mountains. As the weather shifted from day to day and warmth ebbed, all manner of wildlife was on the move.

Sandhill cranes and snow geese passed through on the way south. Mule deer moved down from the high country, along with mountain chickadees and juncos.

To delay his return, as Steward knew, would raise the risk of meeting a blizzard in the Rocky Mountains or on the Great Plains and prairie. And he also missed his wife. In three years of marriage they had only twice spent more than a day apart. After some wearing weeks spent alone on the road, the comforts of home—and their new life in suburban Virginia—beckoned. He arrived there in late October, and Jane gave birth to their first child, Gary, in December. A second son, and their last child, Michael, was born two years later.

When Steward left Utah in 1936 and headed east, his departure marked trail's end: the end of his time in the high desert of the Great Basin and the end of what proved to be the major fieldwork of his career. He never found the patrilineal band, and he finally gave up the quest.[60] He found something else instead: rich evidence of what came to be called cultural adaptation.

During the year after his return Steward organized and analyzed that evidence and completed *Basin-Plateau*. He drew on elders' memories and his own observations of land and water sources and old village sites. These showed that a vast arid region, which most outsiders saw as uniformly bleak and barren, had varied greatly from place to place. California's Owens Valley and Utah's Skull Valley perhaps best illustrated the extremes. The Owens Valley Paiutes and the Skull Valley Goshutes had adapted to their particular valleys, to different environmental conditions; and it was cultural adaptation that explained many of their differences—in foraging practices, community size and stability, technology, and so on.

In the final pages of the book, Steward concluded that human behavior is an adaptation "in varying ways and degrees to the requirements of existence in a particular natural environment."[61]

Afterword

Journeys West

In 1843 an explorer set out on a journey through the high desert. Maps of the time showed a space framed by mountains and crosscut by a line. The explorer went in search of the line, labeled the Buenaventura River: a broad band of water that flowed west through the desert and toward the sea. Despite glimpses by trappers and other travelers, the Buenaventura remained uncharted. Discovering its source and charting its course would open a river route through country that outsiders feared as empty waste, that they wished to cross quickly on the way west.

The explorer rode with his band of men for month after month across a dry land, never sighting the Buenaventura. They crossed mountains on the desert's western edge, turned back, and rode through the desert once again, skirting the southern edge. Still they did not find the river.

In time the explorer realized what he *had* found. The Great Basin, as he came to call it, was home to few rivers, and none drained to the sea. Hemmed in on every side by mountain and plateau, the water had no outlet. The Buenaventura River did not exist and could not exist in a land of interior drainage, a place unique in North America.

In the end, explorer John C. Frémont had discovered the opposite of what he set out to find.[1]

Nearly a century later Julian and Jane Steward passed through the same territory. Mexico claimed it in Frémont's time, but the United States soon took it, along with Alta California. Native people had their own enduring claims to the land, claims that they continued to press in the 1930s. Some still lived where their ancestors had lived long before explorers passed by, and before other outsiders, including Jane's ancestors, settled.

Generations of explorers and scientists of all types on expeditions had preceded Steward on searches for this and that in the Great Basin. Maps, old and new, along with the recorded memories of Frémont and others, helped him find his way across the open reaches of space and back in time. So too did the elders' memories.

I continue to wonder whether Steward felt the ghostly presence of those explorers as he and his wife followed some of the same routes. He knew the story of Frémont's search for the Buenaventura River, but I doubt that he ever saw any parallels to his own search for the patrilineal band. Despite failing to find it in the Great Basin, he always believed that it existed—somewhere else. His journey of discovery ended as Frémont's had ended, and as so many do: by finding the unexpected, even the reverse of the expected.

The Buenaventura had turned out to be purely conjectural, the many reports based only on glimpses of water and on speculation and hearsay and hope. But the search did lead to a new understanding of a geographic region that most outsiders knew nothing about, or misunderstood. That helped to open the door to colonization and settlement, creating an ecological crisis for Shoshones and Paiutes and Utes. The settlers' unsustainable farming, ranching, and mining practices led to a second, but shared, ecological crisis during the dust bowl years of the 1930s. Steward observed the results directly even as he searched for elders who remembered the time before settlement and the first crisis.

Nearly every search, and re-search, begins with reports of a Buenaventura River. There are almost always predecessors and previous reports, acknowledged or not. Romantic notions about journeys of discovery in unknown places have enduring appeal. But in reality there is practically no untrodden territory, geographic or intellectual, in this world. Some places simply have less traffic. Steward entered one of those less trafficked places when he asked questions about culture and environment in the late 1920s and 1930s.

He drew on fragmentary reports about hunters in remote places who seemed to live in male-centered groups. Although he did not find the patrilineal band in the Great Basin, his search did lead to new questions and understandings about environment and culture. By questioning and listening carefully to elders; by recording what they remembered doing and seeing; by documenting a portion of their broad and deep ecological knowledge, he slowly learned how they had lived on the land, and how that varied from place to place. He saw how people had adapted—not biologically, like plants and most animals, but culturally—to particular environments in the high desert.

His search also led to a different way of understanding a natural and cultural region that most outsiders dismissed as uniformly barren and impoverished. Steward, in contrast, found some striking variation in the Great Basin. Some places had more water and edible plants and animals, others had less, and people lived differently in those places. Far more people lived in the well-watered Owens Valley, and in larger and more stable groups, than in Skull Valley and Deep Creek Valley, which border a nearly waterless desert.

Today it is commonplace to say that humans have occupied every part of the earth by using culture to adapt, and that they have survived environmental changes by adapting. That basic understanding, about adapting culturally in order to survive, flows in part from Darwin's ideas in the nineteenth century about biological adaptation to environment; and in part from the ideas of Steward and others in the twentieth century about environment, culture, and human survival. It also comes in part from the elders' personal memories. They told Steward how they lived before American settlement—and some spoke of how they survived after settlement, although few of those memories reached print in *Basin-Plateau*.

Perhaps *because* Frémont looked for a great river flowing out of the desert, he discovered that all the water stayed there. A search for gold might have resulted in the discovery of silver or copper, but probably not of the unusual hydrology. Perhaps *because* Steward set out to find a rather rigid, uniform, and exclusionary structure—as he defined the patrilineal band—he discovered flexibility and adaptability. What he was searching for influenced what he found, as it almost always does. But it cannot be said that "he found what he was looking for," to use a well-worn phrase of skeptics everywhere. He found what was there—to the credit of his method, ethnographic fieldwork, and his (and his wife's) long months of hard work.

In the Great Basin Steward learned that social groups and the social practices of native people were unexpectedly flexible and variable, adapted to specific local environments and to shifting conditions in those places. What elders recalled about people and places and events suggested flexibility in an array of social practices: from how many spouses a man or woman could have at one time, to where married couples lived, to which people lived together at a given time, to where they foraged in good times and in bad. In a few instances he documented monogamous, polygynous, and polyandrous unions in a single community. He staked a claim to one discovery, filing the first report of polyandry among Shoshones—but he could have claimed another one as well: marriage systems so flexible that both men and women could have multiple spouses.

Flexibility in a variety of social practices, as Steward's research showed, had proven highly adaptive in arid environments with scattered and shifting resources. Flexibility promoted survival. Rigid rules and exclusionary practices (which defined the patrilineal band and the ownership of land, as Steward conceived of them) were not adaptive in those environments.

Their goals, and the questions that Frémont and Steward asked at the start of their journeys, influenced the routes they took, what they saw as they searched, and what they finally found. Without questions and goals, which form a kind of map, they would have wandered aimlessly in the desert. For its time, Steward's fieldwork was distinctive in its strong grounding in theory, its sense of what came to be termed *problem*. He framed it as a hypothesis, just as a behaviorist psychologist planning an experiment might do. His goal was more than simple salvage, more than a description of the past—just as Frémont's goal was more than general exploration.

A signal difference between the two is that Frémont later told his readers what he was looking for, what route he took, what he did not find, and what he found instead. Steward did not reveal the original goal of his fieldwork in *Basin-Plateau*—or tell readers what he did not find. Instead, he presented findings on "ecology in cultural studies" and his general conclusion that native people of the Great Basin had adapted by means of cultural behavior to each "particular natural environment."[2]

What explains his almost complete silence, in print and otherwise, about the original aim of his search? He mentioned it in writing once, but privately and in passing. In a letter that he wrote near the end of his life, Steward remarked that he undertook fieldwork "after formulating the patrilineal band idea, and I fully expected to find it." The letter was addressed to Robert F. Murphy, one of his former students at Columbia University. He had known Murphy for twenty years and trusted him as an unusually friendly colleague.[3]

Then in his midsixties, Steward had a long history of feeling embattled. His ideas continued to draw attacks thirty years after first reaching print, even while some younger cultural anthropologists and archaeologists were reading his early work for the first time, and carefully, as they planned their own research on hunter-gatherers. His sense of being under siege may help to explain his long silence.[4]

His strong identification as a scientist might also account for the silence. Steward did not comment on his failure to find evidence of the patrilineal band in fieldwork just as an experimental scientist might not report a hypothesis that received no support from repeated experiments. Following a common convention of science, perhaps he decided not to report a negative result.

And of course he had no way of knowing in 1938 that he would *not* find the patrilineal band in future fieldwork. The future is a blank space on the map of time. Just as *Basin-Plateau* appeared in print, Steward was about to search again, this time in western South America. He said nothing later about that, perhaps because he gave up on the plan before reaching a field site. Nor did he reveal the reason for the final unsuccessful attempt in 1940, once again in western North America but farther north, in Canada with Carrier Indians.[5]

Frustration or puzzlement or even some sense of failure may also explain his later silence. Despite searching in what seemed the likeliest places, he had failed to find evidence of patrilineal bands—and others had apparently succeeded in finding that evidence. Earlier writings by some of his Berkeley colleagues appeared to suggest such bands among Shoshonean-speaking Indians of Southern California. So did reports from other parts of the world.

Nearly forty years after his fieldwork, and eleven years after his death—and after long years of fieldwork by other anthropologists— his concept of the patrilineal band was pronounced a product of "empirically groundless assumptions." Research showed that flexibility in social practices, which Steward had documented in the Great Basin, defined foragers in many other places as well.[6]

Basin-Plateau and Steward's other writings about the native people of the Great Basin had helped to foster much more ethnographic research on hunter-gatherers, although that research did not produce strong support for his ideas about patrilineal bands. Later anthropologists undertook long-term fieldwork with "living cultures" or "functioning cultures" of hunter-gatherers rather than carrying out salvage research on the past and on "memory cultures."[7] The terms *hunter-gatherers* and *foragers* slowly replaced *hunting societies*, which nearly disappeared from the vocabulary of anthropology.

Later research with foragers showed that in most cases plant foods provided a mainstay, surpassing the importance of animals in the daily diet. As Steward's own fieldwork had shown, women's labor was often crucial in the food quest. However, it fell to later anthropologists to make that point. Steward said almost nothing about it in print, despite his comment about Panamint Shoshones in a letter to Kroeber: "This comes near to being a woman's economy."[8]

By the end of the twentieth century the concept of hunter-gatherers came into question, as had the earlier concept of hunting societies. It seemed simplistic in some cases. As Steward himself had learned in the Owens Valley and in parts of Nevada and western Utah, some Paiutes and Shoshones had not just gathered nature's bounty. They had acted to increase productivity, diverting water to irrigate wild plants or using fire to burn unwanted brush or sowing wild seeds. Kroeber had learned years earlier that Mojave Indians planted wild seeds. A still earlier predecessor, writing in the 1860s, had reported the irrigation ditches of the Owens Valley Paiutes. Most anthropologists, and others, had long drawn a firm boundary between foraging and farming, but that boundary began to blur by the end of the twentieth century. New perspectives on foraging, or hunting and gathering, may eventually result in new terms.[9]

Cultural adaptation may prove more resilient as a term and concept—or it may one day be revised, discarded, or simply forgotten. *Basin-Plateau* offered extended illustration of cultural adaptation, an implicit, guiding concept in the book. Steward mentioned it mainly in passing and in the closing pages. He wrote more about it later, sometimes using the term *cultural ecological adaptation* to highlight his ideas about cultural ecology. It became an explicit, core concept in research on hunter-gatherers.[10]

Over time cultural adaptation achieved the status of a unifying concept in American anthropology, and led to new research and to new understandings about human life. It was one of only a few such concepts in a sprawling discipline that ranged from the biological to the cultural, from remote prehistory to the present. University students routinely heard about cultural adaptation in courses on cultural anthropology, archaeology, and physical anthropology, if not linguistic anthropology. By the late twentieth century it had moved beyond anthropology to other fields, and beyond the university to the mainstream press.[11] Cultural adaptation proved so useful and durable as a concept that it found a long-lasting place in the intellectual common.[12]

The work of Steward and others helped to create another way of understanding why people live as they do, and why that changes: how they survive through adapting, often quickly and by cultural means, to changing environmental conditions. Eventually the concept of cultural adaptation came to stand on its own, without close association to any named persons. That attested to its wide acceptance. It was simply taken for granted.

Steward's struggle for recognition and acceptance of his ideas, an unavoidable and consuming part of the work of scholars and scientists, occupied many years of his long career. The unexpected outcome, years after his death, was to be largely forgotten by later generations as a creator or early advocate of the widely shared concept of cultural adaptation. In some quarters, Steward even faded from memory as the architect of cultural ecology, although his approach survived and evolved into variants. Those were creations of later anthropologists who branded the new variants with new names.[13]

As I surveyed Steward's lifework and reconstructed the story of his 1930s fieldwork, I came to think that struggles for priority, and survival, on the battleground of ideas have ironic results. Even someone whose ideas do survive and reach later generations may be forgotten as a creator of those ideas. (Contrary to many claimants, few ideas seem to be the *sole* creation of one person. There are nearly always precursors and, often, parallel thinkers: consider the famous case of Charles Darwin and Alfred Russel Wallace.) Engaged in the perennial competition for recognition and their own struggles to claim priority and originality, later generations have good reason to forget most of their predecessors. The reward structure of many fields directly fosters a kind of intellectual or professional amnesia.

Contributing to the intellectual common is, in the end, its own reward—and perhaps the only certain reward for long years of training, research, thinking, and writing.

When I first began to learn about Steward's fieldwork, I wondered if it *was* fieldwork. Staying in rented auto cabins (between visits with dozens of colleagues and kith and kin in California and Utah); using interpreters; paying informants an hourly wage; spending only a few hours with them in some cases, and then moving on—always moving on: none of that fit my own experiences or prevailing conceptions of fieldwork.[14]

As I learned more I realized that Steward's approach was not unique, although its regional scope was unusual. Others in Steward's generation, and an earlier one, depended heavily on retrospective interviews with elders to reconstruct the past and record old ways of life, or so-called memory cultures; and they did not usually linger at the sites where they carried out those interviews. Kroeber, Lowie, and the British social anthropologist A. R. Radcliffe-Brown, among many others, had approached fieldwork with indigenous people in that way. Radcliffe-Brown, for example, alluded to making "careful enquiries among old men." He wrote of undertaking a "long and tiresome journey" to a remote place in Australia in order to question, briefly, some "old members of the tribe" about the past.[15]

By contrast, ethnographic fieldwork with "living cultures" increasingly came to center on staying for an extended time at the journey's destination, termed the *field site*. Bronislaw Malinowski, the Polish-born British social anthropologist, generally receives credit for establishing this as standard practice. He was not the first to remain at a field site for years, to learn the local language, and to engage in participant observation. He did write at length about the experience, however, in a series of well-known ethnographies about Trobriand Islanders, and in a now-famous private diary that appeared in print twenty-five years after his death.[16]

As I began to think more inclusively and historically about ethnographic fieldwork, I saw that Malinowski's experience, while iconic, was not completely representative. I came to see fieldwork as "going there," making a journey to an unfamiliar place for ethnographic purposes—but not necessarily as "being there," in the sense of settling in one locale and working with the same informants for a period of years as Malinowski did. In North America, fieldwork grew out of journeys west: journeys of exploration such as the Lewis and Clark Expedition across the continent, and later scientific expeditions such as Powell's in the Great Basin and the Southwest. Ethnographic fieldwork began as a means of learning about indigenous people. Indigenous studies began with fieldwork: ethnographic, archaeological, linguistic.

Journeying, but not necessarily settling in a community of indigenous people, defined what Powell and his fellow scientists and explorers did, along with early generations of ethnographers. A journey, and distance from home, also defined the fieldwork of Malinowski, a European man who lived for a time on islands in the Western Pacific. Consider his words in the opening pages of *Argonauts of the Western Pacific*: "Imagine yourself suddenly set down, surrounded by all your gear, alone on a tropical beach close to a native village, while the launch or dinghy that has brought you sails away out of sight."[17]

Over time the element of being "set down," staying in one place, seemed to eclipse another element, that of going to an unfamiliar place. Prevailing definitions of ethnographic fieldwork equate it with cultural immersion, close and long-term contact with a community or other social group. They privilege participant observation, treating it as the hallmark feature of fieldwork—as I too once did. (Even ethnographic research carried out close to home, on a part-time basis and in familiar places such as schools or hospitals, now often carries the label *fieldwork* if it centers on participant observation. The term *ethnographic research* may be more appropriate.)

With the prevailing model of fieldwork in mind, at first I saw only striking differences between Malinowski's approach to fieldwork in the Trobriand Islands of the tropical Pacific and Steward's in the high desert of the American West. The differences faded as I learned more about Steward's research, and I came to see many more shared features. Those features help to define ethnographic fieldwork in all of its variable forms, past and present.

In the broadest sense, as both Malinowski's and Steward's experiences suggest, fieldwork is a quest, a journey made for ethnographic purposes to an unfamiliar place. Its methods are particularly suited to discovery and to the goal of understanding the unfamiliar. They are not well suited to testing a hypothesis, which is generally the aim of experimental and survey research. That requires familiarity: knowing a great deal in advance about the subject of inquiry—and far more than Steward knew when he framed his hypothesis about hunting bands.

Fieldwork begins with questions about cultural matters, and it centers on acquiring and recording primary data that bear on those questions. The term *ethnographic data*, which cultural anthropologists commonly use, does not make clear exactly what they are acquiring and recording: *primary* data of various types, from the words of informants, who describe and explain and who often recount memories, to their own observations and experiences as ethnographers.

Looking and listening, purposefully and attentively, are the means of acquiring most of that data. Malinowski and Steward, like all ethnographers, used their senses as well as intellect. The standard terms *observation, participant observation*, and *interviewing* refer to modes of sensory experience, looking and listening, yet those methods always involve other senses as well. Steward felt the heat and the wind; he smelled the acrid dust and the sagebrush; he tasted wild seeds and pine nuts. It is commonly said that in fieldwork the ethnographer is the research instrument; and that in contrast to other research instruments (for example, questionnaires in survey research) ethnographers use all of the human senses. Steward was no exception.

Acquiring primary data through ethnographic fieldwork, as Steward's—and Malinowski's—experiences also show, is a labor-intensive, lengthy, costly, and complex process, often with high personal demands. Fieldwork contrasts sharply in these respects with other ways of acquiring primary data. Survey and experimental research methods produce primary data much more rapidly, at lower cost, and make far fewer personal demands on the researcher. In still other forms of research—such as historical research based on the use of documents— the primary sources, or documents, need only to be located. They contain the primary data, eliminating the labor needed to *produce* such data.

Like nearly all ethnographers, Steward had to search for willing and able cultural informants, guides to help him understand the natural and cultural landscapes they inhabited. The dozens of elders who agreed to work with Steward constituted the main primary sources for his research project. When the search for informants involves going to dozens of different places in a vast region, as Steward did—rather than staying in one area, as Malinowski did—it is a time-consuming and often frustrating process. (Malinowski, in contrast, described his sources as "easily accessible," but added that what he heard and observed was "also supremely elusive and complex."[18])

Depending on circumstances, Steward resorted to varying means to locate informants. Most often he used what came to be called the *snowball technique* (a name that might well have amused him given the sweltering summer heat of the desert). Referrals by one informant usually led him to the next. Grouse Creek Jack, for example, most likely told Steward about Ray Diamond, a longtime acquaintance and former neighbor at Washakie. He also located informants by other person-to-person means, with the help of other knowledgeable people. The superintendent of the Duck Valley Reservation probably gave Steward the names of Tom Premo, Charley Thacker, and others. And serendipity, always an element in fieldwork, also played a role.[19] While he was looking for Peter Sport, Steward just happened to pass John Alston on the street in Bishop, California, and Alston recognized him and smiled. However he found each informant, each primary source, the search took time and effort.

Steward then worked actively with every informant to acquire much of his primary data about the past. He did that mainly in formal interviews, and sometimes in informal conversations. At least once he acquired data in the course of participant observation, while taking part in seed gathering with Jennie Washburn and other Ely elders.

Steward did not simply "collect ethnographic data," to use a common but unfortunate phrase. That wording does indicate the connection of ethnographic fieldwork to earlier scientific expeditions, which collected all manner of specimens, from the botanical and geological to the cultural. (The last took the form of artifacts, usually acquired by purchase or trade, from indigenous people.) But the word *collecting* misleads. It does not clearly express what the ethnographer and informant are doing as they work together, or the time and effort, the thought, the patience, and the goodwill required for that work.

In truth, Steward spent long hours with most of the elders, *co-constructing*, or *co-producing*, primary data: asking questions, listening carefully, and thinking; asking again in hope that the elder could clarify or amplify an explanation; and recording what he understood his informant to say. The process was interactive, collaborative, and highly personal.

Again and again he confronted one of the perennial puzzles of ethnographic research, about differences in rapport and communication. Why did some informants understand his questions and intentions so readily while others did not? Why could he understand some of them so much more easily than others? A high level of fluency in English helped but did not guarantee a good result. He questioned two of his most highly prized informants, Johnnie Pronto and James Pegoga, for many days with the help of interpreters Tom Premo and Adolph Pavitse, both exceptionally skilled. He questioned Joe Pikyavit directly, but soon gave up in frustration, with doubts about reliability. (What Pikyavit thought about the encounter can only be guessed.)

Steward left some interviews, happily if wearily, with a mass of primary data. He left others, unhappily and wearily, with very little. He liked some of his informants more than others. The short entries in his journal offer glimpses of the emotional landscape of fieldwork. (The far longer and more detailed entries in Malinowski's diary reveal more about the emotional demands and his emotional responses.) Steward clearly felt irritated or disappointed or angry in some instances, and happy or amused or optimistic in others. There were peaks and valleys among patches of emotionally neutral terrain.

As some of his journal entries also illustrate, ethnographic interviews are not simple question-and-answer sessions with uniform results. Steward had quickly learned that asking open-ended questions was more productive. That type of questioning, now seen as a hallmark of ethnographic interviewing, encourages greater thought and active collaboration. It allows informants to teach. Beyond simply giving a direct reply to a question, informants may volunteer other information or insights not directly sought; or explain why the question misses the point; or correct misunderstandings that they detect in the ethnographer's follow-up questions or comments; or ask questions themselves, in order to explain something indirectly or in a comparative way; or show the ethnographer something, or invite the ethnographer to take part in a shared activity, in order to enhance understanding. The elders who were Steward's best informants actively taught him.

Dozens of elders scattered across four western states were the major, but not the sole, primary sources for Steward's project. By thinking creatively, he also identified other primary sources. They included the high desert landscape, maps of the desert, archaeological sites, old photographs, and published texts. His observations of particular valleys and mountain ranges, of features on U.S. Geological Survey maps, and of the sites of old camps and villages constituted primary data. So did the photographs from Powell's scientific expeditions, which he examined first in Pendleton, Oregon, and later in Washington DC. The observations of early explorers about the land and about Indians, which Steward found in old books and reports, also qualified as primary data.

Once I understood Steward's use of a broad range of primary sources, I had to think again about his field site. I had to reconsider the notion of staying versus moving on—a difference that turned out to be more apparent than real. Steward's field site was in fact the Great Basin, the entire region of desert valleys and mountains, not just the series of localities where he interviewed elders; and he did stay at his field site for months at a time. As he traveled from one place to another, he engaged in observation. Those observations—of the landscape and of the surface remains at old camps and village sites—constituted fieldwork at his field site, just like the interviews.

The dimensions of the field site matter less, I eventually realized, than that ethnographers work in naturalistic settings—not in the artificial and controlled setting of a laboratory. One outcome is the well-known physical discomforts and risks and demands of so much fieldwork. In Steward's case these ranged from the heat and gusting winds and dust storms of the desert, to campsites without water or privacy, to a steady diet of canned food—to say nothing of the poisonous spiders and snakes he encountered now and then. The nearly constant presence of his wife, however, spared him one of fieldwork's most common discomforts: loneliness, which is a recurring theme in Malinowski's diary.

Yet another outcome of working in naturalistic settings was that Steward, like every ethnographer, had to tailor the research to unique circumstances: those he knew about in advance and those he encountered in the field. His project may look unusual in its surface appearance, but in truth every project is unique. Conditions not only vary from place to place (the Great Basin obviously differs from the Trobriand Islands), but most conditions are also beyond the ethnographer's control. Control is never an aim, in any case, in naturalistic research. Control would interfere with the goal of understanding what *is*—or what once was.

Given the absence of researcher control, conditions may also change in the course of fieldwork, and in unexpected ways. Steward put off working with Ray Diamond at Washakie and drove instead to Kanosh, Utah, because of a smallpox epidemic. He treated Powell and other explorers as informants when he failed to find a Ute elder to answer his questions. He searched for a new informant and located Tom Horn when the Johnnie family at Fallon, Nevada, decided to spend the day trapping ground squirrels. He left Tonopah, Nevada, when John Best refused to work with him for another day.

Cultural informants have agency—and acting as a cultural informant requires time and effort. It can also cause social and emotional discomfort. How did elders feel as they answered Steward's questions about the past, about the time before invasion and conquest? Later generations expressed an acute sense of loss for "an ancient way of life in an abundant land."[20] They did not remember a barren and impoverished homeland. Outsiders saw it that way.

Does that sense of loss explain in part why Pat Hicks, Steward's first informant at the Fallon Reservation in Nevada, answered questions reluctantly? Did his brother Barney Hicks respond so differently because he had left exile on that distant reservation? Steward found him living hundreds of miles away in Railroad Valley, near his homeland. The two brothers, in any case, had markedly different reactions to the curious stranger and his questions, and Steward adjusted his work accordingly.

If there is a certain surface similarity in experiments with strict protocols, and in survey research based on standardized questionnaires, the same cannot be said of fieldwork. The unplanned and unexpected are so common in fieldwork that flexibility is essential. Ethnographers too can learn something from Coyote.

Perhaps because Steward received no training in research methods—as was common then and now—he drew on his earlier formal study of geology and geography and history, and on three years of experience in archaeology, to identify a broad range of primary sources. By using multiple types of primary sources, and multiple, or mixed, methods of research, Steward engaged in what came to be termed *triangulation*, another hallmark of fieldwork. He did not depend solely, for example, on what he learned by interviewing. This approach allowed him to crosscheck the interview data. His own observations, along with recorded observations of explorers, helped to verify what the elders told him. In some cases those observations extended or amplified what the elders said or led him to ask new questions.

Producing the trait lists contributed to triangulation as well. Along with the censuses, the lists qualified as a form of what was later termed *structured data collection* (or better, structured data *production*). Despite his dislike of the task and his doubts about Kroeber's project, his work yielded comparative primary data from dozens of local places across a large region. In the end it contributed to Steward's research project as well as Kroeber's. What he recorded about hunting and gathering and social organization proved helpful to him, despite the limitations of the present/absent format.

Recording primary data, for the trait lists and for his ecological project, was an integral part of fieldwork. That time-consuming and laborious work occurred in stages, as is typical. He took notes during interviews, then he and his wife drew up revised drafts of the trait lists, working at night or taking a day off from interviewing to spend time on the lists. For most ethnographers the complex process of recording includes adding comments or questions as they arise; analyzing or interpreting in a general way what has just been recorded; correcting misinterpretations as understanding deepens; and otherwise revising the notes as needed while fieldwork continues or after it ends.

Steward was still at that work five months after the first round of fieldwork ended. When Kroeber wrote to him in Washington to inquire, again, about the lists for Nevada Shoshones, Steward sent a sullen reply, insisting that he and his wife needed more time. He complained that they had spent many nights working on the lists until midnight. He also explained that notes for his ecological study were mixed in with the notes for the trait list. That had slowed their work.

Jane Steward finished typing the lists and mailed them to Kroeber a few weeks later, days after her husband left on a trip. The magnitude of the task—including the exhausting toil of keeping a mass of recorded primary data in order, detecting omissions and correcting errors that crept in, and putting the text and the lists in final typed form—challenged even her normal good cheer. She told Kroeber in the cover letter to contact her if he had questions, adding, "But I'd rather not hear anything more about it for a few days!"[21]

Fifty years later Jane said wistfully that she felt like an unrecognized partner in an important enterprise. Her labor and other assistance had gone unacknowledged in print and in her husband's profession, as was common. The conventions of the time rendered everyone but the author invisible.[22]

The more I learned about Jane and Julian Steward's journeys in the desert, the more I saw how typical they were as fieldwork. Among the most typical features was the considerable cost. Fieldwork has always been expensive, far more expensive than survey research and many other stay-at-home forms of research. In addition, funding has always been limited, and the competition for it, fierce. Although Steward succeeded in getting a grant for the first round of fieldwork, he also expressed the routine worries about running out of money before the fieldwork was finished. He might well have had to end the 1935 fieldwork earlier but for the food and lodging provided by his old school in Deep Springs Valley.

Like many ethnographers Steward also experienced the so-called honeymoon period at the beginning of fieldwork. His 1935 research in California and Nevada was a honeymoon both literally and metaphorically. He was happily married to his second wife, a marriage that would endure until his death decades later; and he had launched a quest, confident that he would find the evidence he sought for his ecological study. The two years between Julian Steward's marriage to Jane Cannon and his entry into the federal bureaucracy in fall 1935 may qualify as the happiest period of his life.

In the last year of her long life Jane still recalled the first spell of fieldwork as "Eden." She said almost nothing about the 1936 research. By then the honeymoon period of fieldwork had ended, as it often does during the strain of completing a difficult and demanding task.

The importance of personal memories in ethnographic fieldwork is rarely recognized. As Steward's research illustrates, personal memories recalled by individuals—or even memories of others' personal memories—are the source of much of the recorded and reported primary data. They form a foundation of nearly all ethnography, whether it centers on the present or the past or both. For a variety of reasons, this is rarely evident to readers—or even many ethnographers.

From Bill Gibson's memory of what his mother said about being taken away from home by the father of Ruby Valley Johnson, and then walking back (an event Steward categorized as marriage by abduction); to Frank Stick's memories of his mother's two husbands (which Steward categorized as polyandry); to Mary Harry's recollections of who once lived in Fish Lake Valley and of times when they gathered together (recorded as a census and labeled as festivals, respectively, by Steward)—much of this valued primary data, or "raw ethnographic data," to use a common phrase, consisted of personal memories told to Steward. Some of the memories were generic ones, of repeated events or activities; others were memories of particular, unique episodes.[23]

Steward recorded both types—as most ethnographers do, including those who emphasize participant observation. I recall in my own fieldwork often observing actions or interactions or events that puzzled me, and seeking explanations by asking questions. Very often, my cultural informants explained by recounting personal memories, sometimes in a narrative way, as story. I did not fully realize at the time that I was trafficking in autobiographical memory, but I see it in hindsight.[24]

Given this reality of fieldwork, the border blurs between what Steward took for subjectivity (the personal or collective memories, or interpretations, often emotion laden, of insiders, the cultural informants) and objectivity (analytical categories created from or for those memories, and interpretations and representations created by outsiders, the ethnographers). A particular memory may be "raw": recounted by a cultural informant, often in response to questioning by the ethnographer, who then records it. It may also be slightly or thoroughly "cooked": later categorized and interpreted to varying degrees by the ethnographer.

Raw memories, cooked memories: they comprise much of the primary data acquired, or co-constructed, in fieldwork and reported in ethnographies. The elders' words and memories that Steward re-corded—along with his observations and experiences and memo-ries, as well as his interpretation of all the primary data—became ethnography.

Cultural anthropologists carry their own store of personal memo-ries into the field. In some instances, as Steward's fieldwork suggests, those memories can provide useful direction. What he recalled about living in the high desert for three years in boyhood no doubt helped him ask the elders more informed and nuanced questions about how they had once lived in that arid land. Other recollections, about liv-ing and working with a band of brothers in a high desert valley, seem to have influenced his theoretical ideas to some degree, especially his concept of the patrilineal band. He had spent three years in Deep Springs Valley, living and working at a school and ranch that was in many respects a prototype of the patrilineal band. Perhaps it is no co-incidence and even most fitting that Steward put the finishing touches on his essay about bands during the time he spent at Deep Springs in April 1935, just before starting fieldwork.[25]

During fieldwork, however, he listened carefully to the elders' mem-ories. He asked questions about how they had lived, and he heard again and again the evidence that they had *not* lived in such male-centered groups—to his surprise and disappointment. He reported what he understood them to say, using terms such as *family* and *band* and *tribe*.

Only the rare amnesiac can claim complete objectivity—in the sense of complete detachment from emotion-laden memories and interpre-tations of experience—but there is as yet no evidence that amnesia of-fers any real benefit in fieldwork.

It comes as no surprise that Steward's fleeting encounters with elders gave him the sense of being almost completely detached, an external observer, and thus an objective scientist. Objectivity was taken for granted as a standard for good science, and good anthropology, during his time. Many anthropologists, including Lowie and Radcliffe-Brown, also had brief, one-time exchanges with informants that no doubt heightened their sense of distance and objectivity.

Later debates—about objectivity and subjectivity, and what came to be termed *reflexivity* ("a process of self-reference")—had roots in a way of doing fieldwork that centers on long-term, repeated contact with informants.[26] That way does *not* lead cultural anthropologists to feel detached and distant. In many cases they feel close, even uncomfortably close, and deeply involved in the lives of cultural informants. Newer, narrative ways of writing ethnography, using first person, convey their sense of involvement in the lives of other people in other places.

The impression given by *Basin-Plateau*, in contrast, is one of scientific detachment and distance—and again, Steward had some reason to feel detached. His mostly one-time encounters with elders rarely lasted for as much as a week. In every case but one (his old acquaintance Tom Stone), after a few hours or a few days he and his wife drove off toward the horizon, never to see those informants again. This also explains in part why Steward paid wages; engaging in acts of reciprocity, which is now the rule in fieldwork, requires more time and longer acquaintance. He did know far more about their life histories than an experimental psychologist knows about the so-called S's, the human subjects of experiments, or a survey researcher knows about individual respondents. But he provided few details in his book, except when it was unavoidable, when he needed to do so in order to make a particular point.

This silence about individual informants promoted an aura of objectivity: objectivity in the sense of impersonality and impartiality. From the outset I wondered why Steward used initials instead of actual names or pseudonyms, the more common practice in cultural anthropology. Kroeber, for example, sometimes named his cultural and linguistic informants. Later in the twentieth century most cultural anthropologists used pseudonyms for informants and the communities where they worked. (As I was to learn, an exception to this practice involved North American Indian informants; their names often appeared in print, but at their request or with their permission.) For ethical reasons, as a protective measure, most ethnographers working in places other than Native North America did not disclose names or use initials of those names. According to the professional code of ethics developed in the late twentieth century, they were obliged not to reveal the identity of their own, or others', informants and field sites.[27]

Mistakenly reading the present onto the past, for a time I assumed that Steward's use of initials had to do with ethics and protection of privacy. It did not. As I came to see, it reflected other concerns. The names of most elders did not sound "authentic." Names such as George Robinson, Tom Stewart, and Mary Howell seemed prosaically Anglo-American and inappropriate for a book about Indians in the time before American settlement. As I learned more about his informants, I realized that identifying elders by their initials, instead of their given names or even pseudonyms, also depersonalized them. It promoted a sense of the research as impersonal and impartial.

The look of science is impersonal, but in reality ethnographic fieldwork consists largely of personal encounters, and many ethnographers spend much of their time during interviews listening to personal memories. That was as true for Steward as for most ethnographers, then and now.

Steward died in 1972, but controversy about some of his ideas and his strong identification as a scientist continued into the twenty-first century. Much of it centered on his testimony as a witness in Indian Claims Commission court cases about compensating Indian tribes for the loss of their land. Steward was one of the anthropologists who served as expert witnesses for the federal government. He drew directly on his Great Basin fieldwork in giving testimony. Kroeber and many other anthropologists testified on behalf of Indians, the plaintiffs, in a series of cases.

The prevailing opinion among anthropologists at the time, and later, was that Steward was "on the wrong side." Two prominent anthropologists who knew him, Sidney W. Mintz and William C. Sturtevant, each used that phrase when I asked about his role in the trials. Others have used sharper language, increasingly in print. Although anthropologists famously disagree about a great deal, I have yet to meet anyone who thinks that Steward and other expert witnesses for the government did no harm to indigenous people whose land had been taken.[28]

Steward believed that he was simply providing scientific evidence, impartial knowledge from fieldwork. He thought it showed that most of the Indians of the Great Basin had not owned land, testimony that lawyers for the federal government found very useful. He reached this conclusion in the course of fieldwork because of the way he defined land ownership. Clear boundaries, and exclusive use of land and other natural resources within those boundaries, were defining features of ownership in Steward's view, and important for his theory of bands.

Most of the elders he questioned did not recall trying to exclude other native people from hunting and gathering grounds with strictly defined borders. (But their people *had* tried to exclude the rising tide of settlers who began to occupy and degrade their lands—suggesting a far greater proprietary sense than Steward recognized.) Because of the theoretical goals that had led to his fieldwork, but were not disclosed to readers of *Basin-Plateau*, he represented most groups as "living off the country" as foragers, not as bands "owning" the land. The concept of the common—of natural (and cultural) resources held in common and passed on to future generations—was so marginal in the American legal system that it does not seem to have influenced his thinking.

Like any ethnography, *Basin-Plateau* was a partial representation. It left out many parts of life—as any ethnography does, by necessity, given particular questions and goals, and given the impossibility of recording everything. Steward, the committed but undeclared behaviorist, had no interest in how people thought about land and concepts of ownership. Behaviorists did not explore such internal, "subjective" matters, located in the "black box" of the mind.

He thereby reduced land ownership to the external, observable features of well-defined borders and acts of exclusion. This very partial definition left out everything else, including the intricate system of rights and duties and statuses and meanings that define the term *property* in many legal systems, or culturally. Steward did not consider that people without formal legal codes may make claims to land and other natural resources based on landmarks rather than on linear boundaries. Kroeber, in contrast, advised a confused graduate student who had just begun fieldwork with California Indians that their territories might center on "a spot, or a group of spots; the edges are hazy."[29]

Whether or not Steward's knowledge was *im*partial, as he thought, it was, more importantly, partial. Like every ethnographer, he understood some matters better than others, and he recorded and reported selectively. He knew far more about land as something natural than land as also cultural.

"All the Indians we meet are harmless as sagebrushes," John Muir wrote from western Nevada in 1878, "though perhaps about as bitter at heart." No wonder. Their land had been taken, as well as a time-tested and sustainable way of living on the land. They adapted and survived, but that chapter of the elders' life histories did not find a place in *Basin-Plateau*. Still, what Steward saw on reservations and at scattered camps off reservations testified to hardship and to the loss of much that was cherished—and to impressive survival skills.[30]

Although American settlement had damaged their land and nearly destroyed a way of life they valued, the native people of the Great Basin found new ways to use old skills and knowledge. They learned other skills in order to make a living in the new conditions. They were masters of flexibility and resilience. The flexibility that Steward documented in their old way of life continued to serve them well. Like Coyote, they had a genius for adaptation and survival.

Many of them, as Steward saw, tried farming. In some cases they succeeded in growing the new kinds of seed plants, such as wheat, even producing crops in places that settlers considered too marginal for agriculture. They also tried raising "wooly locusts," another one of Muir's terms for the sheep that stripped western lands of native plants, including the very plants the elders had once gathered and eaten.[31] Some of the men and women Steward met earned money by selling pine nuts and baskets and buckskin or new products such as strawberries and watermelon and other garden produce. Many of them learned to speak English, and a few learned to read and write.

Nearly all sold their labor at least now and then, even if they farmed. Most of the men who worked with Steward had earned wages as ranch hands or seasonal farm workers or road laborers. As he knew from his own experience at the ranch in Deep Springs Valley, as well as conversations with ranchers, their employers generally valued such men as hardworking and competent. Women, who earned wages as laundresses and housekeepers, had long received praise because, as a resident of Nevada put it decades earlier in print, they "work at cheap rates and make docile and industrious domestics."[32] In other words, they worked very hard to earn a meager wage so that they could buy food for their families. Few food plants remained for them to gather.

As elders, some men and women also sold a portion of their knowledge. They earned money from Steward and other anthropologists who recorded their memories in books. Those personal and collective memories came to comprise part of the record of human knowledge stored in libraries. By the beginning of the twenty-first century some of their knowledge entered cyberspace and became instantly accessible to people around the world.[33]

In these times their life stories, even if known only in outline, also read as cautionary tales about the effects of rapid environmental change caused by human activities. They show that sudden change on such a major scale can bring hardship in many forms: hunger, sickness, dislocation, even violence and war and death—as well as profound cultural change, often traumatic. People suffer, and other forms of life suffer. The elders' life histories also reveal that an unsustainable way of life can destroy others that are sustainable, at great cost to people and environment—and that the costs are not shared equally. Paiutes and Utes and Shoshones, those who died too early in life and those who survived, including the elders, bore the highest costs.

As I listened in the twenty-first century, I heard descendants of the first generation of survivors speak about the disastrous effects of American colonization and settlement. They remembered events of the past in ways that differ from most written histories. They spoke publicly and privately of unhealed trauma, passed on for generations, and of ways to heal people and the earth.[34]

If Steward could hear their words, how might he understand them? He lived and worked and wrote about the links between environment and culture in another time. He lived in an era before the environment emerged as a focus of intense political struggle and deep moral concern. The epic dust storms of the 1930s did testify that all was not well in the world, or at least not in the American West. But the ozone layer was intact, icebergs filled the northern and southern seas, and glacier-clad mountains presided over many parts of western North America. The terms *sustainability* and *ecological crisis* had not yet entered the public vocabulary.

Public concern about endangered species, runaway population growth, and global climate change would not emerge until decades later. By that time professional ecologists had tallied the damage to ecosystems in North America: the loss of four-fifths of the wildlife, at least half of the timber, and most of the old-growth forests; the damming of many rivers and the destruction of freshwater fisheries; the pollution of much of the water and air. By the end of the twentieth century more than a thousand native species had been placed on an official list as endangered. Nevada had experienced years of nuclear testing, above and below ground, leaving parts of the desert contaminated and taking a heavy toll on human health.[35]

Public opinion about human rights, and violations of those rights, had also shifted by the end of the twentieth century. In the 1930s a statement of universal human rights had not yet been written and accepted by most countries in the world. There was almost no public awareness that trauma can have long-term effects on individuals, or even transgenerational effects. The term *genocide* did not yet exist, nor the related concept of *cultural genocide*.[36]

Julian Steward saw the world and the elders he met in the 1930s through the eyes of an Anglo-American man born to a middle-class family in the early years of the twentieth century. He saw his work as science, and he devoted years of his life to studying the material and social world, the external and observable. Some of the questions that he asked in the 1930s, and some of the conclusions he reached, differ sharply from those of today. But the record that he left—a partial account of a sustainable way of life, and of cultural adaptation to arid environments—has new meaning in new times, as scientists warn of drought and other threats to food security.

The lives of his cultural informants, which went largely unreported in *Basin-Plateau*, also hold great meaning. Steward, adopting a common view of his day, regarded the changes they had made as evidence of so-called deculturation and assimilation. Those changes might better be viewed as an instance of remarkably rapid adaptation to drastically altered and perilous conditions.

The process and also the high human costs of adapting quickly to environmental change—to the severe ecological crisis caused by settlement of Paiute and Shoshone and Ute lands—are inscribed in the elders' life histories. When I look at a photograph of Mary Harry, John Shakespeare, Grouse Creek Jack, and others, I see those costs etched in their worn faces as well. I also detect the resilience and courage and creativity of these survivors who were Steward's guides.

Cultural adaptation is no longer an abstraction to me. It now has a face, or rather, many faces—*their* faces. When I hear or read the term *cultural adaptation*, in my mind's eye I see those men and women. I also see the high desert as it was before and after mass settlement, with waving stands of grass in places where later only sagebrush grew. That land, the elders' birthplace and homeland, was a birthplace of the concept of cultural adaptation, which is today more widely known and more relevant than Steward might ever have imagined. And in these times the elders still have much to teach.

Notes

Abbreviations

ALK   A. L. Kroeber Papers, MSS C-B 925, Bancroft Library, University of California, Berkeley

BAE   Bureau of American Ethnology, National Anthropological Archives, Smithsonian Institution, Washington DC

CKP   Charles Kelly Papers, MSS B 144, Utah State Historical Society, Salt Lake City

DAR   Department of Anthropology Records, CU-23, Bancroft Library, University of California, Berkeley

ECM   Eastern California Museum Collections, Independence, California

ICR   Indian Census Rolls, 1885–1940. Records of the Bureau of Indian Affairs, Record Group 75, National Archives, Washington DC

JHS   Julian H. Steward Papers, 1842–1980, Record series 15/2/21, University of Illinois Archives, Urbana, Illinois

LDS   Church of Jesus Christ of Latter-day Saints, Family History Library, Salt Lake City, Utah

RHL   Robert Harry Lowie Papers, MSS C-B 927, Bancroft Library, University of California, Berkeley

RVC   Ralph V. Chamberlin Papers, 1890–1969, Accn 907, Manuscript Division, Marriott Library, University of Utah, Salt Lake City

RWC   Ramona Wilcox Cannon Papers, 1863–1994, Accn 1862, Manuscript Division, Marriott Library, University of Utah, Salt Lake City

Introduction: Remembering

1. John C. Frémont (1813–1890) named the Great Basin in 1844 (Cline, *Exploring the Great Basin*, 215).

2. The Smithsonian Institution's Bureau of American Ethnology published *Basin-Plateau Aboriginal Sociopolitical Groups* in 1938. The University of Utah

Press reprinted it about thirty years later. Steward—like some who cited the book in print—sometimes left out a word or reversed words in the title.

3. Steward, *Basin-Plateau*, 54, 72.

4. Steward, *Basin-Plateau*, plates 1 and 2.

5. Steward, *Basin-Plateau*, 7.

6. Muir, *My First Summer*, 56, 86; Walton, *Western Times and Water Wars*, 17. On John Muir (1838–1914), see Worster, *A Passion for Nature*. I use the term "wild lands" for land that may be inhabited but that has no permanent settlements, roads, herds of domesticated animals, or industrial activity such as mining.

7. Kerns, *Scenes from the High Desert*; Steward, *Theory of Culture Change*, 30–42.

8. Although Julian Steward included Utes in his study, he reconstructed their past primarily by using written sources, not by working with Ute elders (see chapter 8). Jane Steward left Utah before he located Goshute informants (see chapter 10).

9. On the American West's history of conquest and colonialism, see Limerick, *Legacy of Conquest*.

10. Jane Cannon Steward (1908–1988) died in Honolulu sixteen years after the death of Julian Steward (1902–1972).

11. Morgan and Wheat, *Jedediah Smith and His Maps*, 16; Fox, *The Void, the Grid, and the Sign*, 13; McPhee, *Basin and Range*; Harney, *The Way It Is*, 136; Crum, *The Road on Which We Came*, 1.

1. Going There

1. Kerns, *Scenes from the High Desert*, 119, 145.

2. Jane C. Steward to Joseph J. Cannon, Feb. 20, 1934, RWC Box 57; Jane C. Steward to Elizabeth Cannon, n.d. [mid-March, 1934], RWC Box 59; Grant Cannon to Joseph J. Cannon and family, n.d. [ca. 1934–1935], RWC Box 58; Kerns, *Scenes from the High Desert*, 152.

3. Kerns, *Scenes from the High Desert*, 73, 130–31; Jane C. and Julian H. Steward to Joseph J. Cannon, July 3, 1936, RWC Box 57.

4. Jane C. Steward interview; Dorothy B. Nyswander interview.

5. Jane Cannon to Grant Cannon, Aug. 15, 1928, RWC Box 58; "Jane Cannon Steward," n.d. [ca. 1978], RWC Box 57.

6. Joseph J. Cannon to Jane C. Steward, Nov. 20, 1933, RWC Box 57.

7. Jane C. Steward to Ramona W. Cannon, n.d. [1934], RWC Box 57.

8. Kerns, *Scenes from the High Desert*, 91–92, 97–99; Liljeblad and Fowler, "Owens Valley Paiute," 413.

9. Steward, *Basin-Plateau*, 8.

10. Julian H. Steward to Alfred L. Kroeber, July 26, 1928, DAR; Kerns, *Scenes from the High Desert*, 98–99.

11. Jane C. Steward interview.

12. See Steward, "Diffusion and Independent Invention," for his views on diffusion.

13. Steward, "Economic and Social Basis of Primitive Bands," 333; Kerns, *Scenes from the High Desert*, 160–62. Nearly twenty years later, Steward published a slightly revised version of his 1936 essay; he divided it into two chapters, one on the patrilineal band and the other on the composite band (*Theory of Culture Change*, 122–50). He retained the phrase "innate male dominance" (125). See Steward, *Theory of Culture Change*, 5–6, 87–97, for more on culture types.

14. Steward, "Review of *Aboriginal Society*"; Steward, "Economic and Social Basis of Primitive Bands"; Steward, *Basin-Plateau*, 50, 259; Julian H. Steward to Robert F. Murphy, March 31, 1967, JHS Box 6.

15. Steward, *Kroeber*, 14; Jorgensen, *Western Indians*, 10–11; Myers, "Frame for Culture."

16. Steward, *Kroeber*, 20.

17. Journal of Jane C. [and Julian H.] Steward [hereafter, Journal], April 13, 1935, JHS Box 21; Jane C. Steward interview; Jane C. Steward to Elizabeth C. and Frank Haymond, n.d. [1934], JHS Box 10; Jane C. Steward to Ramona W. Cannon, n.d. [1934], RWC Box 57.

18. Jane C. Steward interview; Jane C. Steward to Joseph J. Cannon, May 8, 1935, RWC Box 57.

19. Kerns, *Scenes from the High Desert*, 155–59.

20. Federal Writers' Project of the Works Progress Administration of Northern California, *Death Valley*, 21, 56.

21. The Owens Valley usually receives only five or six inches a year (Sauder, *The Lost Frontier*, 12). Annual precipitation of ten inches or less generally defines a desert.

22. Kerns, "Learning the Land"; Kerns, *Scenes from the High Desert*, 36–37, 43–45. The school, now Deep Springs College, still includes a working ranch.

23. "Great Sierra Road Planned," *Los Angeles Times*, Sept. 11, 1910, VII2. El Camino Sierra, now Highway 395, is still the main road through the valley.

24. Austin, *Land of Little Rain*; "Mary Austin Dead; Noted Writer, 65," *New York Times*, Aug. 14, 1934, 17.

25. Steward, *Basin-Plateau*, 52.

26. Walton, *Western Times and Water Wars*, 16–22; Liljeblad and Fowler, "Owens Valley Paiute," 414–15, 429–30; Leland, "Population," 612.

27. Walton, *Western Times and Water Wars*, 22–23. See also Banner, *How the Indians Lost Their Land*.

28. Steward, *Basin-Plateau*, 89; Walton, *Western Times and Water Wars*, 27, 29, 32.

29. Kahrl, *Water and Power*; Sauder, *The Lost Frontier*.

30. Steward, *Basin-Plateau*, 32, 33.

31. Alfred L. Kroeber to Omer C. Stewart, June 3, 1935, DAR.

32. Chalfant, *The Story of Inyo*, 406; Baugh, "Land Use Changes"; Kahrl, *Water and Power*, 314; Liljeblad and Fowler, "Owens Valley Paiute," 431; Sauder, *The Lost Frontier*.

33. Kerns, *Scenes from the High Desert*, 38–39.

34. Delacorte, *Prehistory of Deep Springs Valley*; Liljeblad and Fowler, "Owens Valley Paiute," 415.

35. Journal, April 14–25, 1935, JHS Box 21.

36. Kerns, *Scenes from the High Desert*, 160, 175; "Autobiographical Appraisal," n.d., JHS Box 16; Steward, "Economic and Social Basis of Primitive Bands"; Steward, *Theory of Culture Change*, 129, 132.

37. Julian H. Steward to Robert H. Lowie, April 20, 1935, RHL Box 13; Steward, "Economic and Social Basis of Primitive Bands"; Kerns, *Scenes from the High Desert*, 160.

38. Julian Steward, Deep Springs Diaries, 1918–1920, JHS Box 21. Jane Steward stored the diaries in the 1970s, and they were largely forgotten until removed from storage in about 2004. Her sons, Michael and Gary Steward, later added the diaries, along with the field journals, to the Julian H. Steward Papers at the University of Illinois Archives.

2. Shoshone Territory

1. Jane C. Cannon to Joseph J. Cannon, May 8, 1935, RWC Box 57; Steward, *Basin-Plateau*, plate 1C, facing p. 16.

2. Steward, *Basin-Plateau*, 71; Kroeber, *Handbook of the Indians of California*.

3. Jane C. Steward to Joseph J. Cannon, May 8, 1935, RWC Box 57; National Park Service, n.d.; Federal Writers' Project of the Works Progress Administration

of Northern California, *Death Valley*, 47–48. The National Park Service now administers Scotty's Castle, which is open to the public.

4. National Park Service, n.d.; United States Federal Census (hereafter USFC), 1930, Inyo County, California; Steward, *Basin-Plateau*, 87, 88.

5. Journal, April 26, 1935, JHS Box 21; Kerns, *Scenes from the High Desert*, 91; Jane C. Steward to Joseph J. Cannon, May 8, 1935, RWC Box 57.

6. USFC 1930, Inyo County, California; Census of the Bishop Agency of the Walker River jurisdiction as of April 1, 1934, ICR. Steward (*Basin-Plateau*, 74) cited JN (not JH, John Hunter) as an informant for Death Valley, evidently a typographical error that he corrected, listing JH (Steward, *Basin-Plateau*, 92; Steward, "Culture Element Distributions: XIII, Nevada Shoshoni," 213). WP (Steward, "Culture Element Distributions: XIII, Nevada Shoshoni," 214) is Wilbur Patterson.

7. Steward, *Basin-Plateau*, 78.

8. Federal Writers' Project of the Works Progress Administration of Northern California, *Death Valley*, 21–23, 30, 31, 41, 61. See Lingenfelter, *Death Valley and the Amargosa*, on mining in Death Valley.

9. Census of the Bishop Agency of the Walker River jurisdiction as of April 1, 1934, ICR; Journal, April 26, 1935, JHS Box 21.

10. Julian H. Steward to Alfred L. Kroeber, April 27, 1935, DAR.

11. Miller, Newe Natekwinappeh, 3; Fowler and Liljeblad, "Northern Paiute," 435; Fowler, "History of Research," 29.

12. Kerns, *Scenes from the High Desert*, 177. For the vocabulary lists, see Steward, *Basin-Plateau*, 272–83.

13. Jane C. Steward to Joseph J. Cannon, May 8, 1935, RWC Box 57.

14. Journal, April 27, 1935, JHS Box 21; Federal Writers' Project of the Works Progress Administration of Northern California, *Death Valley*, 29.

15. Journal, April 28, 1935, JHS Box 21; Slater, *Panamint Shoshone Basketry*, 55–58; Dean et al., *Weaving a Legacy*, 72–75. Steward sent the specimens to the Peabody Museum at Harvard University. GH (Steward, *Basin-Plateau*, 73; Steward, "Culture Element Distributions: XIII, Nevada Shoshoni," 213) is George Hanson.

16. Census of the Bishop Agency of the Walker River jurisdiction as of April 1, 1934, ICR; Irwin, "Introduction," iii; Federal Writers' Project of the Works Progress Administration of Northern California, *Death Valley*, 52, 53. Indian Ranch had status as a reservation from the late 1920s until the 1950s (Clemmer and Stewart, "Treaties, Reservations, and Claims," 533).

17. Federal Writers' Project of the Works Progress Administration of Northern California, *Death Valley,* 19–20, 53; Lingenfelter, *Death Valley and the Amargosa,* 20; Boyles, "He Witnessed the Death Valley Tragedy," 6.

18. Steward called her Mabel Hanson in a journal entry (Journal April 27, 1935, JHS Box 21). In print Steward identified the woman as MHa, "GH's niece" ("Culture Element Distributions: XIII, Nevada Shoshoni," 214). Isabel Hanson, also known as Mabel Hanson, was George Hanson's daughter (Census of the Paiutes, Shoshone, Monache and Washoe Indians of Bishop Agency, June 30, 1927, ICR). See Aird et al., "Venoms and Morphology," 131, on the Mojave rattlesnake.

19. Journal, April 27, April 28, 1935, JHS Box 21; Federal Writers' Project of the Works Progress Administration of Northern California, *Death Valley,* 52; Slater, *Panamint Shoshone Basketry,* 125.

20. Journal, April 28, 1935, JHS Box 21.

21. For photographs of Isabel Hanson, see Slater, *Panamint Shoshone Basketry,* 30, 33. Many photographs of George Hanson reached print, including those in Irwin, "Introduction," xii; Thomas, Pendleton, and Cappannari, "Western Shoshone," 278, fig. 20; and Slater, *Panamint Shoshone Basketry,* 30, 125.

22. De Angulo's *Indians in Overalls* (1970) originally appeared in the *Hudson Review* in 1950, but drew on much earlier fieldwork. On acculturation studies, see Redfield, Linton, and Herskovits, "Memorandum for the Study of Acculturation."

23. Jane C. Steward to Joseph J. Cannon, May 8, 1935, RWC Box 57.

24. Journal, April 27, 1935, JHS Box 21; Steward, *Basin-Plateau,* 73

25. On care of the land, see Harney, *The Way It Is.* On Steward's lack of interest in symbols, values, and religion, and on the influence of behaviorism, see Kerns, *Scenes from the High Desert.* For elders' conflicting testimony about land, see Steward, *Basin-Plateau,* 73, 77–78.

26. Journal, April 27, April 28, 1935, JHS Box 21; Jane C. Steward to Joseph J. Cannon, May 8, 1935, RWC Box 57.

27. Journal, April 28, 1935, JHS Box 21; Federal Writers' Project of the Works Progress Administration of Northern California, *Death Valley,* 34. By the 1930s the pipeline had worn out and water was hauled from another source, also miles from town. Steward named some of the springs used by Panamint Shoshones (*Basin-Plateau,* 81).

28. Journal, April 28, April 29, 1935, JHS Box 21; Irwin, "Introduction," iii; Walton, *Western Times and Water Wars,* 39.

29. Journal, April 29, 1935, JHS Box 21; Irwin, "Introduction," iii; Kerr, *Shoshoni Indians,* 5n6; Steward, *Basin-Plateau,* 82; Sauder, *The Lost Frontier,* 97.

30. Federal Writers' Project of the Works Progress Administration of Northern California, *Death Valley*, 34.

31. In 2005 some charcoal kilns still stood at a site a few miles from Cartago, as well as in Death Valley's Wildrose Canyon.

32. Steward, *Basin-Plateau*, 52, 71.

33. Journal, April 29, 1938, JHS Box 21; Federal Writers' Project of the Works Progress Administration for the State of California, *California*, 520; Census of the Bishop Agency of the Walker River jurisdiction as of April 1, 1934, ICR; Irwin, "Introduction," iii. For photographs, see Slater, *Panamint Shoshone Basketry*, 12; and Irwin, "Introduction," 2.

34. Harold Driver to Mrs. Chilcote, March 18, 1935; Alfred L. Kroeber to Harold Driver, April 10, 1935, DAR. Harold Driver (1907–1992) drew on the lists in comparative research that centered on statistical analysis (see Jorgensen, *Comparative Studies by Driver*). Later generations of anthropologists made use of the lists as well (e.g., Jorgensen, *Western Indians*; Myers, "A Frame for Culture").

35. Steward, "Culture Element Distributions: XIII, Nevada Shoshoni," 273, 279.

36. Federal Writers' Project of the Works Progress Administration of Northern California, *Death Valley*, 34; Jane C. Steward interview.

37. Jane C. Steward interview.

38. Journal, April 30, 1935, JHS Box 21; Irwin, "Introduction," iii. GG (Steward, *Basin-Plateau*, 83; Steward, "Culture Element Distributions: XIII, Nevada Shoshoni," 213) is George Gregory.

39. Elizabeth Mecham to Charles Irwin, Jan. 22, 1978, ECM 1955.913.41; Kerr, Shoshoni Indians of Inyo County, California, 17n39; Slater, *Panamint Shoshone Basketry*, 37–42; Dean et al., *Weaving a Legacy*, 69–70.

40. Slater, *Panamint Shoshone Basketry*, 98; Sennett-Walker, *Basketry*; Sennett-Graham, *Basketry*; Dean et al., *Weaving a Legacy*, 54–60. In 2006 Scotty's Castle still had the collection on display. See Slater, *Panamint Shoshone Basketry*; and Dean et al., *Weaving a Legacy*, on the women who produced fine baskets for sale, and on the collectors.

41. Journal, April 30, May 1, May 3, 1935, JHS Box 21.

42. Journal, May 2, 1935, JHS Box 21; Walton, *Western Times and Water Wars*, 205–6. Bishop Agency (ICR) census takers of the period listed a few men as residents of Los Angeles.

43. Journal, May 2, 1935, JHS Box 21; Steward, "Ethnography of Owens Valley Paiute," 291.

44. See Darnell, "Taciturnity"; and Harney, *The Way It Is*, 6, on "taciturnity" and different styles of expression.

45. Journal, May 2, 1935, JHS Box 21.

46. Kerns, *Scenes from the High Desert*, 215, 344n41; Jorgensen, *Comparative Studies by Driver*, 3. See Price, "How Good Is Graduate Training," on contemporary training. The course in field geography constituted Steward's only formal training in field techniques.

47. Julian H. Steward to Robert H. Lowie, May 6, 1935, DAR.

48. "Evangelist's Kidnaping Case History Replete with Sensations," *Los Angeles Times*, Jan. 11, 1927; "Ormiston's Wife Picks Attorneys," *Los Angeles Times*, Jan. 29, 1927, A18.

49. Journal, May 2, 1935, JHS Box 21.

50. Steward, *Basin-Plateau*, 8; Jane C. Steward interview.

51. Journal, May 3, 1935, JHS Box 21; Census of the Paiute Indians of Bishop Agency, California, on June 30, 1920, ICR; Census of the Paiutes, Shoshone, Monache & Washoe Indians of Bishop Agency, June 30, 1927, ICR; Census of the Bishop Agency of the Walker River jurisdiction as of April 1, 1934, ICR.

52. Kerns, *Scenes from the High Desert*, 96. TSp (Steward, *Basin-Plateau*, 71n7; Steward, "Culture Element Distributions: XIII, Nevada Shoshoni," 214) is Tom Spratt. Steward used the term *full-blood* in his list of informants ("Culture Element Distributions: XIII, Nevada Shoshoni," 212–14). In a letter to Kroeber, he referred to Spratt as "a half breed," common slang at the time but later regarded as very pejorative (Julian H. Steward to Alfred L. Kroeber, May 3, 1935, DAR). Alfred L. Kroeber (1876–1960) and Robert H. Lowie (1883–1957) studied anthropology with Franz Boas (1858–1942) at Columbia University.

53. Journal, May 3, 1935, JHS Box 21; Steward, *Basin-Plateau*, 71, 274, 275; Steward, "Culture Element Distributions: XIII, Nevada Shoshoni," 214; Zigmond, "Kawaiisu," 398–99.

54. Justice Hugo Black wrote those words in 1945 in *Shoshone Indians v. United States*, 324 U.S. 335, p. 357 (www.supreme.justia.com/us/324/335/, retrieved June 15, 2008), a case involving the Northwestern Bands of Shoshones. Black's opinion in this and others cases involving Indian rights was seen as "particularly insensitive" (Reich, "*Mr. Justice Black and the Living Constitution*," 689).

55. Julian H. Steward to Alfred L. Kroeber, May 3, 1935, DAR; Steward, *Basin-Plateau*, 72.

56. Steward, "Ethnology of Owens Valley Paiute"; Steward, *Basin-Plateau*, 50.

3. Valley of the Paiutes

1. Steward *Basin-Plateau*, 52; USFC 1930, Inyo County; Census of the Bishop Agency of the Walker River jurisdiction as of April 1, 1934, ICR; Irwin, "Introduction," xv. In 1939, four years after Steward's fieldwork, the Lone Pine Colony was officially established (Clemmer and Stewart, "Treaties, Reservations, and Claims," 533).

2. "Earhart Flight Delayed," "Barring Out Needy Urged," *Los Angeles Times*, May 4, 1935, 1, 4.

3. Journal, May 5, 1935, JHS Box 21; Steward, "Ethnography of the Owens Valley Paiute," 234.

4. Steward, *Basin-Plateau*, 56; Census of the Bishop Agency of the Walker River jurisdiction as of April 1, 1934, ICR; Ford, Owens River Valley, ECM; Liljeblad and Fowler, "Owens Valley Paiute," 427. Steward identified Glenn as a widower; census takers in the 1930s simply listed him as single.

5. Ford, Owens River Valley, ECM; Sauder, *The Lost Frontier*, 63; Steward, *Basin-Plateau*, 52.

6. Kerns, *Scenes from the High Desert*, 182–83; Steward, *Basin-Plateau*, 57.

7. Spear, "Andrew Glen—1878–1973," 17; Ford, Owens River Valley, ECM.

8. Journal, May 5, May 6, 1935. JHS Box 21; Census of the Bishop Agency of the Walker River jurisdiction as of April 1, 1934, ICR. In some other censuses Lacy was identified as Paiute, not Shoshone.

9. Journal, May 7, 1935, JHS Box 21; Federal Writers' Project of the Works Progress Administration for the State of California, *California*, 519. A plaque, in place in 2005, marks the site of Austin's house.

10. Steward, *Basin-Plateau*, 51; Liljeblad and Fowler, "Owens Valley Paiute," 430; Walton, *Western Times and Water Wars*, 18–22; Clemmer and Stewart, "*Treaties, Reservations, and Claims*," 532; Federal Writers' Project of the Works Progress Administration for the State of California, *California*, 518.

11. USFC 1920, Inyo County, California; Census of the Bishop Agency of the Walker River jurisdiction as of April 1, 1934, ICR; 1993 O.V.I.H.A. calendar, S/H file, Indians, Inyo Co. (Misc.), ECM.

12. Journal, May 7, 1935, JHS Box 21; USFC 1920, Inyo County, California; Ford, Owens River Valley, ECM. A federal census taker in 1920 recorded that Robinson farmed five acres of government land. A 1930 report noted about George and Jennie Robinson, "Each have [*sic*] a 2 ½ acre tract at Ft. Independence" (Ford, Owens River Valley, ECM).

13. Journal, May 7, 1935; Steward, *Basin-Plateau*, 51–52.

14. Steward, *Basin-Plateau*, 57.

15. Journal, May 7, 1935, JHS Box 21.

16. SS (Steward, *Basin-Plateau*, 78; Steward, "Culture Element Distributions: XIII, Nevada Shoshoni," 214) is Susie Shepherd (Expense Record of Julian H. Steward [1936], DAR; Journal, May 8, 1935, JHS Box 21). A census taken soon after Steward met Shepherd gives her birth date as 1874 (Census of the Inyo County, California, Non-reservation Indians of the Carson Agency, Jan. 1, 1937, ICR).

17. Journal, May 8, 1935, JHS Box 21; Steward, *Basin-Plateau*, 78.

18. Journal, May 8, 1935, JHS Box 21; Jane C. Steward to Joseph J. Cannon, May 8, 1935, RWC Box 57; Steward, *Some Western Shoshoni Myths*, 253; Census of the Inyo County, California, Non-reservation Indians of the Carson Agency, Jan. 1, 1937, ICR). The only woman whom Steward identified as PW in his list of informants came from Elko, Nevada; adding to the confusion, she did not actually serve as an informant, although he noted that she was "willing and well informed and would probably be excellent" ("Culture Element Distributions: XIII, Nevada Shoshoni," 214). He paid her for some specimens that he sent to a museum. PW is not Patsy Wilson, the Shoshone woman who told Steward the stories (Kerns, *Scenes from the High Desert*, 361n33).

19. Steward, *Some Western Shoshoni Myths*, 281–82. On the reckoning of months by the moon, as explained by Charlie Wrinkle, see Kerr, *Shoshoni Indians of Inyo County, California*, 3.

20. Journal, May 9, 1935, JHS Box 21; Jane C. Steward to Joseph J. Cannon, May 8, 1935, RWC Box 57; Steward, "Culture Element Distribution: XIII, Nevada Shoshoni," 214. Steward sent Shepherd's basket to the Peabody Museum at Harvard University. Her basket is catalogued as Peabody number 35–78–10/4988.

21. Journal, May 9, 1935, JHS Box 21; Steward, *Some Western Shoshoni Myths*.

22. Journal, May 9, 1935, JHS Box 21; Steward, *Basin-Plateau*, 52; Census of the Bishop Agency of the Walker River jurisdiction as of April 1, 1934, ICR. To judge from other records, Lacy may have only been in his midfifties in 1935 (e.g., Census of the Paiute Indians of Bishop Agency, California, on June 30, 1920, ICR; Ford, Owens River Valley, ECM).

23. Journal, May 9, 1935, JHS Box 21.

24. Journal, May 10, 1935, JHS Box 21; Steward, *Basin-Plateau*, 50, 57.

25. Steward, *Basin-Plateau*, 50–51.

26. Julian H. Steward to Alfred L. Kroeber, July 26, 1928, DAR; Kerns, *Scenes from the High Desert*, 98, 127–29; Janetski, "Julian Steward and Utah Archeology."

27. Journal, May 10, 1935, JHS Box 21; Steward, "Ethnography of the Owens Valley Paiute," 251–52; Steward, *Basin-Plateau*, 40–41, 51; Steward, "Culture Element Distributions: XIII, Nevada Shoshoni," 235.

28. Journal, May 10, 1935, JHS Box 21; Steward, "Ethnography of the Owens Valley Paiute," 266, 345, plate 5G; Steward, "Culture Element Distributions: XIII, Nevada Shoshoni," 235; Liljeblad and Fowler, "Owens Valley Paiute," 421. See Bettinger, "Aboriginal Human Ecology," on the prehistoric ecology of the Owens Valley.

29. Journal, May 10, 1935, JHS Box 21.

30. Steward, "Ethnography of the Owens Valley Paiute," 325; Walton, *Western Times and Water Wars*, 156–57 (photos).

31. Steward to Lowie, May 6 [1935], RHL Box 13; Journal, May 12, 1935, JHS Box 21; Jane C. Steward interview.

32. Federal Writers' Project of the Works Progress Administration for the State of California, *California*, 518; Clemmer and Stewart, "Treaties, Reservations, and Claims," 533. *Colony* refers to a small reservation within city limits or on the outskirts of a town or city (Clemmer and Stewart, "Treaties, Reservations, and Claims," 543).

33. Steward, *Basin-Plateau*, 56.

34. Census of the Bishop Agency of the Walker River jurisdiction as of April 1, 1934, ICR; Steward, "Ethnography of the Owens Valley Paiute," 234. TS (Steward, *Basin-Plateau*, 55; Steward, "Culture Element Distributions: XIII, Nevada Shoshoni," 214) is Tom Stone. The census listed Stone as "¾ Paiute," which suggests that his maternal grandfather was white. Steward thought Stone was born in 1887, four years earlier than the date shown in most censuses ("Culture Element Distributions: XIII, Nevada Shoshoni," 214).

35. Census of the Bishop Agency of the Walker River jurisdiction as of April 1, 1934, ICR; USFC 1930, Inyo County, California; Ford, Owens River Valley, ECM; Liljeblad and Fowler, "Owens Valley Paiute," 430. Earlier censuses of Bishop Agency (1914, 1920) listed Stone's previous wives.

36. Steward, *Basin-Plateau*, 62n6, 314; Lingenfelter, *Death Valley and the Amargosa*, 101ff; Malouf and Findlay, "Euro-American Impact Before 1870," 511–14. MH (Steward, *Basin-Plateau*, 64, 314; Steward, "Culture Element Distributions: XIII, Nevada Shoshoni," 214) is Mary Harry.

37. Kerns, *Scenes from the High Desert*, 40–41. Steward recalled that Captain Harry died in 1919 or 1920 ("Ethnography of the Owens Valley Paiute," 234;

Steward, *Basin-Plateau*, 67, 315; see also Kerns, *Scenes from the High Desert*, 53), but a census taker noted his date of death as February 1921 (Census of the Paiute Indians of Bishop Agency, California, on June 30, 1921, ICR). The death occurred during Steward's third and last year as a student at Deep Springs, not his first year.

38. Steward, *Basin-Plateau*, 46, 61–63.

39. Steward, *Basin-Plateau*, 314.

40. Steward, *Basin-Plateau*, 65.

41. Steward, *Basin-Plateau*, 314. The 1920 federal census taker listed him as able to speak English but unable to read and write; ten years later he was listed as able to speak, read, and write English (USFC 1920 and USFC 1930, Inyo County, California).

42. Steward, *Basin-Plateau*, 58, 60–61, 67, 247, 315.

43. Kerns, *Scenes from the High Desert*, 39, 41; Steward, *Basin-Plateau*, 315.

44. USFC 1930, Inyo County, California; Ford, Owens River Valley, ECM; Census of the Bishop Agency of the Walker River jurisdiction as of April 1, 1934, ICR.

45. Journal, May 13, 1935, JHS Box 21; Jane C. Steward interview.

46. Journal, May 13, May 20, 1935, JHS Box 21; Steward, *Panatubiji, an Owens Valley Paiute*, 185.

47. Journal, May 13, May 20, 1935, JHS Box 21; Steward, *Basin-Plateau*, 314–15; Steward, *Panatubiji, an Owens Valley Paiute*, 185.

48. Steward, *Basin-Plateau*, 62.

49. Steward referred to Paiutes of Fish Lake Valley and adjacent areas, including the Owens Valley, as Northern Paiutes (*Basin-Plateau*, 67). For linguistic reasons, anthropologists later categorized the Paiutes of Fish Lake Valley as Owens Valley Paiutes, distinguishing them from Northern Paiutes (Liljeblad and Fowler, "Owens Valley Paiute," 413).

50. Steward, *Basin-Plateau*, 62.

51. Steward, *Basin-Plateau*, 61–64.

52. Steward, *Basin-Plateau*, 8, 53; Steward, "Irrigation Without Agriculture"; Steward, "Ethnography of the Owens Valley Paiute," 247; Liljeblad and Fowler, "Owens Valley Paiute," 417–18; Sauder, *The Lost Frontier*, 16–18. See also Lawton et al., "Agriculture among the Paiute of Owens Valley," who argue that the Owens Valley Paiute were practicing a form of horticulture.

53. Steward, *Kroeber*, 46; Kerns, *Scenes from the High Desert*, 180, 293.

54. Journal, May 18, May 19, 1935, JHS Box 21; Jane C. Steward interview; Dorothy B. Nyswander interview.

55. Journal, May 19, 1935, JHS Box 21.

56. Steward, "Ethnography of the Owens Valley Paiute"; Steward, *Basin-Plateau*, 59; Clemmer and Stewart, "Treaties, Reservations, and Claims," 532.

57. USFC 1920, Inyo County, California; Sauder, *The Lost Frontier*, 63; Steward *Basin-Plateau*, 58; Ford, Owens River Valley, ECM.

58. USFC 1920, Inyo County, California; Steward, *Basin-Plateau*, 58, 61; Lingenfelter, *Death Valley and the Amargosa*, 22.

59. Journal, May 21, 1935, JHS Box 21; Steward, "Culture Element Distributions: XIII, Nevada Shoshoni," 213; Census of the Paiute Indians of Bishop Agency, California, on June 30th, 1916, ICR. JA (Steward, *Basin-Plateau*, 58; Steward, "Culture Element Distributions: XIII, Nevada Shoshoni," 213) is John Alston.

60. Journal, May 21, 1935, JHS Box 21; Census of the Paiute, Shoshone, Monache & Washoe Indians of Bishop Agency, June 30, 1927, ICR; Census of the Bishop Agency of the Walker River jurisdiction as of April 1, 1934, ICR; Ford, Owens River Valley, ECM; "Indian Woman's Memories of Coso Told in Appeal," *Owens Valley Progress-Citizen*, Oct. 1, 1970. Steward used her name in print—incorrectly spelled as Babock—rather than just her initials (*Basin-Plateau*, 59). This was apparently an oversight since he listed other cultural informants and interpreters by initials. He gave her name as Babcock in other records (Kerns, *Scenes from the High Desert*, 186). Her marital status was shown as married in some records (USFC 1930, Inyo County, California) and divorced in others (Ford, Owens River Valley, ECM).

61. Journal, May 21, 1935, JHS Box 21; Jane C. Steward interview.

62. Steward, *Basin-Plateau*, 246–47. See, for example, works by Morton H. Fried (1923–1986) and Elman R. Service (1915–1996), two of Steward's students during his tenure at Columbia University (1946–1952).

63. Steward, *Basin-Plateau*, 58–61. See also Delacorte, "The Prehistory of Deep Springs."

64. Steward, *Basin-Plateau*, 60.

65. Journal, May 21, 1935, JHS Box 21; Steward, *Basin-Plateau*, 57.

4. Coyote's Country

1. Journal, June 17, 1935, JHS Box 21. On U.S. Geological Survey maps, see, for example, Steward, *Basin-Plateau*, 63.

2. Lingenfelter, *Death Valley and the Amargosa*, 106, 340; Carlson, *Nevada Place Names*, 155.

3. USFC, 1930, Nevada.

4. Steward, *Basin-Plateau*, 93; Carlson, *Nevada Place Names*, 36–37.

5. Journal, May 25, 1935, JHS Box 21; Steward, "Culture Element Distributions: XIII, Nevada Shoshoni," 213.

6. Moerman, *Native American Ethnobotany*, 438; Linda L. Miller, U.S. Fish and Wildlife Service, Ash Meadows National Wildlife Refuge, personal communication; Steward, *Basin-Plateau*, plate 2b, between pages 16 and 17.

7. Journal, May 25, 1935, JHS Box 21; Steward, "Culture Element Distributions: XIII, Nevada Shoshoni," 214; USFC 1930, Nye County, Nevada.

8. Journal, May 25, 1935, JHS Box 21; Carlson, *Nevada Place Names*, 152–53; Writers' Program of the Works Progress Administration in the State of Nevada, *Nevada*, 4.

9. Lingenfelter, *Death Valley and the Amargosa*, 168; USFC 1880, Lincoln County, Nevada; USFC 1900, Nye County, Nevada.

10. Journal, May 25, 1935, JHS Box 21; Rusco and Rusco, "Tribal Politics," 569; USFC 1930, Nye County, Nevada; USFC 1900, Lincoln County, Nevada; USFC 1900, Nye County, Nevada.

11. Journal, May 28, 1935, JHS Box 21; Census of the Bishop Agency of the Walker River jurisdiction as of April 1, 1934, ICR; USFC 1930, Nye County, Nevada. The federal census taker, unlike Steward, thought Albert Howell was working on his "own farm." AH and MHo (Steward, *Basin-Plateau*, 182; Steward, "Culture Element Distributions: XIII, Nevada Shoshoni," 213, 214) are Albert Howell and Mary Howell.

12. Steward, *Basin-Plateau*, 182–84.

13. Journal, May 25, 1935, JHS Box 21.

14. Journal, May 26, 1935, JHS Box 21.

15. Kelly, "Southern Paiute Bands." Isabel Kelly (1906–1983) never found a permanent position as an anthropologist in the United States. She lived and worked in Mexico for many years (Kerns, *Scenes from the High Desert*, 171). Her marginal professional status was not unique (see, for example, Parezo and Hardin, "In the Realm of the Muses").

16. Steward, *Basin-Plateau*, 181.

17. Steward, *Basin-Plateau*, 185. See also Kelly and Fowler, "Southern Paiute."

18. Journal, May 26, 1935; Steward, "Culture Element Distributions: XIII, Nevada Shoshoni," 214.

19. Journal, May 26, 1935, JHS Box 21.

20. Journal, May 27, 1935, JHS Box 21; Steward, "Culture Element Distributions: XIII, Nevada Shoshoni," 214.

21. Journal, May 28, 1935, JHS Box 21.

22. Ethnographic photographs, JHS Box 20; USFC 1930, Nye County, Nevada.

23. USFC 1910, 1930, Nye County, Nevada; Census of the Bishop Agency of the Walker River jurisdiction as of April 1, 1934, ICR.

24. "Indians Receive Scanty Rations," *Los Angeles Times*, March 22, 1925, 2.

25. Journal, May 28, 1935, JHS Box 21; Steward, *Basin-Plateau*, 274–75; Steward, *Some Western Shoshoni Myths*, 253. MS (Steward, "Culture Element Distributions: XIII, Nevada Shoshoni," 214) is Mary Scott.

26. Steward, *Some Western Shoshoni Myths*, 265–66. He included six versions of the story.

27. Lingenfelter, *Death Valley and the Amargosa*, 168, 192–94. Hugh J. Cannon (1870–1931) was seven years older than Jane's father and was one of his full brothers. Her father also had many half brothers because her paternal grandfather, a Mormon polygamist, had more than thirty children (Bitton, *George Q. Cannon*, 385, 463–64). See also Zanjani, "Indian Prosepectors," for information on Indian prospectors.

28. Lingenfelter, *Death Valley and the Amargosa*, 192; Journal, May 28, 1935, JHS Box 21.

29. Journal, May 28, 1935, JHS Box 21; Steward to Kroeber, May 30, 1935, DAR. In 2003 the Exchange Club was still open for business.

30. Journal, May 28, 1935, JHS Box 21.

31. Journal, May 29, 1935, JHS Box 21; USFC 1930, Inyo County, California. BD (Steward, *Basin-Plateau*, 76; Steward, "Culture Element Distributions: XIII, Nevada Shoshoni," 213) is Bill Doc. The surname Doc is spelled Dock in some sources. Steward thought Doc was just seventy in 1935, five years younger than the age estimated by census takers ("Culture Element Distributions: XIII, Nevada Shoshoni," 213). See Sennett-Graham, *Basketry*, 185, for his employment records.

32. McCracken, *A History of Beatty, Nevada*, 98–99.

33. Census of the Paiute, Shoshone, Monache & Washoe Indians of Bishop Agency, June 30, 1927, ICR.

34. Journal, May 29, 1935, JHS Box 21; USFC 1930, Inyo County, California;

Census of the Bishop Agency of the Walker River jurisdiction as of April 1, 1934, ICR.

35. See Slater, *Panamint Shoshone Basketry*, 74, fig. 34, for a photograph of Tina Doc.

36. Journal, May 29, 1935, JHS Box 21.

37. Steward, *Basin-Plateau*, 82, 87, 88. See also Bettinger and Wolgemuth, "California Plants," 279; Fowler and Rhode, "Great Basin Plants," 340–41.

38. Steward, *Basin-Plateau*, 76, 88, 90.

39. Steward, *Basin-Plateau*, 89; Kerns, *Scenes from the High Desert*, 58.

40. Steward, *Basin-Plateau*, 89.

41. Lingenfelter, *Death Valley and the Amargosa*, 219–29; Carlson, *Nevada Place Names*, 202.

42. Lingenfelter, *Death Valley and the Amargosa*, 20, 207; Christman, "Johnny Shoshone." Steward identified "Shoshoni John" as Bill Doc's half brother (*Basin-Plateau*, 87; but see Sennett-Graham, *Basketry*, 189, who was not able to verify this). He was probably the man listed as John Shoshone by census takers (Census of the Paiutes, Shoshone, Monache & Washoe Indians of Bishop Agency, June 30, 1927, ICR). See also Zanjani, "Indian Prospectors."

43. Journal, May 30, 1935, JHS Box 21; Writers' Program of the Works Progress Administration in the State of Nevada, *Nevada*, 232–33.

44. Journal, May 30, 1935, JHS Box 21.

45. Journal, May 31, 1935, JHS Box 21; Steward, *Some Western Shoshoni Myths*, 262–63; Hultkrantz, "Mythology and Religious Concept," 637–49.

46. Journal, June 1, 1935, JHS Box 21.

47. Census of the Paiute Indians of Bishop Agency, California, on June 30, 1920, ICR. TSt (Steward, *Basin-Plateau*, 94; Steward, "Culture Element Distributions: XIII, Nevada Shoshoni," 214) is Tom Stewart. See Sennett-Graham, *Basketry*, 194, for Stewart's employment records.

48. Journal, June 2, 1935, JHS Box 21; Steward, "Culture Element Distributions: XIII, Nevada Shoshoni," 214.

49. Steward, *Basin-Plateau*, 93–99.

50. See Sauder, *The Last Frontier*, 29–30, on the symbiotic relationship of ranching and mining.

51. Steward, *Basin-Plateau*, 94, 97–98.

52. Journal, June 4, June 5, 1935, JHS Box 21; Steward, *Basin-Plateau*, 69.

53. Carlson, *Nevada Place Names*, 123; Journal, June 5, 1935, JHS Box 21.

54. USFC 1930, Inyo County, California; Sennett-Graham, *Basketry*, 190.

55. Journal, June 5, 1935, JHS Box 21.

56. Journal, June 6–June 10, 1935, JHS Box 21.

57. Journal, June 17, 1935, JHS Box 21.

58. Steward, *Basin-Plateau*, 64, 314.

59. Steward, *Basin-Plateau*, 16, 68–69.

60. Steward, *Basin-Plateau*, 69; USFC 1920, Esmeralda County, Nevada; Census of the Paiute, Shoshone, Monache & Washoe Indians of Bishop Agency, June 30, 1927, ICR; Census of the Bishop Agency of the Walker River jurisdiction as of April 1, 1934, ICR. JS (Steward, *Basin-Plateau*, 70; Steward, "Culture Element Distributions: XIII, Nevada Shoshoni," 214) is John Shakespeare.

61. USFC 1920, Esmeralda County, Nevada; Journal, June 17, 1935, JHS Box 21.

62. Journal, June 17, June 20, 1935, JHS Box 21; Ethnographic photographs, JHS Box 20; Kerns, *Scenes from the High Desert*, 234–35 (the fifth photo shows John Shakespeare). Steward identified ES as "daughter of JS; basket weaver" ("Culture Element Distributions: XIII, Nevada Shoshoni," 213). ES was more likely John Shakespeare's wife, Ella, not his daughter Elizabeth, who was just nineteen years old at the time. According to most records Ella was about twenty-five years younger than her husband (see, for example, Census of the Bishop Agency of the Walker River jurisdiction as of April 1, 1934, ICR).

63. Steward, *Basin-Plateau*, 70.

64. Steward, *Basin-Plateau*, 70. See Crum's critique in "Steward's Vision of the Great Basin," 120–21.

65. Carlson, *Nevada Place Names*, 179, 233; Writers' Program of the Works Progress Administration in the State of Nevada, *Nevada*, 224; Zanjani, "Indian Prospectors," 53–54.

66. Journal, June 20, 1935, JHS Box 21; Steward, *Basin-Plateau*, 69, 112; Census of the Bishop Agency of the Walker River jurisdiction as of April 1, 1934, ICR. LJB (Steward, *Basin-Plateau*, 69) is John Best, also known as Long John Best. He had earlier lived around Dyer, Nevada, and at Oasis (Census of the Paiute Indians of Bishop Agency, California, on June 30, 1917, ICR; Census of the Paiute, Shoshone, Monache & Washoe Indians of Bishop Agency, June 30, 1927, ICR).

67. Journal, June 21, 1935, JHS Box 21.

5. The People's Land

1. Journal, June 21, 1935, JHS Box 21; Writers' Program of the Works Progress Administration in the State of Nevada, *Nevada*, 217–18; Crum, *The Road*

on Which We Came, 64–65; Clemmer and Stewart, "Treaties, Reservations, and Claims," 532.

2. On the career of C. Hart Merriam (1855–1932) as a naturalist and government scientist, see Sterling, *Last of the Naturalists*. The Division of Biological Survey was the precursor of the U.S. Fish and Wildlife Service.

3. Merriam and Stejneger, *Results of a Biological Survey*. See also Phillips, House, and Phillips, "Expedition to the San Francisco Peaks."

4. Steward, *Basin-Plateau*, 14–18.

5. Julian Steward to Ralph V. Chamberlin, May 19, 1935, RVC Box 5; Kerns, *Scenes from the High Desert*, 159. Jane Steward noted the chance encounter with Merriam, stating only that they "chatted with him" (JJS, June 21, 1935). Her husband never passed up an opportunity to talk shop with other researchers, but the topics of those discussions went unrecorded in the journal's cryptic entries.

6. Slater, *Panamint Shoshone Basketry*, 12 (photo).

7. Journal, June 21, 22, 1935, JHS Box 21; Steward, *Basin-Plateau*, 100.

8. Journal, June 22, 23, 1935, JHS Box 21; Steward, *Basin-Plateau*, 100; Writers' Program of the Works Progress Administration in the State of Nevada, *Nevada*, 144–45.

9. Steward, "Ethnography of the Owens Valley Paiute." As Liljeblad and Fowler note, Steward "did not recognize a sharp linguistic distinction" between the Owens Valley Paiutes and Northern Paiutes although the former in fact speak dialects of Mono, and the latter speak Northern Paiute ("Owens Valley Paiute," 412, 432). See Liljeblad and Fowler, "Owens Valley Paiute"; and Fowler and Liljeblad, "Northern Paiute."

10. Journal, June 24, 1935, JHS Box 21; Steward, *Basin-Plateau*, 108, 110; Steward, "Culture Element Distributions: XIII, Nevada Shoshoni," 213; Steward, *Some Western Shoshoni Myths*, 253; Census of the Walker River Reservation of the Carson Agency jurisdiction, as of Jan. 1, 1937, ICR; USFC 1930, Ormsby County, Nevada. JK (Steward, *Basin-Plateau*, 110; Steward, "Culture Element Distributions: XIII, Nevada Shoshoni," 213) is Jennie Kawich. A photograph reproduced in Crum, *The Road on Which We Came*, between pages 57 and 58, shows Jennie Wilson Kawich and her husband in 1905, when she was in her thirties or forties. Her surname came from marriage, and she did not serve as informant for the region around the Kawich Mountains, north of the Belted Mountains and east of Tonopah. Steward's account of the Kawich Mountains area drew on what he learned from John Best and John Shakespeare (*Basin-Plateau*, 110–13).

11. In passing, Steward explicitly distinguished between data based on "the informant's own observation" and other data ("Culture Element Distributions: XXIII, Northern and Gosiute Shoshoni," 265). On warfare and women, see, for example, the case of Utes who captured Western Shoshone women and children in Little Smokey Valley (Steward, *Basin-Plateau*, 116).

12. Journal, June 24, June 25, 1935, JHS Box 21; Steward, *Basin-Plateau*, 110.

13. Steward cited Powell and Ingalls's "incomplete census of 1873," which he evidently tried to verify or correct and extend (*Basin-Plateau*, 114). See also Crum, *The Road on Which We Came*, 35, on Powell and Ingalls.

14. Steward, *Basin-Plateau*, 110, 113; Steward, "Culture Element Distributions: XIII, Nevada Shoshoni," 214; Badè, *The Life and Letters of John Muir*, 106, 108; Carlson, *Nevada Place Names*, 49.

15. D'Avezedo, "Washoe," 466, 473, 494, 495; Dorothy B. Nyswander interview; Carlson, *Nevada Place Names*, 83–84. The Washoe are considered transitional in a cultural sense, with links to Californian as well as Great Basin peoples.

16. Julian H. Steward to Joseph J. Cannon, Dec. 16, 1933, RWC Box 57; Grant Cannon to Joseph J. Cannon, April 11, 1934, RWC Box 58; Jane C. Steward interview; Grant Cannon to Joseph J. and Ramona W. Cannon, April 21, 1935, RWC Box 58.

17. Journal, June 27, June 28, 1935, JHS Box 21.

18. Journal, June 29, 1935, JHS Box 21; Kerns, *Scenes from the High Desert*, 160, 172–74. His mother, Grace Steward, was assumed to have divorced her husband sometime before or after moving to California (Jane C. Steward interview; Dorothy B. Nyswander interview), but Grace and Thomas Steward may have agreed instead to a permanent separation.

19. Journal, June 30, July 1, 1935, JHS Box 21.

20. Crum, *The Road on Which We Came*, 64–65, 165; Clemmer and Stewart, "Treaties, Reservations, and Claims," 533.

21. Journal, July 2, 1935, JHS Box 21; Steward, *Basin-Plateau*, 110, 113; Census of the Paiute Indians of Fallon Sub-agency, Nevada, June 30, 1927, ICR; Census for the Fallon reservation of the Walker River jurisdiction, as of April 1, 1934, ICR; Crum, *The Road on Which We Came*, 65. PH (Steward, *Basin-Plateau*, 117; Steward, "Culture Element Distributions: XIII, Nevada Shoshoni." 214) is Pat Hicks.

22. Jane C. Steward to Joseph J. Cannon, May 8, 1935, RWC, JHS Box 21; Journal, July 3, 1935. See Crum (*The Road on Which We Came*, 52), who explains that Shoshones and Paiutes used Fourth of July celebrations for their own purposes, as occasions for traditional dances and games.

23. Journal, July 3, 1935. Muir famously complained that Ralph Waldo Emerson had the "house habit" when Emerson, who was visiting in California, preferred the comfort of a bed to camping out in the mountains.

24. Hultkrantz, "Mythology and Religious Concept," 637–40; Liljeblad, "Oral Tradition," 658.

25. Steward, *Some Western Shoshoni Myths*, 253, 266–67, 290.

26. Journal, July 4, 1935, JHS Box 21. The barbecue is generally believed to have origins among native people in the Caribbean, and parades, in the Old World.

27. On the hand game, see Thomas, Pendleton, and Cappannari, "Western Shoshone," 275, fig. 16; Steward, "Culture Element Distributions: XIII, Nevada Shoshoni," 248.

28. Journal, July 3, July 4, 1935, JHS Box 21.

29. Steward, "Culture Element Distributions: XIII, Nevada Shoshoni," 210; Kerns, *Scenes from the High Desert*, 207. Steward recorded stories during fieldwork, but he published them (as *Some Western Shoshoni Myths*) without analysis or commentary, simply as products of salvage ethnography.

30. Steward, *Basin-Plateau*, 250; "Dr. Steward Finishing Study of Cultureless Shoshoni Tribe," *Washington Post*, June 23, 1937, 10. Why the newspaper chose the word "cultureless" is open to question. Steward used the words "'low' culture" in a report he wrote for the BIA months earlier, but not "cultureless" (Julian H. Steward, "Shoshonean Cultures," Nov. 1936, JHS Box 11).

31. Steward, *Basin-Plateau*, 100; Journal, July 3, 1935, JHS Box 21.

32. Journal, July 5, 1935, JHS Box 21; Census for the Fallon reservation of the Walker River jurisdiction, as of April 1, 1934, ICR. See Crum, *The Road on Which We Came*, 65–66, on the effects of legal regulation of hunting.

33. Census for the Fallon reservation of the Walker River jurisdiction, as of April 1, 1934, ICR. TH (Steward, *Basin-Plateau*, 106; Steward, "Culture Element Distributions: XIII, Nevada Shoshoni," 214) is Tom Horn.

34. Steward, *Basin-Plateau*, 100. See Crum, *The Road on Which We Came*, 24, 35, 76, 106, on Tu-tu-wa.

35. Steward, *Basin-Plateau*, 104, 105–6; Steward, "Culture Element Distributions: XIII, Nevada Shoshoni," 254.

36. Steward, *Basin-Plateau*, 105; JJS July 5, 1935, JHS Box 21; Steward, "Culture Element Distributions: XIII, Nevada Shoshoni," 262.

37. Steward, "Culture Element Distributions: XIII, Nevada Shoshoni," 224; Steward, "Culture Element Distributions: XXIII, Northern and Gosiute Shoshoni," 257–58.

38. Journal, July 7, 1935, JHS Box 21; Steward, *Basin-Plateau*, 101–3; Census of the Western Shoshone Reservation of the Western Shoshone jurisdiction as of April 1, 1934, ICR. GJ and JF (Steward, *Basin-Plateau*, 107; Steward, "Culture Element Distribution: XIII, Nevada Shoshoni," 213) are George Johnnie and Joe Frank.

39. Steward, "Culture Element Distributions: XIII, Nevada Shoshoni," 213, 214; Field Expense Account of Julian H. Steward, July 1–July 31, 1935, DAR; Census of the Paiute Indians of Fallon Indian Agency, Nevada, on June 30, 1924, ICR. Jane Steward mistakenly identified Joe Frank as Frank Johnnie (Journal, July 7, 1935, JHS Box 21). MJ (Steward, *Basin-Plateau*, 105; Steward, "Culture Element Distributions: XIII, Nevada Shoshoni," 214) is Maggie Johnnie. Steward also named Gus Thomas as an informant for this region, but he did not list him as a paid informant or mention him in a journal entry (*Basin-Plateau*, 106). Thomas was just forty years old in 1935 (Census for the Fallon reservation of the Walker River jurisdiction, as of April 1, 1934, ICR).

40. Steward, *Basin-Plateau*, 105–6.

41. Steward, *Basin-Plateau*, 106.

42. Lincoln Highway Association 1935; Leon A. Dickinson, "Across the States: Many Transcontinental Routes Available to Tourists—Roads Much Improved," *New York Times*, May 17, 1931, 126; Victor H. Bernstein, "Trails Toward the Pacific," *New York Times*, May 3, 1936, 1, 11. The main road across central Nevada, formerly part of the Lincoln Highway, is now Highway 50 and labeled on many maps *The Loneliest Road in America*, an official designation (see also Tingley and Pizzarro, *Traveling America's Loneliest Road*).

43. Writers' Program of the Works Progress Administration in the State of Nevada, *Nevada*, 261.

44. Journal, July 8–13, 1935, JHS Box 21; Writers' Program of the Works Progress Administration in the State of Nevada, *Nevada*, 258–61; Carlson, *Nevada Place Names*, 43. The International Hotel was still open for business in 2004.

45. Census of the Austin Reservation of the Carson jurisdiction as of April 1, 1933, ICR. WJ (Steward, *Basin-Plateau*, 100) is Wagon Jack. Steward also mentioned Jack by name, not initials, as a past director of rabbit drives (*Basin-Plateau*, 105). He typically used full names for leaders who were no longer alive. Whether Jack was still alive at the time of Steward's visit is not clear.

46. Journal, July 8 [–13], 1935, JHS Box 21; Steward, "Culture Element Distributions: XIII, Nevada Shoshoni," 223, 235, 237.

47. Journal, July 8 [–13], 1935, JHS Box 21; Crum, *The Road on Which We Came,* 63; USFC 1930, Nye County, Nevada.

48. Journal, July 14–20, 1935, JHS Box 21; Jane C. Steward interview; Kerns, *Scenes from the High Desert,* 189–90.

49. Journal, July 22, 1935, JHS Box 21; State of Nevada Department of Highways 1937. See Harney, *The Way It Is,* 136, for a map of Newe Sogobia, the Western Shoshone Nation, which covers portions of California, Nevada, Utah, and Idaho.

50. Journal, July 22, 1935, JHS Box 21; Steward, *Basin-Plateau,* 118, 119; Writers' Program of the Works Progress Administration in the State of Nevada, *Nevada,* 244; Crum, *The Road on Which We Came,* 96; Clemmer and Stewart, "Treaties, Reservations, and Claims," 533.

51. Journal, July 22, 1935; Census of the Paiute Indians of Fallon Sub-agency, Nevada, June 30, 1927, ICR. BH (Steward, *Basin-Plateau,* 116; Steward, "Culture Element Distribution: XIII, Nevada Shoshoni," 213) is Barney Hicks.

52. Journal, July 22, 1935, JHS Box 21; Jane C. Steward interview.

53. Ethnographic photographs, JHS Box 20; Steward, "Culture Element Distribution: XIII, Nevada Shoshoni," 213.

54. Bancroft, *History of Nevada,* 285; Carlson, *Nevada Place Names,* 110; Tingley and Pizarro, *Traveling America's Loneliest Road,* 72; Crum, *The Road on Which We Came,* 30.

55. Carlson, *Nevada Place Names,* 171.

56. Steward, "Culture Element Distribution: XIII, Nevada Shoshoni," 213.

57. Steward, *Basin-Plateau,* 114, 116.

58. Steward, *Basin-Plateau,* 116, 117.

59. See, for example, Steward, *Basin-Plateau,* 46, 109.

60. Bill Gibson, a subsequent informant in Elko, Nevada, recalled hearing that his grandmother had made such a walk.

61. Steward, *Basin-Plateau,* 115.

62. USFC 1930, White Pine County, Nevada; Writers' Program of the Works Progress Administration in the State of Nevada, *Nevada,* 249. More than seventy years later, in 2006, the Hotel Nevada and casino remained open for business.

63. Jane C. Steward interview.

64. Journal, July 24 [–Aug. 2], 1935, JHS Box 21.

65. Steward, *Basin-Plateau,* 122; Crum, *The Road on Which We Came,* 30; Bancroft, *History of Nevada,* 277, 279.

66. USFC 1930, White Pine County, Nevada; Census of the Ely reservation of the Carson jurisdiction as of April 1, 1934, ICR.

67. Crum, *The Road on Which We Came*, 74–75; Clemmer and Stewart. "Treaties, Reservations, and Claims," 553; Inter-Tribal Council of Nevada, *Newe*, 88–89; USFC 1930, White Pine County, Nevada.

68. Journal, July 24 [–Aug. 2], 1935, JHS Box 21; Census of the Ely reservation of the Carson jurisdiction as of April 1, 1934, ICR. JW (Steward, *Basin-Plateau*, 118; Steward, "Culture Element Distributions: XIII, Nevada Shoshoni," 214) is Jennie Washburn. On Frank Stick, see note 87.

69. Journal, July 24 [–Aug. 2], 1935, JHS Box 21; Census of the Ely Indians of the Carson Agency [June 30, 1927], ICR; Census of the Ely reservation of the Carson jurisdiction as of April 1, 1933, ICR; Census of the Ely reservation of the Carson jurisdiction as of April 1, 1934, ICR; Crum, *The Road on Which We Came*, 83, 98, 130. AC (Steward, *Basin-Plateau*, 117; Steward, "Culture Element Distributions: XIII, Nevada Shoshoni," 212) is Aggie Stanton, which suggests that Steward eventually realized the first name was Aggie, not Maggie, but never understood that the surname was Stanton.

70. Journal, July 24 [–Aug. 2], 1935, JHS Box 21. HJ (Steward, *Basin-Plateau*, 120; Steward, "Culture Element Distributions: XIII, Nevada Shoshoni," 213) is Harry Johnny. He corresponded with a Northwestern Shoshone man who referred to him variously as Harry George, Harry Johnny George, and Harry Johnny (see Kreitzer, *Washakie Letters*, 100, 171, 232). Census takers listed Johnny's middle initial as G., which suggests that his full English name may have been Harry George Johnny.

71. Clemmer and Stewart, "Treaties, Reservations, and Claims," 543–46.

72. Frank Ernest Hill, "A New Pattern of Life for the Indian," *New York Times*, July 19, 1935, SM 10, 22. See Clemmer and Stewart, "Treaties, Reservations, and Claims," 546–49; and Crum, *The Road on Which We Came*, 91–99, on the "Indian New Deal."

73. Journal, July 24 [–Aug. 2], 1935, JHS Box 21. The vote at Ely Colony was eight in favor and six opposed, but because of twenty-one abstentions, the act was rejected (Crum, *The Road on Which We Came*, 104). On Harry Johnny's activities as a leader, see Crum, *The Road on Which We Came*, 74, 84, 129–30.

74. Steward, "Culture Element Distributions: XIII, Nevada Shoshoni," 212–13, 214.

75. Steward, *Basin-Plateau*, 118; Steward, "Culture Element Distributions: XIII, Nevada Shoshoni," 214; Carlson, *Nevada Place Names*, 130.

76. Steward, *Basin-Plateau*, 118–19, 120.

77. Steward, *Basin-Plateau*, 26, 27, 122.

78. Jane C. Steward interview; Ethnographic photographs, JHS Box 20.

79. Steward, *Basin-Plateau*, 121–22, 128. AR (Steward, *Basin-Plateau*, 122, 124; Steward, "Culture Element Distributions: XIII, Nevada Shoshoni," 213) is Annie Riley.

80. Steward, *Basin-Plateau*, 128; Steward, "Culture Element Distributions: XIII, Nevada Shoshoni," 210, 213. He later inscribed Annie Riley's question on her photograph (Ethnographic photographs, JHS Box 20).

81. Steward, *Basin-Plateau*, 124, 130, 131. JR (Steward, *Basin-Plateau*, 124; Steward, "Culture Element Distributions: XIII, Nevada Shoshoni," 213) is John Riley.

82. Steward, *Basin-Plateau*, 14. For the photograph of the Snake Range (now part of Great Basin National Park) and Spring Valley, see Steward, *Basin-Plateau*, plate 3a.

83. Information provided in 2003 by the Humboldt-Toyaibe National Forest office, Ely, Nevada.

84. Steward, *Basin-Plateau*, 48–49, 111, 124.

85. Steward, *Basin-Plateau*, 142; Steward, "Culture Element Distributions: XIII, Nevada Shoshoni," 214. SF (Steward, *Basin-Plateau*, 141; "Culture Element Distributions: XIII, Nevada Shoshoni," 214) is Frank Stick. Steward mistakenly recorded his English name as Stick Frank.

86. Steward, *Basin-Plateau*, 141–43.

87. Steward, *Basin-Plateau*, 144. Frank Stick struck Steward as a "willing" informant, unlike Pat Hicks, who was "reluctant" (Steward, "Culture Element Distributions: XIII, Nevada Shoshoni," 214). He had mixed feelings about Harry Johnny, questioning his motives but not his reliability (Steward, "Culture Element Distributions: XIII, Nevada Shoshoni," 213).

88. Steward, *Basin-Plateau*, 121, 143–44, 171–72.

89. Steward, "Shoshoni Polyandry."

6. River from Snow Mountain

1. Journal, Aug. 3–10, 1935, JHS Box 21; Utah Road Commission 1935.

2. Jane C. Steward interview; Polk & Co., *Polk's Salt Lake City Directory, 1935*, 229.

3. Journal, Aug. 3–10, 1935, JHS Box 21; Julian H. Steward to Ralph V. Chamberlin, May 19, 1935, RVC Box 5.

4. Steward, *Basin-Plateau*, 21, 26–27; Moerman, *Native American Ethnobotany*, 370–71, 904. See Steward, *Basin-Plateau*, 31–32, for the list of plants that remained unidentified by scientific name. It is not clear whether Cottam looked at specimens of those plants.

5. Martz, *Why Hurry Through Heaven*, 118. Among the many students of Henry Chandler Cowles (1869–1939) Walter Cottam (1894–1988) is regarded as one of the most eminent (Cassidy, *Henry Chandler Cowles*, 5).

6. Evans, "An Ecological Study," 284; Chamberlin, *Life Sciences at Utah*, 243–44, 290, 398, 403. Despite earning a PhD and teaching for five years Alice Evans (1890–1975) did not gain a lasting foothold in the new field. In 1928 she married and evidently did not continue her academic career (Chamberlin, *Life Sciences at Utah*, 398). Given the hiring policies in universities of the time, her marital status may have prevented that (Kerns, *Scenes from the High Desert*, 137, 171–72, 243).

7. Martz, *Why Hurry Through Heaven*, 8–9, 26, 118. See also, for example, Cottam and Stewart, "Plant Succession"; and Stewart, "Historic Records."

8. Cottam, "Man as a Biotic Factor"; Martz, *Why Hurry Through Heaven*, 118–19; Arrington, *The Mormon Experience*, 174. The site of his study in southern Utah is far more famous as that of the Mountain Meadows Massacre of September 11, 1857. Overlanders from Arkansas, on the way to California, were killed in an attack planned and largely executed by Mormon settlers but initially, and falsely, blamed on Utah Paiutes (Alexander, *Utah, the Right Place*, 129–34; Bagley, *Blood of the Prophets*, 175, 177, 294, 295; see also Novak and Rodseth, "Remembering Mountain Meadows"; and Walker, Turley, and Leonard, *Massacre at Mountain Meadows*). Attempts by Utah Indians to correct the record have continued into the twenty-first century (Forrest Cuch, executive director, Utah Division of Indian Affairs, personal communication, Dec. 6, 2007; Tom and Holt, "The Paiute Tribe of Utah," 131–39).

9. Martz, *Why Hurry Through Heaven*, 119. For other environmental effects, including later wildfires, see Young and Sparks, *Cattle in the Cold Desert*.

10. Steward, *Basin-Plateau*, 2; Steward, *Theory of Culture Change*, 30; Kerns, *Scenes from the High Desert*, 156, 276. In the intervening years he also used the term *social ecology*, but dropped it, perhaps because others had already used it and with different meanings (Kerns, *Scenes from the High Desert*, 157, 356–57n21). On Lyndon Hargrave (1896–1978), see Kerns, *Scenes from the High Desert*, 156–57, 356n20.

11. Kerns, *Scenes from the High Desert*, 149, 159; Steward, *Basin-Plateau*, 21. Steward's first wife was an educational psychologist. She was a trained and, at

that time, a committed behaviorist who shared many intellectual interests with him (Dorothy B. Nyswander interview; Kerns, *Scenes from the High Desert*, 12). Steward does not seem to have read widely in ecology. In *Basin-Plateau* he acknowledged Cottam for his help with plant specimens but did not identify him as an ecologist (Steward, *Basin-Plateau*, 21). He attributed influence only to a chance encounter on Mount Tamalpais in Northern California with a botanist who was studying plant ecology (Jane C. Steward interview; Kerns, *Scenes from the High Desert*, 153).

12. Kerns, *Scenes from the High Desert*, 269; Steward, *Basin-Plateau*, 230.

13. Journal, Aug. 11, 1935, JHS Box 21; Utah Road Commission 1936. On Wells Indian Village, see Inter-Tribal Council of Nevada, *Newe*, 100–102.

14. Starrs, *Let the Cowboy Ride*, 159, 168; Carlson, *Nevada Place Names*, 107. See Starrs, *Let the Cowboy Ride*, 159–91, on Elko, the town and the county, past and present.

15. Writers' Program of the Works Progress Administration in the State of Nevada, *Nevada*, 121; Starrs, *Let the Cowboy Ride*, 168. In 2006 the Commercial Hotel (now the Commercial Casino) and the Stockmen's Hotel were still in business.

16. Starrs, *Let the Cowboy Ride*, 184–85; Malouf and Findlay, "Euro-American Impact," 503–6.

17. Crum, *The Road on Which We Came*, 14–15; Starrs, *Let the Cowboy Ride*, 161, 168.

18. Malouf and Findlay, "Euro-American Impact," 507.

19. Steward, *Basin-Plateau*, 152–53.

20. Journal, Aug. 14, 1935, JHS Box 21; Crum, *The Road on Which We Came*, 74; Census of the Elko reservation of the Carson jurisdiction as of April 1, 1933, ICR; USFC 1930, Elko County, Nevada; Inter-Tribal Council of Nevada, *Newe*, 85–88. Elko Colony was enlarged three years later, in 1938 (Clemmer and Stewart, "Treaties, Reservations, and Claims," 533).

21. USFC 1930, Elko County, Nevada; Census of the Elko reservation of the Carson jurisdiction as of April 1, 1934, ICR.

22. Steward, "Culture Element Distributions: XIII, Nevada Shoshoni," 259. BG (Steward, *Basin-Plateau*, 157; Steward, "Culture Element Distributions: XIII, Nevada Shoshoni," 213) is Bill Gibson.

23. Journal, Aug. 12, 13, 1935, JHS Box 21.

24. "Adventure Marked Life of Humorist," *New York Times*, Aug. 17, 1935, 6; Journal, Aug. 15, 16, 17, 1935, JHS Box 21.

25. Journal, Aug. 14, 18, 1935, JHS Box 21.

26. Crum, *The Road on Which We Came*, 67–68. A federal census taker (USFC 1930, Elko County, Nevada) listed Gibson as unable read or write, evidently an error. See Crum, *The Road on Which We Came*, 54–55, on off-reservation Indian schools and their effects on students. On Gibson's activities as a leader, see Crum, *The Road on Which We Came*, 67–68, 83–84, 93, 97.

27. Journal, Aug. 18, 1935, JHS Box 21; Steward, *Basin-Plateau*, 153, 159; "Culture Element Distributions: XIII, Nevada Shoshoni," 226, 254.

28. Steward, *Basin-Plateau*, 153, 157.

29. Journal, Aug. 18, 1935, JHS Box 21; Steward, *Some Western Shoshoni Myths*, 253. Variants of the story existed, and Lowie had recorded one of them years earlier in Idaho (Hultkrantz, "Mythology and Religious Concept," 637, 639). Steward was undoubtedly familiar with the story.

30. Journal, Aug. 18, 1935, JHS Box 21.

31. Journal, Aug. 19 [–30], Aug. 31, 1935, JHS Box 21.

32. Jane C. Steward interview.

33. Journal, Sept. 4, 1935, JHS Box 21; Jane C. Steward to Cannon family, Sept. 4 [1935], RWC Box 57.

34. Steward, *Basin-Plateau*, 160–61.

35. Steward, *Basin-Plateau*, 160.

36. Journal, Sept. 4 [–Oct. 9], 1935, JHS Box 21; Crum, *The Road on Which We Came*, 32.

37. Steward, *Basin-Plateau*, 144, 145; Journal, Sept. 4 [–Oct. 9], 1935, JHS Box 21.

38. Steward, *Basin-Plateau*, 149–50; Crum *The Road on Which We Came*, 25–26, 36. The name is variously spelled Tümok, Tim-oak (Steward, *Basin-Plateau*, 149), Temoke, Te-Moak, and Temoak (Crum, *The Road on Which We Came*, 36, 103, 104).

39. Steward, *Basin-Plateau*, 150; Crum, *The Road on Which We Came*, 84.

40. Steward, *Basin-Plateau*, 144; Census of the Ruby Valley Indians of the Carson jurisdiction, June 30, 1927, ICR; Census of the Scattered Indians of the Carson jurisdiction, as of April 1, 1934, ICR; Crum, *The Road on Which We Came*, 36–38. As Crum points out, "homeless" was inapt since they continued to live in their homeland (73). About five years after Steward's fieldwork, the U.S. Congress placed some acreage under trust status, far less than the six square miles originally intended as a reservation in Ruby Valley (Crum, *The Road on Which We Came*, 94–95; Clemmer and Stewart, "Treaties, Reservations, and Claims," 533).

41. Steward, "Culture Element Distributions: XIII, Nevada Shoshoni," 213,

214. Harry Johnny and Bill Gibson also provided some details on Ruby Valley; see Steward, *Basin-Plateau*, 147, 150.

42. Census of the Scattered Indians of the Carson jurisdiction, as of April 1, 1934, ICR. MM (Steward, "Culture Element Distributions: XIII, Nevada Shoshoni," 214) is Mamie Moore.

43. Steward, "Culture Element Distributions: XIII, Nevada Shoshoni," 285, 317, 350–51; Crum, *The Road on Which We Came*, 52.

44. Census of the Scattered Indians of the Carson jurisdiction, as of April 1, 1934, ICR. RVJ (Steward, *Basin-Plateau*, 145; Steward, "Culture Element Distributions: XIII, Nevada Shoshoni," 214) is Ruby Valley Johnson. BM (Steward, *Basin-Plateau*, 145; Steward, "Culture Element Distributions: XIII, Nevada Shoshoni," 213) is Billy Mose, whom Steward thought was born in about 1855. A census taker recorded the date of birth as "ca. 1848."

45. Steward, *Basin-Plateau*, 37–38, 148; Steward, "Culture Element Distributions: XIII, Nevada Shoshoni," 213, 214.

46. Steward, *Basin-Plateau*, 146–47; Steward, "Culture Element Distributions: XIII, Nevada Shoshoni," 258.

47. Steward, *Basin-Plateau*, 151.

48. Journal, Sept. 4 [–Oct. 9], 1935, JHS Box 21; Steward, *Basin-Plateau*, 148; Steward to Lowie, Sept. 17, 1935, DAR; Ethnographic photographs, JHS Box 20.

49. Elizabeth Cannon Haymond to Ramona W. Cannon, March 8, 1935; Ramona W. Cannon to Elizabeth Cannon Haymond, March 4, 1935, RWC Box 7.

50. Journal, Sept. 4 [–Oct. 9], 1935, JHS Box 21; State of Nevada Department of Highways 1937; Starrs, *Let the Cowboy Ride*, 179.

51. Census of the Western Shoshone Reservation of the Western Shoshone jurisdiction as of April 1, 1934, ICR; Inter-Tribal Council of Nevada, *Newe*, 72–78. Steward referred to the reservation as the Western Shoshoni Reservation ("Culture Element Distributions: XIII, Nevada Shoshoni," 209), which was apparently the official name at one time (Crum, *The Road on Which We Came*, 35–36).

52. Crum, *The Road on Which We Came*, 34–35.

53. Crum, *The Road on Which We Came*, 35–36. See also McKinney, *A History of Shoshone-Paiutes*.

54. Steward to Lowie, Sept. 17 [1935], DAR; Steward, "Culture Element Distributions: XIII, Nevada Shoshoni," 214; Census of the Western Shoshone Reservation of the Western Shoshone jurisdiction as of April 1, 1934, ICR. TP (Steward, *Basin-Plateau*, 169; Steward, "Culture Element Distributions: XIII, Nevada Shoshoni," 214) is Tom Premo. For more about Premo, Beverly Crum's father,

see Crum, "Afterword." See also Crum, *The Road on Which We Came*, viii, 100, 112, 128, 133, 135; photo between pages 57 and 58.

55. Crum, *The Road on Which We Came*, 51, 55, 198n59; Crum, "Afterword," 183; Steward, *Basin-Plateau*, 170; "Culture Element Distributions: XIII, Nevada Shoshoni," 214. See also Crum, "Afterword," 181 (photo).

56. Julian H. Steward to Robert H. Lowie, Sept. 17 [1935], DAR; Steward, "Culture Element Distributions: XIII, Nevada Shoshoni," 214

57. Steward, "Culture Element Distributions: XIII, Nevada Shoshoni," 213; Western Shoshone Tribal Census, 1930, Nevada, ICR; Census of the Duck Valley reservation of the Western Shoshone jurisdiction, 1930, ICR; Census of the Western Shoshone reservation of the Western Shoshone jurisdiction as of April 1, 1933, ICR. JP (Steward, *Basin-Plateau*, 162; Steward, "Culture Element Distributions: XIII, Nevada Shoshoni," 213) is Johnnie Pronto. (Elsewhere, Steward used the same initials for another man, James Pegoga [*Basin-Plateau*, 187ff].)

58. Steward, "Culture Element Distributions: XIII, Nevada Shoshoni," 209, 259.

59. Steward, *Basin-Plateau*, 161n19, 163; Writers' Program of the Works Progress Administration in the State of Nevada, *Nevada*, 127.

60. Steward, *Basin-Plateau*, 162–63. See Crum, *The Road on Which We Came*, 4–5, for a story about why pine nuts were more abundant in central Nevada.

61. Steward, *Basin-Plateau*, 164.

62. Steward, *Basin-Plateau*, 68, 152; Steward, "Culture Element Distributions: XIII, Nevada Shoshoni," 349, 351; Zanjani, *Sarah Winnemucca*, 3, 239–42. Sarah Winnemucca Hopkins (1844?–1891) had several husbands; Bob Thacker may have been the fourth (Zanjani, *Sarah Winnemucca*, 144, 208).

63. Census of the Western Shoshone reservation of the Western Shoshone jurisdiction as of April 1, 1934, ICR. Cth (Steward, *Basin-Plateau*, 164; Steward, "Culture Element Distributions: XIII, Nevada Shoshoni," 213) is Charley Thacker. His name is shown in some censuses as Charlie Thatcher.

64. Steward thought Thacker was about eighty-five ("Culture Element Distributions: XIII, Nevada Shoshoni," 213). His later estimate of seventy was evidently an error (Steward, *Some Western Shoshoni Myths*, 253). Thacker may have served as a scout at Camp McDermit, near the Nevada-Oregon border. His brother Bob Thacker (see note 62) worked there as an interpreter (Zanjani, *Sarah Winnemucca*, 144).

65. Steward, *Basin-Plateau*, 68; Steward, *Some Western Shoshoni Myths*, 253,

299. The section on Winnemucca, a few short paragraphs, is perhaps the briefest account of a locality in *Basin-Plateau.*

66. Census of the Western Shoshone reservation of the Western Shoshone jurisdiction as of April 1, 1934, ICR. Frank Smith is both FS (Steward, *Basin-Plateau,* 107) and FSm (Steward, "Culture Element Distributions: XIII, Nevada Shoshoni," 213).

67. Census of the Western Shoshone reservation of the Western Shoshone jurisdiction as of April 1, 1934, ICR. CT (Steward, *Basin-Plateau,* 165; Steward, "Culture Element Distributions: XIII, Nevada Shoshoni," 213) is Charley Tom.

68. Steward, *Basin-Plateau,* 165–71.

69. Journal, Sept. 4 [–Oct. 9], 1935, JHS Box 21; Steward, "Culture Element Distributions: XIII, Nevada Shoshoni," 209. The so-called snowball technique, in which one informant recommends the next, was especially helpful to Steward in locating elders who lived off the reservations.

70. Journal, Sept. 4 [–Oct. 9], 1935, JHS Box 21; Steward, "Notes on Hillers' Photographs."

71. Elizabeth Cannon Haymond to Ramona W. Cannon, Oct. 9, RWC Box 7; Journal, Sept. 4 [–Oct. 9], Oct. 10, 1935, JHS Box 21.

72. Julian H. Steward to Alfred L. Kroeber, June 9, 1936, DAR; 1937 Census, Nevada, Western Shoshone reservation, Deaths occurring between Jan. 1, 1936, and Dec. 31, 1936, ICR.

7. Basin and Plateau

1. Kerns, *Scenes from the High Desert,* 197–99; Journal, April 18, 1936, JHS Box 21.

2. Julian H. Steward to Alfred L. Kroeber, July 3, 1936, DAR.

3. Julian H. Steward to Alfred L. Kroeber, June 9, 1936; Alfred L. Kroeber to Julian H. Steward, May 18, 1936, DAR.

4. Jane C. Steward to Joseph J. Cannon, July 3, 1936, RWC Box 57; Journal, Aug. 1, 1936, JHS Box 21.

5. On William Duncan Strong (1899–1962) and Matthew Stirling (1896–1975), see Willey, *Portraits in Archaeology,* 74–96, 242–64.

6. Journal, Jan. 12, 1938, JHS Box 21

7. Ashley Montague, "Aleš Hrdlička, 1869–1943," 113, 116. M. F. Ashley Montague (1905–1999) was unusual in taking note, in print, of an attitude about women that many men of the time did not find remarkable.

8. Arrington, *History of Idaho*, 166; Alexander, *Utah, the Right Place*, 85–87, 96; Bitton, *George Q. Cannon*, 46, 55, 172–74.

9. Bitton, *George Q. Cannon*, 55; Carlstrom and Furse, *History of Emigration Canyon*, 36; Van Cott, *Utah Place Names*, 128; Jane C. Steward interview

10. Jane C. Steward interview; Kerns, *Scenes from the High Desert*, 137–45.

11. Bitton, *George Q. Cannon*, 390–401, 463–64; Jardine, "Life on the Cannon Farm"; Cannon, "George Q. Cannon," 348–49. One of the houses of the Cannon compound in Salt Lake City was still standing in 2006.

12. Bitton, *George Q. Cannon*, 283.

13. Debates about how to "manage" polygamy were carried on in various media—newspapers, radio, television—in Salt Lake City in 2005 and 2006. The general debate was ongoing, but the search for Warren Jeffs spurred even more public discussion. Jeffs, the head of a fundamentalist Mormon sect, was on the FBI's Most Wanted list at the time of his capture in Nevada in 2006. The Utah attorney general estimated publicly that there are tens of thousands of polygamists in the West. The Mormon church—officially, the Church of Jesus Christ of Latter-day Saints—has not supported the practice of polygamy since the end of the nineteenth century.

14. Bitton, *George Q. Cannon*, 291–95; Jane C. Steward interview.

15. Alexander, *Utah, the Right Place*, 186–201; Bitton, *George Q. Cannon*, 301, 364; Arrington, *History of Idaho*, 378–80.

16. Joseph J. Cannon to Jane C. Steward, Nov. 20, 1933, RWC Box 62; "Florence G. Cannon Is Suddenly Called," *Deseret News*, Dec. 26, 1912; Wayne Cannon, "Story of Significant and Interesting Incidents That Occurred during the Cannon Family History," Sept. 21, 1974, RWC Box 62; Jane C. Steward, "Jane Cannon Steward," n.d. [ca. 1978], RWC Box 57.

17. Jane C. Steward interview. The University of Utah now gives an annual award for teaching that bears the name of Ramona Wilcox Cannon.

18. Silver, "Ramona Wilcox Cannon," 82, 87. Young Mormon men were expected to serve a two-year mission for the church before marriage and to marry within a few years of returning from their mission.

19. Joseph J. Cannon to Jane Cannon, Sept. 23, 1932, RWC Box 57; Jane C. Steward interview; Kerns, *Scenes from the High Desert*, 143–45. Jane Steward recalled her time in California as an "exile," but her father's letters in fall 1932 suggest that she initiated the move.

20. Bitton, *George Q. Cannon*, 90; Ramona W. Cannon to Joseph J. Cannon,

"Tuesday" [1933]; Joseph J. Cannon to Ramona W. Cannon, July 24, 1933; Elizabeth Cannon to Joseph J. Cannon, July 24, 1933, RWC Box 7.

21. Jane Cannon to Joseph Cannon, n.d. [Oct. 1933]; "Stan" to Jane Cannon, Oct. 2, 1933, RWC Box 57; Charles Kelly journal, Nov. 17, 1933, CKP Box 1.

22. Joseph J. Cannon to Grant Cannon, Jan. 6, 1935; Grant Cannon to Joseph J. Cannon, Feb. 28, 1935, RWC Box 58.

23. Jane C. Steward interview; Joseph J. Cannon to Jane Cannon, Nov. 22, 1932, RWC Box 57; Julian H. Steward to Joseph J. Cannon, Sept. 30, 1937, RWC Box 57.

24. Journal, June 1936, JHS Box 21; Polk & Co., *Polk's Salt Lake City Directory, 1936*, 156; "Mary" to Ramona W. Cannon, July 28, 1936, RWC Box 7; Jane C. and Julian H. Steward to Joseph J. Cannon, July 3, 1936, RWC Box 57.

25. Polk & Co., *Polk's Salt Lake City Directory, 1936*, 756; Kerns, *Scenes from the High Desert*, 148; Stegner, *Mormon Country*; Stegner, *Beyond the Hundredth Meridian*. Wallace Stegner (1909–1993) was also well known as a conservationist.

26. Swensen, "Dorothea Lange's Portrait," 44, 45; Alexander, *Utah, the Right Place*, 323.

27. "Salt Lake Citizens Riot at Tax Auction," *Washington Post*, Feb. 24, 1933, 1; "Sheriff's Sales Barred by Salt Lake City Mob," *Los Angeles Times*, Feb. 24, 1933, 1.

28. Julian H. Steward to Ralph V. Chamberlin, Aug. 1, 1933, RVC Box 4.

29. Greer, *Atlas of Utah*, 122; Kelen and Stone, *Missing Stories*, 99–100.

30. Journal, July 1, 1936, JHS Box 21; Polk & Co., *Polk's Ogden City Directory, 1936–37*, 236; Saunders, "The Utah Writers' Project," 22, 23; Writers' Program of the Work Projects Administration for the State of Utah, *Utah*, 553. Howe accompanied Steward on a trip through the region around the Vermilion Cliffs and the Virgin River (Kerns, *Scenes from the High Desert*, 142–43).

31. Journal, July 1, 1936, JHS Box 21; Polk & Co., *Polk's Ogden City Directory, 1936–37*, 400.

32. Writers' Program of the Work Projects Administration for the State of Utah, *Utah*, 200. The summer of 1936 was reportedly the hottest on record in Utah until 2007.

33. "Idaho's Red Men Begin Age-Old Dance to Sun," *Los Angeles Times*, July 21, 1936, 9; Ethnographic photographs, JHS Box 20. Steward gave the date of that Sun Dance as 1927, evidently a typographical error ("Culture Element Distributions: XXIII, Northern and Gosiute Shoshoni," 290).

34. Journal, Aug. 1, 1936, JHS Box 21. The concept was well known to her

husband, who had earlier reported on what he termed *semicouvade* (Steward, "Ethnography of the Owens Valley Paiute," 306; see also Steward, "Culture Element Distributions: XIII, Nevada Shoshoni," 255; Steward, "Culture Element Distributions: XXIII, Northern and Gosiute Shoshoni," 280).

35. Journal, Aug. 1, Sept., 1936, JHS Box 21; Julian H. Steward to Matthew Stirling, Sept. 12, 1936, BAE Box 83.

36. Arrington, *History of Idaho*, 109.

37. Steward, *Basin-Plateau*, 218. On the life of Chief Pocatello, see Madsen, *Chief Pocatello*.

38. Madsen, *Chief Pocatello*, ix, 119–20; Clemmer and Stewart, "Treaties, Reservations, and Claims," 544; Murphy and Murphy, "Northern Shoshone," 303.

39. Census of the Fort Hall Reservation of the Fort Hall jurisdiction as of Jan. 1, 1937, ICR.

40. Steward, "Culture Element Distributions: XXIII, Northern and Gosiute Shoshoni," 264; Census of the Fort Hall Reservation of the Fort Hall jurisdiction as of Jan. 1, 1937, ICR. AP (Steward, "Culture Element Distributions: XXIII, Northern and Gosiute Shoshoni," 263) is Adolph Pavitse.

41. Census of the Fort Hall Reservation of the Fort Hall jurisdiction as of Jan. 1, 1937, ICR. Earlier censuses identify Lucy as Gussie Pegoga. JP (Steward, *Basin-Plateau*, 187ff) and JPe (Steward, "Culture Element Distributions: XXIII, Northern and Gosiute Shoshoni," 264) are James Pegoga.

42. Census of the Shoshoni, Bannock, and Sheepeater Indians of Lemhi Agency, 1906, ICR; Clemmer and Stewart, "Treaties, Reservations, and Claims," 532, 544. I have named these children because a descendant of James and Lucy Pegoga has identified Cora Pegoga George publicly as her mother (http://www.lemhi -shoshone.com/lemhi_pass_camp_fortunate.html, retrieved November 5, 2006). Cora Pegoga left the Lemhi Valley in 1907 as a teenager, according to her daughter, and at the age of about six, according to census records.

43. Mann, *Sacajewea's People*, 36.

44. The reservation, established in 1873, closed just thirty-four years later (Clemmer and Stewart, "Treaties, Reservations, and Claims," 532). See Mann, *Sacajawea's People*; and Campbell, "The Lemhi Shoshone," on Lehmi Shoshones in the twentieth century.

45. Steward, "Culture Element Distributions: XXIII, Northern and Gosiute Shoshoni," 263–64; Mann, *Sacajawea's People*, 16–20.

46. Steward, *Basin-Plateau*, 186–98; Julian H. Steward to Alfred L. Kroeber, Aug. 12, 1936; Alfred L. Kroeber to Julian H. Steward, Aug. 21, 1936, DAR.

47. Steward, *Basin-Plateau*, 186. On the Mormon mission in the Lemhi Valley, see Mann, *Sacajawea's People*, 22–25. See also Campbell, "The Lemhi Shoshone."

48. Steward, *Basin-Plateau*, 186–87. Elsewhere, however, Steward reported that "the mountain people gradually amalgamated with the Lemhi band and acquired horses" ("Culture Element Distributions: XXIII, Northern and Gosiute Shoshoni," 264).

49. Arrington, *History of Idaho*, 13–14; Murphy and Murphy, "Northern Shoshone," 285.

50. Steward, *Basin-Plateau*, 200; Mann, *Sacajawea's People*, 16. On the disappearance of bison, see Lupo, "Historical Occurrence and Demise of Bison"; and Van Hoak, "The Other Buffalo."

51. Steward, *Basin-Plateau*, 189–92, 200; Steward, "Culture Element Distributions: XXIII, Northern and Gosiute Shoshoni," 266–67.

52. Steward, *Basin-Plateau*, 189. See Walker, "Revisionist View of Julian Steward," for the author's critique and the evidence for rather abundant resources.

53. Steward, *Basin-Plateau*, 186, 192.

54. Steward, *Basin-Plateau*, 136; Steward, "Culture Element Distributions: XXIII, Northern and Gosiute Shoshoni," 274.

55. Steward, *Basin-Plateau*, 200; Arrington, *History of Idaho*, 8; Murphy and Murphy, "Northern Shoshone," 285; Kerns, *Scenes from the High Desert*, 84–85.

56. See, for example, Steward, *Basin-Plateau*, 172–75.

57. Steward, *Basin-Plateau*, 181, 201; Kerns, *Scenes from the High Desert*, 200–201.

58. See Kreitzer, *Washakie Letters*, 175, and passim, on Fort Hall Shoshones visiting and working seasonally in northern Utah.

59. Steward, "Culture Element Distributions: XXIII, Northern and Gosiute Shoshoni," 264; Census of the Fort Hall Reservation of the Fort Hall jurisdiction as of Jan. 1, 1937, ICR. SB (Steward, *Basin-Plateau*, 210; Steward, "Culture Element Distributions: XXIII, Northern and Gosiute Shoshoni," 264) is Silver Ballard.

60. Clemmer and Stewart, "Treaties, Reservations, and Claims," 532.

61. Field Expenses of Julian H. Steward, June–Oct. 1936, JHS Box 10; Census of the Fort Hall Reservation of the Fort Hall jurisdiction as of Jan. 1, 1937, ICR; Steward, *Basin-Plateau*, 202–3; "Culture Element Distributions: XXIII, Northern and Gosiute Shoshoni," 264, 266–67; Ethnographic photographs, JHS Box

20. WH (Steward, *Basin-Plateau*, 210; Steward, "Culture Element Distributions: XXIII, Northern and Gosiute Shoshoni," 264) is Whitehorse.

62. Steward, "Culture Element Distributions: XXIII, Northern and Gosiute Shoshoni," 268.

63. Steward, *Basin-Plateau*, 198–200, 203, 274–75; see also Murphy and Murphy, "Northern Shoshone."

64. Steward, *Basin-Plateau*, 203.

65. Steward, *Basin-Plateau*, 6, 191, 200, 201, 218; Alexander, *Utah, the Right Place*, 60–65.

66. Steward, *Basin-Plateau*, 201–2, 207, 211–12.

67. Steward, *Basin-Plateau*, 210–12; Heaton, *Shoshone-Bannocks*, 114–16.

68. Census of the Fort Hall Reservation of the Fort Hall jurisdiction as of Jan. 1, 1937; Steward, *Basin-Plateau*, 211; Steward, "Culture Element Distributions: XXIII, Northern and Gosiute Shoshoni," 264, 290.

69. Jane C. Steward to Joseph J. Cannon, August 3, 1936, RWC Box 57.

70. Julian H. Steward to Alfred L. Kroeber, Aug. 12, 1936, DAR. An article by E. Adamson Hoebel (1906–1993) on the Sun Dance at Fort Hall, based on fieldwork in 1934, had appeared in print just months earlier, in a 1935 issue of the *American Anthropologist*.

71. Julian H. Steward to Matthew Stirling, Sept. 12, 1936, BAE Box 83; Baker, *Jesse Owens*, 94–107.

72. Steward, *Basin-Plateau*, 173; Steward, "Culture Element Distributions: XXIII, Northern and Gosiute Shoshoni," 264; Census of the Fort Hall Reservation of the Fort Hall jurisdiction as of Jan. 1, 1937, ICR. GCJ (Steward, *Basin-Plateau*, 175; Steward, "Culture Element Distribution: XIII, Nevada Shoshoni," 264) is Grouse Creek Jack.

73. Kreitzer, *Washakie Letters*, 296; Van Cott, *Utah Place Names*, 169; USFC 1930, Box Elder County, Utah.

74. Steward, "Culture Element Distributions: XXIII, Northern and Gosiute Shoshoni," 264; Kreitzer, *Washakie Letters*, 76, 118–19, 296.

75. Census of the Fort Hall Reservation of the Fort Hall jurisdiction as of Jan. 1, 1937, ICR; Kreitzer, *Washakie Letters*, 296.

76. Steward, "Culture Element Distributions: XXIII, Northern and Gosiute Shoshoni," 264; Field Expenses of Julian H. Steward, June–Oct. 1936, JHS Box 10.

77. Steward, *Basin-Plateau*, 173–77; Steward, "Culture Element Distributions: XXIII, Northern and Gosiute Shoshoni," 264.

78. Madsen, *Chief Pocatello*, 23, 112.

79. Steward, *Basin-Plateau*, 172, 174, 175; Murphy and Murphy, "Northern Shoshone," 306.

80. Steward, *Basin-Plateau*, 216–18. For a map of the California Trail, see Malouf and Findlay, "Euro-American Impact," 502 fig. 1d.

81. USFC 1930, Box Elder County, Utah.

82. Steward, "Culture Element Distributions: XXIII, Northern and Gosiute Shoshoni," 264; Julian Steward to Alfred L. Kroeber, July 3, 1936, DAR.

8. Land of the Utes

1. Journal, Sept., 1936, JHS Box 21; Jane C. Steward interview.

2. Dorothy B. Nyswander interview; Kerns, *Scenes from the High Desert*, 127–28; Omer Stewart to Alfred L. Kroeber, June 16, 1936, DAR. Kilton Stewart later achieved fame among Jungian analysts and notoriety among anthropologists for his ideas about dreams (Kerns, *Scenes from the High Desert*, 127).

3. Howell, *Cannibalism Is an Acquired Taste*, 6, 28; Dorothy B. Nyswander interview. Many years later the property became home to a ski resort, Robert Redford's Sundance Resort.

4. Steward, *Basin-Plateau*, 222; Van Cott, *Utah Place Names*, 264, 305.

5. Arrington, *The Mormon Experience*, 118. Historian Donald Worster, using stronger language, calls Young "one of the great imperialists of the [nineteenth] century" in the American West (*A River Running West*, 263).

6. Janetski, "Utah Lake," 5–10.

7. Steward, *Basin-Plateau*, 228, 229.

8. Alexander, *Utah, the Right Place*, 225; Cannon, "Struggle Against Great Odds," 308–9; Pickford, "The Influence of Heavy Grazing," 160.

9. Arrington, "Utah's Great Drought," 247; Greer, *Atlas of Utah*, 110; Starrs, *Let the Cowboy Ride*, 130–31.

10. Stegner, *Mormon Country*, 21.

11. See Alexander, *Utah, the Right Place*, 314–15. The situation of farmers and ranchers varied from county to county (Cannon, "Struggle Against Great Odds," 314–17).

12. Van Cott, *Utah Place Names*, 224, 272.

13. Van Cott, *Utah Place Names*, 165, 208, 262, 382.

14. Beckwith, *Indian Joe: Historical Perspective*, 115; Van Cott, *Utah Place Names*, xviii–xix, 50, 148, 181, 260, 263, 279, 376, 390. Cannonville was named

for George Q. Cannon, Jane C. Steward's grandfather (Van Cott, *Utah Place Names*, 64).

15. Duncan, "Northern Utes of Utah," 187, 190; Bancroft, *History of Utah*, 471; Church of Jesus Christ of Latter-day Saints, First Presidency, 102, 178; "Governor's Message to the Legislative Assembly of the Territory of Utah," *Deseret Weekly News*, December 14, 1854, 3.

16. Callaway, Janetski, and Stewart, *Handbook of North American Indians*, 356–57; Lyman and Newell, *History of Millard County*, 114–15; Duncan, "Northern Utes of Utah," 188, 190–91, 200. The people who lived in what Steward called "Western Ute bands" are now generally known as Northern Utes (*Basin-Plateau*, 222; Duncan, "Northern Utes of Utah").

17. Steward, *Basin-Plateau*, 222; Julian H. Steward to Matthew Stirling, Sept. 12, 1936, BAE Box 83; Kerns, *Scenes from the High Desert*, 130–33.

18. Julian H. Steward to Ralph V. Chamberlin, May 19, 1935, RVC Box 5.

19. Bitton, *George Q. Cannon*, 374–75, 463–64; Van Cott, *Utah Place Names*, 137; Cannon, "Sarah Jenne Cannon." Sarah Jane Cannon bore six children and adopted a seventh child.

20. Kerns, *Scenes from the High Desert*, 129, 147; Julian H. Steward to Ralph V. Chamberlin, Aug. 1, 1933, and Aug. 4, 1933, RVC Box 5. See Janetski, "Steward and Utah Archaeology," 21–25, on Steward's work, and Simms, *Ancient People of the Great Basin*, on current understandings of Great Basin prehistory.

21. Lyman and Newell, *History of Millard County*, 26; Van Cott, *Utah Place Names*, 212.

22. Lewis, "Kanosh and Ute Identity," 334; Bailey, "Last Wife of Chief Kanosh," 22.

23. Lewis, "Kanosh and Ute Identity," 334; Spencer, *Brigham Young at Home*, 24–29, 122–23; Bailey, "Last Wife of Chief Kanosh," 19.

24. The photograph appears in Lewis, "Kanosh and Ute Identity," 335, and elsewhere. Sally Kanosh is sometimes misidentified as "the stepdaughter of Brigham Young" (e.g., Alexander, *Utah, the Right Place*, 146).

25. Bailey, "Last Wife of Chief Kanosh," 22, 50; Spencer, *Brigham Young at Home*, 123.

26. Journal, Sept. 1936, JHS Box 21. Kanosh Reservation had been formally established a few years earlier, in 1929 (Holt, *Beneath These Red Cliffs*, 43; Clemmer and Stewart, "Treaties, Reservations, and Claims," 533).

27. Julian H. Steward to Matthew Stirling, Sept. 12, 1936, BAE Box 83; Census of the Kanosh Settlement reservation of the Paiute jurisdiction as of Jan. 1, 1936,

ICR. Unaccountably, Steward identified the oldest person as just over forty years old, not seventy ("Culture Element Distributions: XXIII, Northern and Gosiute Shoshoni," 263). According to a census of the reservation where Joe Pikyavit was an enrolled member, he was in his fifties (Census of the Kaibab [Arizona] reservation of the Paiute jurisdiction as of Jan. 1, 1936, ICR).

28. Field Expenses of Julian H. Steward, June–Oct. 1936, JHS Box 10; Steward, "Culture Element Distributions: XXIII, Northern and Gosiute Shoshoni," 263; Census of the Kaibab [Arizona] reservation of the Paiute jurisdiction as of Jan. 1, 1936, ICR. Census takers often listed him as Josie Pikyavit; Beckwith (*Indian Joe; Indian Joe: Historical Perspective*) called him Joe or Joseph J. Pickyavit or Pikyavit. JPi (Steward, *Basin-Plateau*, 137, 225) is Joe Pikyavit.

29. Census of the Kanosh Settlement reservation of the Paiute jurisdiction as of Jan. 1, 1936, ICR.

30. Beckwith, *Indian Joe: Historical Perspective*, xiv, 10, 16; Kelly, "Reminiscences of Frank A. Beckwith," viii.

31. "Archeologist Visits Lower Sevier Area," *Millard County Chronicle*, Nov. 5, 1930, 1; Dr. J. H. Steward, "The Discovery of a Kiva in Ancient Mounds at Kanosh," *Millard County Chronicle*, Jan. 1, 1931, 5. On Charles Kelly (1889–1971), see Mortensen, "In Memoriam."

32. Kerns, *Scenes from the High Desert*, 141–42; Charles Kelly Journal, July 31, 1932, CKP Box 1; Hoffman Birney to Charles Kelly, May 17, 1937, CKP Box 1.

33. Charles Kelly Journal, Feb. 3, 1931; July 31, 1932, CKP Box 1. The site he showed Steward was Promontory Cave (see Kerns, *Scenes from the High Desert*, 127–28; Janetski, "Steward and Utah Archaeology," 25–27).

34. Kelly, "Reminiscences of Frank A. Beckwith," viii.

35. Hamblin, *Jacob Hamblin*, 87–88.

36. Beckwith, *Indian Joe; Indian Joe: Historical Perspective*, xiii, 56. I have not been able to corroborate some of the details recorded by Beckwith.

37. Cannon, "Struggle Against Great Odds," 305, 317.

38. Beckwith, *Indian Joe: Historical Perspective*, 59; Holt, *Beneath These Red Cliffs*, 55. According to Holt, however, the Depression years brought certain benefits. The WPA projects and other jobs offered by relief agencies gave them "their first dependable incomes," although household incomes remained low (*Beneath These Red Cliffs*, 54).

39. Lyman and Newell, *History of Millard County*, 125; Beckwith, *Indian Joe: Historical Perspective*, 59; Bailey, "Last Wife of Chief Kanosh," 50. Household income in 1936 came mainly from four sources: earnings from pine nuts, hauling

wood, farming, and wage labor (Holt, *Beneath These Red Cliffs*, 55, 57). A photograph of Emily Pikyavit taken more than forty years later, in 1982, shows her tanning hides (see Holt, *Beneath These Red Cliffs*, 94).

40. Lyman and Newell, *History of Millard County*, 125, 148n5; Beckwith, *Indian Joe: Historical Perspective*, 59.

41. Field Expenses of Julian H. Steward, June–Oct. 1936, JHS Box 10.

42. Steward, *Basin-Plateau*, 227. They are also called Sevier Lake Utes. According to Duncan, who is Northern Ute, *Pahvant* means "close to water" ("Northern Utes of Utah," 174).

43. Steward, *Basin-Plateau*, 227; Beckwith, *Indian Joe: Historical Perspective*, 13. An American explorer in the 1850s gave the House Range its name because it resembled a built structure from the distance (Van Cott, *Utah Place Names*, 194).

44. Steward, *Basin-Plateau*, 227. See Lewis, "Kanosh and Ute Identity," 332; or Alexander, *Utah, the Right Place*, 146, for the photograph.

45. Houghton, *A Trace of Desert Waters*, 202; Greer, *Atlas of Utah*, 49.

46. Field Expenses of Julian H. Steward, June–Oct. 1936, JHS Box 10; Julian H. Steward to Alfred L. Kroeber, Sept. 25, 1936, DAR. Steward worked for a day on a trait list for Pahvant Utes and concluded that it was a futile effort ("Culture Element Distributions: XXIII, Northern and Gosiute Shoshoni," 263). A year later Omer Stewart spent several months working with other Ute (including Pahvant Ute) and Southern Paiute informants (Stewart, "Culture Element," 231).

47. Steward, "Culture Element Distributions: XXIII, Northern and Gosiute Shoshoni," 263.

48. Beckwith, *Indian Joe: Historical Perspective*, xiii, 6; Census of the Kaibab reservation of the Paiute jurisdiction as of Jan. 1, 1936, ICR; Holt, *Beneath These Red Cliffs*, 44.

49. From the perspective of Northern Utes, as expressed by Conetah (*A History of the Northern Ute People*, 24) and Duncan ("Northern Utes of Utah," 177), the two groups had much in common. As Duncan notes about Pahvant Utes, "In many of their characteristics, they were like their neighbors the Kaibab Paiutes." See also Knack, *Boundaries Between*, 246–47. On the slave trade, see Duncan, "Northern Utes of Utah," 182–83; and Brooks, *Captives and Cousins*.

50. Benjamin Pikyavit, personal communication, April 26, 2006.

51. Greer, *Atlas of Utah*, 110.

52. Beckwith, *Indian Joe: Historical Perspective*, 60, 197.

53. Charles Kelly, quoted in Beckwith, *Indian Joe*, x.

54. Julian H. Steward to Alfred L. Kroeber, Sept. 25, 1936, DAR.

55. Greer, *Atlas of Utah*, 17, 19; Duncan, "Northern Utes of Utah," 202–3, 207.

56. "Educators Examine Reservation Babies," *Roosevelt Standard*, Sept. 24, 1931, 8; Kerns, *Scenes from the High Desert*, 130–34.

57. Dorothy B. Nyswander interview. Steward's book-length ethnographies ("Ethnography of the Owens Valley Paiute," *Basin-Plateau*) drew on interviews with multiple informants, mostly men.

58. Dorothy B. Nyswander interview; Kerns, *Scenes from the High Desert*, 133, 134–35, 149.

59. Jane C. Steward interview; Duncan, "Northern Utes of Utah," 219; Kerns, *Scenes from the High Desert*, 130–31, 151.

60. Field Expenses of Julian H. Steward, June–Oct. 1936, JHS Box 10; Julian H. Steward to Alfred L. Kroeber, Oct. 26, 1936, DAR; Steward, *Basin-Plateau*, 222; Duncan, "Northern Utes of Utah," 196–97. A tribal historian for the Uintah-Ouray Ute Tribe has explained that by 1870, surviving Utes from many parts of Utah moved to the Uintah Reservation. Once there, they were "pushed into one group which would become known as the Uintah Band" (Conetah, *A History of the Northern Ute People*, 77, 89). This may help to explain why Steward did not quickly find an informant who identified as Timpanogot, a Utah Lake Ute (Duncan, "Northern Utes of Utah," 176).

61. Stewart, "Culture Element," 236, 238.

62. Steward, *Basin-Plateau*, 222, 229–30.

63. Kerns, *Scenes from the High Desert*, 90.

64. See Steward, *Basin-Plateau*, 224–25, for names and sources, "a summary of some of the more important references to the 'bands' of Western Ute." Joe Pikyavit (JPi) was the sole cultural informant on his list of sources. A published work by Gottfredson (*History of Indian Depredations*), which Steward listed nine times, was actually a compilation of firsthand accounts by settlers and thus greatly increased the number of Steward's author-informants for the Utes. See also Duncan's list of Northern Ute bands ("Northern Utes of Utah," 176).

65. Steward, *Basin-Plateau*, 252, 260.

9. Trails West

1. Journal, Sept., 1936, JHS Box 21; Van Cott, *Utah Place Names*, 390; USFC 1930, Box Elder County, Utah. In June 2004 there were no buildings at the site; only the cemetery remained.

2. Julian H. Steward to Matthew Stirling, Sept. 12, 1936, BAE Box 83; Kreitzer, *Washakie Letters*, 38.

3. Steward, "Culture Element Distributions: XXIII, Northern and Gosiute Shoshoni," 264; USFC 1930, Box Elder County, Utah; Census of the Shoshonie Indians of Goshute Agency, Utah, June 30, 1919, ICR; Census of the Washakie sub-group reservation of the Fort Hall jurisdiction as of Jan. 1, 1937, ICR; Kreitzer, *Washakie Letters*, 199 (photo caption), 239. Burial records for the Shoshoni Tribal Cemetery at Washakie list his birth date as 1830 (www.lofthouse.com/boxelder/cemetery/shoshoni.htm, retrieved Jan. 30, 2006).

4. Steward, *Basin-Plateau*, 177–78; Van Cott, *Utah Place Names*, 304; Kreitzer, *Washakie Letters*, 199 (photo).

5. Spencer, *Brigham Young at Home*, 133.

6. James, "Indian Farm Negotiations," 249, 250, 253.

7. James, "Indian Farm Negotiations," 251, 254; Christensen, *Sagwitch*, 16, 164–65; Kreitzer, *Washakie Letters*, 2–4, 239, 299.

8. Steward, *Basin-Plateau*, 217; Madsen, *The Shoshoni Frontier*. The name Battle of Bear River still commonly appeared in print at the end of the twentieth century, particularly in the writings of military historians (Schindler, "The Bear River Massacre," 306n8). Parry ("The Northwestern Shoshone"), a descendant, provides many details about the people and events that the monuments and earlier published works left unrecorded.

9. I recorded the inscription at the site in June 2004. At the time of my visit, a complex mix of markers stood there, erected by national and state agencies and private organizations, beginning in the 1930s. They provided very different interpretations of the events of January 29, 1863. In a nearby tree, bead necklaces and other objects left by visitors hung from branches. See Brooks, *Sweet Medicine*, for a recent photograph of the site and text from the markers. See Schindler, "The Bear River Massacre," 302, 303, for photographs taken earlier in the twentieth century.

10. According to a document that came to light in the 1990s, an eyewitness account by a soldier who counted bodies of the dead, 23 soldiers and 280 Indians died (Schindler, "The Bear River Massacre," 302, 307). The number of Indians who died may be much higher (Forrest Cuch, executive director, Utah Division of Indian Affairs, personal communication, December 13, 2007).

11. Schindler, "The Bear River Massacre," 302; *Deseret Weekly News*, Feb. 4, 1863, 5; and Feb. 11, 1863, 4.

12. *Deseret Weekly News*, Feb. 4, 1863, 5; Christensen, *Sagwitch*, 41–76.

13. Promontory Summit is now a historic site administered by the National Park Service. Information on the site was provided by the National Park Service, Golden Spike National Historic Site, Utah, in 2006.

14. Peterson, *A History of Cache County*, 116; Christensen, *Sagwitch*, 174–77; Burial Records, Shoshoni Tribal Cemetery (www.lofthouse.com/boxelder/cem etery/shoshoni.htm, retrieved Jan. 30, 2006); Kreitzer, *Washakie Letters*, 5.

15. Parry, "The Northwestern Shoshone," 33–43; Christensen, *Sagwitch*, 41–59; Steward, *Basin-Plateau*, 217, 218. Parry heard the stories often ("The Northwestern Shoshone," 346n17, 346n21). Her grandfather was Yeager Timbimboo.

16. Steward, *Basin-Plateau*, 178; Kreitzer, *Washakie Letters*, 315; Parry, "The Northwestern Shoshone," 38. See Christensen, *Sagwitch*, 56, for a photograph of Ray Diamond and Yeager Timbimboo, taken about 1935. In 2004 the marker on Yeager Timbimboo's grave in the Shoshoni Tribal Cemetery, Washakie, gave his date of birth as 1848 and date of death as 1937. See also Burial Records, Shoshoni Tribal Cemetery (www.lofthouse.com/boxelder/cemetery/shoshoni.htm, retrieved Jan. 30, 2006).

17. USFC 1930, Box Elder County, Utah; James, "Indian Farm Negotiations," 256.

18. Kreitzer, *Washakie Letters*, 14, 18, 104, 166, 188, 213, and passim. Ottogary's reports, thanks to Matthew Kreitzer's extensive editorial work, provide an insider's portrait of community life that has no parallel in the other locales where Steward did fieldwork for *Basin-Plateau*.

19. Kreitzer, *Washakie Letters*, 16, 18, 117, 119, 125, 188, 193, 205, 223, 269n12, 277n21.

20. Kreitzer, *Washakie Letters*, 32, 180, 188, 194, 199; Kreitzer, "Diamonds, Ovals, and Rings." Steward listed wrestling under the category of "Games" and noted that its rules varied, "depending largely upon agreement before a match" ("Culture Element Distributions: XXIII, Northern and Gosiute Shoshoni," 278).

21. Kreitzer, *Washakie Letters*, 18, 65, 240, 268n10, and passim.

22. Greer, *Atlas of Utah*, 333–34; Kreitzer, *Washakie Letters*, 122, 157–58, 231.

23. Alexander, *Utah, the Right Place*, 448; Peterson, *A History of Cache County*, 6, 7; Greer, *Atlas of Utah*, 33–34; Lupo, "Historical Occurrence and Demise of Bison," 180; Van Hoak, "The Other Buffalo," 16, 17. See also Janetski, "Great Basin Animals," 351–52, 355, 356, on bighorn sheep, bison, and bears.

24. OD (Steward, *Basin-Plateau*, 178; Steward, "Culture Element Distributions: XXIII, Northern and Gosiute Shoshoni," 264) is Ray Diamond.

25. USFC 1930, Box Elder County Utah; Census of the Washakie sub-group

reservation of the Fort Hall jurisdiction as of Jan. 1, 1937, ICR; Record of Members and Children [Washakie Ward, Malad Stake], early to 1931, FHL US/CAN film 0,027,406, LDS. Most records list Seth Eagle under his surname of birth, Pubigee, as Kreitzer also does (*Washakie Letters*, 296). Seth Pubigee seems to have changed his name to Seth Eagle in the 1920s, but he sometimes used the name Seth Eagle Pubigee as well. SE (Steward, "Culture Element Distributions: XXIII Northern and Gosiute Shoshoni," 265) is Seth Eagle.

26. USFC 1930, Box Elder County, Utah; Kreitzer, *Washakie Letters*, 310; Steward, "Culture Element Distributions: XIII, Nevada Shoshoni," 265.

27. Steward, "Culture Element Distributions: XXIII, Northern and Gosiute Shoshoni," 283.

28. Steward, "Culture Element Distributions: XXIII, Northern and Gosiute Shoshoni," 283, 284, 345, 346. He had found similar practices among Western Shoshones (see Steward, "Culture Element Distributions: XIII, Nevada Shoshoni," 259–60).

29. Kerns, *Scenes from the High Desert*, 127; Steward, *Basin-Plateau*, 178n21; see also Janetski, "Steward and Utah Archaeology," 25–26.

30. Steward, *Basin-Plateau*, 178–79; Van Cott, *Utah Place Names*, 24; Peterson, *A History of Cache County*, 47, 49.

31. Steward, *Basin-Plateau*, 178, 218; Field Expenses of Julian H. Steward, June–Oct. 1936, JHS Box 10; Steward, "Culture Element Distributions: XXIII, Northern and Gosiute Shoshoni," 264; Record of Members and Children [Washakie Ward, Malad Stake], early to 1931, FHL US/CAN film 0,027,406, LDS; Burial Records, Shoshoni Tribal Cemetery (www.lofthouse.com/boxelder/cemetery/shoshoni.htm, retrieved Jan. 30, 2006); Kreitzer, *Washakie Letters*, 307. According to burial records, Rachel Perdash died in 1954.

32. Peterson, *A History of Cache County*, 8, 11, 13; Beckwourth, *Life and Adventures*, 96, 554.

33. Beckwourth, *Life and Adventures*, 96, 464, 553, 554; Peterson, *A History of Cache County*, 4, 13; Van Cott, *Utah Place Names*, 61.

34. Peterson, *A History of Cache County*, 40; Greer, *Atlas of Utah*, 110; Arrington, *History of Idaho*, 261–62.

35. Steward, *Basin-Plateau*, 218.

36. Steward, *Basin-Plateau*, 41, 42, 218–19.

37. Burial Records, Shoshoni Tribal Cemetery (www.lofthouse.com/boxelder/cemetery/shoshoni.htm, retrieved Jan. 30, 2006); Kreitzer, *Washakie Letters*, 226 (photo), 297; Christensen, *Sagwitch*, 186, 197 (photo).

38. Burial Records, Shoshoni Tribal Cemetery (www.lofthouse.com/boxelder/cemetery/shoshoni.htm, retrieved June 22, 2007); Christensen, *Sagwitch*, 187.

39. Kreitzer, *Washakie Letters*, 173, 297, 307; Peterson, *A History of Cache County*, 157–86; Hull and Hull, "Presettlement Vegetation"; Steward, *Basin-Plateau*, 218; Greer, *Atlas of Utah*, 110.

40. Kreitzer, *Washakie Letters*, 97 (photo of the Joshuas). Perdash is variously identified as OD's sister (Steward, *Basin-Plateau*, 218); by two names, Shoshone (Posiats) and non-Shoshone (Rachel Perdache); by her initials, RP; and by precise relation to Diamond, as his half sister (Steward, "Culture Element Distributions: XXIII, Northern and Gosiute Shoshoni," 264).

41. Steward, *Basin-Plateau*, 219–21; Duncan, "Northern Utes of Utah," 187; Arrington, *The Mormon Experience*, 112; Alexander, *Utah, the Right Place*, 97; Bullock, 1847 Diary Extracts, MSS A 327, 35.

42. Spencer, *Brigham Young at Home*, 75, 285; Alexander, *Utah, the Right Place*, 96; Bullock, 1847 Diary Extracts, MSS A 327, 38. See also Cottam, "Is Utah Sahara Bound," 10–11.

43. Spencer, *Brigham Young at Home*, 273–74; Arrington, *The Mormon Experience*, 101, 104; Alexander, *Utah, the Right Place*, 102; Blanthorn, *History of Tooele County*, 63.

44. Steward mentioned Wanship and Goship (or Gocip, as he spelled the name), drawing on published sources that identified the two men as chiefs (*Basin-Plateau*, 221).

45. Daughters of Utah Pioneers, 1965 historical marker at Warm Springs (still in place in 2006); Young, *The Founding of Utah*, 542; Nebeker, 1884 Early Justice. MSS A 766, 2; Bancroft, *History of Utah*, 278. The site is now a city park. Markers put in place in 1999 and still standing in 2006 identify those who died as members of a "small mixed band of Utes and Shoshones." Steward identified the so-called Utes or Weber Utes (who came from the area around the Weber River) as Goshutes, who spoke Shoshone, not Ute (*Basin-Plateau*, 220–21). See also Duncan, "Northern Utes of Utah," 177; and Thomas, Pendleton, and Cappannari, "Western Shoshone," 282–83.

46. Spencer, *Brigham Young at Home*, 21–23; Greer, *Atlas of Utah*, 110; Bancroft, *History of Utah*, 320; Young, "Religion, Progress, and Privileges," 83.

47. Information on the bathhouse comes from a National Register of Historic Places marker for Warm Springs, in place in 2006. The new bathhouse remained in use for fifty years, until the 1970s.

48. Daughters of American Revolution, 1926 historical marker at Warm Springs,

still in place in 2006; Van Cott, *Utah Place Names*, 389. Newer markers placed at Warm Springs in 1999 tell what happened to Wansip's and Goship's people, restoring their historical visibility to visitors at the site.

49. Spencer, *Brigham Young at Home*, 285. Bullock described the valley as "dotted in 3 or 4 places with Timber," and noted the trees by creeks (1847 Diary Extracts, 38, 40). One of Brigham Young's daughters, Clarissa Young Spencer, born more than a decade after Mormons first entered Salt Lake Valley, reported what she heard about the landscape from her parents and others.

50. Church of Jesus Christ of Latter-day Saints, First Presidency, vol. I, 353; Wilcove, *The Condor's Shadow*, 20–21; Steward, *Basin-Plateau*, 34. Skunks were identified as "pole cats," and weasels as "minx." See also Sorensen, "Wasters and Destroyers."

51. Kreitzer, *Washakie Letters*, 141, 182, 200, 204.

52. Julian H. Steward to Alfred L. Kroeber, July 23, 1936, DAR; Journal, Aug. 1, 1936, JHS Box 21; Jane C. Steward to Joseph J. Cannon, Aug. 25, 1936, RWC Box 57.

53. "Claire" to Ramona W. Cannon, Aug. 13, 1936, RWC Box 7; Jane C. and Julian H. Steward to Joseph J. Cannon, July 3, 1936, RWC Box 57; Joseph J. Cannon to Jane C. Steward, Nov. 10, 1936, RWC Box 62.

54. Jane C. Steward to Joseph J. Cannon, May 8, 1935; Jane C. Steward to Ramona W. Cannon n.d. [1934], RWC Box 57; Julian H. Steward to Matthew Stirling, Sept. 12, 1936, BAE Box 83.

10. Trail's End

1. Julian H. Steward to Alfred L. Kroeber, Sept. 25, 1936, DAR. The BIA report summarized his observations on social and economic conditions of Utes, Shoshones, Northern Paiutes, and Southern Paiutes, in relation to BIA policies and goals ("Shoshonean Tribes," Nov. 1936, JHS Box 11; "Shoshonean Tribes: Utah, Idaho, Nevada, Eastern California," [1936], JHS Box 10). See also Kerns, *Scenes from the High Desert*, 206–8.

2. Muir, *Steep Trails*, 129, 132, 135; Clarke, *The Life and Adventures of John Muir*, 317.

3. Martz, *Why Hurry Through Heaven*, 149.

4. By the end of the twentieth century the copper mine at Bingham Canyon qualified as the world's largest man-made excavation, and one of the few man-made structures visible from outer space. In 2006 the open pit copper mine at Bingham Canyon was more than ¾ mile deep, and 2 ½ miles across at the widest

point at the top of the pit (information courtesy of Kennecott Utah Copper Corporation, Bingham Canyon, Utah, July 15, 2006).

5. Writers' Program of the Work Projects Administration for the State of Utah, *Utah*, 409, 410. See also the photograph, "Smelter Smoke, Garfield," between pages 284 and 285. The town of Garfield no longer exists.

6. Kroeber, "Bannock and Shoshone Languages," 267; Steward, *Basin-Plateau*, 132. Linguist Edward Sapir had proposed a "'comprehensive study of all Shoshonean languages'" in 1909, but could not pursue it (Darnell, *Edward Sapir*, 32). Most of the languages remained poorly known in the 1930s.

7. Steward, *Basin-Plateau*, 132–33; Thomas, Pendleton, and Cappannari, "Western Shoshone," 281.

8. Bancroft, *History of Utah*, 314; Blanthorn, *History of Tooele County*, 65; Defa, "Goshute Indians," 94–96; Greer, *Atlas of Utah*, 110. The name of the valley is possibly of Goshute origin (Van Cott, *Utah Place Names*, 372), or derived from *tule*, a reed (Bancroft, *History of Utah*, 315).

9. See Twain, *Roughing It*, 108, 136, 146, 147; Defa, "Goshute Indians," 96–103.

10. Twain, *Roughing It*, 148; Steward, *Basin-Plateau*, 140; Malouf, "Gosiute Indians," 124–34; Defa, "Goshute Indians," 96, 97, 99–104.

11. Allen and Warner, "The Gosiute Indians," 166; Defa, "Goshute Indians," 98–99; Malouf, "Gosiute Indians," 135, 141.

12. Census of the Skull Valley reservation of the Paiute jurisdiction as of Jan. 1, 1936, ICR; Crum, "The Skull Valley Band"; Allen and Warner, "The Gosiute Indians," 173, 174–76; Defa, "Goshute Indians," 113; Clemmer and Stewart, "Treaties, Reservations, and Claims," 532. Sources vary about when the reservation was established, in 1907 or in 1912.

13. Bitton, *George Q. Cannon*, 24–26, 310–11; Van Cott, *Utah Place Names*, 200; Jane C. Steward interview.

14. Malouf, "Gosiute Indians," 156–57; Panek, "Life at Iosepa."

15. Census of the Skull Valley reservation of the Paiute jurisdiction as of Jan. 1, 1936, ICR; Steward, *Basin-Plateau*, 133; Steward, "Culture Element Distributions: XXIII, Northern and Gosiute Shoshoni," 265; Kreitzer, *Washakie Letters*, 105, 128; Malouf, "Gosiute Indians," 157. M (Steward, *Basin-Plateau*, 137; Steward, "Culture Element Distributions: XXIII, Northern and Gosiute Shoshoni," 265) is George Moody. See Duncan, who alludes to Pahvant Utes "mixing somewhat with Gosiutes and Paiutes" ("Northern Utes of Utah," 176).

16. Kreitzer, *Washakie Letters*, 85, 269n17.

17. Steward, *Basin-Plateau*, 49, 133–35. Steward noted that some Goshutes had a few recently acquired horses when the first Mormons arrived (*Basin-Plateau*, 135).

18. Steward, *Basin-Plateau*, 134; Twain, *Roughing It*, 143. Perhaps the best-known tales centered on explorer Jedediah Smith as well as on the Donner party, nearly half of whose members died before reaching California (see, for example, Defa, "Goshute Indians," 86; Alexander, *Utah, the Right Place*, 76).

19. Malouf, "Gosiute Indians," 36; Defa, "Goshute Indians," 75; Steward, *Basin-Plateau*, 134.

20. Census of the Gashute Indians living at Skull Valley, Iosepa, Gashute Agency on June 30, 1921, ICR; Census of the Skull Valley reservation of the Paiute jurisdiction as of Jan. 1, 1936, ICR.

21. Cottam drew on the memories of the early settler, mentioned in an obituary published in 1942 ("Is Utah Sahara Bound," 11). See also Martz on Cottam's lecture (*Why Hurry Through Heaven*, 121).

22. "5-State Barrier Recommended to Check Dust," *Washington Post*, April 18, 1935, 5; "Reclaims Big Area in Utah Dust Bowl," *New York Times*, August 24, 1936, 17; Cannon, "Struggle Against Great Odds," 307.

23. Steward, *Basin-Plateau*, 137; Blanthorn, *History of Tooele County*, 273–74.

24. Steward, "Culture Element Distributions: XXIII, Northern and Gosiute Shoshoni," 265.

25. Steward, *Basin-Plateau*, 135, 136n14.

26. Steward, *Basin-Plateau*, 137.

27. Steward, *Basin-Plateau*, 138.

28. Steward, *Basin-Plateau*, 138; Chamberlin, "Ethno-Botany of the Gosiute," 27; Chamberlin, "Place and Personal Names," 11; Van Cott, *Utah Place Names*, 250; Bancroft, *History of Utah*, 279. Steward's estimate of the distance to Mill Creek Canyon, "about thirty miles," probably understates it.

29. Steward, *Basin-Plateau*, 34, 138–39; Egan, *Pioneering the West*, 230–31, 245–46; Defa, "Goshute Indians," 77.

30. Young, *Memoirs of Young*, 66; Steward, "Culture Element Distributions: XXIII, Northern and Gosiute Shoshoni," 270; Madsen and Madsen, "One Man's Meat," 60–61; Alexander, *Utah, the Right Place*, 97. Madsen and Madsen document the nutritional value of grasshoppers and the very favorable caloric return rates of grasshopper and cricket collecting. See also Sutton, *Insects as Food*; and Janetski, "Great Basin Animals," 364, on insects as food in the Great Basin.

31. Young, *Memoirs of Young*, 64; Hartley, "Mormons, Crickets, and Gulls," 229; Alexander, *Utah, the Right Place*, 97, 102; Arrington, *The Mormon Experience*, 104.

32. Smith, *Shoshone Tales*, 42. On the rare use of hawks, coyotes, and wolves as food, see Thomas, Pendleton, and Cappannari, "Western Shoshone," 268; Steward, *Basin-Plateau*, 34; and Steward, "Culture Element Distributions: XIII, Nevada Shoshoni," 331. See also Janetski, "Great Basin Animals," 356.

33. Utah Road Commission, Road Map of Utah, 1936. PAM 14392; Field Expenses of Julian H. Steward, June–Oct. 1936, JHS Box 10; "Culture Element Distributions: XXIII, Northern and Gosiute Shoshoni," 265; Writers' Program of the Work Projects Administration for the State of Utah, *Utah*, 389.

34. "Eight Auto Records Are Set by Jenkins," *New York Times*, Sept. 29, 1936, 13; "Salt Lake City Elects Ab Jenkins," *New York Times*, Nov. 8, 1939, 20; Writers' Program of the Work Projects Administration for the State of Utah, *Utah*, 234.

35. Bateman, *Deep Creek Reflections*, 12, 412; Cottam, "Is Utah Sahara Bound," 12; Anderson, *Tending the Wild*, 117; Starrs, *Let the Cowboy Ride*, 59; Daggett, *Beyond the Rangeland Conflict*, 37; Martz, *Why Hurry Through Heaven*, 119.

36. Bateman, *Deep Creek Reflections*, 11; Defa, "Goshute Indians," 113; Field Expenses of Julian H. Steward, June–Oct., 1936, JHS Box 10; Steward, "Culture Element Distributions: XXIII, Northern and Gosiute Shoshoni," 265; Census of the Goshute reservation of the Paiute jurisdiction as of Jan. 1, 1936, ICR; Clemmer and Stewart, "Treaties, Reservations, and Claims," 533; Writers' Program of the Work Projects Administration for the State of Utah, *Utah*, 391.

37. Stewart, "The Peyote Religion," 678, 679; Defa, "Goshute Indians," 80, 111–13; Heaton, *Shoshone-Bannocks*, 222–26. Ottogary visited Deep Creek Valley and Skull Valley in 1913 as a missionary (Kreitzer, *Washakie Letters*, 58, 59, 60). On peyote ceremonies at the Deep Creek Reservation in the 1930s, as reported by Omer Stewart, see Kerns, *Scenes from the High Desert*, 364n97; see also Stewart, "The Peyote Religion." On peyote, the plant, see Moerman, *Native American Ethnobotany*, 319.

38. USFC 1930, Juab County, Utah; Census of the Goshute reservation of the Paiute jurisdiction as of Jan. 1, 1936, ICR. FB (Steward, *Basin-Plateau*, 139; Steward, "Culture Element Distributions: XXIII, Northern and Gosiute Shoshoni," 265) is Frank Bonamont.

39. Steward, *Basin-Plateau*, 20, 137–38.

40. Bergera, "1911 Evolution Controversy," 34; Julian H. Steward to Ralph

V. Chamberlin, Aug. 1, 1933, and Aug. 4, 1933, RVC Box 4; May 19, 1935 RVC Box 5. In *Basin-Plateau* Steward cited only Chamberlin's publications; he probably did not have access to his field notes.

41. Chamberlin, "Ethno-Botany of the Gosiute of Utah," 358; Chamberlin, "Ethno-Botany of the Gosiute"; Chamberlin, *Life Sciences at Utah,* 276, 289–90, 392. At the time of his research, in 1901, Ralph Chamberlin (1879–1967) was a science teacher.

42. Chamberlin, "Ethno-Botany of the Gosiute of Utah," 337; *Life Sciences at Utah,* 21.

43. Ernst Haeckel (1834–1919) used the term *oecology* in 1866. The American writer and naturalist Henry David Thoreau (1817–1862), among others, has been called "a pioneer in the science of ecology" before it existed as a named field (Harding, "Thoreau and "'Ecology,'" 707). I believe that hunter-gatherers can be seen as the original ecologists in terms of knowledge. They have not always been "ecological" in terms of actions. See, for example, Krech, *Ecological Indian.*

44. Steward, *Basin-Plateau,* 138, 309.

45. Steward, *Basin-Plateau,* 34–36, 137, 138; Steward, "Culture Element Distributions: XXIII, Northern and Gosiute Shoshoni," 270–71.

46. Field Expenses of Julian H. Steward, June–Oct. 1936, JHS Box 10; Steward, *Basin-Plateau,* 140; "Culture Element Distributions: XXIII, Northern and Gosiute Shoshoni," 265.

47. Julian H. Steward to Alfred L. Kroeber, Oct. 26, 1936, DAR; Julian H. Steward to Matthew Stirling, Sept. 12, 1936, BAE, Box 83; Steward, *Basin-Plateau,* 135; Steward, "Culture Element Distributions: XXIII, Northern and Gosiute Shoshoni," 265, 279.

48. Ethnographic photographs, JHS Box 19, 20.

49. Jane C. Steward to Joseph J. Cannon, May 8, 1935, RWC Box 57.

50. Julian H. Steward to Alfred L. Kroeber, Sept. 25, 1936, and Oct. 26, 1936, DAR.

51. Julian H. Steward to Alfred L. Kroeber, May 28, 1936, DAR.

52. See, for example, Kreitzer, *Washakie Letters,* 220.

53. Jane C. Steward interview. Diamond died in 1940 (Burial Records, Shoshoni Tribal Cemetery, www.lofthouse.com/boxelder/cemeteries/shoshoni.htm, retrieved Jan. 30, 2006); Ballard, Pavitse, and Jack died in 1937, 1941, and 1942 respectively (Idaho Death Index, 1911–1951, http://rootsweb.com/~deaths/search .htm, retrieved Jan. 10, 2006).

54. Sidney Olson, "Mormons Get Aid Against Cannibal Cricket," *Washington Post*, July 19, 1936, B2. See Rachel Carson, *Silent Spring*, 17–18, 50, 51, on arsenic, "a highly toxic mineral" long known to have the capacity to sicken and kill humans and other animals, and "clearly established as causing cancer in man." It was still a basic component of weed and insect killers when she wrote her book, despite a shift after World War II away from the use of inorganic chemicals as pesticides and toward the use of synthetic chemicals. Carson refers to "heavy applications of arsenical insecticides," which may poison the soil and then be washed into streams, rivers, and groundwater.

55. Field Expenses of Julian H. Steward, June–Oct. 1936, JHS Box 10; Steward, *Basin-Plateau*, 182.

56. Lewis, "Kanosh and Ute Identity," 332–33; Carlson, *Nevada Place Names*, 152–53.

57. Kerns, *Scenes from the High Desert*, 203; Writers' Program of the Works Progress Administration in the State of Nevada, *Nevada*, 182ff.

58. USFC 1930, Clark County, Nevada; [Census of] Paiute (Paiute, Goshute, and Ute Indians), 1936, 1937, ICR; Steward, *Basin-Plateau*, 184; Field Expenses of Julian H. Steward, June–Oct. 1936, JHS Box 10. He identified his informant as ChB (Steward, *Basin-Plateau*, 184). The Moapa River Reservation was established in 1873, and Las Vegas Colony in 1911 (Clemmer and Stewart, "Treaties, Reservations, and Claims," 532).

59. Steward initially planned to include the "Green River, Wyo. Band of Shoshoni" in his 1936 fieldwork (Julian H. Steward to Alfred L. Kroeber, Aug. 12, 1936, DAR; Nov. 18, 1936, DAR). Steward may have ruled out Hitope Joshua as an informant for Wyoming Shoshones, or she may not have been present when he visited Washakie, Utah (see chapter 9). She was born in Wyoming in the 1840s and spent decades of her life there (see Kreitzer, *Washakie Letters*, 297). See Shimkin, "Eastern Shoshone," on the Eastern Shoshones of Wyoming.

60. On Steward's later brief search for the patrilineal band in South America and in Canada, see Kerns, *Scenes from the High Desert*, 210–16, 218–22.

61. Steward, *Basin-Plateau*, 260.

Afterword: Journey's West

1. Morgan and Wheat, *Jedediah Smith and His Maps*, 16, 17; Cline, *Exploring the Great Basin*, 210–15.

2. Steward, *Basin-Plateau*, 260.

3. Steward to Murphy, March 31, 1967, JHS Box 6; Robert F. Murphy interview; Kerns, *Scenes from the High Desert*, 175.

4. Many of his early essays had been republished in Steward, *Theory of Culture Change*, including a slightly revised essay on the patrilineal band.

5. Kerns, *Scenes from the High Desert*, 218–20.

6. Barnard, "Contemporary Hunter-Gatherers," 196.

7. Fowler, "History of Research," 29.

8. Steward, *Basin-Plateau*, 258; Julian H. Steward to Alfred L. Kroeber, May 3, 1935, DAR; Kerns, *Scenes from the High Desert*, 181–82.

9. See, for example, Steward, "Diffusion and Independent Invention"; Steward, *Basin-Plateau*, 53, 104, 138; Kroeber, *Handbook of Indians of California*, 736; and Anderson, *Tending the Wild*.

10. Steward, *Theory of Culture Change*, 173, 187.

11. See, for example, historian John Heaton, "No Place to Pitch Their Teepees," on the adaptation of Cache Valley Shoshones to Mormon settlement of their lands; and many journalists who, in writing about global warming, allude to the prospect of cultural adaptation.

12. By the "intellectual common" I mean the body of knowledge constructed, recorded, and transmitted by scholars, scientists, and other intellectuals—knowledge shared publicly and without prohibitive costs that would exclude many people. Examples include knowledge recorded in books and other print sources and available in public libraries; or available at open sites on the Internet; or disseminated through programs on public radio and public television; and so on.

13. For later variants of cultural ecology, see, for example, Winterhalder, "Behavioral and Other Human Ecologies"; Sutton and Anderson, *Cultural Ecology*, 21–28.

14. Kerns, *Women and the Ancestors*. On ethnographic fieldwork, see Bradburd, *Being There*; Mintz, "Sows' Ears"; and Stocking, *Observers Observed* and *Ethnographer's Magic*, among others.

15. Kerns, *Scenes from the High Desert*, 22–23; Radcliffe-Brown, "Australian Local Organization," 105, 106.

16. Frank Hamilton Cushing's fieldwork at Zuni Pueblo preceded Malinowski's in the Trobriand Islands by more than thirty years (see Mark, *Four Anthropologists*, 98–103). See also Malinowski, *Argonauts of the Western Pacific*, 1967.

17. Malinowski, *Argonauts of the Western Pacific*, 4.

18. Malinowski, *Argonauts of the Western Pacific*, 3.

19. See Bradburd, *Being There*, xiii, passim, on the importance of serendipity

("unexpected, unprogrammed" events) in fieldwork. I can only add that serendipity is inevitable in *naturalistic* research of any kind, including ethnographic fieldwork, and is a defining feature of such research.

20. Inter-Tribal Council of Nevada, *Newe*, 104. These words come from the closing paragraph of a Western Shoshone tribal history.

21. Julian H. Steward to Alfred L. Kroeber, Feb. 17, 1936; Jane C. Steward to Alfred L. Kroeber, March 10, 1936, DAR.

22. Jane C. Steward interview. See Parezo, "Conclusion: The Beginning," 352–53, on the "'two-person single career'" and the general silence about the contributions of wives; and see Parezo and Hardin, "In the Realm of the Muses," on the failure to acknowledge other assistance as well. Although they focus on southwestern anthropology, their comments generally apply to other areas of anthropology, and to other academic fields.

23. Kerns, *Scenes from the High Desert*, 330n17.

24. See, for example, Brewer, "What Is Autobiographical Memory." My informants (Kerns, *Women and the Ancestors*) often recounted personal memories of particular events or episodes as stories. Generic personal memories, resulting from "repeated exposure to a set of related experiences" (Brewer, "What Is Autobiographical Memory," 30–31), were generally expressed in a nonnarrative, expository way.

25. Kerns, *Scenes from the High Desert*, 176; Steward, "Economic and Social Basis of Primitive Bands." Some of the parallels between the school and the patrilineal band include the size of the group, the size of its territory, the primacy of ties between males, the significance of male work groups, and the nature of leadership (Kerns, *Scenes from the High Desert*, 316–17).

26. See Davies, *Reflexive Ethnography*.

27. The American Anthropological Association's current code of ethics is posted at http://www.aaanet.org/committees/ethics/ethcode.htm (retrieved June 1, 2008).

28. William Sturtevant interview; Sidney W. Mintz interview; Kerns, *Scenes from the High Desert*, 259, 282–83. On Steward, see also Crum, "Steward's Vision of the Great Basin"; Blackhawk, "Julian Steward"; Ronaasen, Clemmer, and Rudden, "Rethinking Cultural Ecology"; and Pinkoski, "Julian Steward." More broadly, see Banner, *How the Indians Lost Their Land*; and Smith, *Decolonizing Methodologies*.

29. Alfred L. Kroeber to Omer C. Stewart, June 3, 1935, DAR.

30. Badè, *Life and Letters of John Muir*, 102.

31. Muir, *First Summer in the Sierra*, 128.

32. Julian H. Steward, "Shoshonean Tribes," Nov. 1936, 10, JHS Box 11; Angel, *History of Nevada*, 649. Dorothy Nyswander, who grew up near the California-Nevada border, also spoke highly of the Indian ranch hands at the large ranch her father managed in the early twentieth century (Dorothy B. Nyswander interview).

33. See, for example, Steward, *Some Western Shoshoni Myths* (http://www.sa cred-texts.com/nam/ca/wsm/index.htm, retrieved Nov. 27, 2007).

34. Cuch, "Introduction," xvi–xix; Forrest Cuch, executive director, Utah Division of Indian Affairs, personal communication, Dec. 6, 2007; Inter-Tribal Council of Nevada, *Newe*. See also Novak and Rodseth, "Remembering Mountain Meadows," on collective memory and narratives of traumatic events.

35. Flannery, *The Eternal Frontier*, 336–37; Wilcove, *The Condor's Shadow*, 106–8, 229–32; Harney, *The Way It Is*; Fox, *The Void, the Grid, and the Sign*, 39–41; Solnit, *Savage Dreams*.

36. The term *genocide* entered the world's vocabulary after World War II and the Holocaust. See Lemkin, "Genocide." Anthropologists contributed to the statement of universal human rights that the United Nations adopted in the late 1940s. Steward was among those who did not support a universal statement (see Steward, "Comment on the Statement on Human Rights").

Bibliography

Manuscripts and Archives

Bullock, Thomas. 1847 Diary Extracts, 1847. MSS A 327 (typescript). Utah State Historical Society, Salt Lake City.

Bureau of American Ethnology. National Anthropological Archives, Smithsonian Institution, Washington DC.

Cannon, Ramona Wilcox, Papers, 1863–1994. Accn 1862, Manuscript Division, Marriott Library, University of Utah, Salt Lake City.

Chamberlin, Ralph V., Papers, 1890–1969. Accn 907, Manuscript Division, Marriott Library, University of Utah, Salt Lake City.

Church of Jesus Christ of Latter-day Saints, Family History Library. Salt Lake City, Utah.

Department of Anthropology Records. CU-23, Bancroft Library, University of California, Berkeley.

Eastern California Museum Collections. Independence, California.

Ford, A. J. 1930 Owens River Valley, California, Indian Problem. Right of Way and Land Agent, Department of Water and Power, City of Los Angeles. ECM Collection, Independence, California.

Indian Census Rolls, 1885–1940. Records of the Bureau of Indian Affairs, Record Group 75, National Archives, Washington DC.

Kelly, Charles, Papers. MSS B 144, Utah State Historical Society, Salt Lake City.

Kroeber, A. L., Papers. MSS C-B 925, Bancroft Library, University of California, Berkeley.

Lowie, Robert Harry, Papers. MSS C-B 927, Bancroft Library, University of California, Berkeley.

Nebeker, John. 1884 Early Justice. MSS A 766 (typescript). Utah State Historical Society, Salt Lake City.

State of Nevada Department of Highways. 1937 Official Road Map of the State of Nevada, 1937. Nevada Historical Society, Reno.

Steward, Julian H., Papers, 1842–1980. Record series 15/2/21, University of Illinois Archives, Urbana, Illinois.

Utah Road Commission. 1936 Road Map of Utah, 1936. PAM 14392. Utah State Historical Society, Salt Lake City.

Published Works

Aird, Steven D., Luke J. Thornhill, Corinne Seebart, and Ivan I. Kaiser. "Venoms and Morphology of Western Diamondback/Mojave Rattlesnake Hybrids." *Journal of Herpetology* 23, no. 2 (1989): 131–41.

Alexander, Thomas G. *Utah, the Right Place.* Revised and updated ed. Salt Lake City: Gibbs Smith, 2003.

Allen, James B., and Ted J. Warner. "The Gosiute Indians in Pioneer Utah." *Utah Historical Quarterly* 39, no. 2 (1971): 162–77.

Anderson, M. Kat. *Tending the Wild: Native American Knowledge and the Management of California's Natural Resources.* Berkeley: University of California Press, 2005.

Angel, Myron, ed. *History of Nevada.* Vol. 1. Oakland CA: Thompson & West, 1881.

Arrington, Leonard J. *Great Basin Kingdom: Economic History of the Latter-day Saints, 1830–1900.* Cambridge MA: Harvard University Press, 1958.

———. "Utah's Great Drought of 1934." *Utah Historical Quarterly* 54, no. 3 (1986): 245–64.

———. *The Mormon Experience: A History of the Latter-day Saints.* Urbana: University of Illinois Press, 1992.

———. *History of Idaho.* Vol. 1. Moscow: University of Idaho Press, 1994.

Ashley Montague, M. F. "Aleš Hrdlička, 1869–1943." *American Anthropologist* 46, no. 1 (1944): 113–17.

Austin, Mary. *The Land of Little Rain.* Boston: Houghton Mifflin, 1903.

Badè, William Frederic. *The Life and Letters of John Muir.* Vol. 2. Boston: Houghton Mifflin, 1924.

Bagley, Will. *Blood of the Prophets: Brigham Young and the Massacre at Mountain Meadows.* Norman: University of Oklahoma Press, 2002.

Bailey, Alice Morrey. "Last Wife of Chief Kanosh." *Frontier Times* 54, no. 2 (1980): 50–51.

Baker, William J. *Jesse Owens: An American Life.* New York: The Free Press, 1986.

Bancroft, Hubert Howe. *History of Utah, 1540–1886*. San Francisco: The History Company, 1889.

——. *History of Nevada, 1540–1888*. San Francisco: The History Company, 1890.

Banner, Stuart. *How the Indians Lost Their Land: Law and Power on the Frontier*. Cambridge MA: The Belknap Press of Harvard University Press, 2005.

Barnard, Alan. "Contemporary Hunter-Gatherers: Current Theoretical Issues in Ecology and Social Organization." *Annual Review of Anthropology* 12 (1983): 193–214.

Bateman, Ronald R. *Deep Creek Reflections: 125 Years of Settlement at Ibapah, Utah, 1859–1984*. Salt Lake City: R. R. Bateman, 1984.

Baugh, Ruth E. "Land Use Changes in the Bishop Area of Owens Valley, California." *Economic Geography* 13, no. 1 (1937): 17–34.

Beckwith, Frank A. *Indian Joe, in Person and in Background*. Delta: F. A. Beckwith, 1939.

——. *Indian Joe, in Person and in Background: Historical Perspective into Piute Life*. Delta UT: DuWil Publishing Company, 1975.

Beckwourth, James P. *Life and Adventures of James P. Beckwourth as Told to Thomas D. Bonner*. 1856. Lincoln: University of Nebraska Press, 1972.

Bergera, Gary James. "The 1911 Evolution Controversy at Brigham Young University." In *The Search for Harmony: Essays on Science and Mormonism*, ed. Gene A. Sessions and Craig J. Oberg, 23–41. Salt Lake City: Signature Books, 1993.

Bettinger, Robert E. "Aboriginal Human Ecology in Owens Valley." *American Antiquity* 42, no. 1 (1977): 3–17.

Bettinger, Robert E., and Eric Wohlgemuth. "California Plants." In *Handbook of North American Indians*, ed. William C. Sturtevant, vol. 3, *Environment, Origins, and Population*, ed. Douglas H. Ubelaker, 274–83. Washington DC: Smithsonian Institution, 2006.

Bitton, Davis. *George Q. Cannon: A Biography*. Salt Lake City: Deseret Book Company, 1999.

Blackhawk, Ned. "Julian Steward and the Politics of Representation." In *Julian Steward and the Great Basin: The Making of an Anthropologist*, ed. Richard O. Clemmer, L. Daniel Myers, and Mary Elizabeth Rudden, 203–18. Salt Lake City: University of Utah Press, 1999.

Blanthorn, Oiuda, comp. *A History of Tooele County*. Utah Centennial County

History Series. Salt Lake City: Utah State Historical Society and Tooele County Commission, 1998.

Boyles, J. C. "He Witnessed the Death Valley Tragedy of '49." *Desert Magazine* 3, no. 4 (1940): 3–6.

Bradburd, Daniel. *Being There: The Necessity of Fieldwork*. Washington DC: Smithsonian Institution Press, 1998.

Brewer, William F. "What Is Autobiographical Memory?" In *Autobiographical Memory*, ed. David C. Rubin, 25–49. New York: Cambridge University Press, 1986.

———. "What Is Recollective Memory?" In *Remembering Our Past: Studies in Autobiographical Memory*, ed. David C. Rubin, 19–66. New York: Cambridge University Press, 1996.

Brooks, Drex. *Sweet Medicine: Sites of Indian Massacres, Battlefields, and Treaties*. Albuquerque: University of New Mexico Press, 1995.

Brooks, James F. *Captives and Cousins: Slavery, Kinship and Community in the Southwest Borderlands*. Chapel Hill: University of North Carolina Press, 2002.

Callaway, Donald G., Joel C. Janetski, and Omer C. Stewart. "Ute." In *Handbook of North American Indians*, ed. William C. Sturtevant, vol. 11, *Great Basin*, ed. Warren L. D'Avezedo, 336–67. Washington DC: Smithsonian Institution, 1986.

Campbell, Greg. "The Lemhi Shoshoni: Ethnogenesis, Sociological Transformation, and the Construction of a Tribal Nation." *American Indian Quarterly* 25, no. 4 (2001): 539–78.

Cannon, Annie Wells. "Sarah Jenne Cannon." *Relief Society Magazine* 15, no. 7 (1928): 373–75.

Cannon, Brian Q. "Struggle Against Great Odds: Challenges in Utah's Marginal Agricultural Areas, 1925–1939." In *A World We Thought We Knew: Readings in Utah History*, ed. John S. McCormick and John R. Sillito, 304–18. Salt Lake City: University of Utah Press, 1995.

Cannon, Joseph J. "George Q. Cannon." *The Instructor* (August 1945): 342–51.

Carlson, Helen S. *Nevada Place Names: A Geographical Dictionary*. Reno: University of Nevada Press, 1974.

Carlstrom, Jeffrey, and Cynthia Furse. *The History of Emigration Canyon: Gateway to Salt Lake Valley*. Logan: Utah State University Press, 2003.

Carson, Rachel. *Silent Spring*. Boston: Houghton Mifflin, 1962.

Cassidy, Victor M. *Henry Chandler Cowles: Pioneer Ecologist*. Chicago: Kedzie Sigel Press, 2008.

Chalfant, W. A. *The Story of Inyo*. Revised edition. Bishop CA: Chalfant, 1933.

Chamberlin, Ralph V. "The Ethno-Botany of the Gosiute Indians of Utah." *American Anthropological Association Memoirs* vol. II, part 5 (1911): 331–53.

———. "The Ethno-Botany of the Gosiute Indians." *Proceedings of the Academy of Natural Sciences of Philadelphia*, vol. LXIII (1911): 24–99.

———. "Place and Personal Names of the Gosiute Indians of Utah." *Proceedings of the American Philosophical Society*, vol. LII, no. 208 (1913): 1–20.

———. *Life Sciences at the University of Utah: Background and History*. Salt Lake City: University of Utah, 1950.

Christensen, Scott R. *Sagwitch: Shoshone Chieftain, Mormon Elder*. Logan: Utah State University Press, 1999.

Christman, A. B. "Johnny Shoshone of Death Valley." *Desert Magazine* 16 (December): 10–11.

Church of Jesus Christ of Latter-day Saints, First Presidency. *Messages of the First Presidency of the Church of Jesus Christ of Latter-day Saints, 1833–1964.* 3 vol. Salt Lake City: Bookcraft, Inc., 1965.

Clarke, James Mitchell. *The Life and Adventures of John Muir*. San Francisco: Sierra Club Books, 1980.

Clemmer, Richard O. "Steward's Gap: Why Steward Did Not Use His Theory of Culture Change to Explain Shoshoni Culture Change." In *Julian Steward and the Great Basin: The Making of an Anthropologist*, ed. Richard O. Clemmer, L. Daniel Myers, and Mary Elizabeth Rudden, 144–63. Salt Lake City: University of Utah Press, 1999.

Clemmer, Richard O., and Omer C. Stewart. "Treaties, Reservations, and Claims." In *Handbook of North American Indians*, ed. William C. Sturtevant, vol. 11, *Great Basin*, ed. Warren L. D'Avezedo, 525–57. Washington DC: Smithsonian Institution, 1986.

Cline, Gloria Griffen. *Exploring the Great Basin*. Norman: University of Oklahoma Press, 1963.

Conetah, Fred A. *A History of the Northern Ute People*. [S.I.]: Uintah-Ouray Ute Tribe, c.1982.

Cottam, Walter P. "Man as a Biotic Factor Illustrated by Recent Floristic and Physiographic Changes at the Mountain Meadows, Washington County, Utah." *Ecology* 10, no. 4 (1929): 361–63.

————. "Is Utah Sahara Bound?" *Bulletin of the University of Utah* 37, no. 11 (1947): 1–40.

Cottam, Walter P., and George Stewart. "Plant Succession as a Result of Grazing and Meadow Desiccation by Erosion Since Settlement in 1862." *Journal of Forestry* 38 (1940): 613–26.

Crosby, Alfred W., Jr. *Ecological Imperialism: The Biological Expansion of Europe, 900–1900*. Second edition. New York: Cambridge University Press, 2004.

Crum, Beverly. "Afterword." In *Shoshone Tales*, comp. and ed. Anne M. Smith, 180–88. Salt Lake City: University of Utah Pres, 1993.

Crum, Steven J. "The Skull Valley Band of the Goshute Tribe—Deeply Attached to Their Native Homeland." *Utah Historical Quarterly* 55, no. 3 (1987): 250–67.

————. *The Road on Which We Came* (Po'i Pentun Tammen Kimmappeh*): A History of the Western Shoshone*. Salt Lake City: University of Utah Press, 1994.

————. "Julian Steward's Vision of the Great Basin: A Critique and Response." In *Julian Steward and the Great Basin: The Making of an Anthropologist*, ed. Richard O. Clemmer, L. Daniel Myers, and Mary Elizabeth Rudden, 117–27. Salt Lake City: University of Utah Press, 1999.

Cuch, Forrest S. "Introduction." In *A History of Utah's American Indians*, ed. Forrest S. Cuch, xi–xx. Salt Lake City: Utah State Division of Indian Affairs/Utah State Division of History, 2000.

Dagget, Dan. *Beyond the Rangeland Conflict: Toward a West That Works*. Layton UT: Gibbs Smith and The Grand Canyon Trust, 1995.

Darnell, Regna. "Taciturnity in Native American Etiquette: A Cree Case." *Culture* 1, no. 2 (1981): 55–60.

————. *Edward Sapir: Linguist, Anthropologist, Humanist*. Berkeley: University of California Press, 1990.

D'Avezedo, Warren L. "Washoe." In *Handbook of North American Indians*, ed. William C. Sturtevant, vol. 11, *Great Basin*, ed. Warren L. D'Avezedo, 466–98. Washington DC: Smithsonian Institution, 1986.

Davies, Charlotte Aull. *Reflexive Ethnography: A Guide to Researching Selves and Others*. New York: Routledge, 1999.

Dean, Sharon E., Peggy S. Ratcheson, Judith W. Finger, and Ellen F. Daus. *Weaving a Legacy: Indian Baskets and the People of Owens Valley, California*. With Craig D. Bates. Salt Lake City: University of Utah Press, 2004.

Defa, Dennis Ray. "The Goshute Indians of Utah." In *A History of Utah's American*

Indians, ed. Forrest S. Cuch, 73–122. Salt Lake City: Utah Division of Indian Affairs and Utah Division of State History, 2000.

Delacorte, Michael G. "The Prehistory of Deep Springs Valley, California: Adaptive Variation in the Western Great Basin." PhD dissertation, University of California, Davis, 1990.

Duncan, Clifford. "The Northern Utes of Utah." In *A History of Utah's American Indians*, ed. Forrest S. Cuch, 167–224. Salt Lake City: Utah Division of Indian Affairs and Utah Division of State History, 2000.

Egan, William M., ed. *Pioneering the West, 1846 to 1878: Major Howard Egan's Diary*. Richmond UT: Howard R. Egan Estate, 1917.

Evans, P. Alice. "An Ecological Study in Utah." *Botanical Gazette* 82, no. 3 (1926): 253–85.

Federal Writers' Project. *Idaho: A Guide in Word and Picture*. Second edition, revised. New York: Oxford University Press, 1950.

Federal Writers' Project of the Works Progress Administration for the State of California. *California: A Guide to the Golden State*. New York: Hastings House Publishers, 1939.

Federal Writers' Project of the Works Progress Administration of Northern California. *Death Valley: A Guide*. Boston: Houghton Mifflin, 1939.

Flannery, Tim. *The Eternal Frontier: An Ecological History of North America and Its Peoples*. New York: Atlantic Monthly Press, 2001.

Fowler, Catherine S. "Foreword." In *Shoshone Tales*, comp. and ed. Anne M. Smith, xi–xxxiv. University of Utah Publications in the American West, vol. 31. Salt Lake City: University of Utah Press, 1993.

Fowler, Catherine S., and Sven Liljeblad. "Northern Paiute." In *Handbook of North American Indians*, ed. William C. Sturtevant, vol. 11, *Great Basin*, ed. Warren L. D'Avezedo, 435–65. Washington DC: Smithsonian Institution, 1986.

Fowler, Catherine S., and David E. Rhode. "Great Basin Plants." In *Handbook of North American Indians*, ed. William C. Sturtevant, vol. 3, *Environment, Origins, and Population*, ed. Douglas H. Ubelaker, 331–50. Washington DC: Smithsonian Institution, 2006.

Fowler, Don D. "History of Research." In *Handbook of North American Indians*, ed. William C. Sturtevant, vol. 11, *Great Basin*, ed. Warren L. D'Avezedo, 15–30. Washington DC: Smithsonian Institution, 1986.

Fowler, Don, and Catherine S. Fowler, eds. *Anthropology of the Numa: John Wesley*

Powell's Manuscripts on the Numic Peoples of Western North America, 1868–1880. Washington DC: Smithsonian Institution, 1971.

Fox, William L. *The Void, the Grid, and the Sign: Traversing the Great Basin.* Salt Lake City: University of Utah Press, 2000.

Gottfredson, Peter, comp. and ed. *History of Indian Depredations in Utah.* Salt Lake City: Skelton Publishing, 1919.

Greer, Deon C. *Atlas of Utah.* Provo UT: Brigham Young University Press and Weber State College, 1981.

Hamblin, Jacob. *Jacob Hamblin: A Narrative of His Personal Experiences as Frontiersman, Missionary to the Indians and Explorer.* The Faith-Promoting Series, No. 5. Salt Lake City: Juvenile Instructor Office, 1881.

Harding, Walter. "Thoreau and 'Ecology': Correction." *Science* 149, no. 3685 (1965): 707.

Harney, Corbin. *The Way It Is: One Water, One Air, One Mother Earth.* Nevada City, CA: Blue Dolphin Publishing, 1995.

Hartley, William. "Mormons, Crickets, and Gulls: A New Look at an Old Story." *Utah Historical Quarterly* 38, no. 3 (1970): 224–39.

Heaton, John W. "'No Place to Pitch Their Teepees': Shoshone Adaptation to Mormon Settlers in Cache Valley, 1855–70." *Utah Historical Quarterly* 63, no. 2 (1995): 158–71.

———. *The Shoshone-Bannocks: Culture and Commerce at Fort Hall, 1870–1940.* Lawrence: University of Kansas Press, 1995.

Holt, Ronald L. *Beneath These Red Cliffs: An Ethnohistory of the Utah Paiutes.* Albuquerque: University of New Mexico Press, 1992.

Honker, Andrew M. "'Been Grazed Almost to Extinction': The Environment, Human Action, and Flooding, 1900–1940." *Utah Historical Quarterly* 67, no. 1 (1999): 23–47.

Houghton, Samuel G. *A Trace of Desert Waters: The Great Basin Story.* Salt Lake City: Howe Brothers, 1986.

Howell, Carol L., comp. and ed. *Cannibalism Is an Acquired Taste and Other Notes from Conversations with Anthropologist Omer C. Stewart.* Niwot: University Press of Colorado, 1998.

Hull, A. C., and M. K. Hull. "Presettlement Vegetation of Cache Valley, Utah and Idaho." *Journal of Range Management* 27, no. 1 (1974): 27–29.

Hultkrantz, Ake. "Mythology and Religious Concept." In *Handbook of North American Indians,* ed. William C. Sturtevant, vol. 11, *Great Basin,* ed. Warren L. D'Avezedo, 630–40. Washington DC: Smithsonian Institution, 1986.

Inter-Tribal Council of Nevada. *Newe: A Western Shoshone History.* Reno: Inter-Tribal Council of Nevada, 1976.

Irwin, Charles N. "Introduction." In *The Shoshoni Indians of Inyo County, California: The Kerr Manuscript,* ed. Charles N. Irwin, i–xv. Ballena Press Publications in Archaeology, Ethnology, and History, no. 15. Socorro NM: Ballena Press and Eastern California Museum (Independence, California), 1980.

James, Rhett. "Brigham Young–Chief Washakie Indian Farm Negotiations, 1854–1857." *Annals of Wyoming* 39 (2): 245–56.

Janetski, Joel C. "Utah Lake: Its Role in the Prehistory of Utah Valley." *Utah Historical Quarterly* 58, no. 1 (1990): 5–31.

———. "150 Years of Utah Archaeology." *Utah Historical Quarterly* 65, no. 2 (1997): 100–33.

———. "Julian Steward and Utah Archaeology." In *Julian Steward and the Great Basin: The Making of an Anthropologist,* ed. Richard O. Clemmer, L. Daniel Myers, and Mary Elizabeth Rudden, 19–34. Salt Lake City: University of Utah Press, 1999.

———. "Great Basin Animals." In *Handbook of North American Indians,* ed. William C. Sturtevant, vol. 3, *Environment, Origins, and Population,* ed. Douglas H. Ubelaker, 351–64. Washington DC: Smithsonian Institution, 2006.

Jardine, Winnifred Cannon. "Life on the Cannon Farm." In *Cannon Family Historical Treasury,* ed. Beatrice Cannon Evans and Janath Russell Cannon, 321–23. Salt Lake City: George Cannon Family Association, 1967.

Jorgensen, Joseph G. *Western Indians: Comparative Environments, Languages, and Cultures of 172 Western American Indian Tribes.* San Francisco: W. H. Freeman and Company, 1980.

———, ed. *Comparative Studies by Harold E. Driver and Studies in His Honor.* New Haven CT: HRAF Press, 1973.

Kahrl, William. *Water and Power: The Conflict over Los Angeles' Water Supply in the Owens Valley.* Berkeley: University of California Press, 1982.

Kelen, Leslie G., and Eileen Hallet Stone. *Missing Stories: An Oral History of Ethnic and Minority Groups in Utah.* Salt Lake City: University of Utah Press, 1996.

Kelly, Charles. "Reminiscences of Frank A. Beckwith." In *Indian Joe, in Person and in Background,* by Frank Beckwith, vii–xii. Delta UT: DuWil Publishing Company, 1975.

Kelly, Isabel T. "Southern Paiute Bands." *American Anthropologist* 36, no. 4 (1934): 548–60.

Kelly, Isabel T., and Catherine S. Fowler. "Southern Paiute." In *Handbook of North American Indians*, ed. William C. Sturtevant, vol. 11, *Great Basin*, ed. Warren L. D'Avezedo, 368–97. Washington DC: Smithsonian Institution, 1986.

Kerns, Virginia. *Women and the Ancestors: Black Carib Kinship and Ritual*. Second, expanded edition. Urbana: University of Illinois Press, 1997.

———. "Learning the Land." In *Julian Steward and the Great Basin: The Making of an Anthropologist*, ed. Richard O. Clemmer, L. Daniel Myers, and Mary Elizabeth Rudden, 1–18. Salt Lake City: University of Utah Press, 1999.

———. *Scenes from the High Desert: Julian Steward's Life and Theory*. Urbana: University of Illinois Press, 2003.

Kerr, Mark. *The Shoshoni Indians of Inyo County, California: The Kerr Manuscript*. Ballena Press Publications in Archaeology, Ethnology, and History, no. 15. Socorro NM: Ballena Press and Eastern California Museum (Independence, California), 1980.

Knack, Martha C. *Boundaries Between: The Southern Paiutes, 1775–1995*. Lincoln: University of Nebraska Press, 2001.

Krech, Shepherd. *The Ecological Indian: Myth and History*. New York: W. W. Norton, 1999.

Kreitzer, Matthew E. "Diamonds, Ovals, and Rings: Northwestern Shoshone Sports at the Washakie Colony of Northern Utah, 1903–29." *International Journal of the History of Sport* 23, no. 2 (2006): 232–46.

———, ed. *The Washakie Letters of Willie Ottogary: Northwestern Shoshone Journalist and Leader, 1906–1929*. Logan: Utah State University, 2000.

Kroeber, A. L. "The Bannock and Shoshone Languages." *American Anthropologist* 11, no. 2 (2000): 266–77.

———. *Handbook of the Indians of California*. Bureau of American Ethnology Bulletin No. 78. Washington DC: Government Printing Office, 1925.

———. "Native American Population." *American Anthropologist* 36, no. 1 (1934): 1–25.

Lawton, Harry W., Philip J. Wilke, Mary DeDecker, and William M. Mason. "Agriculture among the Paiute of Owens Valley." *Journal of California Anthropology* 3, no. 1 (1976): 13–50.

Leland, Joy. "Population." In *Handbook of North American Indians*, ed. William C. Sturtevant, vol. 11, *Great Basin*, ed. Warren L. D'Avezedo, 608–19. Washington DC: Smithsonian Institution, 1986.

Lemkin, Raphaël. "Genocide." *American Scholar* 15, no. 2 (1946): 227–30.

Lewis, Hyrum S. "Kanosh and Ute Identity in Territorial Utah." *Utah Histori-cal Quarterly* 71, no. 4 (2003): 332–47.

Liljeblad, Sven. "Oral Tradition: Content and Style of Verbal Arts." In *Hand-book of North American Indians*, ed. William C. Sturtevant, vol. 11, *Great Basin*, ed. Warren L. D'Avezedo, 641–59. Washington DC: Smithsonian In-stitution, 1986.

Liljeblad, Sven, and Catherine S. Fowler. "Owens Valley Paiute." In *Handbook of North American Indians*, ed. William C. Sturtevant, vol. 11, *Great Ba-sin*, ed. Warren L. D'Avezedo, 412–34. Washington DC: Smithsonian Insti-tution, 1986.

Limerick, Patricia Nelson. *The Legacy of Conquest: The Unbroken Past of the Amer-ican West*. New York: W. W. Norton, 1987.

――――. "Haunted America." In *Sweet Medicine: Sites of Indian Massacres, Bat-tlefields, and Treaties*, Drex Brooks (photographer), 119–63. Albuquerque: University of New Mexico Press, 1995.

Lingenfelter, Richard E. *Death Valley and the Amargosa: A Land of Illusion*. Berkeley: University of California Press, 1986.

Lupo, Karen D. "The Historical Occurrence and Demise of Bison in Northern Utah." *Utah Historical Quarterly* 64, no. 2 (1996): 168–80.

Lyman, Edward Leo, and Linda King Newell. *A History of Millard County*. Utah Centennial County History Series. Salt Lake City: Utah State Historical So-ciety and Millard County Commission, 1999.

Madsen, Brigham D. *The Shoshoni Frontier and the Bear River Massacre*. Salt Lake City: University of Utah Press, 1985.

――――. *Chief Pocatello: The "White Plume."* Salt Lake City: University of Utah Press, 1986.

Madsen, David B., and Brigham D. Madsen. "One Man's Meat Is Another Man's Poison: A Revisionist View of the Seagull 'Miracle.'" In *A World We Thought We Knew: Readings in Utah History*, ed. John S. McCormick and John R. Sillito, 52–67. Salt Lake City: University of Utah Press, 1995.

Malinowski, Bronislaw. *Argonauts of the Western Pacific*. London: G. Routledge & Sons, 1922.

――――. *A Diary in the Strict Sense of the Term*. New York: Harcourt, Brace & World, 1967.

Malouf, Carling I. "Gosiute Indians." In *Shoshone Indians*, 25–172. American In-dian Ethnohistory: California and Basin-Plateau Indians, David Agee Horr, comp. and ed. New York: Garland Publishing Inc., 1974.

Malouf, Carling I., and John Findlay. "Euro-American Impact Before 1870." In *Handbook of North American Indians*, ed. William C. Sturtevant, vol. 11, *Great Basin*, ed. Warren L. D'Avezedo, 499–516. Washington DC: Smithsonian Institution, 1986.

Mann, John W. W. *Sacajawea's People: The Lemhi Shoshones and the Salmon River Country*. Lincoln: University of Nebraska Press, 2004.

Mark, Joan. *Four Anthropologists: An American Science in Its Early Years*. New York: Science History Publications, 1980.

Martz, Maxine. *Why Hurry Through Heaven? A Biography-Memoir of Dr. Walter P. Cottam*. Salt Lake City: Red Butte Garden and Arboretum, University of Utah, 1999.

McCracken, Robert D. *A History of Beatty, Nevada*. Tonopah NV: Nye County Press, 1992.

McKinney, Whitney. *A History of the Shoshone-Paiutes of the Duck Valley Indian Reservation*. Salt Lake City: Institute of the American West and Howe Brothers, 1983.

McPhee, John. *Basin and Range*. New York: Farrar, Straus, Giroux, 1981.

Merriam, C. Hart, and Leonhard Stejneger. *Results of a Biological Survey of the San Francisco Mountain Region and Desert of the Little Colorado, Arizona*. North American Fauna Report 3. U.S. Department of Agriculture, Division of Ornithology and Mammalogy. Washington DC: Government Printing Office, 1890.

Miller, Wick R., comp. *Newe Natekwinappeh: Shoshoni Stories and Dictionary*. University of Utah Anthropological Papers no. 94. Salt Lake City: University of Utah Press, 1972.

Mintz, Sidney W. "Sows' Ears and Silver Linings: A Backward Look at Ethnography." *Current Anthropology* 41, no. 2 (2000): 169–89.

Moerman, Daniel E. *Native American Ethnobotany*. Portland OR: Timber Press, 1998.

Morgan, Dale L., and Carl I. Wheat. *Jedediah Smith and His Maps of the American West*. San Francisco: California Historical Society, 1954.

Mortensen, A. R. "In Memoriam [Charles Kelly]." *Utah Historical Quarterly* 39, no. 2 (1971): 199–200.

Muir, John. *My First Summer in the Sierra*. Boston: Houghton Mifflin, 1911.

———. *Steep Trails*. Boston: Houghton Mifflin, 1918.

Murphy, Robert F., and Yolanda Murphy. "Northern Shoshone and Bannock." In *Handbook of North American Indians*, ed. William C. Sturtevant, vol. 11,

Great Basin, ed. Warren L. D'Avezedo, 284–307. Washington DC: Smithsonian Institution, 1986.

Myers, L. Daniel. "A Frame for Culture: Observations on the Culture-Element Distribution of the Snake River Shoshone." In *Julian Steward and the Great Basin: The Making of an Anthropologist*, ed. Richard O. Clemmer, L. Daniel Myers, and Mary Elizabeth Rudden, 128–43. Salt Lake City: University of Utah Press, 1999.

Novak, Shannon A., and Lars Rodseth. "Remembering Mountain Meadows: Collective Violence and the Manipulation of Social Boundaries." *Journal of Anthropological Research* 62, no 1 (2006): 1–25.

Panek, Tracy E. "Life at Iosepa, Utah's Polynesian Colony." *Utah Historical Quarterly* 60, no. 1 (1992): 64–77.

Parezo, Nancy J. "Anthropology: The Welcoming Science." In *Hidden Scholars: Women Anthropologists and the Native American Southwest*, ed. Nancy J. Parezo, 3–37. Albuquerque: University of New Mexico Press, 1993.

———. "Conclusion: The Beginning of the Quest." In *Hidden Scholars: Women Anthropologists and the Native American Southwest*, ed. Nancy J. Parezo, 334–67. Albuquerque: University of New Mexico Press, 1993.

Parezo, Nancy J., and Margaret A. Hardin. "In the Realm of the Muses." In *Hidden Scholars: Women Anthropologists and the Native American Southwest*, ed. Nancy J. Parezo, 270–93. Albuquerque: University of New Mexico Press, 1993.

Parry, Mae. "The Northwestern Shoshone." In *A History of Utah's American Indians*, ed. Forrest S. Cuch, 25–72. Salt Lake City: Utah Division of Indian Affairs and Utah Division of State History, 2000.

Peterson, F. Ross. *A History of Cache County*. Utah Centennial County History Series. Salt Lake City: Utah State Historical Society and Cache County Council, 1997.

Philips, Arthur M., III, Dorothy A. House, and Barbara G. Philips. "Expedition to the San Francisco Peaks: C. Hart Merriam and the Life Zone Concept." *Plateau* 60, no. 2 (1989): 2–31.

Pickford, G. D. "The Influence of Continued Heavy Grazing and of Promiscuous Burning on Spring-Fall Ranges in Utah." *Ecology* 13, no. 2 (1932): 159–71.

Pinkoski, Marc. "Julian Steward, American Anthropology, and Colonialism." *Histories of Anthropology Annual* 4 (2008): 172–204.

Polk, R. L. & Co. of Utah. *Polk's Salt Lake City Directory, 1935*, vol. 44. Salt Lake City: R. L. Polk & Co. of Utah, Publishers, 1935.

———. *Polk's Ogden City Directory, 1936–37*, vol. 39. Salt Lake City: R. L. Polk & Co. of Utah, Publishers, 1936.

———. *Polk's Salt Lake City Directory, 1936*, vol. 45. Salt Lake City: R. L. Polk & Co. of Utah, Publishers, 1936.

Price, Laurie J. "How Good Is Graduate Training in Anthropology?" *Anthropology News* 42, no. 5 (2001): 5–6.

Radcliffe-Brown, A. R. "Australian Local Organization." *American Anthropologist* 56, no. 1 (1954): 105–6.

Redfield, Robert, Ralph Linton, and Melville J. Herskovits. "Memorandum for the Study of Acculturation." *American Anthropologist* 38, no. 1 (1936): 149–52.

Reich, Charles A. "Mr. Justice Black and the Living Constitution." *Harvard Law Review* 76, no. 4 (1963): 673–754.

Rogers, Garry F. *Then and Now: A Photographic History of Vegetation Change in the Central Great Basin Desert.* Salt Lake City: University of Utah Press, 1982.

Ronaasen, Sheree, Richard O. Clemmer, and Mary Elizabeth Rudden. "Rethinking Cultural Ecology, Multilinear Evolution, and Expert Witnesses: Julian Steward and the Indian Claims Commission." In *Julian Steward and the Great Basin: The Making of an Anthropologist,* ed. Richard O. Clemmer, L. Daniel Myers, and Mary Elizabeth Rudden, 170–202. Salt Lake City: University of Utah Press, 1999.

Rusco, Elmer R., and Mary K. Rusco. "Tribal Politics." In *Handbook of North American Indians,* ed. William C. Sturtevant, vol. 11, *Great Basin,* ed. Warren L. D'Avezedo, 558–72. Washington DC: Smithsonian Institution, 1986.

Sauder, Robert A. *The Lost Frontier: Water Diversion and the Growth and Destruction of Owens Valley Agriculture.* Tucson: University of Arizona Press, 1994.

Saunders, Richard L. "The Utah Writers' Project and Writing of *Utah: A Guide to the State*." *Utah Historical Quarterly* 70, no. 1 (2002): 21–38.

Schindler, Harold. "The Bear River Massacre: New Historical Evidence." *Utah Historical Quarterly* 67, no. 4 (1999): 300–308.

Sennett, Beth. "Wage Labor: Survival for the Death Valley Timbisha." In *Native Americans and Wage Labor: Ethnohistorical Perspectives,* ed. Alice Littlefield and Martha C. Knack, 218–44. Norman: University of Oklahoma Press, 1996.

Sennett-Graham, Beth. "Basketry: A Clue to Panamint Shoshone Culture in the Early 20th Century." Master's thesis, University of Nevada, Reno, 1989.

Sennett-Walker, Beth. "The Panamint Indian Basketry of Scotty's Castle." *American Indian Basketry* 5, no. 3 (1985): 12–17.

Shimkin, Demitri. "Eastern Shoshone." In *Handbook of North American Indians*, ed. William C. Sturtevant, vol. II, *Great Basin*, ed. Warren L. D'Avezedo, 308–35. Washington DC: Smithsonian Institution, 1986.

Silver, Ariel C. "Ramona Wilcox Cannon as Woman and Writer." *Annual of the Association for Mormon Letters* (1996): 82–88.

Simms, Steven. *Ancient Peoples of the Great Basin and Colorado Plateau.* Walnut Creek CA: Left Coast Press, 2008.

Slater, Eva. *Panamint Shoshone Basketry: An American Art Form.* Berkeley CA: Heyday Books, 2000.

Smith, Anne M., comp. and ed. (assisted by Alden Hayes). *Shoshone Tales.* University of Utah Publications in the American West, vol. 31. Salt Lake City: University of Utah Press, 1993.

Smith, Linda Tuhiwai. *Decolonizing Methodologies: Research and Indigenous Peoples.* London: Zed Books, 1999.

Solnit, Rebecca. *Savage Dreams: A Journey into the Landscape Wars of the American West.* New York: Vintage Books, 1994.

Sorensen, Victor. "The Wasters and Destroyers: Community-sponsored Predator Control in Early Utah Territory." *Utah Historical Quarterly* 62, no. 1 (1994): 26–41.

Spear, Beveridge Ross. "Andrew Glen—1878–1973." In *Saga of Inyo County*, comp. and ed., Southern Inyo Chapter (AARP), 17–18. Covina CA: Taylor Publishing Co.

Spencer, Clarissa Young. *Brigham Young at Home.* With Mabel Harmer. Salt Lake City: Deseret Book Co., 1940.

Starrs, Paul F. *Let the Cowboy Ride: Cattle Ranching in the American West.* Baltimore: Johns Hopkins University Press, 1998.

Stegner, Wallace. *Mormon Country.* New York: Duell, Sloan, and Pearce, 1942.

———. *Beyond the Hundredth Meridian: John Wesley Powell and the Second Opening of the West.* Boston: Houghton Mifflin, 1954.

Sterling, Keir B. *Last of the Naturalists: The Career of C. Hart Merriam.* New York: Arno Press, 1974.

Steward, Julian H. "Diffusion and Independent Invention: A Critique of Logic." *American Anthropologist* 31, no. 3 (1929): 491–95.

———. "Irrigation without Agriculture." *Papers of the Michigan Academy of Sciences, Arts, and Letters* 12 (1930): 149–56.

———. "The Discovery of a Kiva in Ancient Mounds at Kanosh." *Millard County Chronicle*, January 1, 1931.

———. "A Uintah Ute Bear Dance, March 1931." *American Anthropologist* 34, no. 2 (1932): 263–73.

———. "Ethnography of the Owens Valley Paiute." *University of California Publications in American Archaeology and Ethnology* 3 (1933): 233–350

———. "Review of *Aboriginal Society in Southern California* by William Duncan Strong." *American Anthropologist* 36, no. 1 (1934): 126–28.

———. "The Economic and Social Basis of Primitive Bands." In *Essays on Anthropology in Honor of Alfred Louis Kroeber*, ed. Robert H. Lowie, 311–50. Berkeley: University of California Press, 1936.

———. "Shoshoni Polyandry." *American Anthropologist* 38, no. 4 (1936): 561–64.

———. *Basin-Plateau Aboriginal Sociopolitical Groups*. Bureau of American Ethnology Bulletin No. 120, 1–346. Washington DC: Government Printing Office, 1938.

———. *Panatubiji, an Owens Valley Paiute*. Anthropological Papers No. 6. Bureau of American Ethnology Bulletin No. 119, 185–95. Washington DC: Government Printing Office, 1938.

———. "Notes on Hillers' Photographs of Paiute and Ute Indians Taken on the Powell Expedition of 1873." *Smithsonian Miscellaneous Collections* 98, no. 18 (1939): 1–23.

———. "Culture Element Distributions: XIII, Nevada Shoshoni." *Anthropological Records* 4, no. 2 (1941): 209–359.

———. *Some Western Shoshoni Myths*. Anthropological Papers No. 31. Bureau of American Ethnology Bulletin No. 136, 249–99. Washington DC: Government Printing Office, 1943.

———. "Culture Element Distributions: XXIII, Northern and Gosiute Shoshoni." *Anthropological Records* 8, no. 3 (1943): 263–392.

———. "Comment on the Statement on Human Rights." *American Anthropologist* 50, no. 2 (1948): 351–52.

———. *Theory of Culture Change: The Methodology of Multilinear Evolution*. Urbana: University of Illinois Press, 1955.

———. *Alfred L. Kroeber*. New York: Columbia University Press, 1973.

Stewart, George. "Historic Records Bearing on Agricultural and Grazing Ecology in Utah." *Journal of Forestry* 39, no. 4 (1941): 363–75.

Stewart, Omer C. "Culture Element Distributions: XVIII, Ute-Southern Paiute." *Anthropological Records* 6, no. 4 (1942): 231–356.

———. "The Peyote Religion." In *Handbook of North American Indians*, ed. William C. Sturtevant, vol. 11, *Great Basin*, ed. Warren L. D'Avezedo, 673–81. Washington DC: Smithsonian Institution, 1986.

Stocking, George W., Jr. *The Ethnographer's Magic and Other Essays in the History of Anthropology*. Madison: University of Wisconsin Press, 1992.

———, ed. *Observers Observed: Essays on Ethnographic Fieldwork*. Madison: University of Wisconsin Press, 1983.

Sutton, Mark Q. *Insects as Food: Aboriginal Entomophagy in the Great Basin*. Menlo Park CA: Ballena Press, 1988.

Sutton, Mark Q., and E. N. Anderson. *Introduction to Cultural Ecology*. Walnut Creek CA: AltaMira Press, 2004.

Swensen, James R. "Dorothea Lange's Portrait of Utah's Great Depression." *Utah Historical Quarterly* 70, no. 1 (2002): 39–62.

Taylor, Ronald J. *Sagebrush Country*. Missoula MT: Mountain Press, 1992.

Thomas, David Hurst, Lorann S. A. Pendleton, and Stephen C. Cappannari. "Western Shoshone." In *Handbook of North American Indians*, ed. William C. Sturtevant, vol. 11, *Great Basin*, ed. Warren L. D'Avezedo, 262–83. Washington DC: Smithsonian Institution, 1986.

Tingley, Joseph V., and Kris Ann Pizarro. *Traveling America's Loneliest Road: A Geologic and Natural History Tour through Nevada along U.S. Highway 50*. Nevada Bureau of Mines and Geology Special Publication 26. Reno: University of Nevada MacKay School of Mines, 2000.

Tom, Gary, and Ronald Holt. "The Paiute Tribe of Utah." In *A History of Utah's American Indians*, ed. Forrest S. Cuch, 123–65. Salt Lake City: Utah Division of Indian Affairs and Utah Division of State History, 2000.

Twain, Mark. *Roughing It.* 1872. New York: Oxford University Press, 1996.

Van Cott, John W. *Utah Place Names: A Comprehensive Guide to the Origins of Geographic Names*. Salt Lake City: University of Utah Press, 1990.

Van Hoak, Stephen P. "The Other Buffalo: Native Americans, Fur Trappers, and the Western Bison, 1600–1860." *Utah Historical Quarterly* 72, no. 1 (2004): 4–18.

Walker, Deward E., Jr. "A Revisionist View of Julian Steward and the Great Basin Paradigm from the North." In *Julian Steward and the Great Basin: The Making of an Anthropologist*, ed. Richard O. Clemmer, L. Daniel Myers, and Mary Elizabeth Rudden, 60–73. Salt Lake City: University of Utah Press, 1999.

Walker, Don D. "The Cattle Industry of Utah, 1860–1900: An Historical Profile." *Utah Historical Quarterly* 32, no. 3 (1964): 182–97.

Walker, Ronald W. "Wakara Meets the Mormons, 1848–52: A Case Study in Native American Accommodation." *Utah Historical Quarterly* 70, no. 3 (1964): 215–37.

Walker, Ronald W., Richard E. Turley Jr., and Glen M. Leonard. *Massacre at Mountain Meadows.* New York: Oxford University Press, 2008.

Walton, John. *Western Times and Water Wars: State, Culture, and Rebellion in California.* Berkeley: University of California Press, 1992.

Whitney, Orson F. *History of Utah,* Vol. I. Salt Lake City: George Q. Cannon and Sons, 1892.

Wilcove, David S. *The Condor's Shadow: The Loss and Recovery of Wildlife in America.* New York: W. H. Freeman, 1999.

Willey, Gordon R. *Portraits in American Archaeology: Remembrances of Some Distinguished Americanists.* Albuquerque: University of New Mexico Press, 1988.

Winterhalder, Bruce. "Behavioral and Other Human Ecologies: Critique, Response and Progress through Criticism." *Journal of Ecological Anthropology* 6, no. 1 (2002): 4–23.

Worster, Donald. *A Passion for Nature: The Life of John Muir.* New York: Oxford University Press, 2008.

———. *A River Running West: The Life of John Wesley Powell.* New York: Oxford University Press, 2001.

Writers' Program of the Work Projects Administration in the State of Nevada. *Nevada: A Guide to the Silver State.* Portland OR: Binfords and Mort, 1940.

Writers' Program of the Work Projects Administration for the State of Utah. *Utah: A Guide to the State.* New York: Hastings House, 1941.

Young, Brigham. "Religion, Progress, and Privileges of the Saints, &c." *Journal of Discourses,* vol. 8, ed. George Q. Cannon, 80–84. Liverpool: George Q. Cannon, 1861.

Young, James A., and B. Abbott Sparks. *Cattle in the Cold Desert.* Logan: Utah State University Press, 1985.

Young, John R. *Memoirs of John R. Young, Utah Pioneer, 1847, Written by Himself.* Salt Lake City: The Deseret News, 1920.

Young, Levi Edgar. *The Founding of Utah*. San Francisco: Charles Scribner's Sons, 1923.

Zanjani, Sally. "Indian Prospectors." *Nevada* 46 (November/December 1986): 53–55.

———. *Sarah Winnemucca*. Lincoln: University of Nebraska Press, 2001.

Zigmond, Maurice. "Kawaiisu." In *Handbook of North American Indians*, ed. William C. Sturtevant, vol. 11, *Great Basin*, ed. Warren L. D'Avezedo, 398–411. Washington DC: Smithsonian Institution, 1986.

Interviews

Sidney W. Mintz, telephone interview by author, July 20, 1998.

Robert F. Murphy, interview by author, August 24, 1989, Leonia, New Jersey.

Dorothy B. Nyswander, interview by author, June 24, 1996, Kensington, California.

Jane C. Steward, interview by author, March 6–12, 1988, Honolulu, Hawaii.

Wiliam C. Sturtevant, interview by author, July 29, 1998, Williamsburg, Virginia.

Index